FINANCE RECONSIDERED: NEW PERSPECTIVES FOR A RESPONSIBLE AND SUSTAINABLE FINANCE

CRITICAL STUDIES ON CORPORATE RESPONSIBILITY, GOVERNANCE AND SUSTAINABILITY

Series Editor: William Sun

Recent Volumes:

Volume 2:	Finance and Sustainability: Towards a New Paradigm? A Post-Crisis Agenda – Edited by William Sun, Céline Louche and Roland Pérez
Volume 3:	Business and Sustainability: Concepts, Strategies and Changes – Edited by Gabriel Eweje and Martin Perry
Volume 4:	Corporate Social Irresponsibility: A Challenging Concept – Edited by Ralph Tench, William Sun and Brian Jones
Volume 5:	Institutional Investors' Power to Change Corporate Behavior: International Perspectives – Edited by Suzanne Young and Stephen Gates
Volume 6:	Communicating Corporate Social Responsibility: Perspectives and Practice – Edited by Ralph Tench, William Sun and Brian Jones
Volume 7:	Socially Responsible Investment in the 21st Century: Does It Make a Difference for Society? – Edited by Céline Louche and Tessa Hebb
Volume 8:	Corporate Social Responsibility and Sustainability: Emerging Trends in Developing Economies – Edited by Gabriel Eweje
Volume 9:	The Human Factor in Social Capital Management: The Owner-Manager Perspective – by Paul C. Manning

CRITICAL STUDIES ON CORPORATE RESPONSIBILITY, GOVERNANCE AND SUSTAINABILITY VOLUME 10

FINANCE RECONSIDERED: NEW PERSPECTIVES FOR A RESPONSIBLE AND SUSTAINABLE FINANCE

EDITED BY

BERNARD PARANQUE
KEDGE Business School, AG2R LA MONDIALE "Finance Reconsidered", Marseille, France

ROLAND PÉREZ
Université de Montpellier, Montpellier, France

Emerald

United Kingdom – North America – Japan
India – Malaysia – China

Emerald Group Publishing Limited
Howard House, Wagon Lane, Bingley BD16 1WA, UK

First edition 2016

British Library Cataloguing in Publication Data
A catalogue record for this book is available from the British Library

ISBN: 978-1-78560-980-0
ISSN: 2043-9059 (Series)

CONTENTS

LIST OF TABLES

LIST OF FIGURES

LIST OF APPENDICES

LIST OF CONTRIBUTORS

Belaïd Abrika	Faculté des sciences économiques, Université Mouloud Mammeri de Tizi-Ouzou, Hasnaoua, Algeria
Abdel-Maoula Chaar	Research, Studies and Development Centre, Ecole Superieure des Affaires, Beirut, Lebanon
Bernard Cova	KEDGE Business School, Marseille, France
Elias Erragragui	KEDGE Business School, Marseille, France
Christophe Faugère	KEDGE Business School, Bordeaux, France
Thomas Lagoarde-Segot	KEDGE Business School, Marseille, France
Jacques Ninet	La Française Asset Management, Paris, France
Bernard Paranque	KEDGE Business School, Marseille, France
Roland Pérez	Université de Montpellier, France
Cécile Perret	IUT de CHAMBERY, Bourget-du-Lac, France
Christophe Revelli	KEDGE Business School, Marseille, France
Jean-Michel Servet	IHEID, Genève, Suisse
Hugh Willmott	Cass Business School, City University, London, UK

Preface

André Renaudin AG2R La Mondiale, France

Post-face

Jean-Louis Bancel Crédit Coopératif, Nanterre, France

ABOUT THE EDITORS

Bernard Paranque is Professor of Finance at KEDGE Business Schooland General Delegate for EuroMediterranean Affairs. He is now Director of "Economy and finance reconsidered – emerging countries" research department. He holds the AG2R LA MONDIALE Chair in "Finance Reconsidered: Investment, Solidarities and Responsibility". He is associate member Institute of Labour Economics and Industrial Sociology LEST-CNRS-UMR 7317.

He began his career as an Associate Economist in an accountancy firm in 1984 in Lyon. In 1990, he joined the French Central Bank in Paris. From 1990 to 2000, he produced papers on the financial structure of non-financial companies.

In 1999, he was on secondment from the Banque de France to the Secretary of State to SMEs' where he was in charge of the "Business Financing" department. He was also a member of the French delegation to the SMEs' working party of the Business and Environment Committee of the OECD. From 2001 to 2003, he was Associate Professor at the University Panthéon Sorbonne in Paris.

His research focuses on finance and common pool resources management, with a particular interest in employee ownership organisation as cooperatives and their governance. He is also interested in the issue of economic coordination and collective action and in the solidarity and social economy.

Some of his papers can be consulted online on http://papers.ssrn.com/sol3/cf_dev/AbsByAuth.cfm?per_id=1633. He is the author of "Construire l'Euroméditerranée" L'Harmattan, 2008, and co-author of "Diversité économique et mode de financement des PME" published in 2001, and of "L'Euroméditerranée: de l'espace géographique aux modes de coordinations socio-économiques" published in 2007, both by L'Harmattan.

Roland Pérez, a graduate from ENS Cachan (1960–1963) has been Chairman of the Scientific Board of the AG2R LA MONDIALE Chair "Finance Reconsidered" from 2011 to 2015. He has a PhD in Economic

Sciences from Paris I University (1970) and an agrégation in both Management Techniques (1965) and Management and Economic Science (1971). Having held successive positions in the universities of Lille (1963–1966), Tunis (1966–1968), the Paris CNRS (1968–1971) and Amiens (1972–1981) where he was University Chairman, since 1981 he has been working at Montpellier I University as Director of the Economics and Management Doctoral School. He has also been Scientific Advisor to the Ministry (1982–1985 and 1998–2002) and on secondment (1986–1996) as Director of an International Centre (the Montpellier Institute of Mediterranean Agriculture). He has been professor emeritus since 2003.

He has worked in corporate finance, industrial economics and strategic analysis for firms and groups. He has helped manage numerous research programmes in these areas and led the scientific field. An author of over 100 publications, he has supervised 100 academic theses (PhD, MSc, HDR). His recent work looks at the industrial and financial strategies of multinational agricultural groups and the general issues of management, finance and governance in terms of sustainable development. He is currently coordinator of the international partnership programme "Finance and Sustainability" (2009–2015) and moderates the "Finance and Common Goods" forum.

He has an honorary doctorate and is a member of several academic institutions in both France and abroad. In particular, he founded the AFFI (French Finance Association) and was Chairman of the SFM (French Management Association) in 2006, and of the RIODD (International Network for Research on Organisations and Sustainable Development) from 2007 to 2009.

EDITORIAL ADVISORY AND REVIEW BOARD

ACKNOWLEDGEMENTS

This volume is a revised and augmented edition of *La Finance Autrement? Réflexions critiques et perspectives sur la finance moderne*, Presses Universitaires du Septentrion 2015 – France

The volume editors would like to thank all those that have engaged with and contributed to this volume. In particular individual chapter authors deserve praise and thanks for engaging so willingly with this project.

Many thanks also to AG2R LA MONDIALE and its strong support since 2008, in particular Philippe Dutertre, Frédéric Duchadeuil, Jean-Michel Foucque along with Patrick Viallanex and Robin Edme.

The editors and authors acknowledge the translation from French to English performed by Technics Translation.

PREFACE

'Finance Reconsidered?' is the outcome of an original partnership between the academic and professional spheres. The work comes as the conclusion of the first round of research headed by the AG2R LA MONDIALE – KEDGE Business School Chair, founded in late 2008 and the goal of which is to develop a pioneering alternative view on responsible finance, symbolising the two partners' community-focused approach.

We are convinced that the responses required to address the recent financial and economic crises and current social and environmental challenges must be found by further developing our economic model, one with a democratic government that respects every stakeholder's contribution and works to the benefit of the communities it serves (clients, policyholders and their beneficiaries, social partners, etc.). This model is regularly called into question but now has to reaffirm its legitimacy, in all its richness and its diversity.

The new boom in the cooperative movement and the social and solidarity economy, the micro-finance and crowd-funding sectors, the emergence of markets focused exclusively on sustainable development projects, and the spectacular development of socially responsible investment – in which we play a key role in France – illustrate just how dynamic these 'new' funding models are. These models bring people and their eco-system back to the centre of economic development, reincarnating the *affectio societatis* that is vital between the saver, the investor and the projects they finance.

Social and community-focused commitment is our hallmark. In our eyes, economic performance and social commitment go hand-in-hand and sustainable growth can only be achieved when both come together. We have built our economic model on this belief. It is at the heart of our business plan driving our community-focused approach, and has been an integral part of our strategy and our activities for several years.

Founded on values of solidarity, closeness and democratic governance since the outset, AG2R LA MONDIALE is, through its social commitment and the action of its Foundations, a major stakeholder in the social and solidarity economy. This sector is rich and diverse in terms of socio-economic development projects and provides an alternative to the model that currently prevails, where striving to maximise value for shareholders in the short term is seen as the only way of increasing wealth and collective well-being.

Getting finance to serve a collective need is also at the core of our fiduciary responsibility. Through this collective thinking, bringing together professionals and academics, we seek to enrich the foundations of fiduciary responsibility for institutional investors by reflecting on the way in which a 'financial' asset's value is built up against a background of social consensus, on how to maintain this value by developing new practices and new asset management solutions that meet the socio-economic demands of all stakeholders, and on the scope covered by the notion of protecting the beneficiaries' exclusive interest.

As the leading social protection group in France and a first-rate institutional investor, we are duty-bound to contribute to this innovative thinking which we must, within the framework of our Chair, continue to support over the long term since the themes addressed are still pioneering.

André Renaudin
Managing Director of AG2R LA MONDIAL

PART I
INTRODUCTION

FINANCE RECONSIDERED: NEW PERSPECTIVES FOR A RESPONSIBLE AND SUSTAINABLE FINANCE

Bernard Paranque and Roland Pérez

This book is entitled 'Finance Reconsidered: New Perspectives for a Responsible and Sustainable Finance', echoing the title of the eponymous Research Chair created by Kedge Business School in 2008 in partnership with AG2R LA MONDIALE. It aims to express the epistemological, theoretical and methodological stances taken by the researchers working on the programme for this Research Chair,[1] and by several members of its Scientific Council who have been supporting it for many years. This publication is also one of the deliverables for the Finance and Sustainability (FAS) international programme created on the same date as the Research Chair and for similar reasons;[2] something which led the members of the Research Chair, Thomas Lagoarde-Segot, Christophe Revelli, Christophe Faugère and Elias Erragragui among others, to adopt leading roles within this programme, in particular in recent years,[3] for which they receive our gratitude.

In this introduction, we review the principles and orientations of these converging initiatives, then give a brief presentation of the various

Finance Reconsidered: New Perspectives for a Responsible and Sustainable Finance
Critical Studies on Corporate Responsibility, Governance and Sustainability, Volume 10, 3–13

ISSN: 2043-9059/doi:10.1108/S2043-905920160000010022

contributions towards this book as an illustration of the work that is being carried out.

PRINCIPLES JUSTIFYING THE 'FINANCE RECONSIDERED' RESEARCH PROGRAMME

The motivation for this book was the sustainability of our development in light of the absence of any critical analysis of the paradigm supporting the theoretical model that underlies the chosen social and economic policies. It goes without saying that the difficulties in criticising this model derive from the fact that its two figureheads – the market and private property – mean it has been, and continues to be, strongly established as the natural state of affairs. And yet there is no lack of articles explaining the weakness of, if not the lack of any basis for, the hypotheses used to justify this model (Bourguinat & Briys, 2009; Giraud, 2012; Gomez, 2009, 2011; Graeber, 2013; Keen, 2014; Meiksins-Wood, 2013, 2014; Weinstein, 2010).

(1) In terms of *contextualisation*, the two initiatives – the AG2R LA MONDIALE Research Chair 'Finance Reconsidered' and the FAS programme – both relate to the global financial crisis, its evolution and the resulting need to review not just the conceptual framework of finance but also the analytical methods, operating procedures and how they are taught.

Indeed, since 2007, the financial crisis of that year – the subprime crisis – has evolved considerably and given rise to extensive analysis and commentary.[4] In addition, several countries – beginning with the United States – have seen their economies reboot, with sometimes spectacular growth on their financial markets. The fact remains however that the economic stagnation persists, especially in Southern and Eastern Europe, despite attempts at quantitative easing; and since behaviour has in many cases not yet changed, the world is still at risk from another financial crisis even more violent than the previous one.[5]

There has therefore never been a greater need for a clear and well-grounded discussion of finance in general and on the ways in which it can be 'reconsidered'.

(2) In terms of *conceptualisation*, the research programme can be set out as follows:

A. The starting point was a critique of mainstream finance, a critique that can be directed at many levels:
   - at individual behaviour which, in finance as with all areas of human activity (*although perhaps a little more*) can foster excess, deviance and faults of various kinds, all of which create weak links in the procedures put in place for monitoring the financial system, as can be seen by recent cases.
   - at the analysis tools, whose apparent sophistication (e.g. the options theory) sometimes conceals a weak design with, all too often, the use of overly simplistic hypotheses. The resulting excessive 'normality' (i.e. the use of Gaussian probability distributions) has rightly been criticised by both researchers and practitioners (Mandelbrot & Hudson, 2005; Taleb, 2008).
   - at the conceptual framework itself, whereby the foundations of the so-called 'modern' finance are being called into question (Bourguinat & Briys, 2009; Keen, 2014; Weinstein, 2010), paving the way for a Kuhnian paradigm shift (Kuhn, 1983).

B. To avoid providing only a critique and ensure a positive contribution to 'Finance Reconsidered', a certain number of research topics have been defined and new analysis frameworks requested.
   - In terms of topics, the programme has either furthered or revisited several fields of research begun in recent years to broaden/modify/evolve the traditional representation of finance:
     - modes of financial investment, in particular socially responsible methods (SRI)
     - types of firms distancing themselves from the traditional model of a public corporation, and those belonging to the 'Solidarity Economy'
     - more broadly, relationships between finance and other areas of life within contemporary human society, including philosophical, ethical, political and religious aspects
   - in terms of analysis framework, the programme not only seeks to obtain an essential understanding of mainstream finance (symbolised by the Chicago School) but is also open to several streams of thought and theoretical analysis:
     - the main currents of the political economy, which are sometimes divided, especially on issues relating to value (classical, neoclassical, Marxist, Keynesian, etc.)

- the other human and social sciences, from which 'scientific' finance has attempted to free itself, as with anthropology (Mauss, 1950).
- Critical Management Studies (Alvesson, Bridgman, & Willmott, 2009), which are very useful for questioning the paradigm of Management and Economic Sciences and their categories. The epistemological debate carried by the CMS calls into question, for example, the status of the market and even of the concept of stakeholder ownership. By asking researchers to take a 'stance', this necessarily means stating 'from where they are standing'.
- the approaches in terms of Common Pool Resources (CPR) studied by Elinor Ostrom (Winner of the 2009 Sveriges Riksbank Nobel Memorial Prize). As we know, Ostrom focused on natural resources (water, forests, fishing areas, etc.) and it was not until she was reaching the end of her life that she began studying the management of non-material resources (Hess & Ostrom, 2011). However, neither her nor her network[6] broached the subject of finance, for whom the respective weight of the Market on the one hand, and of the State on the other, seemed too great for any 'third way' to be considered.[7] The topic of 'finance as a pooled resource' is therefore uncharted territory in terms of scientific research.[8]

(3) Finally, in terms of *operationalisation*, the vocation of the Research Chair, having been developed by a graduate management school, is to translate the results of its scientific programme into both support and advice for the firms concerned and input for its own academic programme (initial or continued education). The aim of a research programme, as regards those disciplines which relate to 'practical knowledge' such as financial management and the economy, is in effect to help us not only understand the modern world but, through this better understanding, to also then improve it and help it evolve.

ORIENTATIONS OF THE 'FINANCE RECONSIDERED' PROGRAMME

The paradigm of financial theory tells us that it is by maximising the utility of the stakeholder (the share value) that collective well-being can be achieved in the long-term (Jensen, 2001). The research programme launched in 2008 aims to reverse the issue by first looking at collective well-being, and then turning to the question of what resources are required to achieve that well-being via a specific organisation known as the firm (beyond its various legal forms). This programme is consistent with the following definition of the Solidarity Economy, '*economic solidarity is built* [ought to be built] *on a policy that is both economic, political and social, and which brings about a new way of doing politics and of forging human relations on the basis of consensus and social action*' (translation by Mayer & Caldier, 2007, p. 102).

With this in mind, it is essential to look at investment politics, that is, the policies for funding anticipated activities, from the point of view of both companies and firms, and of the funders themselves through their portfolio management strategies. These policies are in fact what underpin the creation of future wealth and determine a firm's social commitment. However, we believe that Socially Responsible Investing[9] (SRI) is not simply an expression of portfolio management policy but the operational application of Corporate Social Responsibility[10] (CSR) which is what shapes non-financial investment policy. A firm's investment policy supports and reflects its CSR choices: internal or external investment, capital-widening or capital-deepening, immaterial or material, relocation or localisation, etc. In other words, the commitment of financial resources, whether for the daily running of the firm or its portfolio management, is an expression of the way in which it conceives its civic and social responsibility.

There is therefore a need to know how to mobilise those involved (clients, consumers, users, partners) as regards the management of their wealth (or financial assets) and as regards obtaining a commitment towards/based on the firm's values, a task which poses the challenges of symbolic identification and the forging of links. This is a determining factor when it comes to assessing the impact of a firm's investment policy on its territory, and therefore ultimately on the persons attached to or to be attached to the firm and the implementation of its responsibility.

However, this discussion would be incomplete without taking into account the methods for coordinating the collective actions of the partners of the firm/brand in their day-to-day business (Alvesson et al., 2009; Cefai, 2007; Ostrom, 2005, 2010a, 2010b). Beyond that, the challenge is understanding how to create resource-generating activities that meet the daily needs of a community, and to anticipate future consumption requirements through the creation of sufficient savings to overcome unforeseen events, seize opportunities and prepare for the future stages – in short, to manage the uncertainties of that community. Numerous questions are raised by this approach. How can we manage uncertainty and risk, not only at the level of the individual firm, but as regards the impact on society?

This problem can be broken down into the three lines of research covered by the Research Chair:

- Line 1: From creating stakeholder value to promoting communal life and responsible/sustainable funding
- Line 2: Social and solidarity economy, funding, collective action and cooperation
- Line 3: Ethics, responsible investment and corporate responsibility

PRESENTATION OF THE BOOK

The scientific programme of the Research Chair, as described earlier, is more or less reflected in the way this book is structured. In Part II, the dominant paradigm is questioned using complementary approaches. Part III looks at investment and organisational practices. Part IV uses the examples of certain human societies (Buddhist philosophy, Islamic finance) to examine financial behaviour as an expression of how we have embedded our financial life into our social life.

Part II explores and discusses the conceptual framework. In the second chapter, Bernard Paranque questions the possibility of doing away with stakeholder value maximisation as the guiding principle for collective action in today's world. We are living through an unprecedented crisis affecting our finance, economy, society and culture. This chapter suggests a new way of looking at private property, whereby rather than considering its exchange value we begin to consider its usage value, drawing from the development of brand communities and questioning cooperatives. It proposes a 'common' approach (in the sense of common pool resources – CPR – as studied by Ostrom). This would involve rules for coordinating the collective management of CPR, rules which are either predetermined or are the goal of that management. Viewing a business beyond its commercial status (other than company/firm) is a prerequisite for being able to question the means and ends of its collective, civic action. In fact, as regards methodology, abandoning the concept of the business as an organisation, without differentiating it from the commercial company, in order to analyse its corporate collective action, leads to a sticking point. The absence of any legal definition of the business reduces its understanding and any assessment of its performance to that of a company, which still has a legal definition. This implicit switch leads to an assimilation between the two in a sort of funnel-effect, whereby a collective goal is pared back to merely the goals of its capital backers.

This is the line of thought followed by Thomas Lagoarde-Segot, who points out the contradictions between the need for sustainability and the nature of academic finance, and who proposes a strategy for broadening financial research. He introduces the concept of research diversification, meaning a process whereby financial research is expanded to other paradigms, through social science. He believes that new metaphors are required within the existing paradigm and he suggests ensuring that none of the necessary rigour is sacrificed when resolving the problem. Finally, he insists on the need to explore the social, behavioural, historical and institutional processes that shape a financial system's ability to create – or destroy – well-being, using a comparative, international and interdisciplinary approach.

The need to question the whole situation lies at the heart of the contribution by Roland Pérez, who insists on the challenges relating to training. He discusses the need for a critical discussion of the dominant paradigm in finance, known as 'scientific finance' by its advocates, by highlighting the differences that separate it both from traditional finance which preceded it, and from contemporary issues. This comparative essay has been written in the light of the current global financial crisis, whose scope and the shortcomings it has uncovered lead us all to ask whether the 'analysis of the financial crisis' which is often called for does not in fact reveal a 'crisis of financial analysis'. He then expresses a wish to see the birth of a new financial paradigm and its corollary – the much-needed reform of training for financiers.

Part III of this work broaches the topic of finance from the point of view of the practices and tools developed in recent years to make it 'responsible'. Christophe Revelli offers a critical analysis of the concept of Socially Responsible Investing (SRI), from conception through to development and its current role within mainstream finance. The challenge is realising that SRI needs restructuring and modernising if we are to overcome the risk of diluting the financial mass to the detriment of its moral identity. The aim here will be to 'deconstruct' the concept in order to rebuild it better and offer key solutions for refocusing the concept of SRI on its moral identity and in a quest to measure non-financial performance.

However, as regards fund management methods and practices, there is cause to question the future of this field. Jacques Ninet shows that SRI is far from being the norm and has met with very limited success among private investors and distribution networks. He hypothesises that this failure is due to a series of deep-rooted misunderstandings about the SRI/CSR pairing, between the various actors, namely 'responsible' enterprises who are the practitioners of CSR, SRI finance professionals and management companies, non-financial ratings agencies and analysts, and finally academic researchers. If we are truly to reconcile finance and sustainability, he argues that we must first resolve the traditional dilemma between ethics and performance, which sees non-financial factors as a major hindrance, and promote the contribution potential of sustainable prosperity, for both public and private players. This chapter presents a bottom-up approach which reintroduces the long-term perspective into investment decisions and focuses on our ability to adapt and innovate in the face of the unprecedented challenges posed by this new century.

There are many questions raised by the operational deployment of these new practices. This is also true for an area which looks also at the impact of its choices and decisions, as explained by Jean-Michel Servet in his contribution. The author analyses 10 micro-economic, meso-economic and macro-economic criteria – criteria which appear necessary if microfinance is to have a direct, positive and rapid effect on poverty levels. These criteria are very rarely met, whether in sub-Saharan Africa or in any other developing or emerging country, which explains why microfinance has had only a limited effect on poverty relief.

Belaïd Abrika, Bernard Paranque and Cécile Perret present their study of a community committed to the sustainable management of its resources. Albeit without broaching it directly, they also raise the question of how compatible this development can be with the dominant funding norms and practices. Is it possible to design methods for the circulation of goods and services other than capitalist market trade? The authors suggest the possibility of following Polanyi in his deconstruction of the hypothesis that *Homo oeconomicus* is a 'natural' being, a calculating individual who dreams only of maximising his utility. The case study of a Kabyle society shows that market exchange does not necessarily have to involve the trading mechanism theorised by economic science – we must not confuse commerce and market or circulation and market exchange (Testart, 2007).

Bernard Paranque and Bernard Cova in turn study the existing relationship between marketing and finance. The question they ask is twofold: on the one hand, how can interactions between a brand and its most enthusiastic consumers be transformed into 'bankable' shareholder value for investors; on the other hand, how can brand orchestration – specifically supported by stimulating collaboration amongst consumers grouped into communities – increase or, conversely, endanger shareholder value. Thus, their chapter focuses on the connections between three types of actors who are building the new world of brands: consumers, marketers and financiers.

Finally, Bernard Paranque and Hugh Willmott discuss a very specific organisation, the John Lewis Partnership. John Lewis is of special interest since it is celebrated as a successful organisation and heralded as an alternative to more typical forms of capitalist enterprise. JLP is also an example of ownership not based on shares and legal forms but on a specific form of governance and control. In this sense, it could be interesting to investigate this separation whereby the power to decide is not in the hands of the shareholders but in the hands of the partner, through election and different decisional levels.

Part IV seeks to expand the debate to other approaches to finance which specifically incorporate ethical principles into their foundations, principles which 'shape' the practices and decisions taken by their actors. Without wishing to imitate them, it is interesting to discover how one could reverse the usual representation by designing an ethical framework which takes priority over financial techniques, rather than the other way round, which is usually the case in the world of the so-called 'modern' finance.

Christophe Faugère thus studies what would happen to the world of finance if it were to adopt the two mental faculties of 'mindfulness' and 'compassion'. Mindfulness, as defined by Jon Kabat-Zinn, and ruthless compassion, as defined by Chogyam Trungpa Rinpoché, are two powerful mental tools that could help the world of finance achieve this noble aim. Unveiling new levels of conscience for example gives decision-makers a competitive advantage, since it stops them from falling into certain behavioural traps and gives them an ultimate goal of something more important than simply 'making money'.

This concern of a 'purpose' other than money for money's sake can be seen in Islamic finance, as illustrated by Abdel-Maoula Chaar. Rooted in religion, this approach has 're-enchanted' an area of modern finance which aligns itself with strict non-religious rationalism. Some onlookers see this characteristic as being the only substantial difference between this 'finance for Muslims' and contemporary financial practice. Others believe that similarities/differences between these financial methods call into question the universality of the dominant financial paradigm, and thus with it the importance of the notions of material profit and market equilibrium. If this is indeed the case, an analysis of the Islamic financial paradigm could help determine the socio-economic effects of a non-maximising financial system.

This issue of maximisation has been at the heart of discussions into SRI in recent years. Are there any differences in performance between an SRI and a non-SRI approach (see the chapter by Christophe Revelli). Bernard Paranque and Elias Erragragui extend this question to the management of Islamic funds compared to SRI funds. Their chapter explores the compatibility of Islamic investment with SRI practices and examines the price to pay for being both Sharia-compatible and socially responsible. The results reveal the absence of any negative effects from applying a dual Islamic and SRI filter, and demonstrate clearly superior performance as regards good governance over the period 2008–2011.

Finally, a partial and provisional conclusion is drawn, offering certain pointers for viewing finance as 'common'. It encourages research into the relationship of credit which could suggest possible solutions for reorganising funding relationships for the benefit of uses, under the control of citizens working from the bottom-up.

NOTES

1. Since its conception in 2008, and others more recently, especially following the merger of Euromed Management and Bordeaux E.M., resulting in the Kedge Business School.
2. An appendix to this book provides an overview of this programme and its main findings.
3. Period 2013–2015 'FAS 2'; in particular a day event at Kedge on 21 May 2014 as part of the Management Week organised by the FNEGE (see appendix).
4. Some have gone as far as to say that the only sector not affected by the crisis is that of crisis analysis (see R. Pérez, infra, chap. 4).
5. See the financial report of J. Ninet (La Française A.M.), March 2015.
6. Cf. Workshop at Indiana University (Bloomington) and IASC (International Association for the Study of Commons).
7. *Source*: Interview with E. Ostrom – June 2011.
8. We have launched a forum on this topic finance@bienscommuns.org, bringing together around 50 researchers and professionals from the sector and in which the 'Finance Reconsidered' initiative plays a key role, through either its permanent members or the members of its scientific committee.
9. Used in its generic rather than its institutionalised sense.
10. Used in its generic rather than its institutionalised sense.

REFERENCES

Alvesson, M., Bridgman, T., & Willmott, H. (Eds.). (2009). *Oxford handbook of critical management studies*. New York, NY: Oxford University Press.

Bourguinat, H., & Briys, E. (2009). *L'arrogance de la finance*. Paris: La Découverte.

Cefai, D. (2007). *Pourquoi nous mobilisons nous?* Paris: La Découverte MAUSS.

Giraud, G. (2012). *Illusion financière*. Paris: Seuil, Collection Poche.

Gomez, P. Y. (2009). Théorie néolibérale du gouvernement des entreprises: Critique d'un renversement critique. In D. Golsorkhi, I. Huault, & B. Leca (Eds.), *Les études critiques en management* (pp. 233–260). Québec: Presses Universitaires de Laval.

Gomez, P. Y. (2011). Sciences de gestion et conventions: de nouveaux cadres l'analyse critique. In L. Taskin & M. de Nanteuil (Eds.), *Perspectives pour critiques en management, pour une gestion citoyenne* (pp. 49–66). Bruxelles: De Boeck.

Graeber, D. (2013). *Dette. 5 000 ans d'histoire*. Les Liens qui Libèrent.

Hess, C., & Ostrom, E. (2011). *Understanding knowledge as a commons*. Cambridge, MA: MIT Press.

Jensen, M. C. (2001). *Value maximization, stakeholder theory, and the corporate objective function*. Retrieved from http://ssrn.com/abstract=220671. Accessed in October. In *Journal of Applied Corporate Finance*, *14*(3), 2001, 8–21 and *European Financial Management Review*, (7), 2001, 297–317.

Keen, S. (2014). *L'imposture économique*. Ivry sur Seine: Les Éditions de l'Atelier.

Kuhn, T. (1983). *La structure des révolutions scientifiques*. Paris: Flammarion.

Mandelbrot, B., & Hudson, R. (2005). *Une approche fractale des marchés – Risquer, perdre et gagner*. Paris: Éd. Odile Jacob.

Mauss, M. (1950). *Sociologie et anthropologie*. Paris: PUF.

Mayer, S., & Caldier, J.-P. (2007). *Le guide de l'économie équitable*. Paris: Fondation Gabriel Péri.

Meiksins-Wood, E. (2013). Des citoyens aux seigneurs. Une histoire sociale de la pensée politique de l'antiquité au Moyen Âge. Lux/Humanités, Québec.

Meiksins-Wood, E. (2014). *Liberté et propriété. Une histoire sociale de la pensée politique occidentale de la Renaissance aux Lumières*. Québec: Lux/Humanités.

Ostrom, E. (2005). *Understanding institutional diversity*. Princeton, NJ: Princeton University Press.

Ostrom, E. (2010a). *Gouvernance des biens communs*. De Boeck: Bruxelles.

Ostrom, E. (2010b). Response: The institutional analysis and development framework and the commons. *Cornell Law Review*, *95*(May), 807–816.

Taleb, N. N. (2008). *Le cygne noir – La puissance de l'imprévisible*. Paris: Les Belles Lettres.

Testart, A. (2007). *Critique du don – Études sur la circulation non marchande*. Paris: Syllepse.

Weinstein, O. (2010). *Pouvoir, Finances et Connaissance, les transformations de l'entreprise capitaliste entre XXe et XXIe siècle*. Paris: Éditions La Découverte.

PART II
CRITICAL ANALYSIS OF THE DOMINANT FINANCIAL PARADIGM

AN ALTERNATIVE TO SHAREHOLDER VALUE CREATION: SUBVERTING THE DOMINATION OF CAPITALIST EXCHANGES THROUGH THE PRODUCTION OF USES AND COMMON POOL RESOURCES MANAGEMENT☆

Bernard Paranque

ABSTRACT

Purpose – *This chapter reconsiders commonly held views on the ownership and management of private property, contrasting capitalist and simple property, particularly in relation to how a firm shareholder*

☆This chapter is a revised and expanded version of different contributions: Paranque (2013, 2014a, 2014b).

Finance Reconsidered: New Perspectives for a Responsible and Sustainable Finance
Critical Studies on Corporate Responsibility, Governance and Sustainability, Volume 10, 17–87

ISSN: 2043-9059/doi:10.1108/S2043-905920160000010023

governance model has shaped society. This consideration is motivated by the scale and scope of the modern global crisis, which has combined financial, economic, social and cultural dimensions to produce world disenchantment.

Methodology/approach – *By contrasting an exchange value standpoint with a use value perspective, this chapter explicates current conditions in which neither the state nor the market prevail in organising economic activity (i.e. cooperative forms of governance and community-created brand value).*

Findings – *This chapter offers recommendations related to formalised conditions for collective action and definitions of common guiding principles that can facilitate new expressions of the principles of coordination. Such behaviours can support the development of common resources, which then should lead to a re-appropriation of the world.*

Practical implications – *It is necessary to think of enterprises outside a company or firm context when reflecting on the end purpose and means of collective, citizen action. From a methodological standpoint, current approaches or studies that view an enterprise as an organisation, without differentiating it from a company, create a deadlock in relation to entrepreneurial collective action. The absence of a legal definition of enterprise reduces understanding and evaluations of its performance to simply the performance by a company. The implicit shift thus facilitates the assimilation of one with the other, in a funnel effect that reduces collective projects to the sole projects of capital providers.*

Originality/value – *Because forsaking society as it stands is a radical response, this historical moment makes it necessary to revisit the ideals on which modern societies build, including the philosophy of freedom for all. This utopian concept has produced an ideology that is limited by capitalist notions of private property.*

Keywords: Private property; collective action; cooperative; liberalism; exchange value; use value

JEL classifications: B5; P13; Z13

> The method of advancing from the abstract to the concrete is simply the way in which thinking assimilates the concrete and reproduces it as a concrete mental category.
>
> – Karl Marx[1]

There is a major challenge for society in building collective, shareable and shared meaning.[2] There can be no democracy without a shared project and this can neither be delegated nor founded on a return to the past as an expression of fear in the future.

The modern economic crisis reveals an issue that represents a re-appropriation of the world (Fischbach, 2009b), at a time when virtually everyone feels helpless and is, to some extent, experiencing 'a loss of the world' (Fischbach, 2009b, p. 7; Honneth, 2007), a loss of reference points to either believe in another world or the desire to still change this world. This re-appropriation entails the definition of the common project that will bring people together and affirm the need for a new citizen utopia. If 'what is at issue in a utopia is the need to imagine another way of exercising power'/'*Ce qui est en jeu dans une utopie, c'est le fait d'imaginer une autre manière d'exercer le pouvoir*' (Ricœur, 1997, p. 256), then we need to question the conditions of that action. It appears to me that these conditions are of three types: the first is global, the second is institutional and the third is organisational. I will not deal with the first here. Nonetheless, it is important to put forward ideas on what kind of utopia could mobilise people and take over from the model that failed in the 20th century, perverted by Stalinism. This could be the ecological transition (Giraud, 2012). To take Marx's idea and adapt it to the new socio-economic norm, and the challenges associated with the depletion of our environment, this ecological transition is not a given. It 'is for us not a state of affairs which is to be established, an ideal to which reality will have to adjust itself. We call [ecological transition instead of communism] the real movement which abolishes the present state of things/*n'est pour nous ni un état qui doit être créé, ni un idéal sur lequel la réalité devra se régler. Nous appelons [transition écologique] le mouvement réel qui abolit l'état actuel*' (adapted from Marx, 1976/1932, p. 33). It would therefore be 'the complete emancipation of all human senses and attributes/*le moment réel de l'émancipation et de la reprise de soi de l'homme*' (Marx, 1972a/1959, p. 99). This forces us to reflect on our relationship with nature and the fact of 'being estranged from the natural relation with these essential elements that are, for man, natural things and other human beings/*d'être privé du rapport naturel à ces objets essentiels que sont, pour un homme, les choses de la nature et les autres hommes*' (Fischbach, 2014, p. 67). In other words, what social relationship to production do we want to build over our lives? By affirming that 'nature is his [man's] body, with which he must remain in continuous interchange if he is not to die/*la nature est son propre corps [de l'homme] avec lequel il faut qu'il demeure dans un processus continuel pour ne pas mourir*'

(Marx, 1972a/1959, 1972b/1859, quoted by Fischbach, 2014, p. 69) and 'that nature only exists for man through the social activity by which he appropriates it and transforms it/*que la nature n'existe pour les hommes que par l'intermédiaire de l'activité sociale par laquelle ils se l'approprient et la transforment*' (Fischbach, 2014, p. 73), we question the way our Societies operate currently. This means we need to understand the social relationship that governs our activity and which is characterised by the separation of the majority from the conditions under which they exercise 'their own power to take action', prevailed by the 'myth of Promethean human power to control and dominate nature/*mythe d'une puissance humaine prométhéenne de maîtrise et de domination de la nature*' (Fischbach, 2014, p. 78).

The re-appropriation of this 'power to act' entails the realisation that we need to fight against the fact 'that my business is constantly having goals imposed upon it that do not fit with my motives'/*fait que mon activité sociale se voit imposer sans recours des buts inassimilables à mes motifs*' (Sève, 2008, p. 505), which Sève defines as 'alienation'.[3] Such alienation stems from an understanding of true freedom, limited by private capitalist property, which alienates people by making it impossible for them to exercise their freedom and confronts them with a 'feeling of helplessness'/ *expérience vécue de l'impuissance* (Fischbach, 2009b, p. 13).[4] What would people do, given their potential, without the constraints associated with limited access to all kinds of resources?[5] This gap determines the way societies function, such that 'Behind debates on property, lie key issues such as a property system which plays an essential role in the distribution of economic and social powers. It influences the methods that control resources and enterprise itself, the distribution of risks and that of expected gains from business/*Derrière les débats sur la propriété se cachent des enjeux majeurs: un système de propriété participe fondamentalement de la répartition des pouvoirs économiques et sociaux. Il conditionne les modes de contrôles des ressources et des entreprises elles-mêmes, la répartition des risques et celles des gains attendus de l'activité de l'entreprise*' (Weinstein, 2010, p. 36).

While the modern conception of property is strongly marked by the Roman distinction between private and public (Meiksins-Wood, 2013), we must not lose sight of the fact that this came about after a breakaway from a Greek notion that focused on collective rights: 'On the one hand, family and personal friendship links, on the other, public claims from groups of citizens, the polis, where the law is supposedly devised for the common good. In both cases, the term "private" does not fit the non-state domain as the principles of the polis, like those of the non-polis, concern collective duties/*D'un côté, les liens du sang et de l'amitié personnelle, de l'autre, les*

revendications publiques du groupe de citoyens*, de la polis, dont les lois sont censées viser le bien commun. Dans les deux cas, le qualificatif de privé ne convient pas au domaine non étatique puisque les principes de la polis, comme ceux de la non-polis concernent* ***les devoirs collectifs***' (Meiksins-Wood, 2013, p. 218, underlined by me). This is explained by the fact that Roman citizenship concerned individuals with equal rights but who were not equal socially, contrary to the Greek conception (Meiksins-Wood, 2013). Here again, the underlying policy is one of the relationship to power that the selected/recognised property system upholds. In other words, as was the case in the 17th century, we need to question whether 'the current distribution of property is legitimate, especially the distribution of political rights that go with it/*de savoir si la distribution actuelle de la propriété est légitime, en particulier la répartition des droits politiques qui l'accompagne*' (Meiksins-Wood, 2014, p. 528) and thus the related power. From then on, how do we conceive collective action in relation to collective, common rights without restricting them to relationships between private individuals via the liberal market or to the State as sole arbitrator?

This all leads us to question of how to organise collective action through, on one hand, the property systems and the circulation and goods and services and, on the other hand, the legal organisational structures governing the corresponding productive activity. To rise to this challenge, it becomes necessary to think of enterprises out to the company conception, to reflect on the end purpose and means of collective, citizenship action.[6] When studying entrepreneurial collective action, viewing an enterprise as an organisation, without differentiating it from the company/firm, creates a deadlock, because the absence of a legal definition of an enterprise reduces any understanding or evaluation of its performance, such that it becomes equivalent to the company that is the object of the legal definition (Chaigneau, 2014, Chassagnon & Hollandts, 2014; Hiez, 2013; Roger, 2011; Segrestin & Hatchuel, 2011; Veldman & Willmott, 2013). Through this implicit shift, one becomes assimilated with the other through a funnel effect, which transforms common projects into the sole projects of capital providers (Favereau & Robé, 2012). Then the interests of various stakeholders align with those 'interests of the category seen as holding the ultimate legitimacy, or what we refer to as 'residual claimants' that is those seen as the company owners/*des intérêts de la catégorie considérée comme détentrice de la légitimité ultime, ce qu'on appelle les 'residual claimants', c'est-à-dire les acteurs considérés comme les propriétaires de l'entreprise*' (Desreumaux & Brechet, 2013, p. 81), as Jensen (2001, p. 18) argues '*Two hundred years of work in economics and finance implies that in the absence of externalities and monopoly (and when all goods are priced, social welfare is maximized when each firm in an economy maximizes its total market value). Total value is not just the value of the equity but also includes the market values of all other financial claims including debt, preferred stock, and warrants*'. As Postel and Sobel (2013, p. 11) argue, society can neither be a relevant space for 'an ethical discussion' nor offer 'the prospect of allowing a discussion to be organised/*l'horizon permettant à une discussion de se déployer*'.

Agency theory provides a good illustration of this almost culinary reduction of social relations, such that an organisation gets founded solely on the basis of the relationships between the shareholders and the company director, the manager, when owner and management are distinct (Chanlat, 2009; Gomez, 2009). Jensen (2001) attempts to offer an 'enlightened' version, insofar as he argues that maximising the shareholder's utility function requires the well-being of all. After this point though, the organisation's performance indicators converge to evaluate only the company, as it fits the interests of these two operators. Stakeholder theory seeks to broaden the debate but without avoiding the consequences of the initial legal assumptions (i.e. only society exists in law). The difficulty of reconciling everyone's interests then prompts them to accept the interests of some, under the guidance of managers (Jensen, 2001). Stakeholders seek to maximise their individual utility function, but only in the direction preferred by shareholders, who engage in self-seeking interests to achieve collective well-being and perhaps produce social well-being.[7]

The model then implemented is based on the a priori of financial function, and guides corporate strategy: 'The maximization of shareholder value engenders maximization of company value, which itself corresponds to the maximization of social well-being/*la maximisation de la valeur pour l'actionnaire engendre la maximisation de la valeur de l'entreprise, qui elle-même correspondrait à la maximisation du bien-être social*' (Weinstein, 2010, p. 98). More specifically, it is not possible to challenge the financial profession and its systems without questioning the underlying paradigm which is the creation of shareholder value. This 'founding stone' is crucial to the edifice as it underpins the belief that the allocation of previously saved resources to projects under the constraint of maximising the individual utility function produces collective well-being for the long term, which justifies its central position (Bourguinat & Briys, 2009).

The problem is there has never been any demonstration of this virtuous spiral and any attempts made have been built on false premises (Keen, 2014), as Jensen's problem illustrates in the chapter mentioned above where he is forced to specify what this relationship should be in order to respond to the proponents of the stakeholder theory.

As Weinstein said, 'Agency Theory must be considered for what it is; a theoretical and ideological power grab that is part of a movement seeking to impose a new design for business and to justify key changes in the way in which its functions and management are devised/*La théorie de l'agence doit être considérée pour ce qu'elle est: un coup de force théorique et idéologique qui participe d'un mouvement visant à imposer une nouvelle conception de l'entreprise et à justifier des changements majeurs dans la manière de concevoir ses fonctions et sa gestion*' (Weinstein, 2010, p. 99). This 'power grab' is possible only 'by returning to the ideological sources of modernity (rationality, free individual choice opposing bureaucratic oppression etc.), a 'return' that is more mythical than real' and whose power 'comes less from its intellectual content, strictly speaking, than its ability to be in tune with contextual expectations/*est possible par un retour aux sources idéologiques de la modernité (la rationalité, le choix individuel libre contre l'oppression bureaucratique etc.), 'retour' plus mythique que réel*' (Gomez, 2009, pp. 242, 247). Following Fischbach, I thus characterise it as 'a loss of the world'.

When state-based solutions fail to ensure the control and democratic management of resources or projects, and thc 'pure' market fails to reduce inequalities, it becomes necessary to foster 'micro-emancipation' to favour a more citizen-friendly change: 'Micro-emancipations involve specific and focused attempts to create an area of autonomy along institutionalized relations of power' (Spicer, Alvesson, & Kärreman, 2009, p. 553)

IN THE BEGINNING

The feeling of 'disenchantment' originated in private capitalist property – not that sanctioning what each person, by her or his labour, can buy and possess to live, but that which enhances the value of capital as capital (Marx, 1979/1861, p. 75;[8] Weeks, 2010). This dominance of 'personal' private property[9] by private capitalist property stems from the emergence of liberalism, as well as the historical and social conditions in which it asserted itself (de Saint Victor, 2014; Orsi, 2013). 'It is possible to define property rights not only in a general way, such as protecting the freedom of the individual, but also in a more specific way, such as granting the legal option to take action following personal assessments, which ceases to be a subjective choice and acquires a legal status involving material and civil liabilities/*on peut définir le droit de propriété non seulement de manière générale, comme protection de la liberté individuelle, mais aussi de manière plus précise comme donnant la possibilité légale d'agir en suivant ses propres évaluations, qui cessent d'être des choix subjectifs et acquièrent un statut légal, impliquant des responsabilités matérielles et civiles*' (Audard, 2000, p. 157).[10] But because 'the disparity between economic power and the concentration of capital in the hands of an elite are contrary to liberal values/*l'inégalité du pouvoir économique et de la concentration du capital entre les mains d'une élite sont contraires aux valeurs libérales*' (Audard, 2000, p. 289), the question becomes how this disparity lost its impact and relevance, to the extent that 'the barriers to freedom … [exist] in a much more insidious and invisible way in the *social* conditions of individual existence as well as in the inequalities of economic, social and cultural power/*les obstacles à la liberté (…) [se situent] de manière beaucoup plus insidieuse et invisible, dans les conditions sociales elles-mêmes de l'existence individuelle ainsi que dans les inégalités de pouvoir économique, social et culturel*' (Audard, 2000, p. 268). That is, 'Property both expresses and distils the contradiction of the human world. It is born out of labor and the inequalities in ownership, precisely because it was originally based on differences in labor capacity and unequal strengths/*la propriété, exprime, condense la contradiction du monde humain; elle naît du travail, et l'inégalité des propriétés, précisément parce qu'elle est fondée originellement sur la différence des capacités de travail, est fondée sur une inégalité de forces*' (Manent, 1987, p. 167), even if the protection and safeguarding of this property simultaneously enable people to live on their labour and its benefits.[11]

The difference between private capitalist property and 'personal' private property is that the former does not seek to improve a relationship with nature through accumulation; rather, it seeks value for value (Marx, 2010/1864, pp. 208, 219, 238; Weeks, 2010 for example[12]). The latter instead is based on the fruits of labour undertaken by the worker who possesses its means of production and secures pleasure from it (Marx, 1974b/1863, pp. 103–105, 1978b/1887b, pp. 203–205[13]). As Marcuse (1971, p. 139) puts it so well, 'Individual freedom, effectively developed by bourgeois society … is the expression of free competition between product manufacturers/*La liberté personnelle que la société bourgeoise a effectivement développée (…) est l'expression de la libre concurrence des producteurs de marchandises*'.

This contradiction falls within the social, economic and political circumstances of emerging liberalism,[14] first as a utopian critique of the monarchy's divine right, and then as an ideology[15] of budding capitalism (Parance & de Saint Victor, 2014; de Saint Victor, 2014). The protagonists, demanding to make a living from their work, were merchants.[16] According to Jaume (2010, p. 232), 'It is therefore by trade, or more precisely by *anticipating* the future consolidated as a trading 'promise' that the system of conduct or behaviour will find its force, which is the genuine face of (social) freedom. But, for Hume, the driver of this efficiency of the pledge can be found with the merchant/*C'est donc par l'échange, ou plus précisément par l'anticipation de l'avenir, consolidé 'en promesse' échangée, que le 'système des conduites et des comportements' trouvera sa dynamique, qui est le vrai visage de la liberté (sociale). Or, de façon tout à fait concrète, le véhicule de cette efficace de la promesse sera chez Hume le commerçant*'.

If we accept the premise that freedom constitutes humanity, then inequalities in the exercise of individual potential invariably restrict freedom. Addressing liberalism without addressing its utopian ideals prevents a true understanding of the core issue of private property, which can only play into the hands of the (vast) neoliberal trend.[17] This is particularly so because the 'capitalist enterprise operates as a product of liberal society. In other words, there is no enterprise outside that of liberal ideology which defines the acceptability of it as an organisation .../*l'entreprise capitaliste se déploie comme produit de la société libérale. En d'autres termes, il n'existe pas d'entreprise en dehors de l'idéologie libérale qui en définit l'acceptabilité en tant qu'organisation* (...)' (Gomez, 2009, p. 236).

In turn, we need to revisit the initial challenges to liberalism,[18] questioning collective well-being and happiness (Mill, 1988). People enter society, but they also enter business in an effort to combat rarity, which implies a risk of famine or death (Audard, 2000; Manent, 1987). They relinquish their rights to exercise this freedom, in return for a means to deal effectively with threats. The terms of this debate are seemingly set out in advance to define the exercise of power and the collective venture (Boltanski & Chiapello, 2011).

Efforts to address questions of joint action and cooperation have filled many pages of academic writing (Boltanski & Thévenot, 1991; Cefai, 2007; Golsorkhi, Huault, & Leca, 2009; Lehavi, 2008; Ostrom, 2007, 2008; Taskin & de Nanteuil, 2011; Thévenot, 2006), much of which focuses on the famous prisoner's dilemma. In this task, the cooperative solution has little chance, unless confidence and information spread across the different stakeholders concerned. Because the game does not give the 'prisoners' any chance to organise themselves, it is difficult to argue that it reflects human relations in an exchange, using a quid pro quo strategy (Eber, 2013, p. 68).

The prisoners' need to discuss and share information to organise themselves is a condition of joint action and social life (Caillé, 2007, pp. 102ff.). Cooperation can be non-coercive and sought out solely for what it is, namely, an expression of solidarity with a view towards achieving common goals (Dardot & Laval, 2014, pp. 152–153). In this respect, the definition of the social and solidarity economy (SSE) proposed by Mayer and Caldier (2007, p. 102) might extend to the entire economy, by affirming that 'solidarity in the economy is founded on an economic, social and political project which leads to a new way of conducting politics and establishing human relationships on the basis of consensus and citizen action/*la solidarité en économie repose* [devrait reposer] *sur un projet tout à la fois économique, politique et social, qui entraîne une nouvelle manière de faire de la politique et d'établir des relations humaines, sur la base du consensus et de l'agir citoyen*'.[19] The goal is not to impose these principles to all stakeholders but rather to consider SSE as an alternative institution (Hiez & Lavillumière, 2013) that regulates production and consumption relationships. We can follow Sahakian and Servet when they associate social and solidarity economy '*with the notion of reciprocity, understood as a type of transaction that goes beyond 'giving and receiving' (...) to the notion of reciprocity as a form of interdependence, binding people together in solidarity, (...)* [including] *being invested with the potential of solidarity, consciously interdependent on the others (...)*' (Sahakian & Servet, 2015, p. 5). This 'ideal type'[20] offers a principle for coordination based on cooperation rather than competition, without eliminating the latter, where 'An ideal type of economy is ... defined by the coupling between a form of productive organisation and a method of regulating the economy/*un idéal type d'économie est alors défini par le couplage entre une forme d'organisations productives et un mode de régulation de l'économie*' (Defalvard, 2013, p. 77). The goal of an SSE company is to convey ownership and management of the business democratically. From this standpoint, it is an 'alternative economy' (Lorthiois, quoted by Gardin, 2013, p. 134), stemming from a 'de-liberalisation'. In Dacheux and Goujon's (2013, p. 208) terms, 'the purpose is not to consider the economy as separate from society but, on the contrary, to situate it in the broad and complex context of so-called democratic societies/*Il ne s'agit pas de penser l'économie comme extérieur au social mais bien au contraire de la situer dans un contexte large et complexe, celui des sociétés dites ''démocratiques*'.

How then is it possible to equip people with the means to coordinate actions to produce tangible elements that move the achievement of well-being to a far-off, distant horizon?

OUR QUESTIONING

There is no longer much interest in questioning value (the Physiocrats, the Classics, Marx; Martin & Ouellet, 2014; Roubine, 2009), and exchange and markets are at the forefront instead. In fact, the shareholder – from the point of view of the liberal paradigm because if we follow Weinstein, it is more the duo shareholder/manager (2010, 63 and after) – have taken the place of the market,[21] which had itself replaced the 'Prince' as the ordering principle of the real world, responsible for social order and the collective interest. Passions, except the desire to gain – a source of personal and therefore collective interest (Hirschman, 1980) – are subject to this search for collective well-being.

While we accept this exclusive shift, we still need to question the very possibilities of economic action, one of the key vectors of which is the enterprise, the place where wealth is created.

In neo-classic theory (NCT), the enterprise in an agent and the organisation is absent. NCT therefore only looks at the exchange of goods via calculations to optimise the individual utility function. The company (or firm)[22] is then one point on a segment, defined by its choices between labour and capital factors. In other words, it has no substance or content, or is at best an empty bubble.

We can contrast this approach with one founded on 'collective methodology', compared against 'methodological individualism'. It means breaking away from the ontological hypothesis which states that any collective phenomenon can be reduced to the outcome of individual actions, and any conflicts that arise can be settled by means of a contract,[23] affirming the need to explain the rules that coordinate economic action founded on interpersonal relationships (Amable & Palombarini, 2005; Eymard-Duvernay, 2006, Keen, 2014; Orléans, 2004; Salais & Storper, 1993). This is why our approach is fundamentally opposed to methodological individualism, not so much in terms of method but of its epistemological an ontological status.[24] What basic conditions would then be required to mobilise the necessary resources for promotion of (an) alternative way(s) of coordinating economic action to replace, on the one hand, methodological individualism on an epistemological and gnosiological[25] level and, on the other hand, contracts as the only means of coordination on a methodological level?

This very fact of asking this question implies that we acknowledge the diversity of coordination models and the way that the environment, history and institutions shape the competencies mobilised by stakeholders to reach out to third parties. Forms of knowledge are diverse because they are historical and complex. The history of science demonstrates that the process of 'knowing' is far from linear. Galileo (Feyerabend, 1979, 1989; Hallyn, 1987; Redondi, 1983; Simon, 1979) and others are there to remind us that conviction often outweighs demonstration. As such, how can we help rise to the challenges and needs for coordination in our world, without forbidding this thought (Feyerabend, 1979)?

The debate on company governance and performance cannot be addressed without questioning the construction of these figures: the shareholder and the manager. We need to keep sight of the fact that the financial markets are designed to favour the liquidity of investments and not to fund companies, for whom debt and cash flow are the main resources (Myers, 1984; Weinstein, 2010, pp. 66, 132). In this system, under the cover of shareholder value creation, the manager appears to be the key figure driving the system.

There then emerges a brand new configuration, built into a new construction of the way 'in which concret actors define their social situations/*dont des acteurs concrets définissent leurs situations sociales*' and which 'fetishizes the economic calculation instead of treating it as just one form of commitment in the world among others. This perspective has an impact on the evaluation of collective action using the calculation of investment profitability, applying a formula to maximize gains and minimise losses/*fétichise le calcul économique, au lieu de n'en faire qu'un régime d'engagement dans le monde parmi d'autres. Cette perspective a des conséquences dans l'évaluation de l'action collective à partir d'un calcul de rentabilité des investissements, selon une formule de maximisation des gains et de minimisation des pertes*' (Cefai, 2007, p. 227).This configuration is characterised by the following:

- The progression of management by numbers, reflecting 'the increasing power of the calculation and evaluation economy/*la montée en puissance d'une économie du calcul et de l'évaluation*' (Cefaï, p.141).
- The acceleration of 'the introduction of incentive systems which, at every level, drive the search for short-term financial results and which above all favour the use of trading prices for investment, research and orientation of innovation/*la mise en place de systèmes d'incitation qui poussent, à tous les niveaux, à la recherche de résultats financiers à court terme et surtout qui privilégient la référence aux cours boursiers en matière d'investissement, de recherche et d'orientation de l'innovation*'. (Weinstein, 2010, p. 172).

- A knowledge capital 'that is rapidly renewed and difficult to control over time, requiring fast valuation. Tradeable intellectual capitalism and the permanent innovation economy also introduce a certain short-termism/ *qui se renouvelle rapidement et se contrôle difficilement dans la durée, en imposant une valorisation rapide. Le capitalisme intellectuel marchand et l'économie d'innovation permanent induisent ainsi un certain court-termisme …*' (Weinstein, 2010, p. 171).
- The introduction of 'new instruments (that) serve as internal management instruments, not just as ex-post performance indicators, but actually as ex-ante objectives …/*nouveaux instruments* (qui) *agissent comme instrument de gestion interne, non simplement comme indicateurs de performance ex-post mais bien comme objectifs ex-ante …*' (Weinstein, 2010, p. 108).

All of this leads to 'a financiarised managerial economy based on new managerial power related to financial power (…), the consequence being not so much to return power from shareholders to managers but to establish new financial and managerial power …/*une économie managériale financiarisée reposant sur un nouveau pouvoir managérial lié au pouvoir financier (…) la conséquence en a été non pas tant de restaurer un contrôle des actionnaires sur les managers que d'établir un nouveau pouvoir managérial et financier …*' (Weinstein, 2010, p. 178). Likewise, when we question the generic figure of the shareholder, it is not the 'human' shareholder we evoke (even though the latter is liable) but the paradigm around which shareholder value creation is built, steered by managers through company governance.[26] Shareholder value 'becomes effective through a set of formal and informal rules/*trouve son efficacité dans un ensemble de règles, formelles et informelles*' (Weinstein, 2010 p. 100) and serves to justify the maximisation of the profit share that goes to shareholders as the main tool used to steer the firm's performance (Weinstein, 2010pp. 107–108), maximisation on which managers' remuneration is indexed. This is the shareholder ideology as defined by Ricoeur: 'What is at stake in any ideology is ultimately the legitimisation of a certain system of authority …/*Ce qui est en jeu dans toute idéologie, c'est en fin de compte la légitimation d'un certain système d'autorité …*' (1997, p. 256).

With regard to methodological individualism, we consider that for the 'sum of individual optimisations' to form an organised whole – with meaning – there is a need for coordination principles and regulations if that 'whole' is to emerge. There is nothing metaphysical about these principles; they simply express the complexity of possible interactions between the people making up the whole (our individual and collective history) and are the outcome of that. In other words, a connection between people is something other than a collection of individual functions. For 'optimization' to occur – other than the issues of cognitive capacity and information (Karpick, 2007, p. 58; Simon, 1976) – there needs to be a capacity for thought. This latter is necessarily the outcome of a collective/organised educative process (Sève, 2005, pp. 58, 160, 164 note 138).

We therefore need to question relations in the market and private property according to the three core elements identified in critical management studies (Alvesson, Bridgman, & Willmott, 2009):

- 'De-naturalisation', which re-examines all that is given and taken for granted by a naturalising approach to socio-economic reality (e.g. the market, private property, social denominations, the existence of elites, hierarchy), particularly that which obliges people to question organisational forms in place, such as capitalist enterprise (Gomez, 2009).
- 'Anti-performativity', or the domination of performance in relation to maximising outputs for a given input in all walks of life, such that it 'is used in a somewhat technical sense to identify social relations in which the dominance of a means–ends calculus acts to exclude critical reflection on the question of ends' (Alvesson et al., 2009, p. 10). It is not enough to simply state a performance to do it; it is equally important to dismantle representations and given objects as it is to establish conditions for reclaiming collective action (Cobbaut, 2011; Golsorkhi et al., 2009).
- 'Reflexivity', to question the position of all experts (e.g. professors, managers), 'under the guise of production of 'facts', such research is inattentive to (i.e. reflexive about) the values which guide not only the scope and representation of what is researched but also how research is conducted' (Alvesson et al., 2009, p. 10).

Drawing on these elements to analyse property also involves questioning shareholder finance and pursuing critical thinking about the internal contradiction of capital, which seeks to free itself, in vain, from work to gain in value and which affirms private property as the guarantor of freedom, without providing a means to exercise it effectively. Then 'The pressure for capital to escape from the confines of production goes beyond the potential disruptions arising from the class struggle, it comes from the inter nature of capital, the contradiction between value in exchange and value in use' (Weeks, 2010, p. 141).

To re-appropriate freedom, the starting point is the contradiction between use value and exchange value,[27] and the potential for ending the reign of the latter (Marx, 1980b/1973, pp. 103, 193, 196[28]) – not to abolish trade in general, but rather to eliminate the trade of capital to generate capital[29] and thus regain people's confidence (Servet, 2012, p. 369). This also means that we need to see it as an emancipation from the self-valuation of capital which 'submits all social activity' (Martin & Ouellet, 2014, p. 29) to the logic of the exchange value.

Reasserting use value begins with the re-appropriation of production conditions, including uses, practices and 'use activities/*activités d'usage*' (Sohn-Rethel, 2010, p. 121), and then secondarily involves decision making focused on aims, purposes and resources to be assembled, while ensuring control over manufacturing processes.[30] The issue is to contest the situation in which 'social players no longer form relationships with one another other than through the things that they produce with a view to trading them on the market/*que les acteurs sociaux n'entrent plus en relation les uns avec les autres que par l'intermédiaire des choses qu'ils produisent en vue de leur échange sur le marché (…)*' (Fischbach, 2009b, p. 41) and to establish relationships through developing uses[31] rather than capitalist trade, which seeks value for value.

In turn, it becomes necessary to analyse the conditions for a possible promotion of 'production of use', to use Polanyi's (1983, p. 100) expression, which leads to a challenge to the domination of the cycle of capital valorisation that, among other things, reinstates long-term investment decisions.[32] Such production can be based on forms of organisation and principles of governance that move, or return, the expression of freedom to the centre of the decision-making processes. Freedom determines the tactics used to build collective activities geared towards a pre-established, discussed and shared goal, which then may be re-evaluated according to the outputs obtained.[33] Ultimately, the enterprise becomes 'a finalised and organised collective action involving the formal coordination of activities of a group of players in a collective entity with more or less defined boundaries that also involves cooperative behaviour and varying degrees of commitment/*une action collective, finalisée et organisée, qui engage la coordination formelle des activités d'un ensemble d'acteurs eu sein d'une entité collective possédant des frontières plus ou moins bien délimitées, qui engage aussi des comportements de coopération et des engagements plus ou moins forts*' (Desreumaux & Brechet, 2013, p. 82).

Here I seek to demonstrate that it is possible to map out lines to overcome this denomination of exchange value, and therefore capitalist property, starting from two premises: brand communities[34] and cooperatives. These concepts offer potential means to manage 'common pool resources' as a common (Bollier, 2014; Ostrom, 2011), as either natural or non-material resources (Hess & Ostrom, 2011; Parance & de Saint Victor, 2014) or as an objective, built around clearly stated values (Desreumaux & Brechet, 2013).[35] In the former case, the emphasis is on uses. In the latter, it is on organising around purposes that might be use-related aims, because 'in the private property system, an object becomes 'property' when it is used and this use relates either to the object's direct consumption or in its ability to be capitalised/*dans le régime de propriété privée, un objet devient 'propriété' lorsqu'il peut être 'utilisé'; et cette utilisation consiste soit dans la consommation directe de l'objet, soit dans sa capacité à être capitalisé*' (Marcuse, 1969, p. 93), such that it promotes the first term through collective action, founded both on and by uses. An emphasis also cites a form of governance that prioritises the person rather than capital, because the measure applied here is 'one person, one vote', not 'one share/one vote'. As a result, 'although it is true that freedom cannot be organised, the material, technical (and perhaps intellectual) conditions of freedom require an organisation/*s'il est vrai que la liberté ne peut pas s'organiser, les conditions matérielles, techniques (et peut-être intellectuelles) de la liberté exigent une organisation*' (Marcuse, 1971, p. 202).

Brand communities express this possibility of re-appropriating freedom, because what matters in most of them is use, including the aim. Here, we seek to understand how uses get practiced externally in a market that nurtures them outside the capitalist sphere, though without refusing trade.

THE BRAND COMMUNITY[36]

Brand communities bring consumers and users together around a product or service introduced in a market by a company, in an effort to develop practices and form bonds (e.g. symbolic, emotional) (Badot, Carrier, Cova, Desjeux, & Filser, 2009; Cova & Cova, 2009). Emblematic cases include the communities that have formed around Harley-Davidson, Alfa-Romeo, Warhammer and Manchester United and Nutella (Cova, 1997; Cova & Cova, 2002; Cova, Kozinets, & Shankar, 2007; Cova & Pace, 2006; Cova & White, 2010; Fournier, 2009). In such communities, a dynamic exists between the company's brand and the consumers who acquire it for themselves. As a result,

> Brand communities are sources of value for companies but will only exist insofar as the consumers who have got together sense goodwill towards the brand and develop connections around it. As such, value creation of this kind is exogenous to the firm (Vargo, 2009). Consumers search for a positive, warm, and brand context; a context in which they feel welcome, protected, and included. It is in that sense that we can speak of the linking value of brands. (Cova & Paranque, 2010, p. 6)

The process is not uniform though; it can diverge and create conflicts between the community and the company, as occurred

> for the Games Workshop when a number of consumers, outraged at sales prices, began manufacturing fake figurines and offered them online (www.boardgamegeek.com) or at collectors' fairs. At the same time, other consumers opened sites explaining how to create battle decors for Warhammer by oneself (www.military-kits.com). The company countered by criticising the counterfeit figurines or decors for their mediocre quality and use of dangerous materials. (Cova & Paranque, 2010, p. 6)

Two key dimensions underlie the community-company relationship. First, it creates shareholder value, because the brand is an asset (Salinas, 2009), which must be promoted and contribute to maximising shareholders' utility functions.[37] Second, places emerge for uses to develop, including activities based on uses outside the market (e.g. peer-to-peer, open source). These uses are external to the capital cycle but also represent opportunities for it to capture potential exchange value. In turn, the brand becomes a resource for users/consumers in the community, who develop non-market-oriented exchanges,[38] social ties and activities (Kornberger, 2010). They also derive identity from it, though an identity under stress. For companies that can transform these non-market uses or use value (use-derived) into products or exchange value, shareholder value increases. The question about transcending the market thus is not necessarily proactive but rather occurs because value increasingly emerges outside the market (Arvidsson, 2011), which represents both a challenge and an opportunity for companies, as well as for capital-related emancipation.

Moreover, managing this resource is a unique effort, in that it is neither private in its use (but is private in its purchase) nor public (it is initialised by a relationship with the market, through a purchase or some relationship with something sold in a market). Furthermore, it is not available to everyone. When the emphasis becomes at least somewhat external to the company and moves into an action space driven by consumers who generate uses and resources, it is difficult to determine the status of this resource: Is it public, private, or collective? Who has the right to its use or distribution?

Through its uses, the brand represents a two-dimensional link between consumer and company, and then between customers and shareholder value (through the creation of exchange value). Thus, consider two levels of property:

- Marketable private property, such that the brand is contractually owned by the company.
- Collective property, established through a link between consumers, due to their investment and interactions in non-exclusive commercial relationships.

Accordingly, a dual question arises: How can action be coordinated outside the market, and how can it be validated in a market economy? According to Fischbach (2009a, p. 136), 'The question would then be to know if we could escape the coercive and continual power of value by drawing from the well of another timeframe which would no longer be fixed and restricted to actual presence of value, but a moving, fluid and dynamic timeframe/*la question serait alors de savoir si l'on peut échapper à l'emprise coercitive et perpétuelle de la valeur en puisant à la source d'une autre temporalité qui ne serait plus le temps figé et spatialisé de la présence propre à la valeur, mais à une temporalité mouvante, fluide et dynamique*'.

This value could come from uses, not just exchanges, coordinated by the mediation of collective projects that rely on rules with which all partners can identify. These circumstances mark the beginnings of a possibility to contest the notion that 'market value supplants individual creative value. If the latter serves to nurture the former, it is market rather than the individual that dominates/*la valeur marchande supplante la valeur de créativité individuelle; si la seconde sert à accroitre la première, c'est le marché plutôt que l'individu qui s'impose*' (Marcuse, 1971, pp. 186–187).

THE COOPERATIVE

Having illustrated how uses might emerge outside the capital cycle, it is necessary to clarify that this cycle is defined by the pursuit of value (exchange value) for its own sake. Transcending private capitalist property does not mean that private property disappears; rather a certain set of social relationships arises, based on the capital cycle – the process that targets value for value and therefore increases value.[39] The aim is to identify productive forms that have use value as their common objective and that are likely to pass through the market, without entering the capital cycle,[40] to contribute to debates about exercising citizenship within a company.[41]

The cooperative form regards employees as 'shareholders' – ownership, in their company, with similar influence in the decision-making process, regardless of their capital contributions. Thus, it generally can take on projects that exceed a legal organisational framework and feature a broader collective. People's reasons to cooperate are mostly social rather than economic (Arando, Freudlich, Gago, Jones Derek, & Kato, 2010; Bouchon, Michard, & Plasse, 2010), in accordance with the meaning of dominant theory and maximisation of individual utility. Efforts to safeguard jobs (Casadesus-Masanell & Khanna, 2003) or support for local activities usually are central to the project (Arando et al., 2010). The history of cooperatives[42] clearly emphasises the management difficulties they face (Arando et al., 2010; Durance, 2011). They differ from 'traditional' settings not just in their governance practices but also by the lack of dividends; moreover, there is no increase of value of initial contributions (which challenges the emergence of exchange value). The conditions for transferring shares also differ.[43] Cooperatives consist of members, a term that emphasises the collective nature of ownership, even though it remains on an individual basis. The term 'coordinated private property' further emphasises this latter dimension, as well as the initial commitment, while 'collective property' could be understood as an undefined anonymous 'collective body', even if it results from the coordinated, collective action of individuals.

One of the motivations for this work here involved questions about corporate governance (Pérez, 2009) and the corporate social responsibility (CSR) challenges for companies that acknowledge deficiencies in the way they operate but also worry that cooperatives could lead to archaism (Hart & Moore, 1996) and a threat to their survival. For example, dated forms of producer associations must react to the potential failure of their business (Casadesus-Masanell & Khanna, 2003, p. 4). In contrast, I propose that cooperatives actually provide a modern, operational solution to 'non-cosmetic' problems with the governance and exercise of CSR (Bouchon, Michard, Plasse, & Paranque, 2012; Cornforth, 2004; Feng & Hendrikse, 2011). Studies on the topic (Groupe Alpha, 2012) and real-world decisions, such as those by French cooperative banks that form holdings to access financial markets, demonstrate the many challenges to the so-call 'modernity' of legal forms usually assumed to be well adapted to the status of globalisation.

This discussion also echoes a study by Marx (1978c/1894, pp. 105–106[44]) that revealed

> The cooperative factories of labourers themselves represent, within the old form, the first sprouts of the new, although they naturally reproduce, and must reproduce, everywhere in their actual organisation all the shortcomings of the prevailing system. But the antithesis between capital and labour is overcome between them, if at first only by way of making the associated labourers into their own capitalist, i.e. by enabling them to use the means of production for employment of their own labour .... The capitalist stock companies, as much as the cooperative stock factories, should be considered as transitional forms from the capitalist mode of production to the associated one, with the only distinction that the antagonism is resolved negatively in one and positively in the other/*A l'intérieur de la vieille forme* [de la propriété privée], *les usines coopératives des ouvriers elles-mêmes représentent la première rupture de cette forme, bien qu'évidemment elles reproduisent et ne peuvent pas ne pas reproduire partout dans leur organisation effective, tous les défauts du système existant. Mais, dans ces coopératives, la contradiction entre capital et travail est supprimée, même si les travailleurs ne sont d'abord, en tant qu'association, que leur propre capitaliste, c'est-à-dire s'ils utilisent les moyens de production à mettre en valeur leur propre travail.(...) Il faut considérer les entreprises capitalistes par actions et, au même titre, les usines coopératives comme des formes de transition du mode capitaliste de production au mode collectiviste, avec cette différence que, dans les premières, la contradiction est résolue négativement et dans les secondes positivement.*[45]

The qualification of 'positively' refers to how the cooperative form enables stakeholders,[46] starting with employees, to regain the conditions of production activity. They no longer view capital as working against them as an independent and alienating force but instead regard it as the means to their freedom.[47]

In turn, there are two key issues: (1) the ultimate aims and modes of organisation involving employees or citizens in the management of the organisation, in an effort to seek emancipation from the capital valorisation and (2) responses to need by ensuring long-term activity that generates enough income to support the organisation's development, as embedded in its society and social relations. The resulting collective responsibility also acts on two levels:

Firstly, it corresponds to not dividing responsibility based on different degrees of involvement in the final output .... Secondly, the other distinction that we can give to the concept of collective responsibility, is of responsibility towards the community. In other words, there is a willingness to consider the well-being of other cooperative members and make sure that this is not challenged by any member of the organisation/*Tout d'abord elle correspond au fait de ne pas diviser la responsabilité en fonction des degrés d'implication dans un résultat final. (...). L'autre acception que l'on peut donner à la notion de responsabilité collective est celle de responsabilité envers la collectivité. Autrement dit, il y a une volonté de faire en sorte de prendre en compte le bien-être des autres coopérateurs et de faire que celui-ci ne soit remis en question par aucun membre de l'organisation.* (Bouchon et al., 2010, p. 54).

In concrete terms, the genuine risks occur in the economic sphere as much as in the social life of the community.

This standpoint opposes the collective responsibility required in traditional organisations, where 'the concentration of power in the hands of the shareholder leads to an increasingly bureaucratic system of organisation in which the exercise of responsibility by the employee is replaced by the necessity for loyalty, a sense of duty and discipline with respect to the shareholder/*la concentration des pouvoirs dans les mains de l'actionnaire mène à un système d'organisation de plus en plus bureaucratique, où* ***l'exercice de la responsabilité pour le salarié, est remplacé par la nécessité de la loyauté, le sens du devoir et de la discipline vis-à-vis de l'actionnaire***'. (Bouchon et al., 2010, p. 25, emphasis added). In contrast, in cooperative enterprises (e.g. Sociétés Coopératives de Production now called Sociétés Coopératives et Participatives – SCOPs in France), risk-taking related to invested capital and personal commitments (work, family, etc.) invokes specific responsibilities for both relationships and governance. The result is that 'the first condition to fulfil for responsible behaviour is undoubtedly the power to exercise one's responsibility, i.e. there must be a certain room for manoeuvre in one's actions and keeping the option of making a choice/*la première condition à remplir pour avoir un comportement responsable est sans doute de pouvoir exercer sa responsabilité. C'est-à-dire qu'il faut posséder une certaine marge de manœuvre dans son action, et garder la possibilité d'effectuer un choix (…)*' (Bouchon et al., 2010, p. 51).

This room for manoeuvre is the start of a process of dis-alienation, or re-appropriating means for personal purposes. Thus the cooperative reinstates uses, through ultimate goals, and it provides the organisation with a means to combat 'the objective conditions of work [which] when faced with living labor, assume an increasingly colossal independence/*les conditions objectives du travail* [qui] *acquièrent, face au travail vivant, une autonomie de plus en plus gigantesque*' (Marx, 1980b/1973, p. 323,[48] 1980a/1973, p. 401[49]).[50] Thus it calls into question 'this absolute dissociation, separation, between property, i.e. working conditions coming from 'things', and the power of living labor/*cette dissociation, séparation absolues entre la propriété, c.-à-d. les conditions de travail relevant du domaine des choses, et la puissance du travail vivant*' (Marx, 1980a/1973, p. 391). Finally, this responsibility echoes uses and use activities, such as in fair trade settings, where the market allows resources to be redistributed rather than the production of exchange value as such.

The study of cooperatives can be very useful and is well documented (Wright, 2014), though the issue of equality in capital has not been fully resolved, in particular for employees who are not members (Baretto, 2011). A focal topic for such research is the three key principles of cooperatives: interdependence, solidarity and democracy (Gios & Santuari, 2002; Pendleton, 2005, 2011; Webb & Cheney, 2014). Thus a three-fold research agenda emerges: What governance issues arise from the sustainability of the collective project and the requirements for their re-assessment in the long run? What obstacles hinder this form of collective management of production resources, or which social and cultural conditions support its appropriation? What performance-related advantages do cooperatives present compared with traditional forms of business, such as in relation to their social or financial nature? These questions can be answered only if the underlying paradigm – namely, to maximise shareholder value to increase collective well-being – is clearly specified (Paranque, 2010), rather than reducing corporate performance to the efficiency of the firm (Fama & Jensen, 1983), and it involves the collective as a whole (customers, suppliers, citizens). As Casadesus-Masanell and Khanna (2003, p. 4) remind us, despite arguments that 'cooperatives will underperform limited liability firms [cooperative employees could accept lower wages in return for safeguarding their jobs after a takeover by its employees to avoid it going out of business], though it is important that the poor performance causes the cooperative exist, rather than the act of cooperation inducing inefficiency'. Again, a consensus is necessary in the comparison of objectives and relevance, when it comes to the choice of indicators. Whether in terms of work productivity, sustainability or investments, observations of underperformance are far from confirmed (Arando et al., 2010; Schwartz, 2011).

The challenge is to specify rules to distinguish the conditions that can coordinate these collective actions and render them shareable. To do so, I draw on work by Ostrom, who focuses specifically on common pool resources management and the property regimes in which they can be managed.

COLLECTIVE ACTION AND 'COMMON POOL RESOURCES MANAGEMENT'

When analysing the shift in the capitalist economy from human activities to an 'all-economic' approach (Meiksins-Wood, 2014, p. 619), the examples of cooperatives and brand communities provide some critical pointers.

Whether part of brand communities or cooperatives, resources remain private, because they are both outside the public sphere and underpinned by or embedded in the market, even when the uses and practices thus derived are collective. For example, a community might implement uses in a private setting based on a brand, but it eventually gets formalised as an association. The brand reflects a non-material asset, created or produced from the exclusive use of resources acquired contractually by the company, through the sale of goods and services on the market after processing and packaging.

What then are the rights and obligations of stakeholders? Even if the consumer's purchase remains private, if the company has sold a product (goods or services), the brand appropriation can be symbolic and therefore non-material: I may share it with others, and even if I do not buy or sell it, I can identify with the brand and be part of its symbolic development through the brand community. This appropriation does not require market relations; anyone can belong and contribute to a community. The use value (still in a Marxist sense[51]) can develop by escaping, albeit temporarily, from the capital cycle; it does not need the market, or exchange value, to be shared.

Sharing in turn involves rules for mediating and managing collective action. In brand communities (e.g. Apple, Warhammer, Ducati, Burberry ...) with stakeholders who commit to them, I anticipate two risks or opportunities for the community, depending on the point of view. First, some members may use collective work to privatise the community, such as when a solidarity action leads to access to high quality vegetables, creates a new market, and becomes solvent, such that it can seize commercial opportunities directly. For example, social networks such as 'Couch Surfing' can be sold by their founders. Second, when the organisation comes under pressure from the market (particularly banks), it might be tempted to cash in on the fruits of its labours to develop its offer; employability schemes for workers with disabilities might be considered a simple form of cheap labour, or in the case of listing Facebook on the stock market promoted the voluntary activity of its members in a private and exclusive way. In both cases, use value gets transformed into exchange value on the market. That is, an individual might benefit from collective work to create a commodity, such as open source IT resources, or a company might transform use into a commodity. Regardless of the path, use value provides the group with meaning but breaks free of that meaning to enter an exchange value sphere, because it is subject to a private acquisition (individual as opposed to collective) before being launched on the market. For the community to sustain itself, it must recognise the risk-opportunity pairing: One player (individual or company) acquires all or part of the resources generated by the project, to the detriment of others, whether through the withdrawal of a resource (e.g. technology, product) or limited access to a non-material resource (e.g. copyright, licence) (Hess & Ostrom, 2011; Parance & de Saint Victor, 2014).

Use value mediation involves bonds and symbols, employed to manage collective action and its aims. Arvidsson (2006, 2009, 2011) emphasises the transformations that get introduced by developing non-material resources, which have ethical components (balancing passion and emotions). Following Marx, he calls it the 'general intellect' (Marx, 1980b/1973, p. 194,[52] 2010/1864, p. 235). Willmott (2010) notes the dynamic of promoting brands that try to exploit communities to organise co-production between consumers and the company. New ways of promoting capital and the identification of new sources of (exchange) value are central to this process. It aptly expresses the constant tension between value of use versus exchange, community and market.

At the boundary, the brand defines a space for action between the use and exchange spheres. It is a financial resource for the company, through the income it generates, and it belongs to the company. Yet at the same time, consumers acquire it socially to create bonds, which creates another potential opportunity for the company to improve its market performance. Then the brand becomes a common at a social level, through its symbolic appropriation by consumers, though the 'property' still must be defined, as a pool of resources for the community and the company.[53] The latter might decide to privately acquire resources collectively created by the community,[54] so it becomes necessary to define the boundaries of the resource and the community. For non-material products, these boundaries are vague, and the community is irregular, effectively illustrated as concentric circles representing aficionados with varying degrees of involvement. A brand community approach often is based on intangible, 'easily' transferable resources (Hess & Ostrom, 2011)[55] but is limited by the threat that members will perceive being plundered or exploited (Cova & Dalli, 2009). Another difficulty that is also an advantage occurs when a polycentric organisation makes differential investments in members, with the option of authorising everyone's behaviour over time (monitoring), even if collective coordination is complex. In this system of labour ownership and activities, everyone invests in the community, including the company and third parties.

So the shift moves from a logic of possession to one of common property,[56] or in Caillé's (2007, p. 101) words, 'of the necessary subordination …

of interests of 'having' to that of 'being'/*de la nécessaire subordination (...) des intérêts de l'avoir aux intérêts de l'être*' whether as a result of production activity, or as a product of collective action, to appropriate the 'whole world of culture and civilisation/*du monde entier de la culture et de la civilisation*' (Fischbach, 2009b, p. 234). The aim is define a general outline 'of an alternative conception of property as an enjoyment of active self-expression/*d'une conception alternative de la propriété comme jouissance de l'expression active de soi*' (Fischbach, 2009b, p. 238). Is it possible to follow Fichte who defines this conception 'as an exclusive right to a freely determined activity/*dans un droit exclusif à une activité libre déterminée*' (Fischbach, 2009b, p. 244)? In other words, can people agree that 'the real conflict ... is not between private property and collective property, but between private, or exclusive, use and common use/*la véritable opposition (...) n'est pas entre propriété privée et propriété collective, mais entre usage privé ou privatif et usage commun*' (Fischbach, 2009b, p. 249)? I propose building 'a common use of goods and assets as opposed to their private and exclusive consumption which prevails today/*un usage commun des biens et des richesses, contre leur consommation privée et privative qui prévaut aujourd'hui*' (Fischbach, 2009b, p. 262), which requires a method of organising that facilitates this construction.[57]

WHAT TYPE OF COORDINATION?

Another challenge involves managing intermediate collective action between the state and the market (Chanteau & Labrousse, 2013), on the basis of coordinated private property (Bollier, 2011), such that it cannot be reduced to the behaviour of *homo economicus* (Aoyagi, Pede, Kajisa, & Tsusaka, 2013; Chanlat, 2009). As an archetypal example, private property owners might manage a common pool resource, such as fish for fishermen or water for farmers. This distinction involves a public commodity versus a private commodity. The former 'is naturally non-rivalrous, meaning that consumption of the resource does not deplete the amount available to other users, and not excludable meaning that knowledge resources are not naturally defined by boundaries that permits exclusion of users' (Madison et al., 2010, p. 666)[58] (Table 1).

A social space might span the two, enabling the collective use of resources, not derived from public action or a single capitalist market. It would include some prior coordination, to enable the organisation to be

Table 1. Definition of the Type of Goods.

Rivalry Exclusion	Weak	Strong
Difficult	Public goods	CPR
Easy	'Toll Goods – Club Goods'	'Private Goods'

managed but also act as a reminder of the collective objectives (and means) being pursued, while still retaining the clarity and legitimacy of everyone's interests (private and personal).

However, it appears uncertain whether a society-based approach is irreducible from the market and the state (Caillé, 2007, p. 61). To investigate locally institutionalised 'coordination', using Testart's (2007, p. 128) approach, I identify five relationship levels in a system:[59]

- Gifts,
- Reciprocity,
- Non-market-oriented exchange ('in which price and value considerations are not sufficient to prompt the exchange/*dans lesquels les considérations de prix ou de valeurs ne suffisent pas à provoquer l'échange*' (Testart, 2007, p. 44)) and
- Two types of market exchange, one of which specifically denotes a capitalist market exchange in which 'the person exchanging seeks use value from the goods provided in return or its exchange value/[...] *l'échangiste cherche la valeur d'usage du bien fournie en contre partie ou sa valeur d'échange*' (Testart, 2007, p. 156).

This categorisation also corresponds with three levels of activity-based bonds:

- Reciprocity, which involves neither synchronicity or obligation in the implied dual movement;
- Exchange, which requires a causal relationship and an obligation and
- Gifts, for which there is neither an obligation nor right and is unilateral (Testart, 2007, p. 221)[60] (Table 2).

This differentiation serves as a reminder that 'the exchange is just one case, a very specific case, among all other forms of circulation/*l'échange n'est qu'un cas particulier, très particulier, parmi toutes les formes de circulation*' (Testart, 2007, p. 69); there is no single system of exchange (Mauss, 2012, p. 65; Rehn, 2014). Thus it is possible to situate this coordination in a society, as defined by Mauss, namely, 'a group of people sufficiently permanent and sufficiently large to ordinarily form enough sub-groups and

Table 2. Forms of Circulation.

Kind of Relationship	Testart (2007)
Gift	The gift is selfless and timeless. There is neither an obligation nor right for the donor or beneficiary, and is unilateral
Reciprocity	It involves neither synchronicity or obligation in the implied dual movement
Exchanges	They require a causal relationship and an obligation;
Non-market-oriented exchange	The price and value considerations are not sufficient to prompt the exchange
Non-capitalist market-oriented exchange	The person exchanging seeks use value from the goods provided in return
Capitalist market-oriented exchange	The person exchanging seeks exchange value.

enough living generations in a given area ... around an (generally) independent and always determined constitution/*un groupe d'hommes suffisamment permanent et suffisamment grand pour rassembler d'assez nombreux sous-groupes et d'assez nombreuses générations vivant – d'ordinaire – sur un territoire déterminé ... autour d'une constitution indépendante (généralement) et toujours déterminée*' (Caillé, 2007, p. 217).

The 'common' concept appears useful, as long as it extends to analyse the conditions and the forms of its own production, including non-material ones, not simply its use. Ostrom (2011, p. 1) establishes the importance of, for example, 'the issues of how best to govern natural resources used by many individuals in common'.[61] A prevalent response to such management is binary: either the state or the market.[62] An alternative solution combines private property with the common pool resource management, without reducing it to a binary distinction between nationalisation (omnipresent state) and capitalist privatisation (omnipresent market). Rather, the important element is 'how noticeable each person's actions are' (Ostrom, 2011, pp. 6, 7), which defines confidence among participants. Ostrom also emphasises the importance of understanding a common pool resource institution as a specific property system affected by the **distribution rights of use** (bundle of rights); each system of resources has a related system of ownership rights, each with its own system of governance (Chanteau, Coriat, Labrousse, & Orsi, 2013).[63]

Common resources come from nature or are produced by humans; any withdrawal by an individual likely comes at the expense of others, and each person is tempted to take the maximum, to avoid rationing (Ostrom, 2007). Therefore, it is necessary to define the community or group boundaries, then establish forms of property that are congruent with the objectives of this community. Seven rights qualify 'property' and determine the roles and capacities for action for everyone, according to their access and their rights (Hess & Ostrom, 2011, pp. 52–53):

1. *Access*: the right to enter a defined physical area and enjoy non-subtractive benefits.
2. *Contribution*: the right to contribute to the content and quality of the resource to maintain it.
3. *Extraction*: the right to extract the resource and use it for one's own ends.
4. *Removal*: the right to alter one or more components of the resource to develop it.
5. *Management*: the right to manage, regulate and improve the day-to-day working of the corresponding area.
6. *Exclusion*: the right of exclusion, which defines access and extraction rights and the transfer of previous rights.
7. *Alienation*: the right of alienation, specifying the rules of sale or leasing management, as well as exclusion rights.

Creating the conditions for collective action goes beyond managing a business venture, in that it requires defined boundaries that characterise the space for action, as well as the appropriate degree of involvement of various stakeholders. In addition to technical aspects, it therefore is important to define corresponding social space.

An organisation delivering a project must explicate its reasons and values for undertaking the project, then translate the conditions for action and day-to-day management into operations, while also working to achieve the collective goal set by its partners and their commitments. The project often stems from a question or necessity, such as a handicap, access to a resource, or the need for independence. In all cases, projects face resource-related challenges: Who will the customers be? Which suppliers can ensure supply? How should teams be training? How can be the required funds be secured?[64] When such questions arise, it is mostly with time pressure, and the answers may seem glaringly obvious: This supplier is available, that customer has contacted you and so on. Yet in each case, expectations and values may not be compatible with those established by the persons delivering the project, which demands some means to prevent the organisation's constraints from 'contaminating' the project. For example, a fair trade network needs to integrate local producers that respect the environment with end users in the market that demand fresh fruits and vegetables all year round, even out of season.[65]

The response, and therefore the organisation and governance, should reflect the way power is exercised and the procedures for its implementation. To define this exercise, key questions include How are (or should) decisions (be) made? Have the principles been defined? Are decisions made on the basis of everyone's capital contributions, with preference for financial capacity? Are they instead organised according to each person's level of involvement, motivation or abilities? Eight design principles for stable, common pool resource institutions are defined by Ostrom (2011, p. 90, 2010, p. 114, 2005, pp. 258ff.):

1. Clearly defined boundaries, because 'it is necessary to identity the community concerned by the common pool resource/*il convient d'identifier la communauté concernée par le commun*' (Dardot & Laval, 2014, p. 150). What are the community's boundaries? Can its foundations be identified by links?
2. Matching rules for the appropriation and provision of common pool resources in local conditions, because 'They must be well adapted to needs and local conditions and in line with objectives/*elles doivent être bien adaptées aux besoins et conditions locales et conformes aux objectifs*' (Dardot & Laval, 2014, p. 150). The aim is to identify how the community functions, according to its value-based procedures, and the types of contributions by members, as well as the principles authorising each member to use of the output generated through activities by each other person.
3. Collective choice arrangements, which enable members to 'regularly take part in proceedings to amend these rules/*participer régulièrement aux instances chargées de modifier ces règles/regularly take part in proceedings to amend these rules*' (Dardot & Laval, 2014, p. 150) and thereby define how operational rules should be instituted, at what level of formalisation, and how they might be modified.
4. Monitoring, to ensure community spirit is respected and punishments for offenders.
5. Graduated sanctions, including what are they and how they can be defined and applied.
6. Conflict resolution mechanisms, to assess the capacity of the group to manage change and or divergences when faced with corporate behaviour.

7. Minimal recognition of organisational rights, which reflects the community's structure and the way it manages the range of commitments to the project, as well as its constraints.
8. Nested enterprises, accounting for the various levels of action and interaction resulting from these principles, especially among the various organisations closely involved in the process, but also with the outside.

The forms of governance reveal these choices; the rules adopted, such as a 'one person, one vote' or a 'one share, one vote' principle, encourage specific coordination expressions tactics of collective action and stakeholders involvement. These forms of governance in turn have a major influence on how the project is delivered and whether it fulfils the values held by the collective. The right to speak out also recognises the legitimacy of speech in a decision-making context. Finally, a common pool resources management approach can sanction a use-based stance, as long as the purpose of the 'enterprise'[66] is redefined.

THE NEED FOR REDEFINITION

By implicitly reducing enterprise to the sole legal form of the company, the modern finance paradigm takes on indisputable force. However, questioning this implicit assimilation enables a challenge to two underlying hypotheses, namely, maximising individual utility functions and creating shareholder value, the shareholder's utility function as a guarantor of collective (long-term) well-being. The reasoning is as follows:

- Many arguments assume individual selfishness, such that each person seeks out his or her own interests as a way to master one's passion, enabling the community to achieve well-being (Hirschman, 1980). This argument is justified through comparisons to Darwin's natural selection, but doing so ignores the difference in levels of analyses: Darwin explicitly based his work on species, not individuals (Lecointre, 2009; Testart, 2012, p. 136ff., in particular). Recent ethological studies even demonstrate that cooperation tends to override competition (Sciama, 2013).
- Rather than only seeking to maximise their resources, academic work reveals that organisations participate in an optimisation process under pressures that is not merely economic but also social, cultural or even geographic. They seek to achieve project viability over time, through sustainability (for and by) the community (Poteete, Janssen, & Ostrom, 2010).

- What does 'value' mean? In the financial world, the only legitimate value is that which serves a managerial function, such as stakeholder value which can be measured by financial markets. 'Other' values are considered relevant only if they contribute to it. But these other values require definition (Desreumaux & Brechet, 2013; Foster, 2011), as well as evaluation that avoids reducing them to simple monetary performance. A quantitative accounting measurement cannot be the only criterion for legitimacy.
- By integrating values, it may be possible to contest the assumption that the maximisation of shareholder value will lead to collective well-being in the long run.
- And finally, of what does collective well-being consist of (de Nanteuil, 2011)?

Although this work does not claim to answer all these questions, the goal is to challenge neo-classic theory(NCT) which separates 'the analysis of the action at a given time from everything that has created the conditions of that action/*l'analyse de l'action à un moment donné du temps de tout ce qui a créé les conditions de cette action*' (Przeworski, 1991, p. 88), because 'circumstances make men just as much as men make circumstances/*les circonstances font tout autant les hommes que les hommes font les circonstances*' (Marx, 1976/1932, p. 39[67]). Facing this challenge demands questioning practices, as much as the dominant theoretical foundations for finance and management (Alvesson & Willmott, 2012; Golsorkhi et al., 2009; Orleans, 2011; Taskin, 2011).[68]

As I explained previously, the conditions for collective action require boundaries to establish the 'world' for action and the involvement of various stakeholders. For example, the entrepreneurial role must expand, beyond its legal incarnation, to encompass the corresponding social sphere from which it emerges.

The tension, or even contradiction, in companies (firms) has not escaped the attention of theorists, such as in the debate about the dominant position of the shareholder – manager duo in aligning the expectations of other stakeholders. The aim is to provide (or restore) the manager's legitimacy and thereby find a compromise between stakeholder expectations and demands (Chanlat, 2009; Cobbaut, 2011; Gomez, 2011), especially under pressure from financial markets (Rainelli-Le Montagner, 2009). The effort to achieve integration also appears in human resource management policies (Alvesson & Willmott, 2012) that encourage behavioural changes by ensuring employees share in ownership, so that they act like shareholders

(Carberry, 2011). It also resonates with CSR, which seeks to broaden the managerial horizons of company boards by obliging them to include other stakeholder interests (Pérez, 2009). However, this approach only affects shareholder performance in a marginal manner, without reconsidering the heart of the matter which is that of coherence (compatibility) between the following:

- The performance of the enterprise as a company,
- The aims of the enterprise as a collective organisation and
- Society as the democratic context within which people act as citizen.

The result is an ongoing game of power and domination, as illustrated by CSR policies that seek to contain the excesses of finance, whereas a contrary ideal would subject finance to a shared ethic in Society. Consider two (imperfect) pieces of evidence to help envisage this reversal. First, Islamic finance aims to control, rather than redefine, finance by highlighting how ethical principles can come first (without being naïve about their possible circumvention). Social values determine the 'legitimate' space for financial action (Erragragui, 2013, and Chapters 11 and 12 in this book) in the sense of both the security and the act. Second, use value stems from social and socialising practices, emerging from spaces outside the market, such as the brand communities I outlined previously (see also Chapter 8 in this book), as well as local currencies (Servet, 2012) and community exchanges (peer-to-peer, social networks, open source etc.).

COLLECTIVE ACTION AND COMMON POOL RESOURCES MANAGEMENT: AN APPRAISAL OF MARKET/NON-MARKET-ORIENTED RELATIONS

I use Cova and Paranque'previous work (2013b) to illustrate the process of emergence. If capturing (exchange) value refers to the company's ability to recover emerging (use) value from outside its confines (Bowman & Ambrosini, 2000; Pitelis, 2009), the managerial challenge is to capture and then appropriate the additional value created outside the marketing sphere, for example, by the brand community.

This effort is constrained by two dual contradictions, corresponding to public/private and market/non-market processes. To illustrate this, I use a chart from a socio-economic, non-utilitarian approach (Caillé, 2007) that identifies four key points related to brand uses:

- The emergence of the brand within the company as part of the process to produce exchange value;
- Its passage through the brand community with attribution of uses and specific meanings;
- Brand socialisation, which subsequently is enriched but also becomes part of society at large and
- Collective acquisition in markets through dissemination, even banalisation, or is reinstated in the private production process by the company that owns it or another entity (e.g. counterfeits, imitations).

This framework reveals possible trajectories between the private and public spaces and between primary and secondary sociality.

Our distinctions and typologies will undoubtedly be clearer if they are not based only on the opposition between the primary and secondary, but on a cross-reference between this opposition and that of private and public spaces. It is therefore easy, within secondary sociality, to distinguish between a private secondary (firm, market) and a public secondary (State, administration). Similarly and symmetrically, the distinction between private primary (family, domesticity) and public primary (associative, corporations, guilds, the public space of mutual acquaintances) naturally springs to mind/*Nos distinctions et nos typologies serons assurément plus claires si nous ne les fondons pas seulement sur l'opposition entre le primaire et le secondaire, mais sur un croisement entre cette opposition avec celle du privé et du public. Il est ainsi facile, au sein de la socialité secondaire, de distinguer entre un secondaire privé (l'entreprise, le marché) et un secondaire public (l'Etat, l'administration). De même et symétriquement s'impose tout naturellement à l'esprit la distinction entre un primaire privé (la famille, la domesticité) et un primaire public (l'associatif, les corporations, les confréries, l'espace public d'interconnaissances)* (Caillé, 2007, p. 135).

According to this framework, brand communities fall into the primary sociality categorisation, which can be seen in private practice but eventually reveals itself in the public arena.

The analytical framework also helps outline uses, spaces and their rules for collective action, organised to varying degrees and formalised as in the example of brand communities. There is no required route between quadrants; rather, the options include emerging market and non-market opportunities in a space that can generate hybrid forms, such as mutual companies, cooperatives, or the welfare system. This private stakeholder bears the socialisation of a need, managed collectively outside the capitalist market. The term 'public' refers to collective coordination of and by the audience.

This representation suggests an initial approximation of social spaces that allow for collective action. By specifying the approach, as in the case of a brand community, or in other cases, the management of a resource that is common to different groups or persons is at stake, which can give rise to conflict in terms of coordinated or opportunistic appropriation. A methodological tool is thus required to analyse and understand the management of common pool resources, whether material or intangible, and the different, related forms of ownership.

Managing a physical resource clearly differs from managing social relations to produce an intangible resource such as 'collective well-being'. Yet these relationships can create a resource if they are part of a collective project that calls on the skills and ambitions of all, to achieve a collectively defined objective within a territory (De Angelis & Havie, 2014; Desreumaux & Brechet, 2013; Hess & Ostrom, 2011; Ostrom, 2007; Schweik, 2011). Donsimoni, Kemmar, and Perret-Karnot (2010, p. 19) state that 'initiating a process of local development consists in finding and highlighting a specificity to offer a unique product. The space gains in brand image and becomes a territory/*amorcer un processus de développement local consiste à trouver et mettre en valeur une spécificité pour offrir un produit unique. L'espace y gagne en image de marques et se transforme en territoire*'. The territory is the result of a process but also a resource that serves the process, as long as the levers required for its coordination and its promotion, can be identified, which guarantees the sustainability of the organised group. Thus a common aspect emerges. Before managing or producing a resource, the stakeholders must agree. This point is perhaps the key contribution Ostrom makes, by establishing a junction: how can we define a common objective and the means to achieve it? Regardless of the material nature of the resource, the key element is the way stakeholders, under a specific property regime,[69] come to an agreement, or not, to manage a physical resource or deploy the means required to meet a need. To be formally operational, the first agreement requires explicit rules to manage collective action and coordinate private interests. The second mobilises stakeholders around an intangible resource, for a project that requires means (human, financial, technical) to meet a social need.[70]

Furthermore, management must be at least somewhat interested in formalising the practices, whether of the brand community or initiated by a collective project. Such practice management must be long-term and able to deal with contradictions or differences within the group, that is, between private interests.

A common pool resource approach[71] offers an opportunity to position use value at the heart of organisational management. Specifically, it stems from a collective process that 'builds and is built in and by a project, in and by a group of stakeholders/*se construit et se construisant dans et par un projet, dans et par un collectif d'acteurs*' (Desreumaux & Brechet, 2013, p. 91), to enable the coordination of 'personal' private property, including both personal interests and activities that produce use value. Such a method could represent relative liberation from the reign of exchange value over certain collective actions, to set out rules to validate these non-market actions, which does not mean there is no exchange.

This approach empirically questions the hypothesis of maximising individual utility functions (Ostrom, 2011; also see Poteete et al., 2010, pp.194, 198, 215). The collective management of resources involves people seeking something that works in the long run, without knowing whether it will result from maximisation, optimisation, or consensus that enables them to 'live together'. Beyond the diversity of institutional forms, basic rules allow the construction of common pool resource management institutions[72] (Ostrom, 2010), or different types of action that can exist and be deployed (Brechet & Desreumaux, 2010; Boltanski & Thévenot, 1991; Cefai, 2007), so it also refers to underlying regulatory principles.

To alter social relationships, people need access to evaluations and justifications of proposals, bearing in mind the range of methods available to coordinate collective action, which are not mutually exclusive. Three 'worlds' detailed by Boltanski and Thévenot (1991) appear particularly relevant:

- Domestic 'world', which 'appears when seeking fairness places the accent on relationships between people/*apparait chaque fois que la recherche de ce qui est juste met l'accent sur les relations personnelles entre les gens*' (p. 206).
- Civic 'world' that are important to human beings 'insofar as they belong to these [collective persons] or represent them/*en tant qu'ils appartiennent à ces [personnes collectives] ou les représentent*' (p. 231).
- The market 'world', 'used (...) to coordinate local transactions/*sert effectivement (...) à coordonner des transactions locales*' (p. 243).

These 'worlds' identify principles of coordination, for which a commons pool resource-based approach offers an operational methodology for building the corresponding institutions. Each socio-economic 'world' must be able to carry out entrepreneurial use projects, with the condition that the enterprise has a legal and organisational form that is coherent with the collective project of the socio-cultural space,[73] as determined by the territory's citizens. In this respect, the cooperative form is of interest, because the governance principle is similar to those on which citizen 'one person, one vote' relations are founded, so it is not subject to value, as expressed in the 'one share, one vote' rule. This form reflects the 'imaginary cooperative' proposed by Defalvard (2013, pp. 79–80), which he refers to as 'the cooperative form of economic regulations based on common rules defined between and by associates/*la forme coopérative des régulations économiques, basée sur des règles communes définies entre et par des associés*'. The common pool resource approach defined by Ostrom therefore provides the keys to micro-economic regulation (coordination) of projects, backed by the associations linking private property and collective resource management.

Using the framework (Fig. 1), I suggest that quadrant 2 constitutes a relevant space to deploy the common pool resource management. Based on a common project, starting with a use community, various disseminations stem from the 'cooperative' fact (Hiez, 2013), ranging from non-market-oriented (e.g. management of a forest by local people) to market-oriented (developing income-generating activities from resource management) relationships, including relationships with the capitalist market, insofar as enterprises are part of specific social and economic environments (Coriat, 2013a; Weinstein, 2013).

The cooperative, as an organisation, can develop responsibility around uses, similar to practices developed in brand communities, if the vision held by associated members and their possible employees is clearly established (Baretto, 2011). Conventional performance indicators are those of companies focused on the evaluation of exchange value, that is, *in fine* shareholder value. Stakeholder interests instead must be clarified, so that the surplus, required to sustain the project, still meets the uses (needs) and not the (exchange) value, and is not specifically driven by rules to create shareholder value creation rules.[74] In this respect, using the proposed framework (Fig. 1) to undertake a social assessment of the project, based on social and ownership priorities (space), can provide a better understanding of it and the ways it can be shared.[75]

THREE EXAMPLES OF COLLECTIVE ACTIONS

Collective action is defined as 'any attempt to form a group which is more or less formalised and institutionalised, by individuals seeking to achieve a

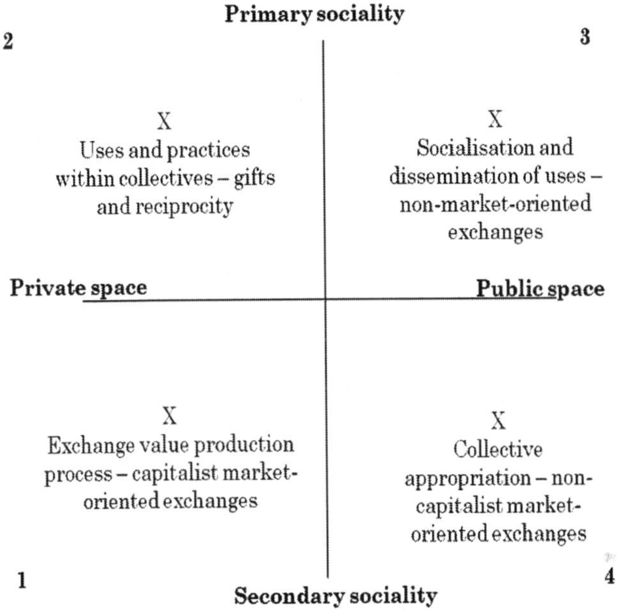

Fig. 1. Sociality and Property (Cova & Paranque, 2013b).

common objective in a context of cooperation and competition with other groups .... Collective action is therefore a joint action or a concerted action/*toute tentative de construction d'un collectif, plus ou moins formalisé et institutionnalisé, par des individus qui cherchent à atteindre un objectif partagé, dans des contextes de coopération et de compétition avec d'autres collectifs. (...). L'action collective est donc une action conjointe ou une action concertée*' (Cefai, 2007, p. 8). For the purposes of this chapter, this objective consists of enhancing a territory that constitutes a symbolic and tangible 'common pool resource', which guides the actions of those involved.

In turn, the collective action requires some clarification and coordination of rules. Both the group and the people involved must agree not only on the reality to be created but also on how to work together to achieve it: 'The issue at stake in these negotiations is the interpretation model chosen to "create the reality" that presents itself [to the operators] in the form of a problem to solve/*L'enjeu de ces négociations est le modèle d'interprétation à retenir pour "construire la réalité" qui se présente à eux [les agents] comme problème à résoudre*' (Salais, Baverez, & Reynaud, 1999, pp. 197–198). This necessary negotiation is an expression of an arrangement, through which 'the agreement of the operators on their description of the world which thus allows them to coordinate their projects/*l'accord des agents sur leur description du monde et leur [permettant] ainsi de coordonner leurs projets*' can be recognized, and its construction 'relies upon social processes to develop models that represent the reality/*repose sur des processus sociaux d'élaboration de modèles de représentation de la réalité*' (Salais et al., 1999, pp. 236, 239). In short, it requires trust to be built in preparation for action.

To illustrate and clarify this approach, this section details three examples: a project conducted at Kedge Business School between 2008 and 2014, entitled Ethomed (Paranque, 2010), the employee takeover of the FRALIB-Unilever site in Gémenos, near Marseille, and Palmas Bank in Brazil (Hudon & Meyer, 2013).

(i) **Ethomed**[76]

The power of modern finance lies in its capacity to synthesise financial profitability (in multiple variants of this single indicator) via the markets. The performance underlying financial results is in fact the company's strategic performance. Furthermore, companies need minimum financial performance so they can control solvency and thus ensure their durability. That solvency depends not only on the financial markets but on the market for goods and services because of the cost of resources. This leads to a kind of vicious circle: financial performance sanctions strategic performance so the latter is 'good' only if it is reflected in financial performance that is independent of the real economy (Plihon, 2002). This neglects the fact that a good strategy is one that generates social well-being (at least that is what the theory justifying the central place of finance in our society tells us), but how do we evaluate it, measure it or define it?

The Ethomed project sought to question modern finance by reversing the traditional configuration, in which shareholders are the heart of social dynamics. Can a societal objective, and corresponding performance measures, be proposed that does not use the creation of shareholder value as an internal central coordination tool? Economic development is a condition for collective well-being. The debate then should focus on the content of this sought-after, expected development. Doing so requires the definition of consultation procedures that enable stakeholders to produce common objectives. The use of the plural here implies the need to rank these objectives. In addition, the method by which to achieve the objectives must be clear, including how to assess an organisation's performance.

Ethomed's goal was to adopt a practical approach. The debate about social well-being is complex and involves consideration of both a Society and its purposes. By reversing the usual sequence – that is, beginning with profit (i.e. maximising shareholder value) devoted to achieving long-term, collective well-being through an optimal allocation of capital – Ethomed defined which objectives citizens set for themselves, in the concrete terms of their daily lives (e.g. starting a nursery, opening a free health clinic, children's education). Only then does it define the resources to be implemented through that enterprise, in both senses of the term, namely setting about to do something new and a specific type of organisation. The sequence starts with the collective needs of a community (specified according to the project), then clarifies the necessary form of organisation and the resources required, including financial ones. The challenge then is to ensure the project's long-term sustainability, in terms of its responsiveness to the collective needs identified at the outset. In particular, the sequence must identify the surpluses required to meet current and future commitments and how to generate them. The related management tools must ensure coherence between economic performance and these previously established objectives, suggesting that economic performance must be established in combination with the means to evaluate it. Then economic performance, or the ability to generate the surpluses necessary to both live up to past commitments (e.g. paying off loans) and ensure future obligations (investments, recruiting, training), is just one, albeit an essential, part of this process, which conditions sustainability and anchors the project in the market.

Ethomed participated in defining these collective objectives and achieving the performance necessary to attain them by providing financial means. The project receives backing from FCP AG2R-LA MONDIALE ETHOMED ISR, a mutual trust fund whose income is partially secured in a dedicated account, prior to funding projects approved by the partners. The project fitted into a continuum that begins with uses and practices in collective bodies and extends to deployment as collective ownership (Fig. 1). On an operational level, this strictly empirical approach seeks to define tools to structure the necessary creation of surplus and the concrete achievement of social well-being, as defined by the stakeholders through a jointly developed collective project.

Ethomed was a double trial. The purpose was to help students realise that finance can't be understood only as a field for shareholder players. Even we need it for liquidity and intertemporal operation, it is necessary not only to control it but also to propose other opportunities and rules of the game. However, it is important to show that we could coordinate ourselves as responsible citizens and producers-consumers if we have a clear understanding of our goals and how proceed. To some extent, this approach is close to Ostrom's (2011) work on common pool resources management.

But unfortunately, the Ethomed experience was shut down because of changes in the French legislation concerning the mutual trust fund.

(ii) **FRALIB**

'FRALIB' was the name given to employees of the company with the same name (Française d'Alimentation et de Boissons), based in Gémenos. It was a subsidiary of the Unilever Group, resulting from a 1977 merger of the Thés Eléphant company (which was bought by Unilever from Ricard in 1972) with the Lipton company, which belongs to Unilever. The history of Thés Eléphant is intrinsic to Marseille. It dates back to the late nineteenth century and became a subsidiary of Ricard in 1969. Gémenos became the company's sole production site in 1989, though packaging of tea and herbal teas took place in Gémenos and in Brussels after 2006. Then in 2010, Unilever decided to centralise production and packaging in Brussels and close the Gémenos site.[77] Employees have been fighting since then to retain the business location, as well as revive the 'Elephant' as a cooperative, with the support of local authorities. The Société Coopérative Ouvrière Provençale des Thés et Infusions (SCOPTI) was established on 14 November, 2012. In 2014, the employees won their court case and the business was relaunched under the 1336 brand after a long period of conflict.

This interesting case illustrates the remarks about collective well-being and common pool resources and property. Collective well-being consists of maintaining an economic activity that generates income for people, so they can continue to plan for the future and their families, with far less uncertainty than if the company were to close completely. The common property is a resource, comprised of a production tool, a brand, a supply network and a territory with a strong history. This territory is both cultural and economic, as exemplified by the strong identity markers, from Frédéric Mistral to 'l'Occitane en Provence'. It even has been institutionalised with a PRIDES recognition (*Pôle Régional d'Innovation et de Développement Economique Solidaire*, or Regional Centre for Inclusive Economic Development) by the PACA Regional Council. It appears possible to find converging interests across differing sectors, with

Carac'Terres (Territorial Solidarity Tourism), PASS (Perfumes, Aromas, Scents and Flavours Competitiveness Cluster), and the European Fruits and Vegetables Innovation Cluster.[78] All these PRIDES seek to create inter-dependencies and thereby develop territories that can support significant economic activity.

From this standpoint, SCOPTI conveys the notion of micro-emancipation (Alvesson & Willmott, 2012, pp. 192, 197), which inherently features 'an emphasis on partial, temporary movements that break away from diverse forms of mundane oppression, rather than successive moves towards a predetermined state of liberation', or more precisely, which allows the approach to focus on 'the living experience of people who are continuously engaged in local decision making and associated struggles to improve working conditions' and their daily living conditions.

The common to be managed is within the given territory, defined by local socio-cultural and economic relations, and the creation of an activity results from principles (values) and resources. In terms of employment, maintaining an industrial activity contributes to the development of the Huveaune Valley, which was once a thriving industrial area but is now subject to significant de-industrialisation. This affects both populations and related businesses, including sub-contractors, tradespeople and public and private services. However, the business venture still must participate in viable commercial relationships if it is to maintain its tea business. Thus there is an opportunity to achieve collective well being, as defined by the employees whose choice of suppliers reveals strategies based on similar values, in terms of the conception of development. The Hom et Ter company, which works in the organic fair trade tea business and could supply SCOPTI with quality produce, defines itself as 'a creator of networks'.[79] This cooperation might offer an opportunity to revive the network of plant producers in the Carpentras area that existed some 15 years ago. Another company, Agro'Novae, processes fruit[80] and markets it under the brand name 'Comte de Provence', for sale in supermarkets. This connection could open an avenue for diversification or even development through contacts with the aforementioned PRIDES to extend the scope of their business in terms of flavouring or with a move into vegetable conserves.

The challenge consists in defining the space for collective action and establishing founding or justifying principles for a cooperative venture that are not solely economic. There are some existing advantages, in terms of common values, a demand for authenticity and encouragements for relevant territories to act together. Thus SCOPTI offers a good example of how to off-set the problem. If, using the common expression, the 'business model' remains centred on the company, the possibilities for development are strongly constrained by competitive environments. If the problem instead expands to a space for action that is centred on a territory, the company can be defined as a place that generates income as part of a wider collective action.[81] Accordingly, the shared resource must be defined and qualified by the project boundaries. In turn, SCOPTI is part of a process based on two spaces for action (Fig. 1): uses and practices within groups, and collective ownership with non-capitalist market exchanges that give rise to a more capitalist-oriented development where required.

(iii) **Palmas Bank**[82]

This bank started with a group, namely a community of fishermen in northern Brazil who were driven out of their village to allow the development of coastal tourism, and relocated 70 km inland, in what would later become the district of Conjunto Palmeiras. Thus uprooted, the population organised itself to coordinate and manage their expulsion, so that they could benefit from the small amount of aid provided, then redefine their collective project, centred on community well-being.[83] Such well-being was defined at the outset with a negative perspective, stemming from the question, 'Why are we poor'? (Neiva et al., 2013). The conclusion was that the cause stemmed from the failure to maintain the territory's (or district's) resources and activities; people went to purchase what they needed 'elsewhere', because they could not get all that they needed locally.

In response, the community decided to encourage diverse business activities and keep the outcomes of these activities within the neighbourhood. By developing micro-credit and a local currency, they could support internal exchanges in the local area and offer solvent outlets for the activities developed there, through the collective organisation of residents.[84] What is particularly interesting is the way the project was delivered, through the creation of a neighbourhood residents' association, the Palma Institute, which included a finance department (Palmas Bank[85]). To ensure overall coordination, they created an 'arena of collective choice represented by the socio-economic local forum (FECOL). This collective deliberative body does not have the explicit goal of changing the operational rules relating to the provision and ownership of the common. It is more of a public space for close interactions between different stakeholders of Conjunto Palmeiras' (Hudon & Meyer, 2013, p. 12).

Hudon and Meyer (2013) analyses the entire system using the framework of a common pool resource management institution (Bollier, 2014; Ostrom, 2010). The intangible resource, though it became tangible through the micro-credit coordination process and access to the local currency, was managed as common property, with appropriate rules (e.g. living in the neighbourhood, being of legal age, non-exclusion for beneficiaries who did not need to provide guarantees). The creation of FECOL as a stakeholder interface both defines Palmas Bank's strategy and ensures democratic control. The rules also apply for monitoring, achieved through the social proximity of the borrowers with not just other residents but also the bank managers, who come from the same neighbourhood. This type of control makes guarantees unnecessary. In addition, a system of progressive sanctions exists, ranging from a reminder phone call to blacklisting through the '*disclosure of the outstanding dues to relations and the FECOL*'. Conflicts are resolved by acknowledging exceptional situations and borrowers' behaviours. The bank also acts as an interface with external organisations, such as the Brazilian Central Bank, which helps ensure the availability of the necessary funds for micro-credit. Projects receive support from public authorities (State of Ceara, Sao Joao di Arraial municipality) and private organisations (BNDES, Banco do Brasil, Caixa Economica). Finally, interventions coordinated with companies and organisations outside the area ensure access to external activities or services required to support the collective project.

The next challenge is to secure the project for the long term. With success, some residents, in particular the youngest, might consider going to live elsewhere, which would weaken the group. The issue becomes finding ways to ensure anchoring, not simply on the basis of local emancipation but instead on a collective project designed to last. In this case, the space covers 'collective ownership' based on 'uses and practices within local groups' that target local development (Fig. 1).

CONCLUSION

The purpose of this chapter has been to help suggest elements to address the 'disenchantment of the world' (Fischbach, 2009b; Rosa, 2012).

The motivation also stemmed from a question Marx likely had in mind when he said that 'cooperative factories should be considered transitional forms from the capitalist mode of production to the associated one [with] the contradiction resolved … positively/*faut considérer (…) les usines coopératives comme les formes de transition du mode capitaliste au mode collectiviste* [avec dans ce cas, le fait que] *la contradiction est résolue (…)* ***positivement***' (1978c/1894, p. 106;[86] our emphasis).[87] The contradiction emerges from the description Marx gives of the peasant or craftsperson in relation to capital, as both an employee and a self-capitalist. It is not a question of people themselves as much as the functions they perform in their economic activity: 'the independent peasant or craftsman is divided into two people …. As a possessor of means of production, he is capitalist and as a labourer, he is his own employee …. In fact, as irrational as this mode might at first seem, it is however right to a certain extent/*le paysan ou l'artisan indépendant sont divisés en deux personnes (…). Comme possesseur des moyens de production, il est capitaliste, comme travailleur, il est son propre salarié* (…) *En fait, ce mode d'exposition, aussi irrationnel soit-il à première vue est pourtant juste dans une certaine mesure*' (Marx, 1974a/1863, p. 477ff.;[88] also see Böhm & Land, 2012). People must be able to 'manage' these two social functions of the system by transcending them, which can be done only if they adopt a different perspective than the organisational view towards creating shareholder wealth. The 'positively' comes about only from a perspective other than that derived from a capital-based company, without condemning themselves to domination by the reign of (exchange) value. This condition prevents each person's work from becoming an external object, with an existence determined by a process over which they have no control but that is instead incumbent on them.[89] Beyond the need to achieve an 'ethical critique of alienated life/*critique éthique de la vie aliénée*' (Rosa, 2012, p. 91), to break with this exteriority and domination, groups and the common must be (re)constructed, using projects anchored in territories.[90] Thus they can identify possible ways to overcome the alienation that makes them a 'stranger in their own worlds', where they feel as if they have no say in the future and have been objectively dispossessed by social relationships of production (Fischbach, 2009b; Honneth, 2007).

In this sense, the cooperative offers 'positive' possibilities for escaping the reign of value, on two levels. First, the absence of capital value creation provides access to the use value market, as part of non-capitalist exchanges. Thus profits are not distributed, nominal value gets maintained as a transfer price and private transfers are controlled by members (Hiez, 2013).

Second, because of its governance principle of 'one person, one voice', it rejects the assumed supremacy of financial contributions as a criterion for regulation. This possibility would then remain in quadrant 4 in Fig. 1, with possible spill-overs into quadrant 1 – a reminder that the break involves a capital company that might proceed through a transition stage and return to a capitalist market. Emancipation never occurs. The limit of this 'positivity' lies in the risk of localism in which the cooperative engages to maintain its principles, or at least to reserve the membership status of its historic founders. Then it might adopt a more capitalist development, creating subsidiaries, similar to what the Basque cooperative Mondragon has done (though it has never claimed to break with capitalism). The cooperative format is not, as such, a 'positive' response; it becomes one only if the organisation is part of a wider collective process, beyond a simple production organisation that generates income.

Research on the commons offers key insights, insofar as it is concerned with uses and practices.[91] Work from the Bloomington School often focuses on management practices for common pool resources; little discussion refers to the way members later develop their production, by selling it on a market in the usual sense of the term. Likewise, there is no mention of the financing of 'common' activities or of the organisation of collective management, Ostrom (2005, p. 248) quotes Berkes to highlight that 'community control over the fishing effort appears to be very difficult to achieve in commercial fishing in general,' highlighting the same issue to emphasise this 'external' aspect, to which Marx also refers. That is, Ostrom analyses the coordinated production of use value by independent producers who pool the management of their production (i.e. as an activity to mobilise a resource for non-commercial or commercial gains). As Marx said, 'Each individual commodity has a double character of use value and exchange value.[92] The commodity is primarily, as English economists call it, 'anything necessary, useful or pleasant in life', an object of human wants, a means of existence in the widest sense of the term …. Use value has only has value in use and is realised only in the process of consumption/*Chaque marchandise se présente sous le double aspect de valeur d'usage et de valeur d'échange.*[93] *La marchandise est d'abord, comme disent les économistes anglais, 'une chose quelconque, nécessaire, utile, ou agréable à la vie', l'objet de besoins humains, un moyen de subsistance au sens le plus large du mot (…) La valeur d'usage n'a de valeur que pour l'usage et ne se réalise que dans le procès de la consommation*' (Marx, 1972b/1859, pp. 7–8[94]). The 'commons' approach potentially allows autonomy for use value, producing value outside the capital sphere, even though it does not lead to independence, because at a given moment, the product of the activity must be sold or is simply a single stage in a wider process.[95] That moment offers a possible emancipation nonetheless, as the Palmas Bank case study shows. Paradoxically, the strength of Ostrom's approach is this focus on the organisational dimension of an internally regulated group, in which each person accepts a share of the 'outside' that each other person represents, as a potential competitor who also relies on the local market.[96] These aspects of the 'positive' provide the basis for a re-appropriation of labour, as long as it entails close attention to boundaries in terms of not just geography or communitarianism, but also common shared objectives, such as producing a surplus not solely to accumulate capital but rather to sustain the collective project.[97]

It is problematic not to think simultaneously about the place and role of the company in this commons approach. In my opinion, it is not just about considering shared management, which is a real challenge, particularly for intellectual property or culture. Rather, it is a matter of thinking about exchange on the basis of productive, activity-generating income, namely the enterprise. A surprising lack of studies explain what happens to products, an item that has 'monetary value and [is] likely to be owned/*une valeur pécuniaire et [est] susceptible d'appropriation*' (Le Roy, 2014, p. 83), derived from common pool resource management. In terms of the examples offered by Ostrom, what happens to rice grown with collectively managed irrigation, fish caught using collectively established rules, or cattle raised on collectively held Swiss or Japanese pastures? The ability of a community to collectively manage a resource that is necessary to produce goods that can be traded on a market says nothing about how those goods get exchanged. This gap is nonetheless vital; addressing it could increase stakeholders' ability to take part in organised exchanges, unless their ambition is self-sufficiency.

Another challenge is to clearly distinguish the foundational principles for group life, in the management of the *input* of principles that underpin trade with the *outside*. We need to consider what forms the basis of the community, such as a simple need to survive or a political project, as well as what connects and make this community fit with the rest of the world. In this respect, rather than a binary, silo mentality, implying inevitable commodification, a continuum of entrepreneurial options and actions should be promoted, as if embarking on an adventure or organising a get-together. The distinction proposed by Testart (2007) is already detailed, but because it is primarily rooted in human relations, it could be expanded with the addition of the concept of sharing, as proposed by Le Roy (2014). From a gift, which is neither based on nor requires a commitment, to reciprocity that involves an exchange as part of what could be called moral obligations, through to non-market-oriented, market-oriented and capitalist market-oriented exchanges, sharing might operate as the political link that creates coherence between the shared management of a necessary resource and the production of goods within aa revised form of private property, enabling everyone (including groups) to generate necessary income. Sharing is a 'mechanism of division and unification/participation/*mécanisme de division et de réunion/participation*' (Le Roy, 2014, p. 89) that can organise the community by fitting it into internal social relationships, as well as into exchanges with the rest of the world. This 'community ontology' (Le Roy, 2014, p. 95) could be defined by a triple-sharing arrangement: 'sharing the same life ..., sharing all the specific characteristics ..., and sharing a common decision-making sphere/*partage d'une même vie [...], partage de la totalité des spécificités [...] et partage d'un champ décisionnel commun*' (Alliot, 2003, pp. 73–76 quoted by Le Roy, 2014, p. 95). Such sharing also involves the collective management of a resource, without the dual dimensions of means of production and regulations on the non-capitalist trade relationship.

Is it possible to break away from the domination of exchange value without assimilating or denying state and collective ownership?

Arvidsson (2009, p. 2) hypothesises that 'exchange value no longer adequately reflects use value', such that the modern world contends with a crisis of transition, amplified by a crisis of value, which itself is linked to growth in intangible assets, such as brands, largely ignored by traditional tools. These developments are because of not only the difficulty associated with appraising such assets but also to their intrinsic characteristics, in that they are immediately shareable upon being distributed, and their value comes from their non-market-oriented appropriation by consumers. Arvidsson's (2009, p. 9) argument thus is that the ' 'New Economy' is an Ethical Economy' and the value created at its core 'is not measured inputs of scarce productive time (labour or machine time), but the ability to build social relations that organize and motivate essentially abundant resources: 'free labor' and collective intelligence' (p. 11). The only way to manage transaction costs related to opportunistic behaviour for example[98] is ethics (p. 13), that is recourse to the social actor and his/her responsibility. The next step is to determine in which context stakeholders can act this way, or would even want to, whereas it is clear that shareholder pressure from financial markets will only increase to capture – potential – exchange value (Bowman & Ambrosini, 2000; Cova & Paranque, 2013a). Arvidsson (2009, p. 19) suggests it is possible only by promoting a new agreement about value (see Orleans, 2011).

The resulting challenge is effectively the redeployment of use value, beyond its diversity, anchored in a new agreement that expresses new principles of coordination, such as the development of common pool resources, starting with research and development, that enable everyone to share and make offers. The importance of the intangible, and of the common good(s) – that is disseminated knowledge – as a resource but also as values/ethics enables organisational principles to be altered and supports clear assessments of projects and goals.

Willmott (2010) stresses the importance of the growth of non-material, intangible assets as increasingly central to shareholder value creation. He also notes an increasing discrepancy between exchange value and use value, proposing the concept of an 'ethico-political complex' that 'underscores how, as value is more or less explicitly placed upon 'this' (e.g. 'exchange') rather than 'that' (e.g. 'use'), the construction of social reality is an endemically ethical undertaking' (Willmott, 2010, p. 518). By studying brands, he seeks to reveal how 'value-productive activity is increasingly occurring in the sphere of circulation' (Willmott, 2010, p. 520),[99] a place where use value can escape from the capital sphere through consumers activities (not to say labour) in their (eventual) appropriation of products. Willmott immediately positions this 'complex' as a means to express tensions between the emergence of new uses through consumer practices and the pressure to integrate (new) uses in the capital cycle, in the form of exchange value.[100] The ethico-political complex thus is a process that mobilises the symbolism at work in practices, such as societal issues expressed by CSR and socially responsible investments. Its management makes cooperative forms very appealing, insofar as it enables collective coordination in governance, based on the individual and not capital (Table 3).

Reciprocal goods transfers have always existed in human communities, though they rarely entail sharing. The market as a site of exchange existed well before capitalism (Braudel, 1979; Polanyi, 1983), at least if we understand it as a site of meetings and symbolic exchanges forming links within and across human communities (Caillé, 2007; Descola, 2005; Fontaine, 2014; Graeber, 2010, 2013; Guesnerie, 2006; Jappe, 2014; Karpick, 2007; Testart, 2007; Servet, 2013; Servet & Hillenkamp, 2015; Vergara, 2006). In this sense, the market is based on symbolic or material media that validate exchanges occurring within it. Whether based on seashells or money or gifts, these exchanges establish a social link and an ability to meet '*others*' (Servet, 2012). Yet the market was also a place or institution, among others, that expressed social relations (Caillé, 2007; Testart, 2012; Weber, 2012). Since the nineteenth century, the market has served as a central

Table 3. The Ethico-Political Context.

Ethico-Political Complex	Collective	<——>	Public (in the Public)
Nature of value or value in the process of production	Use value		Exchange value
Kind of resources and property rights	Commons	***Nature of appropriation***	Private
Ethic of governance	One person one vote	***Of the means of production***	One share, one vote
Nature of the performance	Ethic		Shareholder value maximisation

Source: According to Willmott (2010).

institution for authorising economic activity, such that 'Instead of the economy being embedded in social relations, social relations are imbedded in the economic system/*Au lieu que l'économie soit encastrée dans les relations sociales, ce sont les relations sociales qui sont encastrées dans le système économique*' (Polanyi, 1983, p. 104).[101] My goal here is to proactively implement a change in social relations while recognising the relevance that 'the concept that mankind makes of relationships between nature and culture reflects the way in which their own social relationships are altered/*la conception que se font les hommes des rapports entre nature et culture est fonction de la manière dont se modifient leurs propres rapports sociaux*' (Lévi-Strauss, 2008, p. 681). This proactive ambition stems from an analysis of capitalism as a system that pursues the development of capital for itself, with no thought for the use value produced, other than as a source of profit. Altering social relations requires access to assessments and justifications of other proposals. My comments are based on an acknowledgement of a wide range of mutually non-exclusive ways to co-ordinate collective action, as proposed by Boltanski and Thévenot (1991).

In addition, this chapter offers a methodological framework that supports the development and coordination of collective actions enabling emancipation from the market alone or from any State in order to satisfy collective well-being, expressed in the response provided to the identified needs. To be free from does not mean to refuse; for an agreement to be valid, it must be contestable within a framework that is accepted by all members. To be free means to be able to propose and to build organisation of collective action somewhere between the all-state or all-market approach. Collective action cannot be reduced solely to the interplay of contracting operators (Coriat, 2013a; Orsi, 2013; Weinstein, 2013), nor can it forget that defining rules require an appropriate legal framework that affords possible recourses for members and coordination with those who are not part of the process.

This process in turn must challenge the use value/exchange value relationship (see Jappe, 2014), governance forms for structures that generate necessary income, and overall methods used by private operators to coordinate the project by managing the intangible resources formed out of pooled skills, ambitions and values.

Another overall framework should link different approaches and theories. The process put forward here is certainly eclectic, though it has adopted part of the Marxian paradigm of value. It also reflects what Guerreiro-Ramos (1981, p. 123) calls

> the para-economic paradigm [which] assumes that the market is an enclave within multicentric social reality where there are discontinuities of several sorts, multiple substantive criteria of personal life, and a variety of designs of interpersonal relations … [The individual] is granted to 'work' or even 'beat' the market system, creating and participating in a variety of social settings which differ one from the other in nature. In summary, the space depicted by the paradigm is one in which the individual can properly act, rather than merely behave so as to meet the expectation of market-dominated social reality.

The term 'enclave' could be debated, yet the emphasis on the existence of collective spaces for action that are autonomous, but not independent of one another, issues a challenge to market domination as the sole means for social regulation and the only assessment criterion for individuals.[102] In this respect, Testart's (2007, p. 128) distinction among reciprocity,[103] exchange and gifts suggests an interesting method to qualify exchanges, in the general sense of the term.[104] Primary sociality (Fig. 1) might be a space for gifts or reciprocity (quadrant 2) and non-market-oriented exchanges (quadrant 3). Secondary sociality might encompass market-oriented exchanges, capitalist (quadrant 1), or not (quadrant 4). Institutions that manage common pool resources likely straddle quadrants 1, 2 and 3 between these two socialities, thus collectively associating private stakeholders with a private institution. Then reciprocity and exchanges develop, from non-market to market forms in their relationship with the traditional market, including the capitalist one.

The examples provided and the approach suggested underline the need for empirical studies to refine our understanding of the long-term results of collective action. Such an effort would allow the reclamation of the world in which we live but whose control, if not understanding, escapes us.

From this standpoint, the form of ownership that may emerge is one based on use and not possession of capital or funds. Testart makes a clear distinction, qualifying the first form as 'use-founded/*usufondée*', 'founded on the continuous use over time and for as long as that use can be demonstrated/*fondée sur l'usage continu à travers le temps et pour autant que cet usage puisse être démontré*' (2012, p. 408) and the second 'fund-based/*fundiaire*', encouraging accumulation.[105] It is about favouring the 'nomos', 'a word that suggests sharing what is held in common/*un mot qui suggère le partage de ce qui est en commun* ...' (Meiksins-Wood, 2013, p. 69). By harnessing the opportunities offered by new modes of consumption that unleash consumer's/citizen's creativity and make them less dependent on capital, uses can escape from the domination of shareholder value creation – as long as the rules for collective action are clear. The positive opportunity offered by the cooperative form stems from a definition of common goals, which might be simply to meet stakeholder needs by reclaiming the means and ends of managing their activity. As Dardot and Laval (2014, p. 49) recommend, people should think about the common as the 'practical activity of people/*l'activité pratique des hommes*'.

This activity could be included in a wider perspective of ecological transition as affirmed by the 'the complete emancipation of all human senses and attributes (...)/*moment réel de l'émancipation et de la reprise de soi de l'homme (...)*' (Marx, 1972a/1959, 1972b/1859, p. 99). This transition could form the bases of the 'ethico-political complex' previously referred to and the regulation of non-capitalist circulation of products, and therefore the framework in which to re-embed finance in the economy and the economy in the social, in Society. This issue is well set out by Giraud (2012) when he puts forward the formulation of a new utopia in the sense defined by Ricœur (1997), that is another way of being human with the power to change things. If I cite both Marx and Giraud one after the other, even though they do not share the same paradigm, it is because they do seem to converge on one fundamental dimension. We need to break away from the conception of the world where people are external to nature and exploit it, and a marxist vulgate with an instrumentalist conception of people and nature. The two come together in this paradoxical conception that man is different to nature. The affirmation of our liberty and therefore the need to re-appropriate the means of being free entails the reclamation of our 'natural' foundations, not as a dimension that lies outside our humanity but as the very expression of our human essence that lies in all the social relations in which we are involved and which we produce. We therefore need to re-appropriate our own nature.

> If the essence of individuals is nothing other than activity itself or the power to act that they express in the element of productive relationships they forge with each other, and if those individuals cannot conceive themselves in any other way than as parts of nature, then their own productive activity is nothing other than the essence of the very activity of nature or the activity of nature itself.(Fischbach, 2014, p. 147)

In other words, it is a matter of redefining our relationship with nature not in terms of exteriority but of 'social relations' underpinning our collective citizen project because 'society is a unit of nature and history (…) as long as we understand that the human relationship with nature is still a social relationship and that nature only exists for man through the social activity by which he appropriates it and transforms it/*Si l'essence des individus n'est pas autre chose que l'activité même ou la puissance d'agir qu'ils expriment dans l'élément des rapports productifs qu'ils nouent les uns avec les autres, et si ces individus ne se peuvent concevoir autrement que comme des parties de la nature, alors leur propre activité productive n'est pas autre chose en son essence que l'activité même de la nature ou l'activité de la nature elle-même*' (Fischbach, 2014, p. 129).

There is a need to clearly define the conditions for this appropriation and the institutional regime of ownership in which it applies. As Fischbach said, 'the work to be abolished is the work that, like productive work, (is) enrolled in the capital valuation process (…). However, as Walter Benjamin remarked, this abolition has been done to the benefit of a form of work that, far from exploiting nature, is able to draw out the virtual creations that lie within it/*la société est l'unité même de la nature et de l'histoire (…) qu'à la condition de comprendre que le rapport humain à la nature est toujours un rapport social et que la nature n'existe pour les hommes que par l'intermédiaire de l'activité sociale par laquelle ils se l'approprient et la transforment*' (Fischbach, 2011, p. 134).

Therefore, rather than seeing the ecological transition as an external requirement, it should be seen as the process of developing new social relations required by our human condition, as a stakeholder in nature. However, in order to do so, we need to move on from the neoliberal logic of competition for all to achieve cooperation for all (Dardot & Laval, 2010, 2014), as a realistic option, in line with the latest work on ethology (Sciama, 2013).

NOTES

1. Marx, K. (1971). *Introduction to a contribution to the critique of political economy*. Retrieved from http://www.marxists.org/archive/marx/works/1859/critique-pol-economy/appx1.htm#205

2. Read more about this in the chapter on the construction of meaning in marketing by Caru and Cova (2006), which highlights the operational difficulties that emerge when we make do with taking qualities from the whole without 'linking' them to parts, in this case the consumer's behaviour immerged in the actual consumption situation, and therefore interaction with one or more environments, and the identification of determinants at an individual level to develop commercial applications.

3. Also see Marx (2010/1864, p. 132/1864, http://www.marxists.org/archive/marx/works/1864/economic/ch02.htm) and Sève (2012). For the quotation in English the source is www.marxists.org/archive/marx/works/date/index.htm. In the bibliography the English reference is mentioned with '/' after the French one.

4. Terms are underlined by the quoted authors unless otherwise indicated.

5. In this respect, I qualify this private property of exclusion on the same basis as its legal foundation (Rochfeld, 2013).

6. I could use 'common' instead of collective, or synonymously, as Grandjonc (2013) does in his work on the origin and development of the word 'communism'. Then 'collective' expresses the process of social and socialising interactions, with a structural dimension, to organise.

7. For a more detailed critical appraisal, see Weinstein (2010), Gomez (2009), Rainelli-Le Montagner (2009) and Keen (2014). Also see the work of Meiksins-Wood on the emergence of democracy and the construction of the 'polis'.

8. Marx (1979/1861, pp. 66–92).

9. In this opposition, I refer to a different term that Marx qualifies as private (capitalist) property, the private property of means of production and trade, and 'true human and social property' (Marx, 1972a/1959, p. 68, 34, 1978c/1894, p. 103, 304) and that I qualify as 'personal', where the former grants 'power over the smallest amount of other people's labor' (Marx, 1976/1932, p. 227/1932, communism). For a critique see Dardot, Laval (2012, pp. 641 ff., 2014, pp. 233 ff.). For a historical study, see Meiksins-Wood (2013, 2014).

10. On the emergence of liberalism, it is interesting to re-read what Marcuse (1971) said, particularly on the contribution of Luther and Calvin (Marcuse, 1971, pp. 26, 53, 122, 124–125, 183).

11. 'The relationship of man to nature is defined by labor. Man is not naturally a political animal; he is an owning and labouring animal, owning because he is labouring, labouring in order to own/*Le rapport de l'homme à la nature se définit comme travail. L'homme n'est pas naturellement un animal politique: c'est un animal propriétaire et travailleur, propriétaire parce qu'il est travailleur, travailleur pour être propriétaire*' (Manent, 1987, p. 97).

12. Marx (2010/1864), [479], [483], [491].

13. Marx (1978b/1887b, pp. 535–536, 1978c/1894, pp. 305–306).

14. See Dockes on Hobbes (2008) and Meiksins-Wood (2014), especially Chapter 7.

15. In accordance with Ricœur (1997).

16. See Polanyi (1983), Braudel (1979).

17. A key point related to this term is that, even in the most intensive trend, elitism and – paradoxically on an epistemological level – confirmed authoritarianism is evident (Audier, 2012, p. 410). It also seems surprising that, despite their differences, liberal economists often find themselves in authoritarian or even fascist political positions (Audier, 2012, pp. 492, 494; see also Audier's citation of a quote by

Aron on p. 504). Audier (2012) outlines the liberal project (Chapters 3 and 4), as do Dardot and Laval (2010, pp. 122ff.ff.). Klotz (1985, p. 207) also offers an analysis of its foundations, particularly in terms of Latouche's contributions: 'Natural social order does not just serve as an imaginary foundation for capitalistic liberal society..../*L'ordre social naturel ne sert pas seulement d'assise imaginaire de la société libérale capitaliste ...*'

18. For a discussion about neoliberalism see Cox and Nilsen (2014), Audier (2012) and Dardot and Laval (2010).

19. For a discussion of the link between SSE and liberalism, see McMurtry (2013).

20. The ideal type requires that reasoning does not adopt alternative or dichotomous terms starting from 'standard ideals' but rather uses 'the combination of social standards, formal and informal rules that shape their respective morphologies [the social and solidarity economy and other forms of economic organisations]/*de la combinaison de normes sociales, de règles formelles et informelles qui modèlent leurs [l'économie sociale et solidaire et les autres formes d'organisations économiques] morphologies respectives*' (Chanteau & Labrousse, 2013, p. 72).

21. In *Alternatives Economiques*, no. 249, July–August 2006, pp. 92–94.

22. We take both terms (company and firm) as synonyms even though the first one refers more to an economist's approach and the second one to a manager's approach (Baudry, 2003; Bouba-Olga, 2003).

23. In this respect, see Fleurbaey's essay, in particular the section entitled 'The myth of the contract/Le mythe du contrat' (2006, p.175).

24. See Defalvard (1992), Hodgson (2007) and Birnbaum and Leca (1991) for the presentation of the terms of the debate between methodological individualism, holism, dialectic and convention.

25. According to Sève (2004, p.242, note III) 'epistemology is reflection on science, gnoseology is reflection on all forms of knowledge (...)/*l'épistémologie est proprement réflexion sur la science, la gnoséologie réflexion sur l'ensemble des* ***formes du connaître*** (...)', (our emphasis).

26. For a critique of the way that company boards operate (Weinstein, 2010, pp. 101–109).

27. For a presentation of this contradiction, see Jacot (1974).

28. Marx (1980a/1973, 1980b/1973, pp. 637, 704, 707).

29. 'The result of the capitalist production process is neither a simple product (use value) nor good, i.e. a use value that has a set exchange value. The result, the product, is the creation of surplus value for capital and therefore the actual transformation of money or goods into capital .../*Le résultat du procès de production capitaliste n'est ni un simple produit (valeur d'usage) ni une marchandise, c'est-à-dire une valeur d'usage qui a une valeur d'échange déterminée. Son résultat, son produit, c'est la création de la plus value pour le capital et donc la transformation effective d'argent ou de marchandise en capital ...*' (Marx, 1974a/1863, pp. 467–468/1863, Addenda to part 1, 12d.).

30. 'As soon as the individuals confront each other as free persons, there is no production of surplus value without a wage system. Without the production of surplus value there is no capitalist production, hence no capital and no capitalist! Capital and wage labor (this is what we call the labor of the worker who sells his

own labor capacity) merely express two factors in the same relation/*Dès que les individus se font face comme des personnes libres, sans* salariat *pas de production de survaleur, sans production de survaleur pas de production capitaliste, donc pas de capital et pas de capitaliste! Capital et travail salarié (c'est ainsi que nous appelons le travail du travailleur qui vend sa propre capacité de travail) n'expriment que les deux facteurs d'un seul et même rapport'* (Marx, 2010/1864, p. 159/1864, [469f–469g].). It is difficult to abandon everyday vocabulary to grasp this concept. For example, the phrase 'no surplus value' does not mean a lack of surplus to invest, train, recruit, or pay. Wage-earning employment is a legal regime and title for income that an employee receives, but more also exists, including a social relationship. Therefore, Audier (2012, p. 132) refers to 'the process of alienation as a product of his own labor/*le procès d'aliénation de son propre travail*'.

31. This point raises the question of what to do about commodities and the unrelenting pressure of commoditisation, as well as authenticity, or 'a pure use value defined in a singular relationship with a user/*une pure valeur d'usage définie dans un rapport singulier à un utilisateur*' (Boltanski & Chiapello, 2011, p. 594). Anecdotally, see 'Les bricoleurs préfèrent l'usage à la propriété' (*Les Echos*, July 18, 2013, p. 17, http://entrepreneur.lesechos.fr/entreprise/tendances/actualites/0202902956118-tendance-le-commerce-collaboratif-s-etend-a-de-plus-en-plus-de-secteurs-10031218.php).

32. Much work could be done on civilisations and time. For example, in Islam, time is not linear but lived as the 'accumulation of an instant/*accumulation d'instant*' (Madoui, 2005). I thank Cécile Perret for this observation.

33. This aspect comes closer to the 'deliberation' concept (Dacheux & Goujon, 2013).

34. See Lehavi (2008) for more detail on community and the collective; for the community economy, see Elsen (2013, p. 173 in particular).

35. See Chanteau and Labrousse (2013) on this ambivalence.

36. See Chapter 12 in this book for a more developed analyse.

37. That is, 'the brand equity produced by user consumers becomes a target of valorization as the monetary value attributed to branded goods, such as Lego bricks or Virgin broadband, is factored into the stock price of the companies owning the intellectually property vested in the brand' (Willmott, 2010, p. 521).

38. Testart (2007). See later in this chapter.

39. 'Capital itself is dual, since it consists of commodities. Exchange value (money), but self-valorising value, value which creates value, grows as value, obtains an increment, through the fact that it is value .... **Use value**, and here capital appears according to its particular situation in the labor process/*Le capital même est double, du fait qu'il consiste en marchandises. Valeur d'échange (argent), mais valeur se valorisant, valeur qui par la même crée de la valeur, qui s'accroit en valeur, reçoit un incrément consistant en valeur. (...). Valeur d'usage et ici il apparaît selon les rapports déterminés qui sont les siens dans le procès de travail*' (Marx, 2010/1864, pp. 238–239/1864, [490]).

40. In this respect, the case of the Kibbutz is interesting to analyse. See Warhurst (1996a, 1996b), Bradley and Sosis (2002) and Lehavi (2008), particularly on the question of use value: 'many kibbutz branches operate on use value alone' (Warhurst, 1996a, p. 423).

41. See Dunlavy (2006) and Segrestin and Hatchuel (2011) for a perspective.

42. See Henriksen, Hviid, and Sharp (2011), Feng and Hendrikse (2008, 2011), Prinz (2002), Espagne (1997) or Gios and Santuari (2002) for review. See Goglio and Leonardi (2010), Cuevas and Fischer (2006) and Cutcher and Mason (2014) for credit cooperatives. For North American experiences see Wright (2014).

43. Other forms of property also place employees at the heart of the process, such as the John Lewis Partnership plc in the United Kingdom, though in that case, 'ownership' is a mode of governance rather than a control on capital (see Chapter 9. Paranque & Willmott, 2014).

44. Marx (1978c/1894, p. 305).

45. Note that the dominant form was family-oriented capitalism, based on inheritance.

46. For a description of the introduction of SCICs (Société Coopérative d'Intérêt Collectif) in France, please see http://www.les-scic.coop/sites/fr/les-scic/documentation/guides. Accessed on the December 14, 2016, in French.

47. This freedom can be found in the operating rules for cooperatives. If dividends are not distributed, and the speculative development of equity is impossible, there can be no capitalistic exchanges.

48. Marx (1980b/1973, p. 831); see also p. 459.

49. Marx (1980a/1973, pp. 450–451).

50. Which is therefore the means to tackle reification (Fischbach (2009a, 2009b; Honneth, 2007; Lukacs, 1960; Marcuse, 1969, 1971; Orleans, 2011).

51. 'A commodity is, in the first place, is an object outside of us, a thing that by its properties, satisfies human wants of some sort or another. The nature of such wants, whether they spring from the stomach or from fancy, makes no difference .... Each one is a collection of a variety of properties and can consequently be useful in different ways. Discovering these different sides and at the same time, discovering the various uses of things is the work of history/*La marchandise est d'abord un objet extérieur, une chose qui par ses propriétés satisfait des besoins humains de n'importe quelle espèce. Que ces besoins aient pour origine l'estomac ou la fantaisie, leur nature ne change rien à l'affaire (...). Chacune est un ensemble de propriétés diverses et peut, par conséquent, être utile par différents côtés. Découvrir ces côtés divers et, en même temps, les divers usages des choses est une œuvre de l'histoire*' (Marx, 1978a/1887a, p. 51/1887a, p. 26).

52. Marx (2010/1864, [489], 1980b/1973, p. 704).

53. In the distinction between 'common ownership resources' and 'common pool resources' and 'common' (Bollier, 2014; Hess & Ostrom, 2007, 2011, p. 5), the latter can be managed as public assets (without excluding beneficiaries) or private assets (consumption by one reduces the available stock for others).

54. For the community, the feeling of ownership is tangible not only by law but by belonging.

55. Ostrom (2010) provides interesting insights, commenting on a 'commons' approach of open source software (Madison, Frischmann, & Strandburg, 2010; also see Schweik, 2011).

56. See Fischbach (2009a, pp. 233 ff.) and Marx (1972a/1959, pp. 90–91/1959, Private Property and Communism, p. 42).

57. This debate expands thinking about 'commons', which treat resources as natural and tangible, or non-material and intangible, even when they give rise to goods

(books, software). By extending the work of the PROPICE Project (Coriat, 2013b), this study aims to produce a 'common', as an expression of a collective project, by mustering material resources (shared assets, but also mobilised, such as access to raw materials) together with non-material resources to be developed (common values for the collective project itself and the territory), similar to Banca de Palma (Hudon & Meyer, 2013).

58. It is also a societal choice, as Boltanski and Chiapello (2011, p. 639) recognise: 'what must be defended is firstly the equal dignity of all people which opens up to them equal access to primary commodities/ce qu'il s'agit de défendre, c'est d'abord l'égale dignité des personnes qui leur ouvre un accès égal à des biens primaires (…)'

59. See Descola on the 'relationship schemes' (2005, p. 425), who characterises the gift as a relationship without any expectation of return. Contrary to Descola, I do not include predation, that is taking something without giving something in return, in that here I refer to cooperation. See pages 426 and thereafter.

60. This can still be debated as shows the definition of gift given by Caillé (2007) and what Bourdieu says (1994, p. 178).

61. Also see Ostrom et al. (2002).

62. Dockes (1985, p. 81) offers a historical and epistemological analysis of these commons: 'A progressive fight is led to free rural goods from community practices and servitudes or rights of collective use/Une lutte progressive est menée pour libérer les biens ruraux des pratiques communautaires et des servitudes ou droits d'usage collectif ….', and Dardot and Laval (2014); yet we are far from the 'natural' evolution that the prevailing view implies. Luxembourg (1967, pp. 43 ff.ff.) also specifies how on this conceptms of collective property largely has been an issue of colonisation.

63. See Gaël Giraud (Chapter 7 ssq, 2012) about the concept of finance and currency as 'common pool resource institution'. He recalls the fact that it is not a matter of 'goods' in a material sense but of 'systems governing collective actions, modes of existence and community activities/des systèmes régissant des actions collectives, des modes d'existence et d'activités de communautés' (p. 142) and adds that 'liquidity and credit should be organised as commons/la liquidité et le crédit devraient être organisés à la manière de communs' (p. 143).

64. See Graeber (2013) for a study of the role of credit in human history.

65. This integration was debated by students during a lecture, using the banana trade as an example. How could local producers be supported by the growth of fair trade while reducing the environmental impact of supply associated with transporting the product to Europe? Seemingly, the two could be separated by consumers asserting, 'I will only buy products in season'. However, due to historical influences and previous choices, producers may have no other option; they are so embedded in relationships of power that they need time to diversify their production. Then the challenge becomes defining the level of compromise, including of our own demands.

66. And, we might add, finance. This appears all the more important since Ostrom's work never raises the question of funding the activities studied. In fact, there is no question of financing. We do not know how the collective management institutions were funded, nor the stakeholders' activity, and we know even less about their relationship with the market. For example, in the case of the fisheries

(Ostrom, 2010, p. 209), we know nothing about the real or potential interactions between the constraints linked to selling fish on the conventional market and those arising from the collective coordination and compliance with its rules.

67. Marx (1976/1932) retrieved from http://www.marxists.org/archive/marx/works/1845/german-ideology/ch01b.htm

68. See pages 59 and thereafter '... for the neo-classic economy, the relationship with objects outweighs the relation with other individuals or society/*pour l'économie néoclassique la relation aux objets prime sur la relation aux autres individus ou à la société*' (Orleans, 2011, p. 59). For a critique of the analysis of 'value-work' as 'substance' (Orleans, 2011), see Dardot (2014).

69. See the examples of kibbutz (Bradley & Sosis, 2002; Lehavi, 2008; Warhurst, 1996a, 1996b).

70. See Fradin (1985) for a critical analysis of what makes up the social concept, to be compared with Latouche (1985).

71. I use the expression 'common pool resource' as synonymous with 'common good', to avoid any confusion with the sense of 'living together', though this meaning remains part of our approach and inseparable from the living together construct (Desreumaux & Brechet, 2013).

72. As indicated by Dardot and Laval (2014, p. 149), Ostrom stresses the specific features of collective management institutions whose rules 'represent what people really do, ' such 'that you must not believe that there can be institutions outside those created by the State/qu'il ne faut pas croire qu'il ne peut y avoir d'institutions en dehors de celles crées par l'Etat', even if these institutions cannot exist without rules of law that enable them to be established.

73. A territory can be defined 'as a space considered and recognized as relevant by economic operators for their actions/*comme un espace considéré et reconnu comme pertinent par les agents économiques pour leurs actions*' (Paranque, 2008, p. 11).

74. See Ostrom (2005, pp. 16 ff.ff.) on this concept.

75. In this respect, following Weinstein's (2013) analysis of Ostrom's work, the corporation could be a form of common property, as long as the hegemonic status granted to shareholders and managers is simultaneously challenged.

76. This case is based on Paranque (2010).

77. See https://fr.wikipedia.org/wiki/Thé_Eléphant and http://www.cgt-unilever-hpc-france.com/tag/fralib/. Accessed on December 14, 2015.

78. See http://www.regionpaca.fr/economie-emploi/innovation-et-recherche/les-prides/labellisation.html. Accessed on December 14, 2015.

79. See http://www.hom-ter.com/web/index.php. Accessed on December 14, 2015.

80. See http://confiblog.wordpress.com/tag/recettes-de-confitures/ Accessed on December 14, 2015.

81. The use of the word 'enterprise' simplifies the message but also reinforces its ambiguity. We have the terms firm, company, corporation, and productive organisation. The term enterprise has no legal definition but company does. As soon as we use the word enterprise, we give the impression that we are setting aside the question of ownership. Moreover, a company does not belong to its shareholders. Whether the latter are employees or investors does not make any difference to that fact. As such, the question of ownership of the production facilities is less about understanding in purely legal terms but in terms of power, that is the capacity for

coordinated, organised action. This is why the focus should be put on the forms of governance and organisation of decision-making and implementation.

82. Based on Meyer (2012).

83. See http://www.ceras-projet.org/index.php?id = 5521. Accessed on April 26, 2013.

84. See similar examples in Cutcher and Mason (2014).

85. See http://www.autogestion.asso.fr/. Accessed on June 15, 2015.

86. Marx (1978c/1894, pp. 305–306).

87. See the issue of debate on the question in Dardot and Laval (2012, pp. 641ff. ff.). See also Jossa (2005) for an approach on the difficulties of such an appraisal.

88. Marx (1974a/1863, pp. 1329–1328), at http://www.marxists.org/archive/marx/works/1863/theories-surplus-value/add1.htm#s12f

89. 'The alienation of the worker in his product means no only that his labor becomes an object, an external existence, but that his work exists outside of him, independently, a stranger to him, that the life that he gave to the object, opposes him, is hostile and alien/*L'aliénation* de l'ouvrier dans son produit signifie non seulement que son travail devient un objet, une existence *extérieure*, mais que son travail existe, *en dehors* de lui, indépendamment de lui, étranger à lui, que la vie qu'il a prêtée à l'objet s'oppose à lui, hostile, étrangère' (Marx, 1972a/1959, p. 58/1959, p. 29).

90. This appropriate project scale is a complex and delicate decision, if the goal is to avoid being confined by localism, protectionism, or anti–state-ism. What is the right scale? What is a territory? How can different spaces for action connect? Localised collective action cannot happen in a state that legally supports the credibility of local commitments (Ostrom, 2005, p. 278).

91. See for example Bodier (2014) and Bodier and Helfrich (2015).

92. According to Aristotle, in De Republica, Book 1, Chap. IX (edition I. Bekkeri, Oxonii, 1837 [Opera, Vol. X, pp. 13ff.ff.]): 'As any good can have two uses .... One belongs to the object itself but not the other. As such, a sandal can serve as a shoe but also an object for exchange. In both cases, this is about the use values of the sandal because the person who exchanges the sandal for something they need (e.g. food) also uses it as a sandal. However, in this case, this is not its natural use because it is not designed to be exchanged and the same applies to other goods/*Car tout bien peut servir à deux usages … L'un est propre à la chose en tant que telle, mais pas l'autre; ainsi une sandale peut servir de chaussure, mais aussi d'objet d'échange. Il s'agit, dans les deux cas, de valeurs d'usage de la sandale, car celui qui échange la sandale contre ce qui lui manque, des alimenta par exemple, se sert lui aussi de la sandale. Mais ce n'est pas là son usage naturel. Car elle n'est pas faite pour être échangée. Il en est de même pour les autres biens*'.

93. Aristote: De Republica, Livre 1er, chap. IX (édition I. Bekkeri, Oxonii, 1837 [Opera, Vol. X, p. 13 et suiv.]): 'Car tout bien peut servir à deux usages … L'un est propre à la chose en tant que telle, mais pas l'autre; ainsi une sandale peut servir de chaussure, mais aussi d'objet d'échange. Il s'agit, dans les deux cas, de valeurs d'usage de la sandale, car celui qui échange la sandale contre ce qui lui manque, des alimenta par exemple, se sert lui aussi de la sandale. Mais ce n'est pas là son usage naturel. Car elle n'est pas faite pour être échangée. Il en est de même pour les autres biens'.

94. Marx (1972b/1859) at http://www.marxists.org/archive/marx/works/1859/critique-pol-economy/ch01.htm

95. Groundwater management in California is a good illustration (Ostrom, 2010, p. 130 ff).

96. An important, and little addressed, point is the difficult relationship with the global context, which requires a means to avoid being embroiled in the local context in opposition to a global situation in exchanges with the 'Oother'. This debate is well represented by Scott Cato (2014) and Ganesh and Zoller (2014).

97. Similarly, the community economy maintains certain criteria to integrate common pool resource management institutions (Elsen, 2013 p. 171).

98. Boltanski and Chiapello provide a reminder of the definition of this as 'the fact of not acknowledging debts incurred with other people, individuals or collectives (Sarthou-Lajus, 1997)/*le fait de ne pas reconnaître les dettes contractées à l'égard d'autres personnes – individuelles ou collectives* (Sarthou-Lajus, 1997)' (2011, p. 517). See Graeber (2013) for an history of the concept of debt.

99. On this subject, see developments by Roubine (2009, p. 42).

100. This form of exploitation, of consumers, after that of employees, is not new; such socialised investments allow companies to limit the amount of capital that is tied up when it might be required to produce new goods.

101. Or as Meiksins-Wood says 'In its essene, the capitalist economy is an economy in which the economic domain is assigned a whole range of human activities which, in other times and other places, were subject to different communal and state rules' (Meiksins-Wood, 2014, p. 619).

102. See Guerreiro-Ramos (1981) on pp. 106, 108, 118–119, 121, 141 etc.

103. Reciprocity which is central to the common 'highlights a vital dimension that standard economic theory cannot see, i.e. the close tie between the norm of reciprocity, democratic management and active participation in the production of a certain number of resources/ *met en évidence une dimension essentielle, que la théorie économique standard ne permet pas de voir: le lien étroit entre la norme de réciprocité, la gestion démocratique et la participation active dans la production d'un certains nombre de ressources*' (Dardot & Laval, 2014, p. 151), as illustrated by brand communities.

104. Reciprocity implies no causal relation or obligation whatsoever for the transferor or the beneficiary (Testart, 2007, p. 221).

105. Again see Meiksins-Wood (2013, pp. 57–58, 172).

ACKNOWLEDGEMENT

The author thanks all those who took part in the discussions on the French edition, and specifically Nadine Richez-Battesti, Jean Michel Servet, Jean-Marie Bouquery and Henri Jacot for their remarks and suggestions, as well as Camille Meyer. He remains solely responsible for any errors or omissions.

REFERENCES

Alliot, M. (2003). *Modèles sociétaux: les communautés, Le droit et le service public au miroir de l'anthropologie*, Paris, Karthala, pp. 73–76.

Alvesson, M., Bridgman, T., & Willmott, H. (Eds.). (2009). *Oxford handbook of critical management studies*. New York, NY: Oxford University Press.

Alvesson, M., & Willmott, H. (Eds.). (2012). *Making sense of management. A crucial introduction*. London: Sage.

Amable, B., & Palombarini, S. (2005). *L'économie politique n'est pas une science morale*. Paris: Raisons d'Agir. Cours et Travaux.

Aoyagi, K., Pede, V. O., Kajisa, K., & Tsusaka, T. W. (2013). Neighbourhood effects and social behavior: The case of irrigated and rainfed farmers in Bohol, the Philippines. Munich Personnal RePEc Archive. n° 50162. Retrieved from http//mpra.ub.uni-muenchen.de/50162/

Arando, S., Freudlich, F., Gago, M., Jones Derek, C., & Kato, T. (2010, November). *Assessing Mondragon: Stability and managed change in the face of globalization*. Working Paper No. 1003. William Davidson Institute. Retrieved from SSRN http://ssrn.com/abstract=1726449

Arvidsson, A. (2006). *Brands meaning and value in media culture*. New York, NY: Routledge.

Arvidsson, A. (2009). After capitalism: Ethics? Five ideas on value and the crisis. Paper presented at the 4th Journée du marketing méditerranéen, Université Bocconi, 22 et 23 juin. Milan.

Arvidsson A. (2011). *General sentiment – How value and affect converge in the information economy*. Retrieved from SSRN http://ssrn.com/abstract=1815031. Accessed on April 19.

Audard, C. (2000). *Qu'est ce que le libéralisme? Ethique, politique, société*. Paris: Folio, Essais.

Audier, S. (2012). *Néo-libéralisme: Une archéologie intellectuelle*. Paris: Grasset.

Badot, O., Carrier, C., Cova, B., Desjeux, D., & Filser, M. (2009). L'ethnomarketing: Un élargissement de la recherche en comportement du consommateur à l'ethnologie. *Recherche et Applications en Marketing*, *24*(1), 91–111.

Baretto, T. (2011). Société coopérative de production et démocratie dans l'entreprise. In R. Baudoin (Ed.), *L'entreprise, formes de la propriété et responsabilités sociales* (pp. 347–366). Paris: Collèges des Bernardins.

Baudry, B. (2003). *Economie de la Firme*. Paris: La Découverte.

Birnbaum, P., & Leca, J. (1991). *Sur L'individualisme (sous la direction de)*. Paris: Presse de la Fondation Nationale des Sciences Politiques.

Bodier, D., & Helfrich, S. (2015). *Patterns of communing*. The Commons Strategies Group.

Böhm, S., & Land, C. (2012). The new 'hidden abode': Reflections on value and labour in the new economy. *The Sociological Review*, *60*(2), 217–240.

Bollier, D. (2011). The growth of the commons paradigm. In C. Hess & E. Ostrom (Eds.), *Understanding knowledge as a commons* (pp. 27–40). Cambridge, MA: MIT Press.

Bollier, D. (2014). *La renaissance des communs*. Paris: Editions Charles Léopold Mayer.

Boltanski, L., & Chiapello, E. (2011). Le nouvel esprit du capitalisme. Tel, Gallimard, Paris.

Boltanski, L., & Thévenot, L. (1991). *De la justification: Les économies de la grandeur*. Paris: NRF, Essais, Gallimard.

Bouba-Olga, O. (2003). *L'économie de L'entreprise*. Paris: Seuil, Collection Points Economie.

Bouchon, C., Michard, B., & Plasse, A. (2010). Influence du statut juridique et de la gouvernance sur les conditions de mise en œuvre d'une politique efficace de Responsabilité Sociétale des Entreprises. Etude comparative des Sociétés Anonymes (SA) classiques et des Sociétés Coopératives de Production (SCOP). *Mémoire Master*, Euromed Management, Marseille.

Bouchon, C., Michard, B., Plasse, A., & Paranque, B. (2012). Coopératives et Gouvernance: Modernité ou archaïsme? *Annals of Public and Cooperative Economics*, *83*(3), 317–335. doi:10.1111/j.1467-8292.2012.00465.x

Bourdieu, P. (1994). *Raisons pratiques sur la théorie de l'action*. Essais, point, Paris.
Bourguinat, H., & Briys, E. (2009). *L'arrogance de la finance*. Paris: La Découverte.
Bowman, C., & Ambrosini, V. (2000). Value creation versus value capture: Towards a coherent definition of value in strategy. *British Journal of Management, 11*, 1–15.
Bradley, J. R., & Sosis, R. H. (2002). *Just how cooperative are Kibbutz members? Field experiments on Israeli Kibbutzim and in Israeli cities*. Retrieved from http://ssrn.com/abstract=311962 or http://dx.doi.org/10.2139/ssrn.311962
Braudel, F. (1979). *Civilisation matérielle, Economie et Capitalisme du XVe au XVIIIe siècle*. Paris: Armand Collin.
Brechet, J.-P., & Desreumaux, A. (2010). Agir projectif, action collective et autonomie. *Management International, 14*(4), 11–21.
Caillé, A. (2007). Anthropologie du don. Paris: La Découverte/Poche.
Carberry, E. J. (Eds.). (2011). *Employee ownership and shared capitalism: New directions in research*. Ithaca NY: Cornell University Press.
Caru, A., & Cova, B. (2006). How to facilitate immersion in a consumption experience: Appropriation operations and services elements. *Journal of Consumer Behaviour, 5*(1), 4–14.
Casadesus-Masanell, R., & Khanna, T. (2003, June). *Globalization and trust: Theory and evidence from cooperatives*. Working Paper No. 592. William Davidson Institute. Retrieved from http://papers.ssrn.com/sol3/papers.cfm?abstract_id=577703
Cefai, D. (2007). *Pourquoi nous mobilisons nous?* Paris: La Découverte MAUSS.
Chaigneau, A. (2014). L'entreprise à la croisée des doctrines des biens communs. In B. Parance & J. de Saint Victor (Eds.), *Repenser les biens communs* (pp. 155–174). Paris: CNRS Editions.
Chanlat, J.-F. (2009). L'agir humain selon la théorie de l'agence: Une critique anthropologique. In D. Golsorkhi, I. Huault, & B. Leca (Eds.), *Les études critiques en management* (pp. 329–360). Québec: Presses Universitaires de Laval.
Chanteau, J.-P., Coriat, B., Labrousse, A., & Orsi, F. (Dir.). (2013). *Autour d'Ostrom: Communs, droits de propriété et institutionnalisme méthodologique*. Revue de la régulation [on line], 14 | 2e semestre/Autumn, December 23, 2013. Retrieved from http://regulation.revues.org/10365. Accessed on février 17, 2014.
Chanteau, J.-P., & Labrousse, A. (2013). L'institutionnalisme méthodologique d'Elinor Ostrom: Quelques enjeux et perspectives. Chanteau J-P., Coriat B., Labrousse A., Orsi F. (Dir.) *Autour d'Ostrom: Communs, droits de propriété et institutionnalisme méthodologique*. Revue de la régulation [En ligne], 14 | 2e semestre/Autumn, December 23, 2013. Retrieved from http://regulation.revues.org/10555. Accessed on février 17, 2014.
Chassagnon, V., & Hollandts, X. (2014). Who are the owners of the firm: Shareholders, employees or no-one? *Journal of Institutional Economics, 10*(1), 47–69.
Cobbaut, R. (2011). La gouvernance de l'action collective. In L. Taskin & M. de Nanteuil (Eds.), *Perspectives critiques en management, pour une gestion citoyenne* (pp. 67–81). Bruxelles: De Boeck.
Coriat, B. (2013a). Le retour des communs. Chanteau J-P., Coriat B., Labrousse A., Orsi F. (Dir.) *Autour d'Ostrom: Communs, droits de propriété et institutionnalisme méthodologique*. Revue de la régulation [on line], 14 | 2e semestre/Autumn 2013, 14 février 2014., Retrieved from http://regulation.revues.org/10463. Accessed on février 16, 2014.
Coriat, B. (2013b). Des communs fonciers aux communs informationnels. Traits communs et différences. PROPICE, *Propriété et Communs, Les nouveaux enjeux de l'accès et de l'innovation partagés*. Paris 25 et 26 avril 2013. Retrieved from http://

www.mshparisnord.fr/ANR-PROPICE/25-26_avril/coriat_communs-fonciers-informationnels.pdf. Accessed on March 14, 2014.

Cornforth, C. (2004). The governance of co-operatives and mutual associations: A paradox perspective. *Annals of Publics and Cooperative Economics*, *75*(1), 11–32.

Cova, B. (1997). Community and consumption: Toward a definition of the linking value of product or services. *European Journal of Marketing*, *31*(3/4), 297–316.

Cova, B., & Cova, V. (2002). Tribal marketing: The tribalisation of society and its impact on the conduct of marketing. *European Journal of Marketing*, *36*(5/6), 595–620.

Cova, B., & Cova, V. (2009). Les figures du nouveau consommateur: Une genèse de la gouvernementalité du consommateur. *Recherche et Applications en Marketing*, *24*(3), 82–100.

Cova, B., & Dalli, D. (2009). Working consumes: The next step in marketing theory. *Marketing Theory*, *9*(3), 315–339.

Cova, B., Kozinets, R. V., & Shankar, A. (2007). *Consumer tribes*. Burlington, MA: Elsevier/Butterworth-Heinemann.

Cova, B., & Pace, S. (2006). Brand community of convenience products: New forms of customer empowerment – The case my Nutella the community. *European Journal of Marketing*, *40*(9/10), 1087–1105.

Cova, B., & Paranque, B. (2010). When brand community and brand valuation collide: A case study. *6th thought leaders international conference on brand management*, Lugano, April.

Cova, B., & Paranque, B. (2013a). How to enhance value? A comparative approach between marketing and finance. *Global Business and Economics Review*, *15*(2/3), 279–292.

Cova, B., & Paranque, B. (2013b, March 15). *Value capture and brand community management*. Retrieved from http://ssrn.com/abstract=2233829 or http://dx.doi.org/10.2139/ssrn.2233829

Cova, B., & White, T. (2010). Counter-brand and alter-brand communities – The impact of Web 2.0 on tribal marketing approaches. *Journal of Marketing Management*, *26*(3), 256–270.

Cox, L., & Nilsen, A. G. (2014). *We make our own history*. London: PlutoPress.

Cuevas, C. E., & Fischer, K. P. (2006). *Cooperative financial institutions. Issues in governance, regulation and supervision*. World Bank Working Paper No. 82, pp. 1–59.

Cutcher, L., & Mason, P. (2014). Credit unions. In M. Parker, G. Cheney, V. Fournier, & C. Land (Eds.), *Routledge companion to alternative organisation*. London: Routledge.

Dacheux, E., & Goujon, D. (2013). La délibération: Nouvelle frontière de l'économie? In H. Defalvard, Y. L'Horty, F. Legendre, & M. Narcy (Eds.), *Les nouvelles frontières de l'économie sociale et solidaire*. Charleroi: Presses Universitaires de Louvain.

Dardot, P., & Laval, C. (2010). *La nouvelle raison du monde, essai sur la société néolibérale*. Paris: La Découverte/Poche.

Dardot, P., & Laval, C. (2012). *Marx, prénom: Karl*. Paris: NRF Essais, Gallimard.

Dardot, P., & Laval, C. (2014). *Commun*. Paris: La Découverte.

De Angelis, M., & Havie, D. (2014). The commons. In M. Parker, G. Cheney, V. Fournier, & C. Land (Eds.), *The Routledge companion to alternative organisation*. London: Routledge.

de Nanteuil, M. (2011). Un autre monde … ou un monde plus juste? Pour une anthropologie critique du management. In L. Taskin & M. de Nanteuil (Eds.), *Perspectives critiques en management, pour une gestion citoyenne* (pp. 239–269). Bruxelles: De Boeck.

de Saint Victor, J. (2014). Généalogie historique d'une propriété oubliée. In B. Parance & J. de Saint Victor (Eds.), *Repenser les biens communs* (pp.51–79). Paris: CNRS Editions.

Defalvard, H. (1992). Critique de l'individualisme méthodologique revu par la théorie des conventions. *Revue Economique*, *43*(1), 127–144.

Defalvard, H. (2013). L'ESS comme idéal type de l'économie. In H. Defalvard, Y. L'Horty, F. Legendre, & M. Narcy (Eds.), *Les nouvelles frontières de l'économie sociale et solidaire*. Charleroi: Presses Universitaires de Louvain.

Descola, P. (2005). *Par-delà nature et culture*. Paris: NRF Gallimard.

Desreumaux, A., & Brechet, J.-P. (2013). L'entreprise comme bien commun. *RIMHE*, (7), 77–93.

Dockes, N. (1985). Un ordre naturel communautaire du XVIIIe siècle. In G. Klotz (Ed.), *Ordre, nature, propriété* (pp. 63–118). Lyon: Presse Universitaire de Lyon, collection Analyse, Epistémologie, Histoire.

Dockes, P. (2008). *Hobbes, économie, terreur et politique*. Paris: Economica.

Donsimoni, M., Kemmar, M., & Perret-Karnot, C. (2010). *Les bijoutiers d'Ath-Yenni*. Tizi-Ouzou: Editions Acchab.

Dunlavy, C. A. (2006). Social conceptions of the corporation: Insights from the history of shareholder voting rights. *Washington and Lee Law Review*, *63*, 1347. Retrieved from http://ssrn.com/abstract=964377

Durance, P. (2011). La coopérative est elle un modèle d'avenir pour le capitalisme? Retour sur le cas Mondragon. *Gérer et Comprendre*, (106), 69–79.

Eber, N. (2013). *Théorie des jeux*. Paris: Dunod.

Elsen, S. (2013). Travail social et économies sociales communautaires, réflexions sur le rôle du développement sociopolitique. In D. Hiez & E. Lavillumière (Eds.), *Vers une théorie de l'économie sociale et solidaire* (pp. 163–190). Bruxelles: Ed. Larcier.

Erragragui, E. (2013). Socially responsible investment and Islamic investment: The ethical bridge. Séminaire de Recherche Internationale, chaire Ethique et Normes de la Finance de l'Université Paris 1 Panthéon-Sorbonne (en partenariat avec King AbdulAziz University à Djeddah), April 13, Paris.

Espagne, F. (1997). *Histoire miniaturisée des coopératives ouvrières de production en France*. Retrieved from http://cocomagnanville.over-blog.com/article-histoire-miniaturisee-des-cooperatives-ouvrieres-de-production-en-france-96853516.html. Accessed on May 2, 2012.

Eymard-Duvernay, F. (Ed.). (2006). *L'économie des conventions, méthodes et résultats*. Paris: La Découverte.

Fama, E. F., & Jensen, M. C. (1983). Separation of ownership and control. *Journal of Law and Economics*, *26*, 301–326.

Favereau, O., & Robé, J. P. (2012). RSE et propriété de la firme. Allouche J. (dir.), *Encyclopédie des ressources humaine*. 3ième édition, Vuibert, Paris.

Feng L., & Hendrikse, G. W. J. (2008). On the nature of a cooperative: A system of attributes perspective. Paper prepared for presentation at the 12th EAAE Congress 'people, food and environment: Global trends and European strategies'. Gent, Belgium, August 26–29.

Feng, L., & Hendrikse, G. W. J. (2011). *Chain interdependencies, measurement problems, and efficient governance structure: Cooperatives versus publicly listed firms*. ERIM Report Series, No. ERS-2011-001-ORG. Retrieved from http://ssrn.com/abstract=1793627

Feyerabend, P. (1979). *Contre la méthode*. Paris: Seuil, Sciences.

Feyerabend, P. (1989). *Adieu la raison*. Paris: Seuil.

Fischbach, F. (2009a). Comment le capital capture le temps. In F. Fischbach (Ed.), *Marx Relire le capital* (pp. 101–138). Paris: PUF, Débats philosophiques.

Fischbach, F. (2009b). *Sans objet: Capitalisme, subjectivité, aliénation.* Paris: Librairie Philosophique Jacques Vrin.

Fischbach, F. (2011). *La privation de monde, temps, espace, capital.* Paris: Librairie Philosophique Jacques Vrin.

Fischbach, F. (2014). *La production des hommes, Marx avec Spinoza.* Paris: Librairie Philosophique J. Vrin.

Fontaine, L. (2014). *Le marché.* Paris: NRF Essais, Gallimard.

Foster, R. J. (2011). The uses of uses value: Marketing, value creation, and the exigencies of consumption work. In D. Zwick & J. Cayla (Eds.), *Inside marketing: Practices, ideologies, devices.* Oxford: Oxford University Press.

Fournier, S. (2009). Getting brand community right. *Harvard Business Review, April*, 105–111.

Fradin, J. (1985). Marx et l'ordre social. L'héritage leibnizien de Marx. Y-a-t-il une pensée du social chez Marx? In G. Klotz (Ed.), *Ordre, nature, propriété* (pp. 213–255). Lyon: Presse Universitaire de Lyon, collection Analyse, Epistémologie, Histoire.

Ganesh, S., & Zoller, H. (2014). Organizing transition. Principles and tensions in eco-localism. In M. Parker, G. Cheney, V. Fournier, & C. Land (Eds.), *Routledge companion to alternative organisation.* London: Routledge.

Gardin, L. (2013). Entrepreneurs sociaux et économie sociale et solidaire, continuités et rupture. In H. Defalvard, Y. L'Horty, F. Legendre, & M. Narcy (Eds.), *Les nouvelles frontières de l'économie sociale et solidaire.* Charleroi: Presses Universitaires de Louvain.

Gios, G., & Santuari, A. (2002). Agricultural cooperatives in the county of Trento (Italy): Economic, organizational and legal perspectives. *Journal of Rural Cooperation, 30*(1), 3–12.

Giraud, G. (2012). *Illusion financière.* Paris: Seuil, Collection Poche.

Goglio, S., & Leonardi, A. (2010). *The roots of cooperative credit from a theoretical and historical perspective.* Euricse Working Papers No. 011|10. Retrieved from http://ssrn.com/abstract=1698611

Golsorkhi, D., Huault, I., & Leca, B. (Eds.). (2009). *Les études critiques en management.* Québec: Presses Universitaires de Laval.

Gomez, P. Y. (2009). Théorie néolibérale du gouvernement des entreprises: Critique d'un renversement critique. In D. Golsorkhi, I. Huault, & B. Leca (Eds.), *Les études critiques en management* (pp. 233–260). Québec: Presses Universitaires de Laval.

Gomez, P. Y. (2011). Sciences de gestion et conventions: De nouveaux cadres pour l'analyse critique. In L. Taskin & M. de Nanteuil (Eds.), *Perspectives critiques en management, pour une gestion citoyenne* (pp. 49–66). Bruxelles: De Boeck.

Graeber, D. (2013). *Dette. 5000 ans d'histoire.* Paris: Les Liens qui Libèrent.

Grandjonc, J. (2013). *Communisme. Origine et développement international de la terminologie communautaire prémarxiste des utopistes aux néo-babouvistes 1785–1842.* Paris: Editions des Malassis.

Groupe Alpha. (2012). Bilan de neuf années d'application de la Loi NRE en matière de reporting social, comment le reporting modèle la RSE? Paris. Retrieved from http://www.groupe-alpha.com/data/document/2012-reporting-social-etude-cep.pdf. Accessed on May 3.

Guerreiro-Ramos, A. (1981). *The new science of organizations. A reconceptualization of the wealth of nations.* Toronto: University of Toronto Press.

Guesnerie, R. (2006). *L'économie de marché.* Paris: Le Pommier.

Hallyn, F. (1987). *La structure poétique du monde: Copernic, Kepler*. Paris: Seuil, Des Travaux.
Hart, O., & Moore, J. (1996). The governance of exchanges: Members cooperatives versus outside ownership. *Oxford Review of Economic Policy*, *12*(4), 53–69. Retrieved from http://ssrn.com/abstract=60039
Henriksen, I., Hviid, M., & Sharp, P. R. (2011). *Law and peace: Contracts and the success of the Danish dairy cooperatives*. Discussion Paper No. 11-11. University of Copenhagen Dept. of Economics. Retrieved from http://ssrn.com/abstract=1806935
Hess, C., & Ostrom, E. (2011). *Understanding knowledge as a commons*. Cambridge, MA: MIT Press.
Hiez, D. (2013). *Coopératives*. Paris: Editions Delmas, Dalloz.
Hiez, D., & Lavillumière, E. (2013). *Vers une théorie de l'économie sociale et solidaire*. Bruxelles.
Hirschman, A. O. (1980). *Les passions et les intérêts*. Paris: Presse Universitaire de France.
Hodgson, G. M. (2007). Meanings of methodological individualism. *Journal of Economic Methodology*, *14*(2), 211–226.
Honneth, A. (2007). *La réification, petit traité de théorie critique*. Paris: NRF Essai, Gallimard.
Hudon, M., & Meyer, C. (2013). *Microfinance and common goods: A study of Brazilian community development banks*. CEB Working Paper No. 13/049. Université Libre de Bruxelles – Solvay Brussels School of Economics and Management Centre Emile Bernheim.
Jacot, H. (1974). Substance, grandeur et forme de la valeur dans le capital. Analyse, Epistémologie, Histoire. Cahier numéro 4, Lyon, novembre.
Jappe, A. (2014). Une histoire de la critique de la valeur à travers les écrits de Robert Kurz. In E. Martin & M. Ouellet (Eds.), *La tyrannie de la valeur*. Montréal: Écosociété, Collection Théorie.
Jaume, L. (2010). *Les origines philosophiques du libéralisme*. Paris: Flammarion – Champs Essais.
Jensen, M. C. (2001, October). *Value maximization, stakeholder theory, and the corporate objective function*. Retrieved from http://ssrn.com/abstract=220671; in *Journal of Applied Corporate Finance*, 14(3), 2001, p. 8–21 and *European Financial Management Review*, 7, 2001, p. 297–317.
Jossa, B. (2005). Marx, marxism and the cooperative movement. *Cambridge Journal of Economics*, *29*(1), 3–18.
Karpick, L. (2007). *L'économie des singularités*. Paris: Gallimard, NRF.
Keen, S. (2014). *L'imposture économique*. Ivry sur Seine: Les Éditions de l'Atelier.
Klotz, G. (Ed.). (1985). Ordre, nature, propriét. Lyon: Presse Universitaire de Lyon, collection Analyse, Epistémologie, Histoire. Retrieved from http://presses.univ-lyon2.fr/produit.php?id_produit=464
Kornberger, M. (2010). *Brand society. How brands transform management and lifestyle*. Cambridge: Cambridge University Press.
Latouche, S. (1985). L'ordre naturel comme fondement imaginaire de la science sociale. In G. Klotz (Ed.), *Ordre, nature, propriété* (pp. 193–211). Lyon: Presse Universitaire de Lyon, collection Analyse, Epistémologie, Histoire.
Le Roy, E. (2014). Sous les pavés du monologisme juridique. Prolégomènes anthropologiques. In B. Parance & J. de Saint Victor (Eds.), *Repenser les biens communs* (pp. 81–101). Paris: CNRS Editions.
Lecointre, G. (Ed.). (2009). *Guide critique de l'évolution*. Paris: Belin.
Lehavi, A. (2008). How property can create, maintain or destroy community. *Theoretical Inquiries in Law*, Community and Property (Vol. 1). Berkley, CA: The Berkley Electronic Press.

Lévi-Strauss, C. (2008). *Œuvres*. Paris: Bibliothèque de la Pléiade, NRF, Gallimard.
Lukacs, G. (1960). *Histoire et conscience de classe*. Paris: Les Editions de Minuit.
Luxembourg, R. (1967). *L'accumulation du capital*. Maspéro, BS11.
Madison, M. J., Frischmann, B. M., & Strandburg, K. J. (2010). Constructing commons in the cultural environment. *Cornell Law Review*, *95–94*(May), 657–710. Retrieved from http://papers.ssrn.com/sol3/papers.cfm?abstract_id = 1265793
Madoui, M. (2005). Temps et usage du temps par les entrepreneurs algériens: Entre l'idéal céleste et les réalités terrestres. *Temporalité*, (3). Retrieved from http://temporalites.revues.org/456#tocto1n2
Manent, P. (1987). *Histoire intellectuelle du libéralisme*. Paris: Hachette.
Marcuse, H. (1969). *Philosophie et révolution*. Paris: Denoël, Médiations.
Marcuse, H. (1971). *Pour une théorie critique de la société*. Paris: Denoël, Médiations.
Martin, E., & Ouellet, M. (2014). *La tyrannie de la valeur*. Montréal: Écosociété, Collection Théorie.
Marx, K. (1972a/1959). Manuscrits de 1844. Editions Sociales, Paris/Economic and philosophic manuscripts of 1844. Moscow: Progress Publisher. Retrieved from http://www.marxists.org/archive/marx/works/download/pdf/Economic-Philosophic-Manuscripts-1844.pdf
Marx, K. (1972b/1859). Contribution à la critique de l'économie politique. Editions Sociales, Paris. A contribution to the critique of political economy. Moscow: Progress Publishers. Retrieved from http://www.marxists.org/archive/marx/works/1859/critique-pol-economy/index.htm
Marx, K. (1974a/1863). Théorie sur la plus-value. Tome 1. Editions Sociales, Paris. Theories of surplus value. Moscow: Progress Publishers. Retrieved from http://www.marxists.org/archive/marx/works/1863/theories-surplus-value/index.htm
Marx, K. (1974b/1932). L'idéologie allemande. The German Ideology. MECW. Paris: Editions Sociales. Retrieved from http://www.marxists.org/archive/marx/works/1845/german-ideology/index.htm
Marx, K. (1978a/1887a). Le Capital, Livre 1, Tome 1., Editions Sociales, Paris Capital (Vol. I). Moscow: Progress Publishers. Retrieved from http://www.marxists.org/archive/marx/works/download/pdf/Capital-Volume-I.pdf
Marx, K. (1978b/1887b). Le Capital, Livre 1, Tome 3.. Editions Sociales, Paris. Capital (Vol. III). New York, NY: International Publisher. Retrieved fromhttp://www.marxists.org/archive/marx/works/download/pdf/Capital-Volume-I.pdf
Marx, K. (1978c/1894). Le Capital, Livre 3, Tome 2. Editions Sociales, Paris. Capital (Vol. III). New York, NY: International Publisher. Retrieved from http://www.marxists.org/archive/marx/works/download/pdf/Capital-Volume-III.pdf
Marx, K. (1979/1861). Manuscrits 1861–1863. Paris. Editions Sociales, Paris. Economic Manuscripts of 1861–1863. MECW. Retrieved from https://marxists.anu.edu.au/archive/marx/works/1861/economic/ch17.htm
Marx, K. (1980a/1973). Manuscrits de 1857–1858. Grundrisse, Tome 1. Editions Sociales, Paris/*Grundrisse*. Penguin.. Retrieved from http://www.marxists.org/archive/marx/works/1857/grundrisse/index.htm
Marx, K. (1980b/1973). Manuscrits de 1857–1858. Grundrisse, Tome 2. Editions Sociales, Paris/*Grundrisse*. Penguin.. Retrieved from http://www.marxists.org/archive/marx/works/1857/grundrisse/index.htm
Marx, K. (2010/1864). *Le chapitre VI, manuscrits de 1863–1867, Le Capital, Livre 1*. Éditions Sociales – GEME, Paris/The process of production of capital, Draft Chapter 6 of

Capital. Book I. MECW, vol. 34, pp. 339–467. Retrieved from http://www.marxists.org/archive/marx/works/1864/economic/index.htm
Mauss, M. (2012). *Essai sur le don*. Paris: PUF, Quadrige.
Mayer, S., & Caldier, J.-P. (2007). *Le guide de l'économie équitable*. Paris: Fondation Gabriel Péri.
McMurtry, J. J. (2013, May). *Prometheus, Trojan horse or Frankenstein? The social and solidarity economy as community creation, market wedge or state monster*. Working Paper. The United Nations Non-Governmental Liaison Service.
Meiksins-Wood, E. (2013). *Des citoyens aux seigneurs. Une histoire sociale de la pensée politique de l'antiquité au Moyen Âge*. Québec: Lux/Humanités.
Meiksins-Wood, E. (2014). *Liberté et propriété. Une histoire sociale de la pensée politique occidentale de la Renaissance aux Lumières*. Québec: Lux/Humanités.
Meyer C. (2012). Les finances solidaires comme biens communs durables: étude de cas de la Banque communautaire de développement Palmas (Brésil). Mémoire pour le Master en sciences de la population et du développement, Université Libre de Bruxelles.
Mill, J. S. (1988). *L'Utilitarisme*. Paris: Champs, Flammarion.
Myers, S. C. (1984). The capital structure puzzle. *Journal of Finance*, *39*(July), 575–592.
Neiva, C. A., Braz, J., Tsukumo, D. J., & Melo, J. (2013, May). *Solidarity finance and public policy: The Brazilian experience of community development banks*. Working Paper. The United Nations Non-Governmental Liaison Service.
Orléans, A. (Ed.). (2004). *Analyse économique des conventions* (2e éd.). Paris: Presse Universitaire de France, Quadridge.
Orleans, A. (2011). *L'empire de la valeur*. Paris: Points, Economie.
Orsi, F. (2013). Elinor Ostrom et les faisceaux de droits: l'ouverture dun nouvel espace pour penser la propriété commune. Chanteau J-P., Coriat B., Labrousse A. & Orsi F. (Dir.) *Autour d'Ostrom: Communs, droits de propriété et institutionnalisme méthodologique*. Revue de la régulation [on line], 14 | 2e semestre/Autumn, December 23. Retrieved from http://regulation.revues.org/10471. Accessed on février 17, 2014.
Ostrom, E. (2005). *Understanding institutional diversity*. Princeton, NJ: Princeton University Press.
Ostrom, E. (2007). *The challenge of crafting rules to change open access resources into managed resources*. Workshop in political theory and policy analysis. Indian University. Retrieved from http://ssrn.com/abstract = 1304827. Accessed on April 2, 2012.
Ostrom, E. (2008). Building trust to solve commons dilemmas: Taking small steps to test an evolving theory of collective action. In L. Simon (Ed.), *Games, groups and the global good* (pp. 207–228). New York, NY: Ed. Springer. Retrieved from http://ssrn.com/abstract = 1304695. Accessed on May 2, 2012.
Ostrom, E. (2010). Response, the institutional analysis and development framework and the commons. *Cornell Law Review*, *95-4*(May), 807–816.
Ostrom, E. (2011). *Governing the commons*. New York, NY: Cambridge University Press.
Ostrom, E., Dietz, T., Dolsak, N., Stern, P. C., Stonich, S., & Weber, E. U. (2002). *The drama of the commons*. Committee on the Human Dimensions of Global Change (Ed.). Washington, DC: National Research Council.
Parance, B., & de Saint Victor, J. (2014). *Repenser les biens communs* (pp. 9–32). Paris: CNRS Editions.
Paranque, B. (2008). *Construire l'Euroméditerranée*. Paris: L'Harmattan.
Paranque, B. (2010). La nécessité d'une alternative à la création de valeur actionnariale? *Économie et Société*, série Entreprise et finance, KF, no. 1, 11, pp. 1721–1744.

Paranque, B. (2013). Solidarity as a "commons" to be promoted. Organisation of collective action for a more responsible management. In D. Vrontis & A. Thrassou (Eds.), *Innovative business practices: Prevailing a turbulent era*. Cambridge: Cambridge Scholar Publishing.

Paranque, B. (2014a). Microfinance as cooperation between private property and collective action to reconnect consumption and societal development. In P. Phan (Ed.), *Conversations and empirical evidence in microfinance*. London: Imperial College Press.

Paranque, B. (2014b). Private property and collective action: Co-operation instead of competition. *EuroMed Journal of Business*, *9*(1), 37–59.

Paranque, B., & Willmott, H. (2014). Cooperatives – saviours or gravediggers of capitalism? The ambivalent case of the John Lewis partnership. *Organization* [special issue], *21*(5), 604–625.

Pendleton, A. (2005). Employee share ownership, employment relationships and corporate governance. In B. Harley, J. Hyman, & P. Thompson (Eds.), Participation and democracy at work. Essays in honour of Harvie Ramsay (pp. 75–93). London: Palgrave MacMillan.

Pendleton, A. (2011). Employee ownership in Britain: Diverse forms, diverse antecedents. In E. J. Carberry (Ed.), *Employee ownership and shared capitalism: New directions in research*. Ithaca, NY: Cornell University Press.

Pérez, R. (2009). *La gouvernance de l'entreprise*. Paris: Repères, La Découverte.

Pitelis, C. (2009). *The co-evolution of organizational value capture, value creation and sustainable advantage*. MPRA Paper No. 23937. University Library of Munich, Germany.

Plihon, D. (2002). *Rentabilité et risque dans le nouveau régime de croissance*. Paris: La Documentation Française.

Polanyi, K. (1983). *La grande transformation*. Paris: Collection Tel, Gallimard.

Postel, N., & Sobel, R. (2013). *Dictionnaire critique de la RSE*. Villeneuve d'Ascq: Presses Universitaires du Septentrion.

Poteete, A. R., Janssen, M. A., & Ostrom, E. (2010). *Working together. Collective action, the commons and multiple methods and practice*. Princeton, NJ: Princeton University Press

Prinz, M. (2002). German rural cooperatives, Friedrich-Wilhelm Raiffeisen and the organization of trust 1850–1914. Paper presented at the XIII IEHA Congress, Buenos Aires, July.

Przeworski, A. (1991). Le défi de l'individualisme méthodologique à l'analyse marxiste. In P. Birnbaum & J. Leca (Eds.), *Sur l'individualisme*. Paris: Presse de la Fondation Nationale des Sciences Politiques, Références.

Rainelli-Le Montagner, H. (2009). La nouvelle finance est-elle une finance critique? In D. Golsorkhi, I. Huault, & B. Leca (Eds.), *Les études critiques en management* (pp. 185–206). Québec: Presses Universitaires de Laval.

Redondi, P. (1983). *Galilée hérétique*. Paris: Gallimard.

Rehn, A. (2014). Gifts, gifting and gift economy. On challenging capitalism with blood, plunder and necklaces. In M. Parker, G. Cheney, V. Fournier, & C. Land (Eds.), *Routledge companion to alternative organisation*. London: Routledge.

Ricœur, P. (1997). *L'idéologie et l'utopie*. Paris: Seuil Essais.

Rochfeld, J. (2013). Quel(s) modèle(s) juridique(s) pour les communs? PROPICE, *Propriété et Communs, Les nouveaux enjeux de l'accès et de l'innovation partagés*, Paris 25 & 26 avril. Retrieved from http://www.mshparisnord.fr/ANR-PROPICE/25-26_avril/rochfeld_modeles-juridiques.pdf. Accessed on Mars 14, 2014.

Roger, B. (2011). L'entreprise et la personne. In R. Baudoin (Ed.), *L'entreprise, formes de la propriété et responsabilités sociales* (pp. 105–149). Paris: Collèges des Bernardins.

Rosa, H. (2012). *Aliénation et accélération.* Paris: La Découverte.

Roubine, I. I. (2009). *Essai sur la théorie de la valeur de Marx.* Paris: Syllepse.

Sahakian, M., & Servet, J.-M. (2015). Separating the wheat from the chaff: Sharing versus self-interest in crowdfunding. In D. Assadi (Ed.), *Strategic managerial approaches to crowdfunding online* IGI Global Publishers.

Salais, R., Baverez, N., & Reynaud, B. (1999). *L'invention du chômage.* Paris: Presse Universitaire de France, Quadrige.

Salais, R., & Storper, M. (1993). *Les Mondes de Production – Enquête sur l'identité économique de la France.* Paris: École des Hautes Études en Sciences Sociales.

Salinas, G. (2009). *The international brand valuation manual.* Chichester: Wiley.

Sarthou-Lajus, N. (1997). *L'éthique de la dette.* Paris: PUF.

Schwartz, J. (2011, July). *Where did Mill go wrong? Why the capital managed firm rather than the labor managed enterprise is the predominant organizational form in market economies.* The John Marshall Law School. Retrieved from http://ssrn.com/abstract=1886024 or http://dx.doi.org/10.2139/ssrn.1886024

Schweik, C. M. (2011). Free/open software as a framework for establishing commons in science. In C. Hess & E. Ostrom (Eds.), *Understanding knowledge as a commons* (pp. 277–310). Cambridge, MA: MIT Press.

Sciama, Y. (2013). Penser coopération plutôt que compétition. *Sciences et Vie, avril*(1147), 139–148.

Scott Cato, M. (2014). The bioregional economy. Reclaiming our local land. In M. Parker, G. Cheney, V. Fournier, & C. Land (Eds.), *Routledge companion to alternative organisation.* London: Routledge.

Segrestin, B., & Hatchuel, A. (2011). L'entreprise comme dispositif de création collective: Vers un nouveau type de contrat collectif. In R. Baudoin (Ed.), *L'entreprise, formes de la propriété et responsabilités sociales* (pp. 219–272). Paris: Collèges des Bernardins.

Servet, J.-M. (2012). *Les monnaies du lien.* Presses Universitaires de Lyon.

Servet, J.-M. (2013). Monnaie: Quand la dette occulte le partage. *La Découverte, revue Française de Socio-Économie, 2*(12), 125–147.

Servet, J.-M., & Hillenkamp, I. (2015). *Le marché autrement. Marchés réels et marché fantasmé.* Paris: Classique Garnier.

Sève, L. (2004). *Penser avec Marx Aujourd'hui, Tome 1 Marx et nous.* Paris: La Dispute.

Sève, L. (2005). *Emergence, complexité et dialectique.* Paris: Odile Jacob.

Sève, L. (2008). *Penser avec Marx aujourd'hui.* Tome 2 L'Homme. Paris: La Dispute.

Sève, L. (2012). *Aliénation et émancipation.* Paris: La Dispute.

Simon, G. (1979). *Kepler, astronome astrologue.* Paris: Gallimard.

Simon, H. A. (1976). From substantive to procedural rationality. In S. Lastis (Ed.), *Methods and appraisals in economics.* Cambridge: Cambridge University Press.

Sohn-Rethel, A. (2010). *La pensée-marchandise,* Editions du Croquant, Bellecombe-en-Bauges.

Spicer, A., Alvesson, M., & Kärreman, D. (2009). Critical performativity: The unfinished business of critical management studies. *Human Relations, 62*(4), 537–560.

Taskin, L. (2011). Entre réalisme et citoyenneté: Pour une critique interne aux sciences de gestion. In L. Taskin & M. de Nanteuil (Eds.), *Perspectives critiques en management, pour une gestion citoyenne* (pp. 29–47). Bruxelles: De Boeck.

Taskin, L., & de Nanteuil, M. (Eds.). (2011). *Perspectives critiques en management, pour une gestion citoyenne.* Bruxelles: De Boeck.

Testart, A. (2007). *Critique du don, études sur la circulation non marchande*. Paris: Syllepse.
Testart, A. (2012). *Avant l'histoire. L'évolution des sociétés, de Lascaux à Carnac*. Paris: NRF, Gallimard.
Thévenot, L. (2006). *L'action au pluriel, sociologie des régimes d'engagement*. Paris: La Découverte.
VargoS. (2009). Towards a transcending conceptualization of relationships: A service-dominant logic perspective. *Journal of Business &Industrial Marketing*, *24*(5/6), 373–379.
Veldman, J., & Willmott, H. (2013). What is the corporation and why does it matter? *M@n@gement*, *16*(5), 605–620.
Vergara, F. (2006). Libéralisme: Mythes et réalités. *Alternatives Économiques*, (249), 92–97, juillet-août.
Warhurst, C. (1996a). The management of production and the changing character of the Kibbutz as a mode of production. *Economic and Industrial Democracy*, *17*, 419.
Warhurst, C. (1996b). High society in a worker's society: Work, community and Kibbutz. *Sociology*, *30*(1), 1–19.
Webb, J. T., & Cheney, G. (2014). Worker-owned-and-governed cooperatives and the wider cooperative movement: Challenges and opportunities within and beyond the global economic crisis. In M. Parker, G. Cheney, V. Fournier, & C. Land (Eds.), *The Routledge companion to alternative organisation*. London: Routledge.
Weber, F. (2012). Vers une ethnographie des prestations sans marché, présentation de Maus. *Essai sur le don*, PUF, Quadridge, Paris.
Weeks, J. (2010). *Capital, exploitation and economic crisis*. London: Routledge Frontiers of Political Economy.
Weinstein, O. (2010). *Pouvoir, Finances et Connaissance, les transformations de l'entreprise capitaliste entre XXe et XXIe siècle*. Paris: Editions La Découverte.
Weinstein, O. (2013). Comment comprendre les communs: Elinor Ostrom, la propriété et la nouvelle économie institutionnelle. In J.-P. Chanteau, B. Coriat, A. Labrousse, & F. Orsi (Eds.), *Autour d'Ostrom: Communs, droits de propriété et institutionnalisme méthodologique*. Revue de la régulation [on line], 14 | 2e semestre/Autumn 2013, Retrieved from http://regulation.revues.org/10452. Accessed on February 17, 2014.
Willmott, H. (2010). Creating value beyond the point of production: Branding, financialization and market capitalization. *Organization*, *17*(5), 517–542.
Wright, C. (2014). *Worker cooperatives and revolution. History and possibilities in the United States*. Bradenton, FL: BookLocker.

PROLEGOMENA TO AN ALTERNATIVE STUDY OF FINANCE

Thomas Lagoarde-Segot

ABSTRACT

Purpose – *To lay the ground for a future diversification of academic finance in line with on-going sustainability issues.*

Methodology/approach – *We situate academic finance within the broader spectrum of social sciences and highlight its ontological, epistemological and methodological assumptions. This brings out the limitations of paradigmatic unity in finance and the ideological aspects of academic finance, and allows us to characterise diversification in finance with reference to the nested epistemological structure of scientific discourse.*

Findings – *We define the diversification of academic finance as a process by which (i) finance research is extended to other existing paradigms in social sciences; (ii) new research metaphors are developed within the current paradigm and (iii) puzzle-solving robustness is achieved. We develop a new research agenda which are divided down into themes, paradigmatic hypotheses, and research questions.*

Finance Reconsidered: New Perspectives for a Responsible and Sustainable Finance
Critical Studies on Corporate Responsibility, Governance and Sustainability, Volume 10, 89–110

ISSN: 2043-9059/doi:10.1108/S2043-905920160000010024

Research limitations/implications – *We do not test any particular implications of our research agenda.*

Practical implications – *This chapter will be a useful reference for any researcher or practitioner seeking to contribute to the diversification of academic finance, and make finance work for society.*

Originality/value – *This chapter looks at academic finance from an interdisciplinary angle in order to bring out its limitations and carve out an innovative research agenda.*

Keywords: Finance; sustainability; epistemology; diversification

This chapter starts with the finding that standard financial theory is an obstacle to ecological and social sustainability. We therefore attempt to deconstruct that theory by pointing out the proven limits of its epistemological, ontological and methodological assumptions. These considerations lead us to introduce the concept of diversification in financial research, which we present as a process via which (i) *research in finance will expand to encompass other paradigms inherent in the social sciences*, (ii) *new metaphors will be put forward within the existing paradigm*, and (iii) *rigour in puzzle-solving will be conserved.* We thus expose a number of valid avenues for future research, emphasising the need to explore the social, behavioural, historical and institutional processes that determine the capacity of financial systems to generate well-being in a comparative, international and interdisciplinary perspective. Finally, we set out this research topic alongside several relevant assumptions and research questions.

INTRODUCTION

The current economic, social and ecological crisis has forced us to reconsider the content of the management sciences and especially academic finance (Bay & Schinkus, 2012; Epstein, 2005; Epstein & Habbard, 2011; Faugère, 2014; Giraud, 2012; Lagoarde-Segot, 2010, 2014; Lazonick, 2013). However, the paradigmatic unity of academic finance means that, to a very large extent, researchers restrict their work to a monolithic approach derived from positivism. Against this background, many economists now fear that the introduction of ethical considerations into their analyses would mean relegating finance to the level of disciplines deemed less 'rigorous' such as history, sociology or political science. Taking this paradox on-board, this chapter establishes the bases for *diversification in finance research*.

We thus begin by situating academic finance in the wider sphere of social sciences, reviewing its main ontological, methodological and epistemological assumptions. We then demonstrate that these assumptions, although widely accepted by most researchers (often without them even realising), come with a number of limits. Far from reflecting the company and financing decisions in a neutral, objective manner, financial theory has insidiously contributed to structuring economic and social reality, ultimately forming an obstacle to ecological and social sustainability. Finally, we expose some tangible perspectives for the diversification of finance research, identifying a number of relevant topics, assumptions and questions for research.

EPISTEMOLOGY OF MODERN FINANCE

Finance and Social Sciences

The matrix put forward by Burrel and Morgan (1979) helps shed light on the scope of finance (Adler, Forbes, & Willmott, 2007; Lagoarde-Segot, 2014). This framework categorises research work according to the assumptions made on the nature of science and the nature of society. As shown in Fig. 1, the assumptions on the nature of science can be set out along a subjective-objective axis. This is underpinned by ontological, epistemological and methodological assumptions and the adopted vision of human nature.

- The ontological assumptions refer to the essence of the phenomena studied: are the phenomena objective and external to individuals or are they, on the contrary, subjective that is generated by the human mind?
- The epistemological assumptions refer to the nature of knowledge: is knowledge an external reality that can be acquired in an objective manner or is it, on the contrary, a relative concept influenced by an individual's personal and social experience?

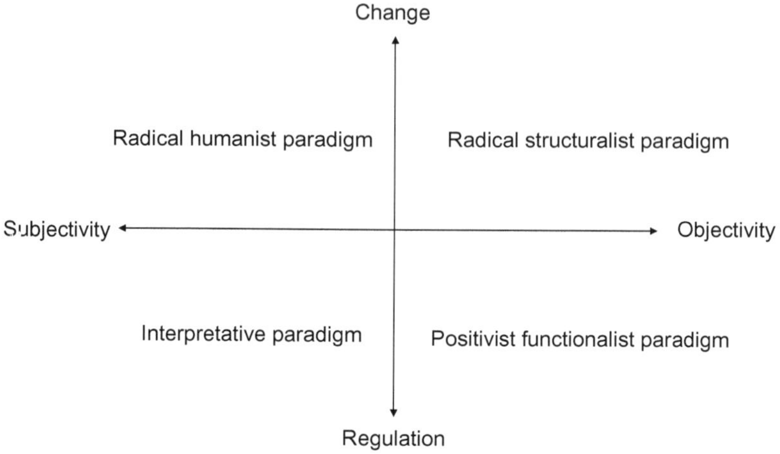

Fig. 1. The Four Paradigms. *Source*: Burrel and Morgan (1979).

- The assumptions on human nature are linked to the relationship between humans and society: are humans determined by their social environment or do humans create their environment?
- The methodological assumptions refer to scientific investigation processes: should researchers set themselves the task of updating universal causal mechanisms or instead seek to understand the processes by which humans create, modify and interpret their social environment in each specific situation?

The assumptions related to the nature of society can be set out along an axis of order/conflict, exploring two competing sociological approaches:

- The 'regulation' approach is based on a premise of social cohesion and unity and seeks to understand the mechanisms that enable a given society to reproduce itself.
- The 'change' approach analyses theories that emphasise the existence of structural conflicts and domination modes, and seeks to contribute to the development of alternatives to the status quo.

As shown in Fig. 1, the interaction of these four hypotheses reveals four main paradigms found in social sciences: the positivist functionalist paradigm, the interpretative paradigm, the radical humanist paradigm and the radical structuralist paradigm.

Given that each of these paradigms is based on philosophical choices, it is impossible to demonstrate the superiority or inferiority of an approach without first accepting a vision of the underlying world. By extension, this matrix demonstrates that the financial world can be analysed from some very different viewpoints and that a given theory can only be considered 'valid' if, and only if, we are ready to accept its implicit paradigmatic assumptions.

The Paradigmatic Unity of Academic Finance

From the outset, financial theory defined three interconnected areas of study: value estimation, the economic analysis of contracts, and the identification and calculation of investment risks. However, we can identify two distinct periods in the historical development of academic finance.

Until the 1950s, finance aimed to analyse corporate accounts, which were assumed to contain all the information required for the study of financing and investment transactions. Research questions focused on evaluating the present value of assets and interpreting financial information by analysing ratios (rate of return on equity, rate of return on investments, debt to equity ratio, etc.).[1] This 'first finance', which was mainly descriptive and anchored in the real economy, comprised numerous institutional details linked to corporate life. It did not seek to issue overall recommendations but instead contented itself with developing decision-making tools, leaving the company owner-manager to set their objectives. Finally, it largely disregarded the existence of capital markets, which were strictly regulated at the time.

Academic finance then underwent major transformation in the early 1960s. During that period, marked by the rapid development of the financial markets, the increased power of shareholders in corporate governance and the expansion of the macro-economy, academic finance moved away from its initial project – describing the *real* behaviour of individuals and companies – to try and establish a set of 'scientific' management principles based on hypothetic-deductive reasoning. In other words, academic finance made a positivist shift: researchers took on the task of developing theoretical models and empirically testing their predictions *to establish laws.*

This shift implied the adoption of an objectivist ontology where the social world is assumed to be made up of stable, tangible entities. These entities, regardless of whether or not they are perceptible to individuals, are assumed to be autonomous and external to the observer. The financial world – like the natural world – would therefore exist independently of the representations that individuals have of it, and would be governed by a set of regularities and balances that could be shown through the use of protocols derived from the natural sciences. The area of study (e.g. the stock market) is thus seen as an autonomous entity, characterised by the presence of regularities that can be identified through the study of causal mechanisms (e.g. the impact of macroeconomic announcements on the anticipated rates of return). Modern finance is therefore based on the observation of facts and experimentation, doing away with moral and ethical considerations and reflections on social well-being, deemed to be outside of its scope.

Furthermore, on an epistemological level, modern finance favours methodological individualism: it assumes that the properties of the whole (society) are determined by the properties of the sub-parts (individuals). The neoclassical representation of the financial market is thus based on two assumptions: first, the rationality of economic agents and second, the equilibrium, which implies that the combination of actions by the agents produces stability within the system. In this context, an exogenous shock (e.g. a fall in key rates) modifies individual behaviour and establishes a new balance (a rise in asset prices). Individual choices therefore produce social reality. 'Social sets' are only theoretical entities, deprived of real substance and can be reduced to the elements that they comprise, that is the individuals. Moreover, the conditions for this aggregation of parts are virtually constant: other than a few minor adjustments, the characteristics of social reality are assumed to be invariant. Like the physical world, the financial world can thus be reduced to indecomposable elements (*atoms*) and can accordingly be rebuilt using those elements.

Finally, from a methodological viewpoint, the project of modern finance meant transposing methods used in the natural sciences to the study of the financial sector. There was therefore a switch from a descriptive methodology to a hypothetic-deductive methodology. Modern finance borrowed four simplifying assumptions from neoclassic microeconomics in order to model the financial markets. These assumptions, which were to lay the foundations for the subsequent theoretical edifice, were:

1. *The perfect market concept*, with the following conditions:
   - Atomicity: the market comprises a multitude of investors who, individually, have no influence of the asset price discovery process;
   - Perfect information, all participants on the financial market have, at all times, access to all the relevant information on the evaluation of tradable assets;

- Absence of transaction costs: at all times, investors are at liberty to enter and exit the market at no cost to them;
- Homogeneity: the various assets traded have similar institutional and fiscal characteristics;

2. *Economic rationality model*: investors conduct themselves in a rational, self-serving manner. This can be represented in a model that maximises expected gains (generally based on the risk/return profile);
3. *Certainty*: the risk of debtors defaulting is assumed to be zero. The various financial instruments (shares and bonds) are therefore analysed as if they formed a single financial security;
4. Existence of a *risk-free asset*: investors can acquire an asset with a certain rate of return at all times.

Modern finance therefore endeavours to form an objective theory, free from all value judgement, to explain and predict reality by demonstrating universal relations uniting the observed phenomena. As we will see, this unified paradigmatic framework founders with a number of ontological, methodological and epistemological questions.

THE LIMITS OF POSITIVISM IN FINANCE

The Entanglement of 'Facts' and 'Values'

According to a 2010 study by the Davos Economic Forum, 68% of people surveyed thought that the financial crisis was '*also a crisis of ethics and values*'. Paradoxically, the use of these terms is impossible in finance research work. Positivism postulates a dichotomy between the realm of 'facts' and that of 'values': facts are tangible, measurable and verifiable, whereas values are metaphysical and cannot therefore be subject to rational analysis. The aim of science is to test hypotheses through experimentation, so financial economists have to set aside their ethical judgements when carrying out research.

This reasoning is based on the Humean notion where *real judgements* can be *analytical judgements* (i.e. logical tautologies as in mathematical deductions) or *synthetic judgements* (i.e. substantive affirmations backed up by empirical tests). However, value judgements do not fall into this new classification: they are not analytical and cannot be tested empirically. As such, this dichotomy between analytical and synthetic judgements *excludes value judgements from the scope of real judgements*. Since ethical judgements are incompatible with the positivist research agenda, they have to be excluded from the scope of academic finance (Robbins, 1935).

However, the dichotomy between analytical and synthetic judgements has been much criticised since the 1950s. It is now accepted that 'facts' and 'values' are not two separate realms of the 'real' world but are in fact inextricably entangled. Putnam (2002) addresses two main criticisms of the fact/value dichotomy:

- Firstly, scientific theories are based on unobservable theoretical terms (such as atoms, gravitational fields or representative investors). From the positivist perspective, the use of such terms remains acceptable if it leads to the formulation of theories whose predictions can be tested: these are the theories that, as indivisible entities, are put to the test in experiments (Carnap, 1966). However, if factual knowledge implies knowledge of the unobservable theoretical terms, it must necessarily presuppose values. The claim to purely factual knowledge is thus based on principles that are themselves prescriptive. Putnam calls these principles *epistemic values*. These values, whose role is to regulate the 'adequate description of the world', have the virtues of 'coherence, simplicity and upholding of the existing doctrine'. It thus implies that *it is impossible to make a statement about facts without making a value judgement.*
- Secondly, the facts/values dichotomy is based on the very restrictive definition of the realm of 'facts'. This dichotomy implicitly implies that the evaluative and descriptive functions of the language used are separate. In fact, statements that attempt to describe a 'fact' (descriptive function) are generally based on a set of beliefs, knowledge, a world vision and, ultimately, 'values' (evaluative function). Putnam theorises on the entanglement of facts and values via the notion of *thick ethical concept.*[2] For example, if I affirm that a man who beats a child is cruel, I describe a fact (use of violence against a weaker individual) and I simultaneously express a value judgement (the word 'cruel' implies the condemnation of the act). It is therefore impossible to separate the evaluative and prescriptive elements of a message.

If we accept the idea that the evaluation of facts presupposes epistemic ideas and that facts and values are entangled in language, this means that *financial theories are not content with pinning down facts but also contain implicit value judgements.*

Every term in a statement aimed at describing a financial 'fact' is always implicitly based on a set of beliefs and knowledge and therefore indirectly refers to a conception of the world and, ultimately, values.

The basic concepts in financial reasoning, such as 'risk premium', 'alpha' or 'VaR' do not therefore reflect economic and social reality in a neutral way. Their formulation reveals certain categories of thought that implicitly constitute an ethical judgement: the role of the financial markets and of the company is to enable the owners of capital to maximise their rates of return, where the latter is evaluated in comparison to the return from alternative investment possibilities. As such, the intellectual attitude that consists in setting ethical considerations aside to boost the scientific robustness of finance seems wrong. *Academic finance has moral, philosophical and political aspects.*

The Controversy over Social Ontology

Within the positivist framework adopted by modern finance, the researcher's goal is to apply rigorous methods to identify the causal mechanisms governing the research topic. Research then allows for the development of a stock of objective, universal knowledge through a cycle of theorisation, operationalisation and empirical tests. However, this vision, which implies a clear separation between researcher and the research topic, has come under fire over recent decades.

Post-modern authors (such as Richard Rorty, Jean-François Lyotard, Michel Maffesoli and the like) have challenged the neutrality-objectivity-rationality triptych of positivist social sciences. They insist that the production of scientific knowledge requires standards, instruments and structures such as a common culture, a language (jargon), methodologies, standards of conduct and so on. 'Knowledge', which is also the product of social interaction, can therefore only be relative to the context in which it was produced. Research cannot therefore lead to objective knowledge but only to interpretations of reality – different, competing interpretations that reflect the social and political fragmentations that are inherent to reality. Although it is interesting, this approach still leads to a paradox whereby there are as many realities as there are visions of reality – which undermines the very object of scientific investigation.

Critical realism, as developed by Bhaskar (1978), seems to provide a relevant analytical framework overcoming the pitfalls of positivism and post-modernism. In this approach, social reality is given an autonomous existence, but it cannot be perceived directly by individuals. Critical realism therefore establishes an ontological distinction between knowledge about reality and reality itself, in other words between scientific laws and the reality of events. According to Bhaskar, social reality comprises three interconnected levels:

- The *empirical*, which means immediately observable data used in scientific investigations (e.g. the time series of stock markets or interest rates);
- The *actual*, which simultaneously contains the observable and non-observable events that occur when real causal mechanisms are activated;
- The *real*, which contains the causal mechanisms and structures that govern the actual.

The *empirical* is therefore seen as a sub-part of the *actual*, which is itself a sub-part of the *real*. Critical realists thus underline the superficial nature of positivist social sciences: any attempt to deduce laws by simply observing facts (i.e. the *empirical*) while ignoring deeper levels (the *actual* and the *real*) can only produce incomplete or even inaccurate statements. They thus urge researchers to try and uncover the hidden mechanisms and structures that govern institutions, practices and social roles (Lawson, 2003).

The Performativity of Academic Finance

In finance, scientists mainly attempt to examine, operationalise and measure detailed implications of the metaphorical insight upon which their research is implicitly based. However, despite the sophistication of the quantitative techniques used, academic finance remains a *social science*. As such, it comprises several fundamental differences with the natural sciences.

While the works of a physician are based on the existence of constant and universal forces (e.g. gravity or the movement of planets), financial economists work in a context of *uncertainty*. The phenomena studied in finance (e.g. price movements) are in fact subject to unpredictable variations resulting from human action. The financial models manage this uncertainly by linking it to the statistical notion of *variance*. They thus assume that it is possible to predict different possible scenarios for the future state of the economy and to assign a probability of occurrence to each of these scenarios. Contrary to physics, the results of the financial models can therefore only have limited scope: the predictions made are always probabilistic and conditional on a set of ex ante hypotheses on the state of the world.

In addition, the behaviour of the phenomena studied in natural sciences (e.g. the trajectory of a meteorite) is in no way influenced by the theory tested (e.g. the theory of universal gravitation): regardless of whether the theory is valid or not, the meteorite will follow the same trajectory. This is far from being the case in social sciences, which study interactions between human beings. Social behaviour is shaped by shared conceptual frameworks that actually make up the final results of social sciences. The language and results of social sciences are gradually infused in the daily life of individuals and therefore contribute indirectly to the modelling of the reality that are supposed to describe.

This general observation is especially relevant in the field of finance. Finance as a discipline is formed by the merging of accounting (i.e. a professional technique) and neoclassic microeconomics (a theoretical branch of economic science). As Nobel economics prize-winner Merton Miller pointed out in 1998 (in an inaugural speech for the German finance association), academic finance has two distinct streams but in reality they overlap:

- A *micro-normative* stream which endeavours to examine that way an economic agent (e.g. an individual investor or company owner-manager) can maximise their objective-function (e.g. the rate of return of an investment) without worrying about price formation processes. This way of approaching finance is characteristic of *business schools*, where the goal is train future stakeholders.
- A *macro-normative* stream, seeking to characterise price trends of financial assets, in a hypothetical world characterised by a multitude of rational agents. This stream, which above all strives to understand how the financial system works, is developed in economics departments.

Once validated by the academic community and transposed in textbooks, financial theory – although based on simplifying hypotheses – thus helps guide the behaviour of economic stakeholders. As knowledge is passed on in economics and management departments, the concepts and metaphors from academic finance (alpha, beta, VaR, risk premium, etc.) eventually form an integral part of the daily life of commentators and financial markets stakeholders. *Financial theory is therefore a constituent element of the reality it aims to analyse.* It contributes to the mechanisation of behaviours and the emergence of 'autonomous rationalities' within organisations. The creation and reproduction of the socio-economic reality thus hinges on assumptions tacitly accepted and incorporated into the vocabulary, the ways of thinking and social standards of stakeholders in the financial system.

FINANCIAL THEORY AND SHAREHOLDER IDEOLOGY

The Repressive Function of Financial Theory

What are the initial conclusions to be drawn from the preceding discussion? Firstly, the claim to 'neutral', 'objective' and 'scientific' financial theory is an illusion: the development of academic finance corresponds to a dual movement with the construction of economic and social reality on the one hand, and the simultaneous expunging of this construction process by the superimposing of a 'veil' of scientificness on the other.

Successive generations of economics and management students have thus interiorised the concepts, methods and language of academic finance. Given their mathematical content, these methods are usually seen as simple technical tools. However, we have demonstrated that finance does not make do with describing reality in an objective manner but instead also forms a *language* that structures the categories of thought of those using it. Financial theory is therefore something of an *ideological superstructure*. Let us explain this in more detail. Modern social and political life is based on the domination of Reason. Against this background, any element of society that awards itself the monopoly of science can easily consolidate its supremacy. This possibility inevitably leads to the development of an ideological vision concealing existing social contradictions under supposed scientificness to the benefit of the dominant social group.[3] The development of academic finance and the gradual dissemination of financial 'knowledge' in the company – knowledge based on the maximisation of the shareholder's utility – have indirectly fixed the balance of power between social groups to the exclusive benefit of the owners of capital. The increasing importance of financial indicators and financial techniques in guiding corporate strategy and governance has thus reinforced shareholder control over companies' units and employees, structuring the managerial language and establishing an 'objective' performance standard. In this way, the development of financial theory has help to reorient business leaders' rationality, in principle focused on analysis and forecasting of the complex context in which the organisation operates, towards the maximisation of financial indicators from a short-term perspective. By linking the question of company management to a set of algebraic concepts and algebraic relations between the latter, financial theory has thus served as an 'invisible technology' insidiously structuring the social relations of production (Berry, 1983).

The supposed scientificness of academic finance can then be addressed as a 'repressive function' contributing to upholding asymmetric relationships between stakeholders in the company, to the benefit of the owners of capital. We can therefore state that financial theory is an aspect of the *ideological domination of capital* (i) by giving theoretical legitimacy to the self-serving behaviour of business leaders and executives, (ii) by legitimising economic policies that reinforce the power of financial stakeholders (Ghoshal, 2005). The next section takes this idea further, looking at the four founding contributions to academic finance.

THE 'FOUR HORSEMEN OF THE APOCALYPSE'

It[4] is customary to date the birth of modern finance to the publication of an article entitled '*Portfolio Selection*' in the *Journal of Finance* in 1952, taken from the thesis of PhD in economics, Harry Markowitz. This article provided a mathematical basis for the concepts of return and risk. It defined the *return expectation* of an investment as the weighted average of anticipated returns according to different probabilistic scenarios; and risk as the variance in return expectation (i.e. the sum of the squared deviations of anticipated return rates around their mean value). Moreover, Markowitz uses the mathematical definition of the variance of a weighted sum of random variables (i.e. the weighted sum of individual variances, plus twice the weighted sum of covariances) to define portfolio risk. This approach let him demonstrate the principle of 'diversification': an investor can minimise risk by selecting assets with low correlation.

For each level of return sought, this work uncovered the possibility of selecting a set of assets minimising portfolio variance by placing the portfolio at the 'efficient frontier'. From then on, the investment selection process implies a choice of assets with the desired characteristics in terms of average return, variance and covariance. Looking beyond these technical aspects, which paved the way for the development of quantitative finance, Harry Markowitz's article, with its typically *micro-normative* approach (although ironically written in an economics department) was of major importance for the development of academic finance because it helped define return and financial risk as *statistical objects* and not as economic, moral or political categories.

A few years later, William Sharpe (1964) published an article in the *Journal of Finance* analysing the rate of return of a theoretical asset on a balanced financial market. To do so, Sharpe borrowed Markowitz's statistical definition of return, then established a set of simplifying assumptions on the functioning of the financial market. These assumptions helped him mathematically derive the rate of return obtained by investors at a point of equilibrium. These assumptions were as follows:

- Investors are assumed to agree on the prospects of various investments;
- Investors all have the same portfolio of assets, which implies (because all risky assets have to be held) that this single asset portfolio is a 'market portfolio' where the rate of return is an average of the return on the existing listed assets (weighted by their outstanding volumes);
- Investors have heterogeneous risk aversion profiles, expressed by the proportion of their wealth assigned to 'risk-free assets' in relation to the proportion invested in the 'market portfolio'.

William Sharpe thus demonstrated that the balanced return rate of a financial asset is a *linear function* of a single variable: the sensitivity of the performance on that asset to variations in the performance of the market portfolio (the *beta*). This capital asset pricing model (CAPM) therefore connects, in an imaginary world, the expected rate of return of an investment in company equity to the *beta* of that company (i.e. the covariance between the time series of the statistical performance of the company's shares and the time series of the performance of the market index, expressed as a proportion of the variance of performance of the market index).

The CAPM is a canonical example of *macro-normative* finance (aimed at understanding how markets work with no concern for practical implications). Ironically, however, it was widely accepted and incorporated in almost all finance textbooks. Thus taken for granted, the CAPM's conclusions – which refer to an idealised market situation – are used on a daily basis by analysts seeking to determine the rate of return that can be legitimately expected by a shareholder.

In other words, the use of the CAPM for financial markets links capital remuneration to a linear function of the average profitability observed on the financial market, doing away with all references to economic and social factors and to the specific characteristics of the company in question.

The CAPM was thus an important turning point in the history of financial theory as it established a *scientific standard of profitability*. Academic finance thus enters the economic and social debate on the distribution of added value by tipping the balance of power to the benefit of shareholders.

In 1970, Eugène Fama published an article in the *Journal of Finance* in which he put forward a set of arguments in favour of the assumption of 'informational efficiency' of the financial markets. This idea, which stipulates that asset prices reflect the full extent of market information at all times, is a very old one. It dates back to the work of Louis Bachelier (1900) on random market statistical processes, and of Paul Samuelson (1965) on arbitration operations that help re-establish market prices at their equilibrium value.

Before Fama's work, economists generally believed that 'informational efficiency' required a very restrictive set of conditions, making it pretty implausible in reality. These conditions included, for example, the absence of transaction costs, the perfect dissemination of information to all market operators, and the use by the latter of a single cognitive framework for interpreting that information. Fama's main contribution was to demonstrate that these three assumptions can be rejected without affecting the relevance of the notion of 'market efficiency'. For a market to be efficient, it simply requires the *majority* of investors to have access to information and to refer to a homogenous analysis framework. Moreover, irrational investors are, by definition, inclined to make losses and are therefore gradually eliminated from the market. In addition, as their decisions are random and uncorrelated, they cannot have an impact on price dynamics, which remain focused on the fundamental value. To measure the 'informational efficiency' of markets, Fama identified three empirical forms: a *strong* form (where market prices reflect public information and private information), a *semi-strong* form (where prices reflect public information), and a *weak* form (where prices reflect past information). He then conducted a series of empirical tests to establish that markets are efficient in *semi-strong* and *weak* form.

These tests are now criticised, especially with the development of calculation capacities, econometric theory and neuroeconomics which have helped identify and explain numerous 'anomalies' in the pricing of financial assets. However, the market efficiency theory is still taught in almost all finance textbooks. It provides very powerful justification for financial deregulation policies and has probably helped consolidate the power of finance over the last 30 years.

A few years later, Jensen and Meckling (1976) published their Theory of the Firm in the *Journal of Financial Economics*, depicting a 'knot of contracts' whereby individual actions with contradictory interests converge to establish a balance. This theory highlights the possibility of a conflict of interests between the company owner-manager and the shareholder.

The shareholder's wealth depends on the market value of the firm's equity, whereas the company owner-manager is independent of that. As a result, the company owner-manager has no incentive to make decisions that comply with the shareholder's interests, which can generate tensions in the firm. The firm's survival then depends on its capacity to minimise these 'agency conflicts' that end in a reduction in the market value of equity to a point below its potential. It is thus necessary to introduce an employment contract requiring the *agent* (the owner-manager) to work in the best interests of the *principal* (shareholder). This contract may contain clauses allowing the shareholder to monitor the owner-manager's decisions or to pin his remuneration on the value of the company's equity (by issuing stock options, for example).

It should be noted that in this model, the firm's performance is measured in terms of the stock market capitalisation of its shares, and therefore the value of the shareholder's assets. The implicit message of Jensen and Meckling's work is therefore that the main goal of management must be to 'maximise the shareholder's wealth'. This model also assumes that the market accurately measures the value of the company's equity, which indirectly refers to Fama's 'informational efficiency' assumption.

These four founding contributions have thus helped:

- Assimilate the notion of financial return as a statistical category, with no economic or moral bases (Markowitz);
- Determine a standard for return on investment for shareholders, established in a tautological manner in relation to the average profitability observed on the market (Sharpe);
- Confer the financial market with the theoretical capacity to measure the fundamental value of real assets (Fama);
- Reduce the notion of value creation purely to the measurement of shareholder wealth (Jensen and Meckling).

OUTLOOK: DIVERSIFYING FINANCE

A Move towards a New Conceptual Framework

The discussion above highlights the epistemological limits and dangers involved in modern finance. As a result, it appears necessary to rebuild – or at least diversify – finance. To clarify the issues at stake with this transformation, it will be useful to first look at the epistemological nature of the academic controversies. As shown in Fig. 2, all scientific discourse contains three superimposed layers – paradigms, metaphors and puzzle-solving (Morgan, 1980).

- A *paradigm* is a world view defined by a set of core assumptions governing the rules and standards of scientific activity. This world view is interiorised by researchers during their studies and provides a common reference framework for scientific work and debate.
- A *metaphor* refers to the construction and use of mental images within a given paradigm. By structuring researchers' language, metaphors define their vision of reality and orient empirical research towards the analysis of similarities between the research topic and common language. In academic finance, research questions are therefore often based on metaphorical presuppositions (e.g. are markets 'efficient'? what is the impact of 'agency conflicts' on the 'risk premium'? how do you explain the 'domestic bias' and 'international diversification' of portfolios?).
- Finally, when it comes to *puzzle-solving*, researchers discuss the choice of tools and models used to answer research questions. Puzzle-solving claims a lion's share of financial science debate *with scientists attempting to examine, operationalise, and measure detailed implications of the metaphorical insight upon which their research is implicitly based.*

The paradigmatic unity of academic finance therefore needs us to simultaneously determine the content of the questions asked, the nature of

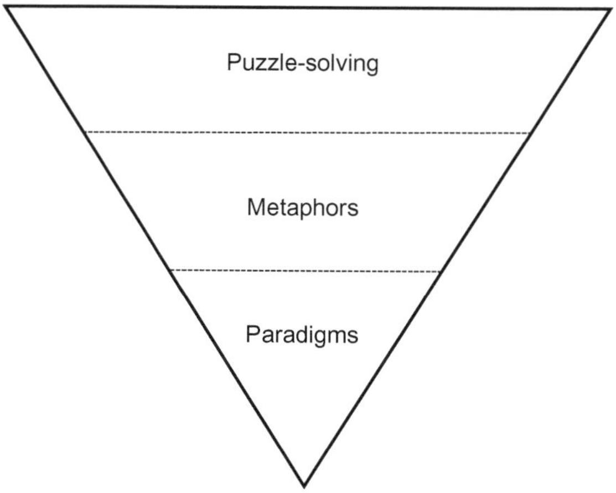

Fig. 2. The Structure of Scientific Discourse. *Source*: Morgan (1980).

acceptable solutions and the phases via which those solutions can be attained. As we have previously established, the majority of finance research work involves perpetually reaffirming the tacit world vision on which the discipline is based: *companies and society must be organised to serve the interests of the owners of capital.*

Fig. 2 characterises the diversification of finance research in a process via which (i) *research in finance will expand to encompass other paradigms taking in the social sciences*, (ii) *new metaphors will be put forward within the existing paradigm*, and (iii) *rigour in puzzle-solving will be conserved.*

The effective diversification of financial theory also requires two essential conditions:

- The notions of ethics, values and intentionality have to be discussed openly. These considerations are inappropriate in the positivist functionalist paradigm but become indispensable when we acknowledge the existence of 'thick ethical concepts' and the performativity of financial theory. Given the current context of social and ecological crisis, we urge researchers to take the fact that *the human being is the relevant measurement of value* (Benedikter, 2011) as the premise for all investigations. In other words, *the existence of money, profit, financial institutions and markets can only be justified as long as they contribute to human development* – and not the contrary.
- Research work will have to adopt varied, appropriate ontological assumptions depending on the question being asked. Objectivist ontology is preferable when studying how markets work from a 'macronormative' perspective. On the other hand, subjectivist ontology, acknowledging that the financial world is only the meeting point of several individual subjectivities, is required for 'micronormative' work.

A New Research Programme

How do we bring about the desired change? We believe that an analysis of the social, behavioural, historical and institutional processes determining the capacity of financial systems to generate well-being in a comparative, international and interdisciplinary perspective would contribute to the goal of diversifying academic finance. This ambitious project would encompass all the aspects mentioned earlier:

– *Macro-normative* research will enrich existing work by generating new metaphors (taking contributions from related disciplines into account).

For example, the concept of *financialisation* has been highlighted in a broad spectrum of social sciences to analyse the multidimensional complexity of the global economy. Used by economists, political scientists and geographers, this concept refers to the 'increased domination, at many levels, of financial stakeholders, financial markets, financial practices, financial indicators and financial narratives, ultimately leading to a structural transformation of economies, firms (including financial institutions), States and households' (Aalbers, 2015). The study of financialisation could form a point where critical researchers converge and thus encourage interdisciplinary dialogue. A set of relevant research questions could, for example, include:

1. Which indicators are relevant for measuring financialisation? How far can these indicators help us understand the temporal and cross-disciplinary variation of the financialisation process?
2. What links unite financialisation and the economic behaviour of firms, shareholders, banks, households and States? What are the implications for well-being? What consequences can we establish for the validity of the various economic theories?
3. Do the technological, legal and geographic transformations of the international financial system explain financialisation? Is financialisation a 'change of regime' in the worldwide economic organisation?
4. Can we identify phases in financialisation over economic and business history? What conclusions can we draw from these experiences?
   - *Micro-normative* research will focus on the emergence of alternative financial practices based on the expression of ethical values (ethical banks, microcredit, social and solidarity enterprises, social stock exchange, alternative currencies, etc.). The business model of these institutions is incompatible with standard financial theory which assumes utilitarian rationality. Adopting alternative finance as a research topic raises a number of questions on the ontological status of currency, finance, entrepreneurship and organisations.

This research will necessarily be based on *subjectivist* ontology. It will seek to understand how alternative finance affects the well-being of beneficiaries, investors and stakeholders. The starting point for these investigations could be the definition put forward by Benedikter (2011) for *dependency on capital*. For those who do not own capital (e.g. households and entrepreneurs), this dependency takes the form of material restrictions and the submission of their existence to criteria defined by the owners of capital. Those who do not own capital see their freedom restricted because, if they are to survive, they are forced to accept to serve another's interests. For the owners of capital (investors), dependency takes the form of a psychological addiction to growth in capital stock (the 'equilibrium return'). This kind of addiction could inhibit the creative potential of savings. The work being considered will help determine whether 'ethical' financing circuits are able to attenuate this dual dependency. A set of relevant research questions could, for example, include:

1. What is the ontological status of currency? Can currency be conceived as a common good? What is the relationship between interest rates and ecological sustainability?
2. Can alternative finance be reconciled with utilitarian rationalism? Can we link discussions on social ontology with the emergence of this alternative finance?
3. Does alternative finance contribute to the development of sustainable organisational models? Does it contribute to the redefinition of managerial tools and the concept of 'value'?
4. What are the characteristics of impact investment on performance and the risks of default? What is the international geography of the social investment sector?

CONCLUSION

This chapter started out with the finding that standard financial theory is an obstacle to ecological and social sustainability. We thus began with an attempt to deconstruct this theory by pointing out the proven limits of its epistemological, ontological and methodological assumptions, and its ideological and political role. These considerations then let us introduce the concept of diversification in financial research, which we presented as a process via which (i) *research in finance will expand to encompass other paradigms inherent to the social sciences*, (ii) *new metaphors will be put forward within the existing paradigm*, and (iii) *rigour in puzzle-solving will be conserved.* We thus exposed a number of valid avenues for future research, emphasising the need to explore the social, behavioural, historical and institutional processes that determine the capacity of financial systems to generate well-being in a comparative, international and interdisciplinary perspective. Finally, we set out this research topic alongside several relevant assumptions and research questions. Our future research work will endeavour to cover this programme.

NOTES

1. For example, the work done by the financial department of American firm Dupont applied algebraic decomposition to accounting ratios to highlight the impact of leverage on returns on equity and corporate risk.
2. These thick ethical concepts includes terms such as 'generous', 'elegant', 'skilful', 'strong', 'weak' and 'vulgar'. They can be distinguished from thin ethical concepts such as 'good', 'bad', 'duty', 'fair', 'vice', 'virtue' and the like (Putnam, 2002, p. 35).
3. It may, for example, represent a phenomenon (e.g. price discovery on financial markets) as natural, whereas it is in fact the outcome of a social relationship, or represent a situation (e.g. an increase in dividends paid to shareholders) as harmonious, whereas it is a source of a conflict of interests.
4. I would like to thank Ciaràn Mac an Bhaird (Dublin City University) for suggesting this phrase.

REFERENCES

Aalbers, M. B. (2015). Corporate financialization. In N. Castree (Ed.), *The international encyclopedia of geography: People, the earth, environment, and technology*. Oxford: Wiley.

Adler, P. S., Forbes, L. C., & Willmott, H. (2007). Critical management studies. *The Academy of Management Annals*, *1*, 119–179.

Bachelier, L. (1900). Théorie de la spéculation. *Annales de l'Ecole Normale Supérieure*, *17*, 21–86.

Bay, T., & Schinkus, C. (2012). Critical finance studies: A manifesto for an interdisciplinary perspective. *Journal of Interdisciplinary Economics*, *24*(January), 1–6.

Benedikter, R. (2011). *Social banking and social finance: Answers to the economic crisis*. New York, Dordrecht, Heidelberg, London: Springer Briefs in Business, Springer New York Dordrecht Heidelberg London.

Berry, M. (1983). Une technologie invisible? L'impact des instruments de gestion sur l'évolution des systèmes humains, *CRG, École polytechnique*.

Bhaskar, R. (1978). *A realist theory of science* (2nd ed.). Hassocks: Harvester Press.

Burrel, G., & Morgan, G. (1979). *Sociological paradigms and organizational analysis*. Aldershot: Gower Publishing Company Limited.

Carnap, R. (1966). *Philosophical foundations of physics*. New York, London: Basic Books Inc.

Epstein, G. (2005). Introduction: Financialization and the world economy. In G. Epstein (Éd.), *Financialization and the world economy* (pp. 1–16). Cheltenham: Edward Elgar Publishers.

Epstein, G., & Habbard, P. (2011). *Dette souveraine et spéculation: Une interaction insidieuse*. Document de travail ITUC General Council.

Faugère, C. (2014). Ruthless compassion in banking and finance. *Research in International Business and Finance*, *32*, 106–121.

Ghoshal, S. (2005). Bad management theories are destroying good management practices. *Academy of Management Learning and Education*, *4*, 75–91.

Giraud, G. (2012). *Illusion financière*. Paris: Les Éditions de l'Atelier.

Jensen, M., & Meckling, W. (1976). Theory of the firm: Managerial behavior, agency costs, and capital structure. *Journal of Financial Economics*, *3*, 305–360.
Lagoarde-Segot, T. (2010). *After the crisis: rethinking finance*. New York, NY: Nova Science.
Lagoarde-Segot, T. (2014). *La finance solidaire, un humanisme économique*. Brussels: De Boeck.
Lawson, T. (2003). *Reorienting economics*. London: Routledge.
Lazonick, W. (2013). *The financialization of the US corporation: What has been lost and how it can be regained*. INET Research Note 007.
Morgan, G. (1980). Paradigm, metaphors, and puzzle solving in organization theory. *Administrative Science Quarterly*, *25*, 605–622.
Putnam, H. (2002). *The collapse of the fact/value dichotomy and other essays*. Cambridge, USA: Harvard University Press.
Robbins, L. (1935). *An essay on the nature and significance of economic science* (2nd ed.). London: Macmillan.
Samuelson, P. (1965). Proof that properly anticipated prices fluctuate randomly industrial management review. *Industrial Management Review*, *6*, 41–49 Spring.
Sharpe, W. F. (1964). Capital asset prices – A theory of market equilibrium under conditions of risk. *Journal of Finance*, *12*, 425–442.

ANALYSIS OF THE FINANCIAL CRISIS, OR CRISIS IN FINANCIAL ANALYSIS?

Roland Pérez

ABSTRACT

Purpose – *The goal of this chapter is to discuss the foundations of 'modern finance', its paradigm and conceptual framework, its methods and tools, its practices and results, its governance and regulation.*

Approach – *The first part presents the characteristics of 'modern finance' and its negative effects. The second part analyses the efforts made to remedy those effects and argue about the need for a real reform.*

Findings – *Several aspects are pointed, for example an unreasonable 'normality', incentives that encourage excess, the spread of subprime crisis, etc. The contemporary finance is a 'giant with clay feet'.*

Originality/value – *We need to proceed with a dual* reembeddedness *of finance in the economy and economy in society.*

Keywords: Finance; conceptual framework; paradigm; crisis; social reembeddedness

Finance Reconsidered: New Perspectives for a Responsible and Sustainable Finance
Critical Studies on Corporate Responsibility, Governance and Sustainability, Volume 10, 111–141

ISSN: 2043-9059/doi:10.1108/S2043-905920160000010025

'*It looks like the worst of the major crises is behind us*' said a well-known economist (Sorman, 2008) in spring 2008. The author, a champion of liberalism, stated that '*the economy is no longer a matter of opinion but a science*'. While most economists were less conclusive and somewhat more cautious in their opinions, there are still plenty of them who, especially when it comes to finance, have long since adopted a rather haughty position, considering that finance is now a separate scientific discipline, just like physics or biology, calling on similar approaches to those applied by the so-called 'hard sciences' in terms of epistemological paradigms, conceptual frameworks and empirical validation protocols. This scientistic posturing has resulted in a widespread mathematisation of finance, which previously made do with simple actuarial calculations and which, in just a few decades, has virtually taken over the entire scope, leading to some impressive modelling and a tendency to talk about the 'arrogance of finance' (Bourguinat & Briys, 2009).

The goal of this chapter is not to embark upon another biased challenge of the use of a highly formalised modelling and analysis approach but to question that applied since the founding works of Markowitz (1952), Tobin (1956), Modigliani and Miller (1958), and those that followed, including Sharpe (1964), Fama (1970), Black and Scholes, 1973) and Ross (1977). I intend to set out a few thoughts on this scientific movement, dubbed 'modern finance' or 'scientific finance' by its supporters, highlighting the differences that set it apart from the 'traditional finance' that preceded it[1] and from contemporary issues; this comparative essay has been written in the light of the current global financial crisis, the scope and impact of which have led to questions as to whether 'analysis of the financial crisis' is not in fact the reflection of 'a crisis in financial analysis'.

The first part of the chapter will present the characteristics of 'modern finance' and its negative effects. I will then look at the efforts made to try and remedy those effects and talk about the need for a real reform of finance.

'MODERN FINANCE' AND ITS NEGATIVE EFFECTS

Firstly, I will draw up a comparison of the characteristics that seem to define 'modern finance', highlighting its most significant features, then I will take the subprime mortgage crisis to illustrate this analysis, as this is recognised as the trigger of the recent banking crisis and ensuing stock market and economic slump.

A FEW MARKERS AND COMMENTS

This presentation will respectively deal with:

- the epistemological posture,
- the conceptual framework for formalisation,
- the 'toolkit' used by researchers and practitioners,
- regulations, professional conduct and ethics,
- governance and regulation.

The Epistemological Posture

Traditional or classic finance, as developed over a number of centuries (Braudel, 1967–1979), never really questioned its epistemological posture. However, if we observe the institutions in place or the practices of the stakeholders involved, we can note the importance of contingent factors (regulations, customs, etc.) that really 'embed' finance within the social fabric. Commercial law has been marked by this, referring to *affectio societatis* when a company is founded, approaching the client-banker relationship from a *fiducie* (or trust) angle, severely penalising the bankrupt, deemed to have damaged the relationship established in the trust.

Modern or scientific finance, sustained by its aim of becoming a real science, did away with these contingency factors to try and become a universal discipline, like its model, physics. It thought it had achieved this by applying mathematic formalisation comparable to that used by its model. In doing so, it committed a major epistemological error stemming from the specific nature of human and social sciences (HSS), not because those sciences refuse all rational approach to the subject under study, but because they are directly related to it.

(a) The argument sometimes known as the 'Levi-Strauss theorem' applies to HSS: it says that '*when an observer is of the same kind as the observed phenomenon, he/she is part of the observation*' (Levi-Strauss, 1950). This does not only apply to the study of populations in distant countries but to all of us, especially those studying the economic world. This proximity between researchers and stakeholders is not without risk: it specifically raises serious epistemological, methodological and deontological questions in the fields of the HSS most concerned, such as psychoanalysis, pedagogy or – most relevant to us here – finance.

(b) A second observation, related to the previous one, concerns the complex and sometimes reciprocal relationship between facts and their representations, especially in terms of predictions. In the so-called 'exact' sciences, the facts are what they are and the representations we produce, made up of expressions, may be simplistic or more sophisticated, enabling those who issue or receive them to understand the subject of the study without that subject being modified (apart from some very minor exceptions, e.g. modifications to a subject under study due to laboratory conditions).

I often give the example of a 'badly behaved' volcano. To summarise, a few years ago, a volcano started rumbling and, given the risk of an eruption, the government commissioned an appraisal by two well-known personalities. The latter gave conflicting opinions – for one of them, an eruption was imminent while the other said there was no risk. Applying the principle of precaution, the authorities evacuated the area but no eruption occurred. The subject under study (the volcano) was 'doing its thing' regardless of the given representations. On the other hand, if a finance minister or central bank governor issues an opinion on a particular economic phenomenon, especially a financial matter, it is clear that this representation of the future will have a direct impact on its realisation.

In fields related to HSS, facts and their representations are often intimately linked, sometimes taking the form of 'self-referential speculations' (Orléan, 1999) leading, as a result of mimetic behaviour, to self-fulfilling prophecies. This concept was identified in sociology a long time ago, most notably by American sociologist/epistemologist Merton (1948).[2] Therefore, the prediction contributes to the construction of reality. This specific feature of HSS was particularly well highlighted, for financial markets, not only by the work of researchers such as Orléan (1999), but also by testimonies from practitioners such as Soros (1998). Hence, the inclusion of finance within the scope of HSS leads to a 'need to take mimetic and self-referential rationalities into consideration' (F. Lobez – discussion with the author).

(a) A third observation, which is also congruent with the previous two, can be made on the complementary nature between the 'processes' and the 'products' of activities relating to 'knowledge of action' in HSS. The production 'process' of a given product (goods or service) is itself a social product 'induced' relative to the main product. This process-product interaction is especially sensitive when the main product is immaterial in nature and therefore directly relating to human activity. We can then legitimately ask whether, as in Escher's images, the representation of a phenomenon not only interferes with that phenomenon, but – to a potentially vital degree – blends into it or even replaces it.

However, this specific feature of HSS is not without risk: the researcher may move on from thinking 'I believe it because it's true' to 'it's true because I believe it'! The limits are that of good old-fashioned self-persuasion ... or more precisely, a switch from an attitude based on Reason and experience to another founded on Revelation and affirmation, with the risk of not venturing out from that 'enchanted' world (as defined by Gauchet, 1985).

As we will attempt to show below, this appears to be particularly true of finance.

The Conceptual Framework for Formalisation

Classic finance developed within a relatively simple conceptual framework.

- distinction between equity and borrowings
- distinction between the 'equity financing' and 'debt financing'
- lender's risks measured in terms of liquidity (at the different maturity dates) and solvency; the latter could be consolidated with a guarantee (mortgage or pledge), insurance or deposit.

Modern finance has simultaneously simplified and complicated this conceptual framework.

A. The simplifications are often major and cover, on the one hand, the conceptualisation of risk and, on the other hand, the distinction between assets and debts according to their term.
   a. Risk analysis, the main element in any financial theory, focuses on a perception of risk limited to the variability in the flow of income generated by a given financial asset and therefore that asset's return rate. The other dimensions of risk – especially a borrower defaulting with respect to their creditor – were initially either neglected (seen as 'incidents' occurring outside the usual framework), taken into consideration in interest rates (which could be differentiated according to the borrower's capacity), or dealt with separately. In this simplified approach, debts are thus seen as 'risk-free capital' (i.e. remunerated at a fixed rate or at least a rate established *ex ante*), contrary to equity which is 'risk capital' (i.e. subject to the risk of variability in remuneration rates).

      As we know, Markovitz's major contribution (1952) – earning him the Nobel Prize for Economics – was to consider the rates of return on risky assets as random variables – '*Let Y be a random variable, i.e. a variable whose value is decided by chance*' (Markowitz, 1952) – opening the way for a 'mean-variance' approach to the 'return-risk' pairing. This initial posture has remained fundamental and is sometimes even used as a general definition of financial risk.[3]

b. The distinction between assets and debts according to their term, pitching 'equity financing' (long-term assets vs. so-called 'permanent' capital) against 'debt financing' (assets vs. liquid or short-term funding) is no longer seen as major. As such, the working capital requirement approach is neglected to the benefit of a more global 'resource pool-jobs pool' approach (Levasseur, 1976). This second simplification adds to the first, refocusing financial analysis on the expected return from assets, and risk in terms of variability of that return and the effect of financing structure; the latter is considered as neutral (outside tax biases) in the well-known demonstration given by Modigliani and Miller (1958).

B. However, increased complexity appears to more than have made up for the simplification described above. Here, I will limit myself to listing a few of the main steps taken in the 1970s and 1980s when the major components of modern financial theory were established, on the basis of the founding works of the 1950–1960s (among others, see the work of Tirole, 2006).
   - a deepening of portfolio theory (Fama, 1970; Myers, 1977, etc.)
   - the theory of rational optional pricing (Black & Scholes, 1973; Merton, 1973)
   - the signalling theory (Ross, 1977)
   - the theory of the firm (Jensen & Meckling, 1976)
   - the pecking order theory (Myers & Majluf, 1984)

These developments occurred at such a rate that we can qualify the period in question as exceptional, leading modern finance to claim the status of a separate scientific discipline, setting itself apart from economic and management sciences.[4]

It should be noted that this construction, however rich it might be, is mainly based on the fundamentals initially referred to. '*It is as if the agents were aware of the actual structure of the economy in which they were acting*' (Rainelli, 2008). This explicit or implicit assumption of a universe that already existed before research began to look at it brings us back to the epistemological debate that pitched 'positivists' against 'constructivists' for decades (Le Moigne, 1994–1995). In HSS, the debate was apparently clarified by Levi-Strauss's theory: as the observer is an integral part of the phenomenon observed, the representation that they give of it helps to 'construct' it. In finance, this 'truism'[5] was highlighted in the works of researchers such as Orléan (1999), MacKenzie (2006)[6] and Amatte (2009)[7] and by practitioners such as Soros (1998).

The 'Toolkit' Used by Researchers and Practitioners

Analysis, modelling and forecasting tools have significantly developed over the last few decades in the field of finance, with creativity seemingly boundless. When modelling finance, the perception of a structured universe with random variables leads to immoderate use of axioms and probability calculations, which now appears highly debatable.

An Unreasonable 'Normality'

As we have seen, the fundamental basis of the portfolio theory is founded, since Markowitz (1952), on a 'mean-variance' analysis supposed to represent the 'return-risk' pairings that characterise the various types of asset on the financial market. According to him, virtually all work on modern finance has been devised on this same basis and has, explicitly for certain and implicitly for others, considered that the laws of probabilities concerned were 'normal' laws or came very close to 'normality'.

This explicit/implicit assumption comes with huge advantages in terms of modelling and calculation. Researchers in finance have made the most of it and from the thesis presented by W. Sharpe in Chicago in 1959 to the latest finance theses defended in Paris, London or Shanghai, hundreds of papers have built something akin to a 'cathedral' devoted to modern finance. Observers of this impressive construction can only admire its breadth and the apparent rigour backed by sophisticated formalisation.

Nonetheless, those same observers might take a closer look and wonder about the conceptual framework and analysis tools used and in that case will be astonished by the narrow scope of the initial basis – especially how risk is focused on the variability of return rates alone – and on the systematic use of Gaussian laws as a matter of course (as implied by their assumed status as 'normal laws').

Yet, in my view *the realm of finance does not seem to be governed by these normal laws*; it is this finding that forms the main criticism of so-called scientific finance, because it refers to the fundamentals of the conceptual framework and formalisation tools defined by Markowitz.

My position is backed by three successive observations:

1. in fields of the earth sciences, many phenomena – and not the least important – are not related to laws of probability as simple as normal law. To take meteorology as an example, a scientific field to which market finance is often compared: despite the powerful calculation resources available, attempts at modelling and forecasting come up against difficulties inherent to the complexity of the processes at work. This is not Laplace-Gauss's reassuring context but instead a configuration linked to catastrophe theory (Thom, 1972–1983); modelling has to include analysis in term of fractals (Mandelbrot, 1973) rather than conventional probabilities.
2. in the field of life sciences, this situation is even more marked. In biology and the related disciplines (medicine), modelling has undergone significant progress over the last few decades within the framework of major finalised research programmes (e.g. cancer or AIDS). Even more so than in physical sciences, the processes of evolution of living species are complex and rarely fit in a Gaussian analysis framework.
3. in the field of HSS that concerns us here, this finding is even more striking and appears to be directly related to Levi-Strauss's observations and the epistemological consequences in terms of bijective relations between the researcher and the phenomena observed, through the co-construction of those phenomena and their representation.

In finance in particular, as we have seen with different authors expressing it in their own words (P. Jorion, D. A. MacKenzie, A. Orléan, R. J. Shiller, G. Soros, N. N. Taleb, etc.), this permanent interference is the source – with mimetics amplifying the self-referencing – of cumulative phenomena frequently seen in the form of 'bubbles'. This clearly falls outside the reassuring context of normal laws and comes closer to the more turbulent realm of storms or indeed chaos. This leads us to the use of the tools mentioned above (R. Thom, B. Mendelbrot) to represent these evolutions.

Analysis instruments such as '*Value at Risk*' *(VaR)*, until recently seen as the ultimate steering tool, are now criticised and users are rightly taking an interest in the potentially damaging consequences of events that were seen as rare and therefore neglected. Even supporters of probabilistic calculation agree: *'On financial markets ... we are looking very closely at these rare events. The financial crisis has renewed interest in these questions'* (El Karoui, 2009). The conventional image is often that of turkeys, well fed every day but sacrificed once a year for Thanksgiving. For them, VaR is excellent, bordering on 99.7! We could use similar examples such as reserve parachute or airbags … all items with low probability of use but where the consequences may be dramatic. See the 'black swans' that Taleb (2006) talks about when reporting the criticism made by Mandelbrot (1997).

Likewise, with regard to accounting, the hasty application of 'fair value' – and more generally the IFRS standards – drew criticism (Bignon, Biondi, & Ragot, 2009; Capron, 2005; Casta & Colasse, 2001; Colasse, 2009; Marteau & Morand, 2009).

Hence, the excessive 'normality' on which the entire scientific finance edifice has been built actually weakens it: despite the considerable developments it has been subject to, the entire finance conceptual framework is akin to the legendary 'giant with feet of clay'.

Incentives that Encourage ... Excess!

While researchers have taken portfolio theory to the extremes of sophistication, practitioners have developed a vast number of management instruments which, in their view, can serve as incentives for the stakeholders concerned, rewarding their performance which is itself a guarantee of the smooth functioning of the markets. This direction, congruent with the political philosophy of the liberal model, is not debatable in itself.

However, these new tools have often been the source of disruption or difficulties, the origin of which lies in their design, structure or the conditions in which they are used. I will list of few here:

- remuneration methods (bonuses, stock options, etc.) for market operators and their leaders encourage them to take very risky positions and with unreasonable volumes.[8] One of the specific – often criticised – features of these remuneration methods is that they are *asymmetrical*: even though amounts are often very high, they reward gains but do not penalise losses (other than potential reputation loss). As a result, the incentives encourage risk-taking. It is a situation that could possibly be acceptable in a 'normal' universe, exterior to the agent. However, it cannot be accepted when we acknowledge that the financial markets are neither 'normal' nor exterior to the agents operating on them.
- market intervention techniques (e.g. short selling) clearly illustrate the potential for drift; the self-referencing postures taken by certain are amplified by the mimetic behaviour of others and can result in 'self-fulfilling prophecies' or even price manipulation.

- the creation of special purpose vehicles (SPV) has enabled the development of a series of operations not subject to any control (see below).
- the 'too big to fail' approach results in governments propping up large financial establishments, given the systemic risk that their failure would incur, and has also encouraged risk-taking.[9]

There are plenty of other examples; together, they form an image of a very well-developed, quite animated financial landscape but one that shows all the signs of excess.

Regulations, Professional Conduct and Ethics

When it comes to economic behaviour, it is not always easy to draw the line between aspects related to the regulations in force, those related to professional conduct (deontology) and those linked to the personal ethics of the agent in question.

- Regulations are more or less stringent according to country – and period. They express the public authorities' reaction after a crisis and thus tend to flourish at regular periods (e.g. Sarbanes-Oxley Act in the United States and the LSE law in France after the 2001 recession).
- professional codes of conduct express self-regulation among the agents themselves, in the form of codes of ethics and recommendations on 'best practices', a mixed bag making up the 'soft law' that replaces or completes public regulations.
- personal ethics go beyond regulations and codes of conduct and concern the behaviour of the agent in line with their own set of values, shaped by their history, education and philosophical positions.

  At this level, I will merely outline a few thoughts:

  Traditional finance put great focus on these different aspects to the extent that it became known as 'institutional finance', taking a different form from one era to another, from one country to another and even within one country, from one sector or social group (usages) to another.

Modern finance, taking the posture of a 'scientific' discipline, freed itself from these aspects, seen as obstacles to the universalisation required by any science worthy of that name. As such, the regulations-professional conduct-ethics triptych has been minimised:

- public rules guarantee the smooth running of the market. Furthermore, compliance with the terms of a regulatory provision does not always imply compliance with the spirit of that provision. In fact, it is the role of tax experts to seek out 'deadweights' so that their clients can benefit from an advantage or evade a constraint (e.g. tax) with no bearing on the spirit that led to the introduction of the provision in question.
- professional organisations are not referred to; codes of conduct express a '*soft law*'.
- personal ethics are those of *Homo economicus* described by the doctrine.

Governance and Regulation

Here I will look at the ways a sector of activity is organised and at the different levels of management, governance and regulation systems (Pérez, 2003–2009).

- level 1 concerns the management of entities by their directors
- level 2 is governance, seen as 'management of the management' by an institutional system and behavioural practices
- level 3 is regulation of the sector in question by specific provisions (professional orders, administrative bodies and legal bodies)
- at higher levels (4–5) we find 'meta governance' with the harmonisation of the regulatory devices and the international agreements that condition them.

Due to its sovereign dimensions – via currency and the protection of savings – finance has always been a very closely monitored sector, at all the levels mentioned above.

Traditional finance was, as I have recalled above, very institutional, with states playing a significant role that has been more or less implicit depending on the period and the configurations adopted. For example, in France various bodies regulate different aspects of the financial sector: banking commission, insurance commission, the AMF (stock market regulator) and so on.

Modern finance has had to take on-board this requirement for regulation in the sector via the central banks and stock market authorities. However, we witness a growing proportion of operators, products and actions related to financial activity falling outside the scope of these controls and thus the controls themselves. Among the most significant examples, there is the aforementioned use of SPV, often domiciled in tax havens, escaping restrictive regulations. More generally, *shadow banking* concerns a growing portion of the contemporary global financial universe.

Moreover, we will see that the increasing sophistication of financial activities makes it difficult to comply with one of the principles guiding multivariate systems – the principle known as the law of requisite variety defined by Asby[10]; a difficulty that results in insufficient internal control, as illustrated by the Kerviel affair, and incomplete controls between agents or sub-systems, as illustrated by the subprime mortgage crisis, which I will analyse below.

AN EXAMPLE: THE SUBPRIME MORTGAGE CRISIS

Since summer 2007 and even more so since autumn 2008, the contemporary world has been subject to a severe crisis that began in the banking sector and was initially limited to the United States (the so-called subprime mortgage crisis) but later spread to the entire global financial system triggering a major recession with drastic social and political consequences. We can thus ask the following question: 'what does this financial crisis teach us, especially with regard to the evolution of finance and its claim of being "scientific"'?

Much has been said and written about this affair, sometimes by those who shortly before were lauding the dynamics and creativity of modern finance. However, well before the current crisis, researchers had already drawn attention to the issues at stake. In France, for example, M. Aglietta, H. Bourguinat and E. Briys, F. Morin, A. Orléan, O. Pastre, or outside France, the Observatoire de la Finance (Geneva – CH) and its review *Finance et bien commun* (Finance and the common good, P. H. Dembinski), or in the United States the work of P. Jorion, de Shiller and de Taleb.

To focus on the key points, I will explain the extent and uniqueness of this crisis by breaking it down into three successive components, each one fed by and amplifying the previous one.

- its beginnings in a compartment of the American mortgage market,
- its contamination of other compartments of finance,
- its spread to the rest of the world.

The Beginnings of the Subprime Mortgage Crisis Lie in a Shift in the Debt Paradigm

There are many debt techniques and procedures, varying according to the society in question and its institutional and regulatory systems, culture and the conduct of the agents concerned (Pérez, 1973). However, we can place these different forms of debt alongside a few simple principles that govern most transactions made between economic agents in contemporary industrial societies.

The first is the consideration of a decision by a lender to grant a loan according to the borrower's capacity for repayment.

The second is the assessment of that capacity taking into account future evolutions in the borrower's income and expenditure and thus their saving capacity; the loan granted can be seen as anticipated savings flow (annuities law).

The third is protection against the risk inherent to all estimates of future events, by taking a number of precautions:

- firstly, limiting expenditure to service the loan granted (interest served and repayment portion) to a 'reasonable' fraction of the agent's income for the given period.
- secondly, obtaining a guarantee (pledge, mortgage, etc.) on the item funded by the loan – or on other property – and making sure that the value of those items, if they were sold (on secondary markets), is sufficient to cover the debt maturities.
- finally, if necessary, other institutional instruments may be called on (insurance, third-party guarantee, etc.) to reduce the risk or cover it at reasonable cost.

All of these principles and the ensuing measures form the classic debt paradigm.

It was this classic paradigm that was compromised with the arrival of subprime mortgages. For this category of loan, from the outset seen as 'inferior to better loans' (hence the name), the first two principles of the classic paradigm were cast aside; the loan was no longer viewed through the conventional annuities law but from the viewpoint of the durable good (real estate) to be acquired and the presumed increase in the market value of that good. In this new debt paradigm, the security system is in fact the opposite of the previous configuration: the first dimension (link between debt servicing and the agent's income) was neglected to the benefit of the second (link between the debt and the asset); a stock-based approach replaced the flow-based approach. The other institutional security instruments (insurance, guarantee, etc.) are not called on, except in exceptional cases.

This paradigm shift is clearly debatable in ethical terms. Failure to consider the borrower's repayment capacity in line with future income and expenditure flows implicitly recognises that the durable good thus funded will one day have to be sold to cover the debt maturity. When real estate prices are rising, this new paradigm can work for so long (wealth effect) but it obviously stalls when there is a downturn in the real estate market; in fact, this downturn is inherent to the very functioning of the system and leads to mortgaged goods being seized from defaulting borrowers and their homes being sold.

Practices in the subprime mortgage sector further aggravated the ethically debatable direction taken by the new debt paradigm:

- mortgage applications filled in superficially – or sometimes falsely
- loans covering up to 100% of the value of the property – or even more
- deferred repayment going beyond reasonable periods
- variable interest rates, starting with abnormally low rates (*teasing rates*)

It is significant that a certain number of intermediaries that put together subprime mortgage applications – commercial agents paid on percentage – disappeared without leaving an address after the outbreak of the affair. In these cases, it is no longer a matter of debatable business ethics but a question of breach of trust and criminal law.

Contamination through Securitisation or Market Transfer of the Lender's Risk

The classic debt paradigm, the conditions of which are described above, has a corollary aimed at the evolution of the loan once it has been taken out. It is usually the credit institution – which defines the conditions of the loan – that oversees its implementation until its term. It therefore assumes what we can call the 'lender's risk' in return for which it receives interest including a portion above the base rate (reflecting the cost of time or a 'preference for the present' discussed by I. Fisher in 1907) as a complement (*spread*) and corresponding to a 'risk premium' that varies according to the quality of the loan and the measures taken to secure it.

Against this background, it was normal for 'subprime' loans, which are riskier than the loans granted to better clients ('prime rate') to be subject to higher spread; thus subprime interest rates are, by definition, higher than the prime rate.

This kind of situation was acceptable as long as the institutions granting these subprime mortgages pretty much indiscriminately were able to assume the consequences themselves. They were running a higher risk and, in return, they benefited from higher remuneration. All perfectly normal!

The balance was upset when securitisation began. The principle of this kind of operation is well-known.[11] Whenever a certain number of bilateral debs between a lender and a borrower can be compared in terms of rate, term and quality, it can be feasible to offer them in the form of representative securities that can be traded on the financial markets The securitisation of debt is not in itself condemnable; it can even contribute to the improved functioning of the economic system by providing better liquidity, adding an additional element to the 'trading instruments' identified by F. Braudel. However, this kind of transfer of receivables/payables to the financial market can only be acceptable if the conversion does not denature the items involved and maintains their main characteristics.

In fact, what happened with the securitisation of subprime mortgages was quite the opposite. We would have thought that the institutions granting them would put them together in a uniform package, but clearly the securities issued against this set of doubtful debts would have had trouble finding a buyer, unless the remuneration conditions absorbed the full spread assigned to the subprime mortgages. The approach taken by the institutions issuing doubtful debt meant transferring the risk at least cost, that is retaining a portion of the initial spread. To this end, the techniques used may appear quite sophisticated at first glance but were really quite simple. Subprime mortgages were mixed with other, less doubtful debts then these sub-packages were themselves broken down into tranches. In the end, the securities issued against a varied set of receivables (*Asset Backed Securities – ABS*[12]) could no longer be linked to the risks inherent to the nature of the subprimes they included.

Hence, securitisation resulted in a contamination of the risks linked to subprime mortgages. The ethical dimension of this contamination is evident and, all other things being equal, can be compared to viral infection. The very fact that they carried out these financial engineering operations implies that the heads of the institutions concerned clearly knew what was involved, namely the transfer to the financial market of the risks inherent to subprime mortgages by concealing them in a composite package of receivables; an operation that may have justified a substantial risk premium but one that was inferior to that initially demanded on the subprime mortgages.

The Spread of the Subprime Risk through the Globalisation of Financial Markets

Securitisation led to financial markets being contaminated with the risks inherent to subprime mortgages; the globalisation of those financial markets did the rest, making sure the risk spread to the rest of the planet. To stay with the medical metaphor, the infection became a pandemic.

The mechanisms of propagation are quite simple: the interconnection of financial markets, the dematerialisation of market operations and ever-increasing data processing capacities enabled the introduction of continual arbitration processes for the various saving-investment products, the vehicles offering them and the markets listing them. A fund manager, regardless of size, seeks to obtain the best conditions (profitability, risk, availability, etc.) for the sums being invested; that is basically their job. As such, from the large American investment funds, handling more than a hundred billion dollars of retirement savings, to the company, local authority or association looking to make the most of their reserves amounting to several thousand euros, investors have a vast choice of investment opportunities.

Asset Backed Securities were of course among the opportunities on offer and appeared very attractive in terms of risk and return, the analysis matrix forming the basis of portfolio theory since Markowitz (1952). This favourable leaning towards ABS was reinforced by a number of initiatives taken by the professionals:

- action by the rating agencies (Standard & Poor's, Moody's, Fitch) whose job is to asset the quality of securities on offer so that investors are as well informed as possible;
- the emergence of *Credit Enhancement*, new specialised (monoline) entities making sure that a given security comes with a sufficient guarantee to allow for better rating by the aforementioned agencies;
- the creation of new investment product compartments – such as 'dynamic money-market funds' mainly made up of fully secured securities but potentially including a small portion of other products (the 'dynamic' element) with better apparent return though in theory not incurring a greater risk than the 'classic' money-market funds.

We could provide plenty of other examples like this as the financial industry has been highly creative over the last twenty years. These initiatives mutually reinforced one another: the application of a credit enhancer allowed for a better rating of a security issued in ABS form, making the latter eligible for dynamic money-market funds, which were put forward as a non-risky, income-earning investment, the whole set-up appearing coherent and well controlled.

However, in ethical terms, these various initiatives and practices need to be balanced.

- At the end of the financial chain – where the 'producers' (of new financial products) are found – it is clear that those behind these innovations knew exactly what they were doing, namely helping to reduce the risks incurred by maintaining a returns differential higher than the cost inherent to the risk reduction operation. Their practices were therefore efficient in terms of portfolio theory. Nonetheless, they are still debatable from an ethical viewpoint, insofar as the risk reduction transaction was more apparent than real, with the event generating the risk – the risk of default by borrowers with subprime mortgages – concealed.
- At the other end of the chain – where we find the 'consumers' (of securitised assets) – it is clear that they are not directly liable but are instead victims of the construction, which – as I said above – appeared soundly built and well controlled. At the most, we could criticise their lack of vigilance, a criticism they could counter, arguing that guarantees were provided with the existence of an AAA rating or the application of a credit enhancer.

In fact, the debate about ethics and the financial crisis should largely focus on the auxiliary stakeholders;

- if the credit enhancers had done their job, they should have reached as far as the event generating the subprime risk and therefore challenge the shift away from the classic debt paradigm. Few subprime mortgages would then have been enhanced, or their insurance cost would have reduced their appeal for the issuing institution;
- if the rating agencies had done their job properly, they would have acted in the same way and downgraded most ABS securities comprising subprime mortgages, indicating a substantial default risk.

On the contrary – as we know – the various categories of intermediary were very flexible, or indeed lax, with their actions and evaluations, directly contributing to the fabrication of the 'giant with clay feet' that is contemporary finance.

THE CHALLENGES FACING MODERN FINANCE: A DRIVE FOR REAL REFORM

The first part of the chapter presented the characteristics of 'modern finance' and its negative effects, as illustrated by the subprime mortgage crisis. In this second part, I will look at the efforts made to remedy the negative effects and, on finding them inadequate, I will discuss the need for real reform affecting the policies governing finance as well as the conceptual framework of this area of knowledge and the training of stakeholders concerned.

The Discordant and Generally Inadequate Reactions of Stakeholders and Researchers

The financial crisis was initially linked to subprime mortgages but went on to trigger a major financial and economic downturn. The effects of the global recession can still be felt (e.g. the Greek crisis) and it is too soon to analyse all of its aspects and draw all the conclusions. The months and years to come will no doubt see a number of events that will modify the context of the recession and hence the analysis we can make of it. Nonetheless, researchers, especially in the field of social sciences, cannot avoid reference to such a far-reaching phenomenon, modifying not only the conditions under which economic systems function but also the analysis matrices concerning them, and indeed the underlying epistemological, theoretical and normative postures. It would thus appear appropriate to provide some thoughts to contribute to the debate.

Financial stakeholders – professionals in the sector and those responsible for its regulation – and researchers in finance do not have the same responsibility (or the same status); it is thus preferable to look at the reactions of these two categories separately, reactions that are discordant and inadequate given the importance of the challenges to be met.

Inadequate Practical Responses

It is clear to all observers that the global financial crisis has political, legal and ethical dimensions, some of which are explicit and others implicit, and related to the way that the financial and economic system functions on a global level. Let us look at some of those dimensions:

(a) on a regulatory level, what new measures have been introduced in light of the current crisis, which demonstrates the excesses of deregulation? This is open to debate but the problem is an international and political one. An effort clearly has to be made to close the loopholes in the current regulatory systems (off-balance sheet entities, tax havens, shadow banking, etc.).

To date, a number of measures have been introduced in several countries, especially the United States and Europe. For example, the pressure applied by the United States on different countries, resulting in the gradual lifting of banking confidentiality in those countries (e.g. Switzerland). Likewise the amount of the fines to be paid for various offences – on the basis of an agreement with the legal authorities to avoid prosecution (as permitted by the American legal system) – now reaches substantial levels, sometimes billions of dollars.

However, serious limits still remain, in two respects:

- on the one hand, not all countries are concerned; in fact, within a given country, a particular zone may benefit from an exception (such as the Channel Islands in the United Kingdom, the state of Delaware in the USA).
- on the other hand, most of the measures decided fall short of what is actually required (the separation of speculative activities and commercial activities in banks has only led to half-measures, despite the consensus among most observers and analysts on its necessity).

Measures between countries are discordant and uncoordinated thus leaving a number of gaps in the supervisory mechanisms, meaning they are pretty much ineffective.

(b) in terms of professional conduct, the weaknesses seen in the financial sphere have largely undermined the self-regulatory systems of the professions concerned and it is likely that this discredit will persist for some time.

What is more, the professional bodies have a natural tendency to become pressure groups serving their members, with professionals in the financial sector able to mobilise considerable know-how and resources for lobbying work. Close observation of the processes used to devise regulatory measures in this sector highlight the effects of this lobbying before the sovereign authorities and largely explains the half-measures described above concerning the separation of speculative and commercial business.

(c) in terms of personal ethics, among the stakeholders in the chain of operations making up the financial crisis, like that of the subprime mortgage crisis, many of them can question their own conduct – from the broker that sold a mortgage to a clearly insolvent family and took his commission, to the 'financial genius' who worked out how to conceal the risks inherent to those mortgages by diluting them in an ABS package, and including the analysts at work within the credit enhancers and rating agencies and who were very lax in their duty of supervision. Looking beyond one particular form of personal conduct, and without going as far as the more criminal behaviour of Kerviel or Madoff, the current crisis has called into question what M. Weber called 'the spirit of capitalism'.

A Divided Scientific Community

The scale of the global financial crisis and its devastating effects led to a challenge on the conceptual framework of finance as an object of scientific knowledge and as a set of professional practices. However, the criticism currently aimed at modern finance is not consistent and can be split into three groups, corresponding to successive levels of questioning.

(a) Questioning of practices alone
On this first level, supporters of modern finance consider that the *conceptual framework* and the exceptional 'toolkit' forged over the last few decades are not to blame. If errors or failings have occurred, they are to be blamed, not on the analysis framework or the tools, but on individual people. History, and especially in finance, has shown that there are always people seeking to play with the rules, such as Jérôme Kerviel, or to fraud savers such as Bernard Madoff.

Human nature being what it is, if those people did not have high enough ethical standards to prevent their inappropriate conduct, the supervisory and control systems simply need strengthening and proper sanctions introduced for clear breaches. This alternative – '*Ethics or Stick*' – is agreed on by all, even the most liberal circles, at least in official statements.

(b) Questioning of the tools and models without changing the paradigm
On this second level, criticism is more precise; without questioning the foundations of the conceptual framework – that is the paradigm – we can criticise the toolkit or, at least, a particular component. Analysis,

modelling and forecasting tools have significantly developed over the last few decades with creativity seemingly boundless. In terms of risk modelling, the perception of a universe structured around random variables led to the immoderate use of axioms and Brownian motion laws, which now appears to be highly debatable (Bourguinat & Briys, 2009; El Karoui, 2009; Mandelbrot, 1997; Mandelbrot & Hudson, 2005; Taleb, 2006; Walter & de Pracontal, 2009, etc.). The current range of tools used (actuarial principles and probabilities) should be expanded to take in other mathematical tools (games theory, fractals, etc.)

Mathematicians, who have gradually acquired a dominant position in the field of finance research, fully support this questioning which, once past errors have been admitted, grants them an almost unlimited 'market'. As an example, take the statement made by a colleague in a large Parisian university: '*It is time for the finance sector to use models that have proven their value to the same extent as those developed in other sensitive industries such as the nuclear industry or pharmaceuticals*' (E. Jouini, colloquium on the reform of finance, November 27, 2009).

(c) Questioning of the current paradigm

On this third level, criticism is more radical and more global: it is not a matter of failings which can be pinned on individual conduct such as Madoff, or biases related to particular modelling tools (e.g. VaR), but instead the challenging of the very foundations of the current conceptual framework, that is the paradigm.[13]

The philosophy of sciences, Kuhn (1983), which looks at the times of crisis encountered by a science during its evolution, states that there is a 'scientific revolution' when a scientific theory established by time – forming a paradigm – is rejected to the benefit of a new theory – a new paradigm.

At the present time, few finance researchers recognise themselves in this level of questioning of the founding paradigm of modern finance; they were mentioned above: M. Aglietta, E. Briys, P. H. Dembinski, G. Giraud, P. Jorion, D. A. MacKensie, F. Morin, A. Orléan, O. Pastre, H. Rainelli, R. Shiller, N. N. Taleb, among others, but differences – or even significant divergences – exist between them, so they cannot be seen as a united front.

We should not therefore be surprised by the permanent nature of the so-called *mainstream* current, that is acceptance of the first level of criticism and, to varying degrees, of the second level, in academic finance today. This configuration of the scientific milieu can be illustrated by the awarding of the 2013 Nobel Prize for Economics to three

American academics, E. Fama and L. P. Hansen (both from the University of Chicago) and R. Shiller (Yale). As observers stated: '*The three winners are from different schools of thought: the first two are neo-classicists – supporting the rationality of economic agents – while the third is a believer in behavioural finance, considering that the rationality of economic agents is not systematic*'.

The Royal Swedish Academy of Sciences, which awards the prize, resorted to understatement to gloss over this disparity: '*The Laureates have laid the foundation for the current understanding of asset prices. It relies in part on fluctuations in risk and risk attitudes, and in part on behavioural biases and market frictions*'.[14] We have rarely seen this kind of recognition of the plurality of conceptual frameworks for a single scientific goal.

FOR A REAL REFORM OF FINANCE

My proposal is based on two complementary lines: of interest respectively for the academic world (for a new paradigm) and for the professional sector (for reembeddedness); I will then bring these two lines together in a conclusion on the training of financial experts.

For a New Paradigm in Finance

I base my belief on the critical assessments described above and come to the conclusion that this is where we are at in finance today. The dominant paradigm, formed in the 1950s by the founding works of Markowitz, Tobin and Modigliani and Miller, despite the immense developments which it has engendered, despite the ten or more Nobel Prizes for Economics marking its history, is currently reaching exhaustion because it just cannot address the issues raised by the current financial crisis, problems for which it is partially responsible.[15] It is no longer a matter of adding another storey to the impressive construction built over fifty years ago and which has now become a 'giant with clay feet', but instead a question of overhauling the entire structure, starting with the foundations. *In brief, contemporary finance needs a new paradigm.*

The definition of this new paradigm should be considered within the framework of a collective programme. However, we can explore several avenues that appear useful to the debate:

- reembedding finance within HSS, leaving behind pipe dream of a separate discipline comparable to physical sciences. In this respect, we need to accept the contingency of facts and financial behaviour, calling for a distinction according to the economic, legal, political and cultural environments in the societies that produce them and to which those facts and behaviour contribute
- expanding the analysis framework – especially risk analysis – to include elements other than price, rates and random variations of those prices and rates
- turning to formalisation as one path (among others) to analysis. In this formalisation, the current range of tools used (actuarial principles and probabilities) should be expanded to take in other mathematical tools (games theory, fractals, etc.)

For the 'Reembeddedness' of Finance in Society

The diagnosis, made by researchers and observers of contemporary finance, is almost unanimous. Apart from some minor differences in style, all these authors consider that the current crisis is linked to the huge emphasis placed on finance compared to the rest of the economy. I can quote a few examples from recent works:

- Simon & Collectif Roosevelt (2014) reminds us that '*the crisis which erupted in finance in 2008 affected the entire world economy*' (p. 8) but despite that '*finance, which is at the root of the crisis, is still more powerful that it was in 2008*' (*ibid.*).
- Durand (2014) considers that '*finance develops according to its own specific dynamic*' (p. 7) and talks about the '*financial eruption*' (p. 11). In his view, '*the accumulation of fictive capital inevitably causes the crisis*' (p. 69).
- Lagoarde-Segot (2014) highlights '*the financial aspects of financialisation*' (pp. 28–31): the concentration of banking risks, the explosion of financial transactions, increased securitisation and the boom in '*shadow banking*'.
- Giraud (2014) makes a similar observation by insisting on the malfunctions inherent to the financial markets (chap. 3) and the banks' *ex nihilo* power of monetary creation (chap. 5), a power increased by policies such as quantitative easing led by the central banks (*ibid.* and chap. 6)

As rightly pointed out by Fimbel and Karyotis (2012), referring to the approaches of K. Polanyi and M. Granovetter, '*ideologically, the financial sphere has conquered self-referential power by embedding the economic realm, which had itself previously embedded society'* (op. cit., p. 539).

The solutions put forward are diverse but converge, except for C. Durand who is pessimistic about the 'lead blanket of fictive capital' (p. 192) and what looks like a dead-end, but other authors put forward solutions or at least avenues to be explored. For example, C. Simon and G. Giraud echo the demands for a separation of commercial and speculative banking activities, a cap on the size of the biggest players in the sector and a tightening of the rules, the Tobin tax and so on. G. Giraud goes further by stating his - support for more drastic solutions such as the 'SMART currency'. Th. Lagoarde-Segot backs 'a reform of knowledge on the basis of ethical considerations', and states that 'the development of the solidarity economy is a real opportunity in response to this kind of challenge' (op. cit., p. 172).

Even though the books quoted here are recent, they were not the first to draw the public's attention to the current financial crisis and its effects on the global economy. On the contrary, in a previous listing, I noted that 'the only sector to sail through the crisis was research and publication on the crisis'. However, despite these repeated warnings and the array of proposals for action put forward by various bodies – in particular, *Finance Watch* – we can see that little has really changed for the financial realm where, apart from a few affairs seen as isolated incidents (Madoff, Kerviel, etc.), it is pretty much 'business as usual'.

Why are stakeholders in finance failing to take appropriate action? Beyond the belief that many of these stakeholders might hold as to the relative superiority of the current system which, for them, is like democracy in that it is 'the least bad option', and beyond the performativity effects pointed out by several previous authors, in my view, the cause lies quite simply in the stakeholders' resistance to any initiative likely to rein in their power. In this respect, I hereby share the opinion of my colleague, A. Cartapanis in his afterword to the book by Th. Lagoarde-Segot: '*finance is also a power ... and this power, which is backed by some powerful lobbies, is not ready to let go of its position in the economy*' (op. cit., p. 177).

To apply a formula in the style of Polanyi-Granovetter, used by Fimbel and Karyotis (2012), we need to proceed with a dual *reembeddedness* of finance in the economy and economy in society.

Conclusion: For a Reform of Financial Training

I feel it would be appropriate to close this 'waypoint' review with a word on the training of financial stakeholders, especially traders who work in the front office on the international markets. As we know, the majority of these professionals are prepared – dare I say – for their jobs in the financial industry with training in exclusively mathematical techniques.[16] This has two unfortunate consequences:

- it consolidates the idea that finance is, like physics and chemistry a separate science that can be controlled using appropriate modelling techniques;
- it trains a pool of financial decision-makers who are often young with no experience of economic and corporate life, and no training in law, economics, management, or more generally, the HSS to prepare them for their future profession. As for a course on ethics ...

Alongside the new finance paradigm that I would like to see emerge, financial training also has to be overhauled.

Again, I will make do with a brief outline here: all 'master's in finance' courses should include:

- basic training in the 'anthropology of finance': – a course based on the work of economics anthropologists/sociologists (Dumont, Godelier, Levi-Strauss, Polanyi, etc.) and historians (Braudel, Wallerstein, etc.);
- substantial training in international economics, law (commercial law) and management (businesses and organisations);
- knowledge of tools and languages (mathematics, statistics, information systems, including accounts and internal control), and the 'decoding' of their conceptual bases and how they are used;
- special modules on:
  - epistemology and methodology,
  - the psycho-sociology of decision-making,[17]
  - professional conduct and business ethics.

The main thing to be learned from the global financial and economic crisis may be that the most advanced societies need to take a good look at themselves, the meaning of their actions and the education of their members.

It is time for those who share these ideas to combine their efforts, not only to advance the analysis of the issues related to the 'financial flood', but also to prepare viable solutions to address it and, last but not least, muster enough weight to help implement those solutions. The idea of working together, recommended by Lin Ostrom, appears to the prerequisite enabling us to look 'beyond fatal financial logic' and one day reply 'I can see the almond tree blossom' (G. Giraud, op. cit., p. 248).

NOTES

1. Sometimes referred to as 'classic finance' or 'institutional finance' or even 'folklore' by M. Jensen who has no hesitation in discrediting his opponents (see below).

2. N.B. Do not confuse Merton (1910–2003), sociology professor at Columbia, with his son Merton (1944–...), finance professor at MIT (and later Harvard), well known in finance for having developed, around the same time as F. Black and M. Scholes, the Theory of Rational Option Pricing, an important step forward for scientific finance, which earned them the Nobel Memorial Prize in Economic Sciences in 1997. Anecdotally, when the Nobel prize was awarded, R. C. Merton rounded off his speech with a quote qualifying the LTCM investment fund he founded with Scholes and other renowned researchers, as '*the best finance faculty in the World*' (ref. speech on ;www.nobelprize.org). This was less than a year before the fund's spectacular collapse, leading to a bail-out under the supervision of the Federal Reserve to prevent a chain reaction.

3. R. Goffin's work begins with the idea that 'a sum is risky if that sum is a random variable where we know the probability distribution' (Goffin, 1998, p. 13).

4. It is significant that in the second edition of *Encyclopédie de la gestion* (Management Encyclopaedia), market finance was taken out and included in its own *Encyclopédie des marchés financiers* (Encyclopaedia of Financial Markets).

5. I purposely use this expression often applied by M. C. Jensen and the modern finance proponents who hammer home the self-proclaimed scientificness of their approach compared to others. M. C. Jensen does not shy from controversy and has repeatedly rubbished his critics and, declared himself as a defender of 'the Science'! On the issue of takeovers (Jensen, 1984), he contrasted 'science' (himself) with 'folklore' (the others). Likewise, his argument on the 'market for corporate control' (Jensen & Ruback, 1983) was '*the scientific evidence*'. In his criticism of the 'stakeholders' approach (Jensen, 2001), he goes even further, caricaturizing Freeman and widening the circle of stakeholders to '*terrorists, blackmailers and thieves*'. For him, the multivariate approach required by the notion of 'stakeholders' is worthless: '*Multiples Objectives is no Objective*'. On the other hand, his position – maximising market value – is based on a long academic tradition, and is therefore true '*Two hundred years of work in economics and finance implies that ... social welfare is maximized when each firm in an economy maximizes its total market value*'.

6. '*One item left out of the debate on financial models is their impact on reality. In fact, this was not left out but indeed theorised by a Scottish sociologist, Donald MacKenzie, in his work "an engine, not a camera" where he presents the history of financial theory according to Markowitz. He shows how Markowitz and Modigliani-Miller took financial theory in a resolutely anti-institutional and mathematical direction, clearly marked by Friedmann's epistemology. He shows how these new financial theorists were driven by the very rapid development of financial markets which created a demand for evaluation methods. However, on a more fundamental level, his demonstration showed that models shaped the reality of financial markets (which explains his title, "an engine, not a camera," or so goes the theory)*' (Rainelli, 2009, correspondence with the author).

7. '*The portfolio management models, and even more so option pricing models, are not only models giving a representation of the market. They are prescriptive and performative. They tell you what to do on that market and shape market reality*' (M. Amatte, comment on N. EL Karoui's presentation, 2009).

8. The amount of positions on the credit default swaps (CDS) came to US$50 trillion in 2008, equivalent to global GDP – with US$17 trillion for JP Morgan alone.

9. The collapse of Lehman Brothers is a counter-example, justifying the rule; observers agree that the supervisory authorities should have intervened as they did several years earlier for the LTMC fund or American saving banks.

10. The degree of variety of the control system will at least be equal to that of the system controlled (Ashby, 1958; Mesarovic, Macko, & Takarkara, 1970).

11. See the chapter on 'Asset-backed securities' in the essay by Lederman (1987), and the chapter on 'Securitisation: Economic and financial analysis' by Simon and Lautier (2009).

12. More specifically, in the realm of ABS, the securities backed by mortgages, such as subprime mortgages, make up a category known as *Residential Mortgage Backed Securities* (RMBS).

13. 'What I call paradigms are the universally recognised scientific discoveries which, for a time, provide the researcher community with typical problems and solutions' (Kuhn, 1983, p. 11).

14. http://www.lemonde.fr/economie/article/2013/10/14/le-nobel-d-economie-couronne-trois-americains-pour-leurs-travaux-sur-les-marches-financiers_3495345_3234.html#BFm1DZv5IdrkVv68.99

15. '*As such, the defence of mathematical finance, according to which it has no responsibility in the formation of bubbles, needs to be balanced. It is true that bubbles were formed before mathematical finance was established. However, it is also true that various forms of drift have rocked the boat on a number of occasions in the past. Mathematical financial theory is the matrix that has, at least to a certain extent, allowed for the recent explosion in financial innovations, or new forms of drift*' (Rainelli, 2009, correspondence with the author).

16. The Ecole Polytechnique Master's in 'Probabilities and Finance' at Paris 6 University (Ms. El Karoui) is the reference training programme for traders, much sought after by fund managers in France and abroad.

17. To refer to a note already mentioned above, training for financial stakeholders has as much to learn from Merton, 1948 (*The Self-Fulfilling Prophecy*) as Merton, 1973 (*Theory of rational option pricing*). We can imagine the father giving his 'Nobel' son a lesson in psychology after the collapse of the LTCM fund in 1998.

18. See FAS programme summary report and bibliography.

ACKNOWLEDGEMENTS

This chapter is a new, updated and extended version of a paper published in 2010 (Pérez R., 2010). At that time, I wrote: 'This paper is not a completed work (insofar as research can be considered complete) but a waypoint in an ongoing research programme. This programme has been provisionally entitled "For a new paradigm in finance." My feeling is that the current paradigm, devised in the 1950s by the pioneering work of Markowitz, Tobin and Modigliani & Miller is now "exhausted" (in the meaning defined by Kuhn), as evidenced by the current global financial crisis. It is therefore necessary to start working on a new paradigm, a task that will involve reasoned criticism of the current paradigm. Our research is part of this critical process. A certain amount of preliminary work has already been done'.

Subsequently, an international research programme entitled 'Finance and Sustainability' (FAS) was devised in 2009 with a view to a contribution at the 10th IFSAM World Conference in Paris in July 2010. It was coordinated by a researchers' collective – R. Pérez (U. Montpellier, France), C. Louche (Vlerick Gent-Leuven, Belgium), W. Sun (Leeds Met U., UK) – brought together on the basis of a partnership between two networks – RIODD (Réseau international de recherche sur les organisations et le Développement Durable) and CGSIG (Corporate Governance and Sustainability International Group), in liaison with a number of other institutions including CRIFA (Club recherche de l'Institut français des administrateurs), FIR (Forum de l'Investissement responsable – French SIF) and ISMEA (Institut de sciences mathématiques et économiques appliquées). Over the last few years, the members of the FAS collective have taken part in a number of scientific meetings and events organised either within the programme framework of on the initiative of partner institutions.

This joint project has resulted in several publications, including a new 'Entreprise et finance' series (KF), derived from the K series 'Economie de l'entreprise' by the review Économies et Sociétés (ISMEA) and the first collective work in a dedicated series from Emerald Publishing: Sun, Louche, and Pérez (2011).[18]

As the author, I would like to thank everyone who has encouraged me with this project and made observations and comments on the first draft and took part in the related discussions. Special thanks to Gérard Charreaux, Pierre-Yves Gomez, Daniel Lebègue, Michel Levasseur, Frédéric Lobez, François Morin, Hélène Rainelli, Yves Simon for the first version of the paper (Pérez R., 2010), then Denis Dupré, Catherine Karyotis, Céline Louche, Jacques Ninet, Bernard Paranque, Jean-Michel Servet, William Sun, Henri Zimnovitch for this current version. Of course, I remain solely responsible for any errors or omissions.

REFERENCES

Aglietta, M. (1997). *Régulation et crises du capitalisme* (2nd ed.). Paris: Editions Odile Jacob.

Aglietta, M., & Rebérioux, A. (2004). *Dérives du capitalisme financier*. Paris: Albin Michel.

Akerlof, G. A., & Shiller, R. J. (2009). *Animal spirits: How human psychology drives the economy and what it matters for global capitalism*. Princeton, NJ: Princeton University Press.

Ashby, W. R. (1958). *Introduction à la cybernétique*. Paris: Dunod.

Bignon, V., Biondi, Y., & Ragot, X. (2009). *Une analyse économique de la "juste valeur": La comptabilité comme vecteur de crise*. Prisme n° 15, Paris: Centre Cournot pour la recherche en Economie.

Black, F., & Scholes, M. (1973). The pricing of options and corporate liabilities. *Journal of Political Economy, 81*(3), 637–654.

Bourguinat, H., & Briys, E. (2009). *L'arrogance de la finance*. Paris: La Découverte.

Braudel, F. (1967–1979). *Civilisation matérielle, économie et capitalisme*. Paris: Flammarion.

Capron, M. (Ed.). (2005). *Les normes comptables internationales, instruments du capitalisme financier*. Paris: La Découverte.

Casta, J.-F., & Colasse, B. (coord.) (2001). *Juste valeur: Enjeux techniques et politiques*. Paris: Economica.

Colasse, B. (2009). La normalisation comptable internationale face à la crise. *Revue d'Economie Financière, 95*, 387–399.

Dembinski, P. H. (2008). *Finance servante ou finance trompeuse*. Genève: Desclée de Brouwer.

Durand, D. (2014). *Le capital fictif*. Paris: Les prairies ordinaires.

El Karoui, N. (2009, November). *Un moment de l'expérience probabiliste. Théorie des processus stochastiques et pratiques dans les marchés financiers. Prisme* n° 17, Paris: Centre Cournot pour la recherche en Economie.

Fama, E. F. (1970). Efficient capital markets: A review of theory and empirical work. *Journal of Finance, 25*(2), 383–417.

Fama, E. F., & French, K. R. (1996). Multifactors explorations of asset pricing anomalies. *Journal of Finance, 51*(1), 55–84.

Fimbel, E., & Karyotis, C. (2012). Titrisation et réflexo-genèse. *Economies & Sociétés, (KF2), 46*(3), 527–551.

Fisher, I. (1907). *The rate of interest*. New York, NY: Macmillan.

Gauchet, M. (1985). *Le désenchantement du monde*. Paris: Gallimard.

Giraud, G. (2014). *L'illusion financière*. Paris: Les éditions de l'atelier.

Giraud, G., & Renouard, C. (2009). *20 Propositions pour réformer le capitalisme*. Paris: Flammarion.

Goffin, R. (1998). *Principes de finance moderne*. Paris: Economica.

Granovetter, M. (1985). Economic action and social structure: The problem of embeddedness. *American Journal of Sociology, 91*(3), 1360–1380.

Jensen, M. C. (1984). Takeovers: Folklore and science. *Harvard Business Review, 62*, 109–121.

Jensen, M. C. (2001). Value maximization, stakeholder theory and the corporate objective function. *Journal of Applied Corporate Finance, 14*(3), 8–21.

Jensen, M. C., & Meckling, W. H. (1976). Theory of the firm: Managerial behavior, agency costs and ownership structure. *Journal of Financial Economics, 3*(4), 305–360.

Jensen, M. C., & Ruback, R. S. (1983). The market of corporate control: The scientific evidence. *Journal of Financial Economics, 11*, 5–50.

Jorion, P. (2008). *La crise. Des subprimes au séisme planétaire*. Paris: Fayard.

Kuhn, T. (1983). *La structure des révolutions scientifiques*. Paris: Flammarion.
Lagoarde-Segot, T. (2014). *La finance solidaire: Un humanisme économique*. Bruxelles: De Boeck.
Le Moigne, J.-L. (1994–1995). *Le constructivisme* (Vol. 2). Paris: ESF Ed.
Lederman, J. (1987). *Handbook of mortgage banking*. Chicago, IL: Probus Publ.193.
Levasseur, M. (1976). *Le comportement des entreprises industrielles en matière de trésorerie*. Thèse. Université Paris Dauphine, Paris.
Levi-Strauss, C. (1950). Introduction à l'oeuvre de Marcel Mauss. In M. Mauss (Ed.), *Sociologie et anthropologie*. Paris: PUF.
MacKenzie, D. A. (2006). *An engine, not a camera, social studies in finance*. Cambridge, MA: The MIT Press.
Mandelbrot, B. (1973). Formes nouvelles du hasard dans les sciences. *Economie appliquée*, *26*, 307–319.
Mandelbrot, B. (1997). *Fractals and scaling in finance: Discontinuity, concentration and risk*. New York: Springer.
Mandelbrot, B., & Hudson, R. (2005). *Une approche fractale des marchés: Risquer, perdre et gagner*. Paris: Ed. Odile Jacob.
Markowitz, H. (1952). Porfolio selection. *The Journal of Finance*, *7*(1), 77–91.
Marteau, D., & Morand, P. (2009). *Normes comptables et crise financière: propositions pour une réforme du système de régulation comptable*. Paris: La Documentation Française.
Merton, K. C. (1948). The self-fullfilling prophecy. *Antiech Review*, *Summer*, 193–210. Also published in *Social Theory and Social Structure*. New York, NY: Free Press, 1949.
Merton, R. C. (1973). Theory of rational option pricing. *Bell Journal of Economics*, *4*(1), 141–183.
Mesarovic, M. D., Macko, D., & Takarkara, Y. (1970). *Theory of hierarchical, multilevel, systems*. London: Academic Press.
Modigliani, F., & Miller, M. (1958). The cost of capital, corporation finance and the theory of investment. *American Economic Review*, *48*, 261–297.
Myers, S. C. (1977). Determinants of corporate borrowing. *Journal of Financial Economics*, *6*(5), 147–175.
Myers, S. C., & Majluf, N. (1984). Corporate financing and investments decisions when firms have information that investors do not have. *Journal of Financial Economics*, *13*, 187–221.
Orléan, A. (1999). *Le pouvoir de la finance*. Paris: Ed. O. Jacob.
Pérez, R. (1973). Une étude théorique de l'endettement dans le calcul économique. *Economies et Sociétés*, *8*(4), 581–646.
Pérez, R. (2003–2009). *La gouvernance de l'entreprise*. Paris: La Découverte.
Polanyi, K. (1944–1983). *La grande transformation*. Paris: Gallimard. traduction de la 2e éd, 1972, de The Great Transformation.
Rainelli, H. (2008). Nouveaux chantiers de la finance. In G. Schmidt (coord.), *Le management* (pp. 175–183). Auxerre: Sciences Humaines Editions.
Ross, S. A. (1977). The determination of financial structure: The incentive-signalling approach. *Bell Journal of Economics*, *8*(1), 23–40.
Sharpe, W. (1964). Capital asset prices: A theory of market equilibrium under conditions of risk. *Journal of Finance*, *19*(3), 425–442.
Shiller, R. (2000). *Irrational exuberance*. Princeton, NJ: Princeton University Press.
Simon, C., & Collectif Roosevelt. (2014). *Stop à la dérive des banques et de la finance*. Paris: Les Editions de l'atelier.
Simon, Y., & Lautier, D. (2009). Titrisation: Analyse économique et financière. In M. Boizard & P. Raimbourg (Eds.), *Ingénierie financière, fiscale et juridique* (pp. 689–715). Paris: Dalloz.
Sorman, G. (2008). *L'économie ne ment pas*. Paris: Fayard.

Soros, G. (1998). *La crise du capitalisme mondial.* Paris: Plon. trad. Fr. de The crisis of Global Capitalism.

Sun, W., Louche, C., & Pérez, R. (Eds.) (2011). *Finance and sustainability: Towards a new paradigm? A post-crisis agenda.* Critical Studies on Corporate Responsibility, Governance and Sustainability (Vol. 2). Bingley, UK: Emerald Group Publishing.

Taleb, N. N. (2006). *La puissance de l'imprévisible.* Paris: Les Belles Lettres.

Thom, R. (1972). *Stabilité structurelle et morphogénèse.* Paris: InterEditions.

Thom, R. (1983). *Paraboles et catastrophes.* Paris: Flammarion.

Tirole, J. (2006). *The theory of corporate governance.* Princeton, NJ: Princeton University Press.

Tobin, J. (1956). Liquidity preference as behavior towards risk. *Review of Economic Studies, 26*(1), 65–86.

Wallerstein, I. (1985). *Le capitalisme historique.* Paris: La Découverte.

Walter, C., & de Pracontal, M. (2009). *Le virus B. Crise financière et mathématiques.* Paris: Seuil.

PART III
SOCIALLY RESPONSIBLE INVESTMENT, MICRO-CREDIT, AND ALTERNATIVE MANAGEMENT

A CRITICAL ANALYSIS OF SOCIALLY RESPONSIBLE INVESTMENT (SRI): META-DEBATE AND DEVELOPMENT PERSPECTIVES

Christophe Revelli

ABSTRACT

Purpose – *The aim of this chapter is to propose a critical analysis of socially responsible investing (SRI) through debate and reconstruction. Our goal is therefore to try to understand how the definition of ethics in finance has steered SRI towards a financial approach where ethics is guided by finance.*

Methodology/approach – *This chapter proposes a two-point approach consisting of a meta-debate and development perspectives. Each approach is divided into three debates (ideological and philosophical, scientific and practical), which are interconnected.*

Findings – *The chapter concludes that the debate on mainstream SRI is necessary but should be re-discussed, as it is preventing in its current*

Finance Reconsidered: New Perspectives for a Responsible and Sustainable Finance
Critical Studies on Corporate Responsibility, Governance and Sustainability, Volume 10, 145–178

ISSN: 2043-9059/doi:10.1108/S2043-905920160000010026

form the concept from developing and being grounded in real ethical values, sacrificing the individual ethics that should be driving investing decisions.

Originality/value – *The chapter proposes to rethink the paradigm around SRI through a conceptual framework that re-inserts finance within ethics, where non-financial performance and impact investment should be at the centre of the scientific debates, leading to an SRI based on exclusion, the consideration of controversies and social impact measurement.*

Keywords: Social and responsible investment; ethics; finance; financial performance; impact investment

INTRODUCTION

Since antiquity, and throughout the centuries, there has always between a conflict between ethics and finance (in the sense of wealth or profit), which has now permanently taken hold in economic and social spheres and has been reinforced by a long-drawn-out financial crisis.

Virtue and ethics have long been set in opposition against the financial principles of wealth creation. By setting 'economics' against 'chrematistics', Aristotle was already suggesting 'definancialising the economy'. According to the philosopher,[1] economics should contribute to 'the community's well-being', whereas 'unnatural' chrematistics[2] is the art of getting rich and acquiring wealth, with the sole aim of accumulation and an increase in profit.

This questioning then developed over the centuries, mainly through religious thought. For instance, some passages in the Bible and the New Testament, and also the Koran, condemn the principle of the possession and accumulation of wealth except for redistribution or sharing. Saint Thomas Aquinas,[3] who was influenced by Aristotelian thought, says that usury should be condemned on the grounds that money 'cannot create money', as Van Roey (1905) writes.

The influence of religion, which could be seen everywhere in the Middle Ages, went on to shape the premises of ethical and 'responsible' investing. The scientific community often refers to the *Quaker*[4] movement as the real starting point for this type of investing. *Quakers* refused to invest in the sale of slaves, prohibited the possession of wealth and advocated equality (Férone, D'Arcimoles, Bello, & Sassenou, 2001), for example. This ethical, religious investing later arrived on the financial markets in the form of investment funds that exclude sectors of activity considered to be immoral or unethical (such as alcohol, tobacco, weapons and pornography) from their portfolios.

The advent of the concepts of corporate social responsibility (CSR) and sustainable development (SD) then resulted in a shift from exclusionary ethical investing to a more inclusive approach of selecting companies that apply environmental, social and good governance (ESG) criteria as the pillars of their management strategies in investment portfolios. This marked the arrival of socially responsible investing (SRI).

SRI may be viewed as the foremost of the concepts encompassed by the 'sustainable finance' theme[5] (Revelli, 2012) given the assets under management that it generates on the financial markets and the interest shown in it by the financial world's institutional players. For example, according to reports published by US SIF (2012) and Eurosif (2012), the US and European SRI markets, which account for more than 90% of the global SRI market, recorded SRI assets under management of more than USD 3,700 billion and EUR 6,700 billion respectively in 2012.

There is a certain lack of consensus regarding the precise definition of the SRI concept, however. The very many, broad designations mean that SRI suffers from real conceptual confusion. Socially responsible investing, ethical investing, responsible investing, sustainable investing, 'ESG' investing, Core SRI, Broad SRI, exclusionary, inclusionary, Best-in-Class, Best effort, shareholder engagement and positive or negative screening are all expressions that prove how difficult it is to find your way through this 'lexical jungle' (Zaouati, 2009, p. 83).

Despite 'the proliferation of abbreviations' (Bernard-Royer, 2009, p. 26), SRI, in its multiform aspect, is nevertheless well established in the financial sphere and is a subject of growing interest to academia. For more than 20 years, scientific studies into the concept of SRI have mainly looked at financial profitability and tried to determine whether it is possible to 'do well while doing good'. The original conflict between ethics and economic performance has evolved over time to assume its current global aspect in keeping with the *Business Ethics* school of thought, where ethical interests and financial stakes cohabit to create performance-based ethics.

The concept of SRI 'performance' is now raising the issue of its ideological grounding and its positioning. The current issues surrounding the 'mainstreamisation' of SRI[6] (Arjaliès, 2010; Crifo & Mottis, 2013) are also raising the question of whether it is genuinely ethical. *L'ISR est-il finalement éthique* (Revelli & Sentis, 2012)? Ethics can be defined by querying the relationship between thought and action. According to Demont (2013), 'ethics is a lens through which to look at an action according to its ends and according to the player's ability to keep their values constant between the end and the attainment of the end'. This supports the reasoning behind the theory of conversion set out by Pierre Hadot, for whom the individual should convert the dogmas and social morals of the society in which they live into ethical action, in other words devote themselves to the link between the self and the world. The challenge is therefore to understand whether SRI 'does what it says as well as saying what it does' by going beyond moral dogma to really engage in ethical action, and also to understand whether it should really now be part of a niche market or be rolled out to the whole financial community at the risk of losing its ethical identity.

We will first try to establish a meta-debate[7] around three aspects: ideological and philosophical (to determine in what ways SRI is doctrinally consistent with its founding concepts of ethics and investing), scientific and practical. This deconstruction by 'debating the debate' should then allow us to understand how SRI needs to evolve in order to adopt an approach that promotes its visibility while retaining a central objective of a social or ethical return on investment.

THE DEBATES CURRENTLY SURROUNDING SRI: FROM ETHICAL IDEOLOGY TO FINANCIAL PRACTICE

Ideological and Philosophical Debate: Can SRI Really Be Viewed as Ethical Investing?

Before trying to understand whether investing may be defined as ethical, an ex ante exploration of the original principles of ethics and morality is called for as an introduction. The first signs of this type of investing stemmed from personal and religious beliefs in keeping with the ideologies of a community. Do ethics and morality really have a place in the definition of these investments?

At first sight, it is easy to believe that ethics and morality are related and that the definitions proposed are similar. In some people's minds, ethics is associated with morality. For other people, ethics is based on codes of conduct, deontology or principles defined by law and charter.

It is very difficult to approach the concept of ethics and really define its outlines, as it has undergone many transformations over time, from antiquity and the approach taken by Greek philosophers such as Socrates, Plato, Aristotle and Epicurus, to the appearance of modern ethics according to Kant (deontological ethics) and more recently according to the ethical principles applied to different areas of inquiry (e.g. bioethics, environmental ethics, social ethics, business ethics and medical ethics).

According to Pesqueux and Biefnot (2002, p. 45), 'ethics has no territoriality and refers to unspoken values. It is neither universal nor territorial, but based on identity. There is no content that pre-exists the act of enunciation and no memory'. This implies that ethics refers to the individual or the idea of a 'person', whether natural or legal. The very essence of ethics is personal conviction. According to Mercier (2002, p. 39), this relationship to the purpose of an action and the individual equates to associating ethics with 'a thought process, before an action is performed, to distinguish between the right and wrong way to act'. Benoît (2005, p. 50) proposes a definition of ethics as 'the specific appropriation of values linked to morality (love, peace, dignity and respect) by a people, an institution, a company or a person'. This definition is in line with the approach adopted by Spinoza, for whom ethics is anything that is done out of love (a function of emotion). Again according to Morin (2004, p. 15), ethics is at the junction of three sources that are correlated with each other (inner, outer and prior) and are revealed 'to us in an imperative fashion, as a moral necessity'.

Unlike the term ethics, whose etymology is Greek (*ethikos*, moral, and *ethos*, habit, customs, character, state of the soul), morality originates from Latin (*mores*, customs). Morality refers to the concepts of Good and Bad and implies rules of conduct and norms to be complied with.

Several French philosophers have attempted to define morality, including Paul Ricoeur,[8] who asserts that it denotes, 'firstly, the area of norms, in other words the principles governing what is permitted and what is prohibited and, secondly, the feeling of obligation as the subjective aspect of a subject's relationship to norms'. Again according to Ricoeur, morality denotes 'everything that, with regard to good and bad, relates to laws, norms and imperatives'. The French philosopher Eric Weil[9] adds to Ricoeur's definition by specifying that 'morality appears first and foremost, and legitimately so, to be the system of rules that people follow (or should follow) in both their personal and social lives'. These definitions are in accordance with the Kantian approach, which defines morality as anything that is done out of duty (a function of will). Ancient or Thomist morality is underpinned by fundamental virtues that every individual must live by. These take the form of four cardinal virtues (according to the Aristotelian and Socratic approach), plus three theological virtues (according to the catholic, Thomist approach) (Table 1). Later, under the Kantian approach, the term 'virtue' was replaced by the notion of value, which is closer to a representation of life as part of a society and more norm-based (the notion of virtue being closer to the individual and therefore to a representation of ethics according to Spinoza).

The various approaches and definitions presented above introduce distinctions between the notions of ethics and morality, but are these really opposing concepts or are they similar?

According to Benoît (2005, p. 52), André Comte-Sponville believes that 'morality commands and ethics recommends'. This assertion tends to suggest a conflict between ethics and morality, which although limited is significant enough to be developed, where morality belongs to a more authoritarian and norm-based context than ethics, which plays a more spiritual role. This proposition may be verified in the conflicting approaches of Kant and Spinoza, where Kant defines moral duty as a goal in itself that in no way satisfies hypothetical interests such as the search for happiness or self-realisation. Spinoza, on the other hand, describes ethics as a form of freedom that is the product of the subject's will, and relates to specific, practical situations. According to him, ethics is part of a quest to 'be good' rather than 'do good'. It has a teleological perspective, in other words it is determined by its purpose, whereas morality takes an axiological point of view (based on value judgement), to which a deontological aspect must be added (Chardel, 2002). Mercier (2002, p. 43) effectively summarises the distinctions between these two concepts when he asserts that 'ethics is not the same as morality. It cannot be imposed, it can only be shared'.

Table 1. Fundamental Virtues of Morality: Cardinal and Theological Virtues.

Cardinal Virtues (Socrates, Aristotle, Plato, Stoic Philosophers)	Theological Virtues (St Thomas Aquinas)
Prudence	Faith
Temperance	Hope
Fortitude	Charity
Justice	

Jacques Benoît presents a typology of morality and ethics in *Pédagogie de l'éthique* (2005), by taking all of the components and characteristics of each notion and directly placing them in opposition to each other. This representation is heavily inspired by the Kant-Spinoza relationship through the definitions provided, but offers additional clarifications, particularly on the relationship to religion and to the personalisation of the individual. The author believes that morality has a religious connotation that can be explained by history and the fact that Judeo-Christian values long played a major role in the introduction of norms and in the management of western societies.

Secular morality did not appear until much later (during the Enlightenment period) and the term 'morality' has retained this dogmatic image in the minds of people today. Morality relates to the universal through norm-based values or rules that are reference points for everyone. It is constantly imposed over time by a third party ('thou shalt not steal', 'thou shalt not lie', and so on), unlike ethics, which leaves room for decision-making ('I have decided that …') and favours consultation and discussion ('we should …). Finally, again according to Benoît, moral perversion may result in intolerance and sectarianism through those who believe that theirs is the only truth, while ethical perversion, which again relates to the individual, will instead result in manipulation for personal ends (see Table 2).

The approach to ethics and morality as conceived of by Kant and Spinoza has not been universally adopted by all academic authors. Some give these two notions the opposite definitions to those described above.

Table 2. Opposition of the Notions of Ethics and Morality According to Benoît's Typology (2005).

Morality (Latin: *morales*)	Ethics (Greek: *êthicos*)
Religious connotation	Secular connotation
Notions of good and bad (absolute judgement)	Notions of positive and negative (relative judgement)
Universal (values)	Specific
'You'	'I' or 'Us'
Relation to the self	Relation to the other
Reference	Judgement
Perversion = Fanaticism	Perversion = Manipulation

Source: Benoît (2005, p. 57).

This is the case for Chalmin (2001, p. 146), for whom 'ethics consists of doing what is fair and morality in doing what is good'. This means that happiness is the search for morality and justice is the search for ethics. According to Chalmin, 'morality equates to using gifts and free generosity', in radical opposition to the theory advanced by Benoît, for whom free generosity incorporates ethics according to the principle of the 'pleasure of doing good'.

Finally, some thinkers see an interdependent relationship between the two notions. This is the case of Ricoeur, who implicitly asserts that the notions of ethics and morality are interconnected and are part of the same process, where ethics comes into play ex ante (ethical intention preceding moral law) or ex post (introduction of sectoral or regional ethics based on moral law, in order to insert norms into practical situations).

The terms ethical investing, moral investing and ethical or moral criteria are used by players in the socially responsible investing market although their exact definition has not really been clarified. All of the academic literature agrees, however, that this type of investing was originally named ethical investing (De Brito, Desmartin, Lucas-Leclin, & Perrin, 2005; Férone et al., 2001; Gollier & Leclair, 2006; Sparkes, 2001; Sparkes & Cowton, 2004; Zaouati, 2009).

But is the term ethical appropriate? Should the more general term 'moral' investing not be used? Based on the definitions above and the introductory debate, morality implies a more universal connotation than ethics, which is specific to each individual. Morality incorporates notions of norms and duties to be obeyed in order to act in a 'good' way. Ethics relates more to a person's own judgement and implies the notion of free will, while viewing 'moral' values as guidelines or the limits of a framework that the person must stay within. Each socially responsible investor has their own ideals and these may vary depending on the person. Some will exclude the 'nuclear' sector from their socially responsible investments, as they believe that it harms the environment, while others will include it because they believe that it is vital for the economic and social emergence of developing countries. The designation ethical investing therefore seems more appropriate than moral investing, as each individual appropriates the moral values that underpin society in their own way. 'Moral' investing would mean the systematic and uniform application of the rules imposed on individuals (justice, security, efficiency, progress, notions of good and bad, and so on) to all decision-making processes. We may therefore say that 'ethical' investing is a component of 'moral' investing, as it informs and guides certain *sui generis* investment decisions.

But beyond the 'ethics – morality' debate to determine whether investment is based more on individual values than on norms and duties, is the term 'investing' compatible with the notion of ethics?

In finance, investing incurs an expense, which should ultimately generate a financial, tangible or intangible return. The principle of a return or profitability is therefore systematically addressed when an expense is effectively incurred. Any financial investment (in the stock market sense) is supposed to maximise shareholder value in the short, medium or long term, which has been the case since the liberal, shareholder revolution of the 1970s–1980s (Gomez, 2001, 2009; Lagoarde-Segot, 2014; Plihon, 2001; Weinstein, 2010), when shareholders assumed control over company strategies to the detriment of corporate governance and directors, against a backdrop of market expansion and the abandoning of production targets for financial targets. In its current form, an investment therefore creates an expectation in the person who makes it; an expectation that is usually high. This implies that ethical investing is still investing and should therefore be profitable. But can profitability and ethics be reconciled? Ethics implies a global relation to the 'Other' (Lagoarde-Segot, 2014, p. 115), where 'the Other disrupts the solitude of the self and interrupts its enjoyment,'[10] which may be seen as a 'quiet egoism'. This notion of egoism may also be viewed according to Fischbach's perspective (2009). According to the author (p. 41), the assertion 'that social players only interact with each other by means of the things that they produce with a view to exchanging them on the market' must be challenged in order to establish types of relation based on ethical values and a common exchange. In the financial spheres, individualism through investing and a search for utility cannot be reconciled with a relation to the Other as defined by Levinas. The decorrelation of the real economy and the financial economy through financialisation prevents consideration of the fact that *homo economicus* is able to grasp the notion of a social relationship shared with the rest of the community. The 'rational' economic agent presented in the neo-classical dogma (Keen, 2014) makes decisions and optimises their choices in accordance with profitability and risk criteria with the sole aim of maximising their personal interest. It is therefore difficult to associate the terms 'investing' and 'ethics' due to a conceptual contradiction. The short-term pursuit of a financial return that in no way takes social and environmental consequences into account cannot be the norm that determines investing behaviour as it is completely incompatible with the building of sustainable societies (Les Amis de La Terre, 2010).

To resolve this standoff, economic utility would literally have to be replaced by ethical utility, as the two are poles apart. Either the investment is ethical (seeking of an ethical gain with a moderate or almost zero financial return) or the investment is financial (seeking of the maximisation of financial profit). Too concerted an attempt to combine the genres may result in the ethical identity being absorbed or digested to the benefit of the financial identity. After all, you cannot produce a hybrid fruit combining 50% of a pear's properties and 50% of a lemon's properties by crossing pears with lemons in equal amounts. The lemon's acidity will always prevail over the pear's sweetness if the two are taken in equal proportions. An overweighting in pears is therefore needed to ensure a sweeter taste. Along the same lines, Glass (1976), who is considered to be the father of meta-analysis, explains that it is pointless to 'compare apples with oranges', and that the two fruits can only be compared within the same family. The purpose of this image was to explain the principle of the heterogeneous nature of methods and approaches and that if a researcher wishes to compare different studies, they must choose studies that are based on similar methodologies. This means that trying to fit ethics and investing together is like trying to mix apples and oranges, in other words concepts that are diametrically opposed (long termism of sustainability and ethics and short termism of stock market investing). However, for more than 20 years, the scientific community has attempted to explain and demonstrate whether ethics through investing results in a profit or a financial sacrifice, within the framework of the neo-liberal dogma that has posited, in the absence of proof,[11] that the foremost concern of the economic agent is the maximisation of their utility.

From the Philosophical Debate to the Scientific Debate: The Financial Performance of SRI

The last point raised in the previous section is fully reflected in the scientific debates on the SRI concept. The research on SRI is mainly focused on the quest for financial profitability. In other words it aims to understand whether or not this type of investing has a financial cost compared to a conventional investment if the other aspects of investing are excluded (such as the economic, social or ecological effects).

Several empirical studies have thus attempted to prove that there is a causal link between the introduction of non-financial criteria into investment processes and the financial performance of SRI funds or indices, each making a specific contribution to the understanding of this relationship.

Following the first criticisms made of the concept of CSR by Friedman (1970), the emergence of the CSR concept, and the gradual appearance of stakeholder theory, the concept of Corporate Social Performance (CSP) took shape. CSP is defined as the result of the measurement of the social and environmental policies introduced by companies, whether as the result of an institutional relationship (the company's obligations towards society in the sense of the State), an organisational relationship (actions specific to the company in connection with its primary or secondary stakeholders) or an individual relationship (actions by the company that are voluntary, in the discretionary sense).

Researchers were initially interested in studying the causal link between a company's social performance and its financial performance. In other words, the goal was to determine whether a company that has a high degree of CSR ultimately enjoys better economic or financial performance.

The contradictory theoretical foundations, based on the nature and the direction of the relationship between CSP and CFP, have undergone many empirical validations. Initially, the literature reviews by Pava and Krausz (1996), Griffin and Mahon (1997), Roman, Hayibor, and Agle (1999) and Margolis and Walsh (2003) tended to show that the link between CSP and CFP, and between CFP and CSP, was mainly positive. The results proposed are often highly contradictory, however, due to the different methods used to measure the social and financial performance, as well as the methodological shortcomings noted. Thanks to several meta-analytical reviews, the existing results can be aggregated and these methodological biases can be overcome (Table 3).

The meta-analyses conclude that, globally and exhaustively, there is a positive causal link between CSP and CFP, while specifying that the social and financial performance measurements used in the research included in the meta-analyses have a moderating effect on the intensity of the causal relationship. It should be borne in mind, however, that the use of highly variable and often inappropriate CSP measurements and sampling issues due to a lack of data may have created a bias in the results observed and weighted the positiveness of the link between CSP and CFP.

The debate on the CSP/CFP relationship then logically shifted to the debate on the financial performance of SRI. Research on SRI portfolios followed, in parallel, the advent and development of the SRI concept, which is far more recent than the debate on companies' social performance versus their financial performance. Although these two subjects do not deal with the same fundamental issues,[12] the aim was nevertheless to measure

Table 3. Inventory of the Meta-Analyses of Research on the CSP/CFP Link.

	Orlitzky, Schmidt, and Rynes (2003)	Allouche and Laroche (2005)	Wu (2006)	Margolis, Elfenbein, and Walsh (2007)
CSP/CFP link[a]	0.1836 (positive link)	0.143 (positive link)	0.166 (positive link)	0.14 (positive link)
CFP/CSP link[a]				0.148 (positive link)

[a]The weighted average partial correlation coefficient r acts as the statistical indicator of the trend in the CSP/CFP or CFP/CSP relationship (positive link if the coefficient is positive, negative link if the coefficient is negative). The figures presented in the table give the global statistical representation of all of the samples for each meta-analysis.

whether or not CSR and ethics in general has a financial cost or creates financial value.

SRI is apparently inefficient when judged from the perspective of financial theory. The mainstream financial model described by portfolio theory (Markowitz, 1952) and market efficiency implies that SRI reduces investing opportunities due to the diversification and selection restrictions and exclusionary criteria that it implies. Portfolio theory states that an efficient portfolio is a diversified portfolio and that SRI should therefore generate lower rates of return than conventional investing. Clow (1999) also asserts that SRI creates a sector bias through its selective approach by restricting itself to a smaller number of investment sectors, thus increasing its risk while reducing its profitability. As well as the theory of SRI's effective inefficiency, the theory of the 'costs' of SRI could also explain SRI's underperformance of conventional investments. Rudd believes (1981) that the brokerage fees and expenses incurred to include or exclude certain blocks of shares during portfolio selection represent costs for every transaction completed.[13] Thus, SRI screening criteria reduce the average liquidity of assets over the long term and could also result in more complex and more expensive asset management as more research is needed to find out whether or not a stock meets SRI criteria. These costs combined could ultimately reduce performance (Barnett & Salomon, 2006; Luther et al., 1992).

In the early 2000s, there was little theoretical research into the performance of SRI, which prevented a lack of support for the empirical arguments. The theoretical contributions in the case of SRI performance might be said to suffer from the same failings as the CSP/CFP debate in its early days (lack of theoretical support and controversial empirical tests), as the field of research was so new. De Brito et al. (2005, p. 9) stated that the SRI concept suffered 'from a lack of theoretical maturity'.

From an empirical viewpoint, the results observed over several decades of research were unable to overcome this lack of consensus, concluding that SRI has either a positive effect on financial performance, or a negative effect, or even no effect at all (null effect). The scientific literature on the impact of SRI on financial performance therefore has a strong empirical aspect, but very few authors have attempted to review it and interpret its results. Recent research proposes a meta-analysis of the financial performance of SRI, along the same lines as the meta-analyses identified in the CSP/CFP field. Revelli and Viviani (2014) identify 85 empirical studies (over the 1972–2012 period) comparing the performance of SRI funds, portfolios and indices with that delivered by conventional investments. The authors conclude that the studies analysed (including 190 links or experiments on links between SRI and financial performance) do not confirm that SRI has an effect on financial performance, as SRI and conventional investing perform at the same level. The authors prove that the studies are heterogeneous and conclude that the methodological characteristics of the studies greatly influence the results (particularly the choice of data studied, the measurement of financial performance used, the investment horizon, the SRI market and the journal where the research is published). This research now allows the refuting of the principle of SRI's inefficiency due to its diversification and selection restrictions.

Some authors acknowledge that the debate on the financial performance of SRI lies beyond the ethical aspect. Lucas-Leclin (2006, p. 6) asserts that 'the debate on the financial performance of SRI funds concerns the management process rather than the analysis process'. This would mean that non-financial analysis is not particularly a factor in performance or alpha. The financial performance of SRI does not perhaps depend on the SRI aspect, but on the management decisions made by managers (De Brito, 2006).

Terms such as alpha, manager, stock market portfolio, analysis and performance are all borrowed from financial jargon, which shows the extent to which SRI has now become an institutionalised part of the markets. The financialisation of ethics or CSR and SD has prompted the scientific community to try to determine whether ethics is 'bankable', to the extent that it is easy to forget that the *Quakers*' original objective was to exclude types of investing practices considered to be unethical. This was a time when finance was inserted within and guided by ethics and not the other way round.

The paradigm on which financial theory is based, which really took shape in the 1950s–1970s through Markowitz's portfolio theory (1952), Sharpe's CAPM theory (1964), Fama's market efficiency theory (1970) and option valuation theory (Black & Scholes, 1973), also emerged during the period when Friedman (1970), who was a product of neo-liberal theory and the Chicago school, openly criticised CSR as a restriction on the maximisation of profit by capitalist enterprises. As such, after SRI took a permanent financial form in the 1970s–1980s, it was absorbed within a theoretical school that was interested above all in understanding whether ethics in the guise of 'investing' was profitable, as a semi-Pavlovian reflex triggered by the stimulus of the search for profit.

Aside from the influence of financial theory, researchers have focused on this research theme due to the simultaneous availability of existing financial data and of the first non-financial data published in the 1980s (as the first empirical research dates back to the early 1990s, researchers have large observation histories). In addition to data providers in the form of the best-known social rating agencies on the non-financial analysis market (such as EIRIS, VIGEO and MSCI ESG Research), financial data suppliers such as Bloomberg and Thomson Reuters, along with brokers and management companies, have also gained a foothold in non-financial analysis (through sell-side and buy-side teams of SRI analysts respectively), flooding the non-financial data and analysis market. The mining of these data has therefore enabled their modelling in the form of independent variables. This modelling backs financial theory's positivist dogma based on hypothetical/deductive analysis processes that only take into account the analysis of facts through experience.

Throughout these years, the influence of the analysis of SRI's financial performance thus legitimised the concept in practical terms, from a financial perspective, particularly through the processes and strategies developed by SRI management teams since the appearance of the Global Compact and the PRIs[14] in 2000 and 2006 respectively, and particularly surrounding the concept of ESG integration.

From the Scientific Debate to the Practical Debate: The Issue of Financial or Performance-Based SRI: ESG Integration

The theoretical and empirical debate on the financial performance of SRI has contributed to the construction and legitimisation of performance-based SRI, particularly through the phenomenon of ESG integration.

Before the concept of ESG integration is described in more detail, the various forms of SRI currently existing should first be described. Revelli (2012) proposes an SRI map covering the various components of SRI, including Best-in-class funds, Best-effort funds, exclusionary sector funds, exclusionary norm-based funds, thematic funds, shareholder engagement and ESG integration.[15] Novethic lists the same components, but groups all of the inclusionary selection criteria together (best-in-class and best-effort, with the addition of best-in-universe[16]) within a category named 'ESG selection'. Generally speaking, the whole of the SRI community is able to identify the most well-known forms (best-in-class and exclusionary sector or norm-based funds), but ESG integration poses problems.

According to Novethic, ESG integration 'consists of taking certain key environmental, social or governance (ESG) criteria into account in conventional (or mainstream) management or making ESG analyses available to all management teams, or encouraging cooperation between financial and non-financial analysts. ESG integration practices cover large amounts of assets under management but are less restrictive than SRI, as they do not result in a systematic impact on portfolio stock picking'.

Although ESG integration is not considered by Novethic to be SRI in the strictest sense of the term, it is included in SRI assets under management by *Eurosif*, the European responsible investment forum (Table 4). The figures presented show that ESG integration represents a large slice of the cake, particularly on the French market, where 95% of the SRI assets under management invested are listed in this category!!

The principle of ESG integration may be viewed as less radical than the Best-in-class or Best-effort approaches, or more inclusionary. It is based on the consideration of ESG analyses in conventional financial channels (De Brito, 2006; De Brito et al., 2005; Hellsten & Mallin, 2006; Renneboog, Ter-Horst, & Zhang, 2008), thus facilitating the transition from a niche SRI to a mainstream SRI (Azoulay & Zeller, 2006). The purpose of integration is to ensure that ESG criteria are integrated within the investment strategies of fund management companies and within the framework of conventional financial analysis. When management companies use ESG integration, they may first of all exclude some companies from their investments if they belong to sectors considered to be unethical and then 'push the companies held in portfolios to improve with regard to other criteria' (De Brito, 2006).

In a study published in 2010, Novethic stresses the fact that ESG integration does not impose the same restrictions as SRI, particularly in terms of the traceability of trade-offs between financial and non-financial considerations. Whereas exclusionary SRI funds are managed based on binary,

Table 4. European SRI Assets under Management by Identified SRI Component.

2011 €millions	1: Sustainability Themed Assets	2: Best-in-Class and other Positive Screens	1 + 2[a]	3: Norms-based Screening	1 + 2 + 3[a]	4: Exclusions	5: ESG Integration	6: Engagement and Voting	1 + 2 + 3 + 4 + 5 + 6[a]
Austria	56	3,009	3,011	3,862	3,877	8,195	108	1,191	8,251
Belgium	367	7,834	8,201	19,744	19,893	96,736	13,830	19,586	96,905
Denmark	43	127	157	213,906	213,906	244,227	40,027	187,718	244,227
Finland	322	24,798	25,120	62,336	87,157	83,637	20,715	44,870	107,600
France	623	115,309	115,932	679,566	730,229	15,975	1,804,781	nc	1,884,000
Germany	4,523	13,115	17,477	11,255	19,988	618,248	11,424	7,927	621,020
Italy	1,051	3,422	3,603	314,248	315,492	446,790	446	18,531	447,592
Netherlands	19,914	1,120	20,602	166,359	168,425	665,108	542,156	472,019	666,248
Norway	676	1,117	1,793	550,843	550,879	550,843	23,206	55,652	574,100
Poland	0	13	13	13	13	1,174	13	0	1,174
Spain	107	1,558	1,665	1,119	2,022	56,226	7,302	11,094	57,091
Sweden	396	86,134	86,530	259,346	343,002	339,754	34,897	137,660	378,300
Switzerland	11,079	23,093	29,565	192	29,757	429,194	7,509	4,946	441,637
UK	8,932	2,559	9,154	63,520	69,959	273,180	697,692	989,211	1,235,201
Europe	48,090	283,206	322,823	2,346,308	2,554,597	3,829,287	3,204,107	1,950,406	6,763,347

Source: Eurosif (2012).
[a]Adjusted for 'double accounting' techniques (e.g. some norm-based funds may also integrate Best-in-class type screening techniques).
nc means non communicated.

radical decisions (to exclude one or more sectors or assets from a stock market portfolio), ESG integration incorporates ESG strategies within these existing, conventional management processes. This offers the advantage of generating significant potential leverage for SRI, by creating the foundations of an SRI approach. In practical terms, managers' concerns regarding this strategy are mainly financial, however. Novethic says that, during its discussions with investors on ESG integration, 'the sustainability or social responsibility objectives of economic players remained almost absent from the debate, in favour of considerations regarding the financial impact or reputational benefits for their clients'. The cards have been put on the table ... It is easy to see, if only from the assets under management generated and identified by *Eurosif* (Table 4), that the principle of the 'mainstreamisation' of SRI through ESG integration has a clearly identified financial objective. This is heavily dressed up through marketing to present investors with a virtuous image. 'Finance is the death of ethics!' This intentionally provocative, and somewhat exaggerated image at this stage in the development of SRI (which still has some life left in it) is intended to highlight the fact that whenever financial power comes into play, it is difficult to stop it. The communication bias developed by financial players in the area of ESG integration is discussed by Novethic in its report ('the lack of restrictions and the difficulty reading the effectiveness of ESG integration are also still in question and the risk of misleading marketing is a constant concern. [...] This trend towards the convergence of ESG integration and SRI creates a risk of confusion and opens the door to marketing that bears no relation to the ESG practices actually adopted'). The issue is clearly whether or not players wish to ultimately benefit from a discounted SRI where sustainability and ethics is the omega rather than the alpha of portfolio construction processes. What is allowing ESG integration to develop while retaining this 'catch-all' image is a lack of transparency and the absence of a strict framework. Novethic believes that 'these qualifications confirm the importance of ensuring that SRI funds continue to be demanding and structured'.

One of the characteristics of ESG integration is also the materiality of ESG criteria. The materiality of an ESG criterion may be defined as its hoped-for impact on the economic or financial (stock market) value of an institution (such as a company or State). Increasingly, the objective of institutional investors is to quantify the management of the long-term risks of the companies included in funds through the consideration of ESG criteria. On the plus side, this shows that investors have appropriated 'the ESG user instructions', but they are preparing to read them back to front. Reducing ESG criteria to a means for meeting the ends of materiality does not result in the inclusion of the most virtuous companies in portfolios. If the environmental or social strategy of a company is found to be having no effect on its economic or financial value in the short or medium term, this company will be ignored by the portfolio manager and therefore by the investor (even if it is one of the most virtuous in its sector or the investment universe). Sustainability, as its name suggests, is in keeping with a long-term investment approach, and should not be reduced to a short-termist performance tool, as this is incompatible with its nature. Novethic also stresses this point in its report on ESG integration ('Another risk is that the search for criteria that have financial materiality could in the future have perverse effects such as the abandoning of very long-term goals in favour of only non-financial criteria that are already having an impact on companies and public players'). This exclusion of virtuous companies can already be seen in screening techniques, where the financial screen (the risk/return ratio) is mostly applied before the non-financial screen (ESG), resulting in the selecting of the most virtuous of the companies that are the strongest financially (rather than the most virtuous in the investment universe as a whole).

The debate on the convergence of SRI and mainstream investing has transformed the original objectives of ethical investing. The absorption of ESG screening processes and of exclusions by management companies has distorted the concept and has given it a financial label that is struggling to get rid of.

The aim of this first section was to show, through a 'debate on the debates', that the introduction of an ethical ideology and philosophy based on a stock market investing approach could have a perverse effect on scientific theory, and ultimately on players' practices. As things currently stand, stock market investing, as defined by our short-termist market laws, cannot be reconciled, as part of a 'mainstreamisation' process, with a long-term vision that favours ethics or sustainability. Is it therefore really necessary to try to 'colonise' the system at any cost? In the second section, we recommend the opening of a number of debates on current SRI development and modernisation issues, so that SRI's visibility is increased while it retains its ethical identity.

SRI DEBATES AND PERSPECTIVES TO BE OPENED UP: FROM ETHICAL IDEOLOGY TO NON-FINANCIAL PRACTICE

Ideological and Philosophical Debate: From Ethical Investing to Ethics of Investment

The development of the financial industry has absorbed traditional ethics into a performance-based approach that makes modern SRI a financialised

SRI where sustainability is often of secondary importance, considered after the financial screen. To return ethics to centre stage, finance must be re-inserted within ethics rather than ethics within finance. The role of ethics should be to fuel a wish to change financial practices, and particularly investing practices.

The ideological positioning of ethics within finance therefore plays a major role in the definition of its place within the investing chain. This means that the notion of ethics must be repositioned within the financial system as the driving force that informs and guides individual decisions, in the Levinasian sense of the term. Ethics should help and guide individuals with the integration of their values within their investing decisions. The ethical approach should not be imposed by any factors external to the individual, whether this means an agent or a financial institution. At this stage, by default, the individual's ethical decisions are based, through the SRI concept, on a 'catalogue' composed of decisions made by other individuals (such as non-financial rating agencies and SRI analysts) with a different ethical vision that does not have priority over the financial objective. Ethics should be seen as a tool that allows individuals to re-appropriate their identity, and therefore the function of finance, by redefining the place of the financial return within a multi-dimensional hierarchy (e.g. economic, financial, social, environmental and personal utility). Morin (2004, p. 28) confirms this link to the individual's free will by asserting that 'ethical decisions lie with individuals: it is for them to choose their values and ends'. Benoît (2005) also believes that ethics is the source of the choice of an individual decision. Such a decision must therefore be made by the individual, who may then perceive their relation to the Other beyond their personal convictions, as highlighted by Levinas.

When engaging in ethical investing, each investor must be their own judge and so decide what they think is good or bad, the aim being to reconcile personal interest with the common good. This process comes first, as Spinoza emphasises, by 'being good' before 'doing good'. Individual convictions should be the product of a search for 'pleasure' and meaning, which is then shared with the Other as part of a collective, humanist process.

Putting ethics back at the centre of the decision-making process ahead of a search for economic utility equates to repositioning the term investing before the term ethics, with a goal of guiding investing through ethics. Financial decisions should therefore be based on ethical choices made beforehand. Ethics of investment consequently seems to be a more appropriate term than ethical investing.

As described in Fig. 1, Ethics of investment guide financial decisions and change the investor from an investor/spectator into an investor/decision-maker. The ethical choices specific to the individual are made within a

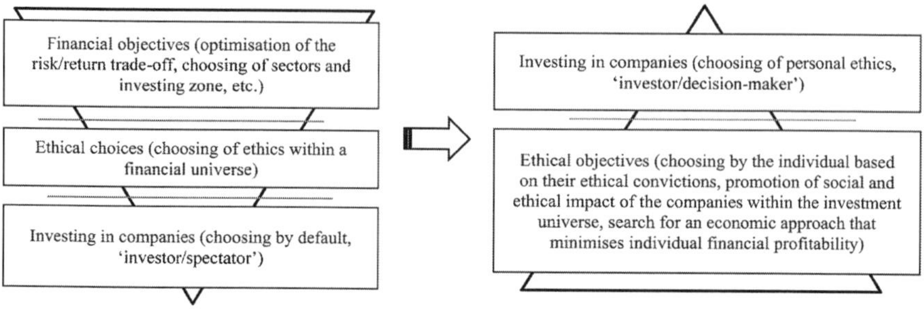

Fig. 1. From Ethical Investing to Ethics of Investment: From a Top-Down Approach to a Bottom-Up Approach.

global universe rather than after the financial objectives have been met, and these objectives are directly incorporated within the ethical thought process (for example, the investor will choose a company that will minimise or limit the distribution of financial income and favour reinvestment in human resources). The repositioning of ethics as a guide for financial decisions therefore allows each individual to first develop a personalised approach to their investing, in accordance with their personal convictions, but still guided by values that should then contribute to a reconciliation with the common good through a relation to the Other's interest.

SRI, through the definition of ethics of investment, should consequently retain its original structured and ethical identity in a bottom-up approach, and not seek to change to please the largest number of investors. Ethics is not self-evident to the world, it should be seen as a path of conscience that is self-evident only to the individual and, in this respect, the objective of SRI is perhaps not to strive for convergence towards the mainstream at all costs. The mainstream will become ethical if a critical mass is reached,[17] where each individual 'hummingbird' has done its bit in the process of change.[18] The objective is not to change the world in the short term, but to promote change. As Lagoarde-Segot emphasises (2014, p. 118), 'we should beware, however, of excessively optimistic assertions that individual consciences just need to be enlightened to initiate a spontaneous shift in global finance towards a system of savings allocation based on ethics and responsibility. This naive vision would inevitably come up against the reality of the markets, whose players share intellectual norms and a professional vocabulary that structure their perception of the economic world at a deep level. These players are also subject to competition, to a battle for survival and to the pressure of 'figures', which punishes any ethical decisions as irrational behaviour leading to financial losses and elimination from the market'.

The first step is therefore to rethink ethical investing or SRI, as defined in the first section, as ethics of investment, in other words prioritising its objective of sustainability and placing higher value on the social and ethical impact than the financial impact. SRI can only be repositioned within an ethical approach through the re-insertion of financial profitability within non-financial performance, which should be the investment driver.

From the Philosophical Debate to the Scientific Debate: Promoting Non-Financial Performance

The debate on the financial performance of SRI is undoubtedly impeding its grounding in a real ethical identity. For more than 20 years, the empirical research has systematically tried to understand how SRI funds perform compared to conventional funds. This was a necessary stage in the process of understanding the concept and its mechanisms. As Capelle-Blancard and Petit (2013) stress, however, 'it seems that a disproportionate amount of attention has been paid to this issue, to the detriment of other investigations, particularly into non-financial returns'.

The scientific community has an important role to play in steering the debate towards SRI concerns. The debate now needs to be refocused on non-financial performance. We should not lose sight of the fact that the term 'socially responsible' implies that companies' environmental, social and ethical performance should be valued more highly than their stock market or economic performance. The original ideology behind SRI was indeed to promote virtuous players and punish non-ethical ones.

In a paper published in 2013, Capelle-Blancard and Petit (2013) try to understand how rating agencies could determine a global non-financial score based on the various social indicators. The authors believe that the first issue to be resolved is the fungibility and commensurability[19] of non-financial criteria. Although the literature states that positive and negative social actions cannot be combined (Mattingly & Berman, 2006, p. 20), most of the time good and bad practices are combined in a single score by analysts (made fungible). But this leaves the issue of commensurability (making criteria comparable for assessment purposes). The majority of the time, rating agencies use scores in the form of ratings (e.g. 0–100) to compare criteria against each other, and can choose whether or not to apply a weighting according to the size of each criterion's contribution to the global score (equally weighted or weighted score).

It is therefore effectively important to start thinking about how to improve ESG rating systems but, aside from the technical debate on the measures to be introduced, there is a major question to which the scientific community must give a definitive response: should companies be assessed on a declarative basis (social reporting) or based on proven results? One of the main areas for improvement is the rating of non-financial performance in itself. The companies that funds invest in are rated according to their social reporting, in other words the information that they declare or their intentions. If SRI is to evolve, it must use a rating system that is based on an analysis of 'results'. Companies rated according to ESG criteria must be rated on their environmental and social results and their incorporation of good governance principles.

Thus Lagoarde-Segot (2014, p. 52) writes about the triple bottom line (environment, social and economic) approach, explaining that 'three-dimensional accounting (economic, social and environmental results) should ultimately allow the incorporation of a company's economic, social and environmental results within one and the same thought process'. There should be a focus on how equally social results and economic results are treated. The aim is to be able to integrate the ESG performance in the same way as risk/return criteria, so that 'ESG criteria become just as important as the EBITDA' in management processes (Zaouati, 2009). But the limitations created by the clashes between social, environmental and economic objectives usually tend to steer the company's discourse towards a utilitarian approach to social responsibility and sustainable development, where the role of the social is to allow the company to generate profits for its shareholders. As such, social performance should no longer be viewed from an informational perspective as it is today (GRIs, PRIs and so on), but be firmly grounded in impact measurement. A company should be judged on what it actually does rather than on what it says that it is doing.

Researchers therefore now need to examine this issue. The difficulty lies in quantifying the social and environmental 'return' and making it commensurable. The assessment frameworks that are currently available include the IRIS (*Impact Reporting and Investments Standards*) framework promoted by *GIIN* (*Global Impact Investing Network*),[20] the *SROI* (*Social Return on Investment*) framework promoted by the *SROI Network*[21] and the *Global Impact Investing Rating System* framework promoted by *B-Analytics*.[22] The disadvantage of these frameworks is that once again they raise the issue of the assessor's legitimacy and the neutrality of the assessment system. A debate is therefore required on the creation of a non-private, independent entity responsible for assessing the social impact of companies, using a single method with several variants, each according to the sector of activity, the stakeholders, etc. The issue of whether or not this entity should be privatised depends on the question of independence and the share ownership or governance structure (some companies rated by non-financial rating agencies are now members of their boards of directors, which inevitably creates an assessment bias). The impact return must include a global aspect based on the triple bottom line triad, to which we might add a governance criterion, to ultimately propose a 'monetised' assessment including economic and ESG criteria.

We need to understand how the methodological limitations of impact measurement should be overcome, however. For example, the many assessment frameworks available mean that there is no standard system of reference allowing the comparison of different companies' impact analyses (how can the social impact of a company A assessed using the method based on framework Y be compared with the social impact of a company B from the same sector assessed using the method based on framework X?). The main assessment method difficulties are listed by Lagoarde-Segot (2014, p. 66), quoting Reeder and Colantonio (2013): impacts that may be interconnected and difficult to measure individually; impacts that may also be interdependent with a global impact that differs from the sum of the impacts; the existence of conflicts between economic, social and environmental objectives or between stakeholders; difficulty knowing whether to attribute a change observed to the actions of the impact creator or other players; difficulty measuring the continuing of the impact over time, and so on. As the author notes, the work is still 'largely incomplete and, at this stage, it is more of an art form than a science', but it is the responsibility of the scientific community alone to open up the debate on these issues more widely to try to propose a credible, robust alternative to the cult of financial performance and social reporting based on intentions and communication.

From the Scientific Debate to the Practical Debate: Towards Transparent, Multi-Exclusionary SRI Based on Impact and the Considering of Controversy

The scientific debate surrounding the importance of considering non-financial performance within the context of SRI logically leads us to a practical debate. This debate should be a source of inspiration for modern SRI grounded in ethical values that drive decisions and take precedence over financial values. Several possibilities for reinforcing SRI and promoting the guiding of financial objectives by ethical values and sustainability are thus proposed.

One of the first proposals is to exclude ESG integration from SRI assets under management. This means 'pruning the tree' and replanting healthy cuttings that convey a deep-rooted ethical ideology. The only medium-term goal of ESG integration is the absorbing of ESG and ethical information to more thoroughly digest and appropriate it. The absorbing of non-financial units by financial units illustrates this, as do the acquisitions of social rating agencies by financial institutions (*Innovest* and *KLD* bought by *Risk Metrics* in 2009, which was itself absorbed in 2010 by *Morgan Stanley Capital International* to create the group *MSCI ESG Research*; *Asset 4* bought in 2009 by *Thomson Reuters*) and the ongoing development of brokers and management companies on the ESG analysis market, forcing non-financial rating agencies to consolidate[23] or diversify[24] to survive (the SRI market was too narrow on its own to absorb all of the massive amount of information provided and to keep all of the agencies in profit). The exclusion of ESG integration from SRI assets under management has been recommended by Novethic since its 2009 report ('*In this spirit, Novethic will only include approaches that have a systematic impact on management in its annual survey of the French SRI market*').

All of SRI's components should then be clearly redefined and only those that genuinely contribute to the goal of supporting well-grounded and proven ethical values should be retained. This means favouring multi-sector and norm-based exclusions to reflect the original ethical investing ideology, while taking things further by considering controversial projects. The report published by 'Les Amis de la Terre' in 2010[25] recommends 'introducing sector exclusion policies that apply to all of the asset classes (nuclear, hydrocarbons, GM organisms, chemical pesticides, weapons, nanotechnologies, biofuels, mines, etc.)' and 'favouring management companies whose approaches are sincere, and therefore verifiable, while avoiding asset managers at financial institutions that finance controversial projects and hold shares in controversial companies'. The principle of controversy is also a major issue to be considered, beyond the excluding of companies that are not operating in sectors considered to be ethical. Indeed, several companies are included in Best-in-class SRI funds despite the fact that they are involved in the financing of controversial projects or hold interests in controversial companies (the report gives the specific examples of Novartis, which has a 33.3% interest in Roche, a company involved in controversial clinical trials in China connected to the transplanting of organs from people who have been sentenced to death, and BNP Paribas, which has financed several controversial projects, such as the Belene nuclear power plant in Bulgaria, the Sakhalin II oil and gas project in Russia and the expansion of the Theun Hinboun dam in Laos). SRI funds based on the inclusion of companies with good environmental and social ratings should systematically compare their ESG analyses against information about participation in controversial projects, through bank or direct financing, to avoid this type of ethical conflict. This is tied to the issue of the promotion of non-financial performance, where Best-in-class type 'positive' SRI should be focused, as a matter of course, on the consideration of 'impacts', and not just CSR communication and the declaration of intentions.[26] 'Impact ESG' therefore requires transparency and changes to SRI analysts' rating methods in order to develop a cult of ESG results. This would involve frequent visits to companies and consideration of all of the primary and secondary stakeholders' discourses in the same way as corporate governance. The ideas raised in the scientific debate should be promoted by the scientific community so that requested rating methods (ESG rating) are no longer just a 'catalogue of good examples'. The taking into account of impacts within selective or positive screening-based SRI funds should also position the new result-based, non-financial screen before the financial screen (risk/return, investment horizon, investment zone and so on). This will be the source of the advantage of an SRI fund over a conventional fund. Otherwise, there is a risk that SRI will be absorbed by financial management principles and become of secondary importance, with the stocks selected possibly being viewed as less ethical than the stocks excluded during the initial financial screening.

Furthermore, if SRI wishes to develop and reach a target market that extends beyond institutional investors, the strategies adopted by SRI funds must be completely transparent, again in the interests of clarity. As Revelli (2013) notes, 'savers must be able to regularly assess the shares that make up the fund in order to identify whether they are in keeping with their investing choices and whether they actually match the image given and communicated by the fund. Communication about strategies must provide detailed information about the asset allocation and weighting and be made public over several periods, in order to judge whether a fund designated as SRI warrants this label'. The Norwegian sovereign wealth fund (*Government Pension Fund-Global*), which is managed by the Norwegian central bank (*Norges Bank*) is a perfect example of this.[27] The Norwegian ministry of finance's website[28] offers a presentation of all of the shares held by the fund and the assets under management invested in each company. An ethics committee meets regularly to decide which companies will be excluded from the global investment universe, particularly based on constantly updated controversial issues and a multi-sector strategy (involvement in the production of nuclear weapons, cluster munitions or anti-personnel mines, in the sale of military equipment to Burma, in the production of tobacco, in environmental destruction, etc.).

The last question that must be answered from a practical viewpoint relates to the principle of transparency. It more specifically regards the principle of punishment if disclosure obligations are not met. Several countries have adopted internal labels and transparency codes to facilitate information disclosure to investors and the general public. Should further steps be taken, however, by authorising penalties if disclosure obligations are not met? SRI management should entail strict compliance with current strategies and methods, and penalties may already be imposed for a failure to comply in some countries. This is the case in Australia, which imposes penalties for false information disclosures. Some penalties go beyond false disclosures, however, and punish non-compliance with SRI strategies (allocation and selection of stocks in portfolios). *Pax World Management*, one of the leading ethical investors and an adherent of the *PRIs*, was ordered by the *Securities Exchange Commission* in 2008 to pay a USD 5,000,000 fine for investing in companies that were not compatible with the ethics promoted in the fund's (legal binding) official prospectus. So is it really necessary to wield a big stick for ESG principles to be taken into account and complied with? The voluntary nature of adherence to the *PRIs* no longer seems to offer a strong enough guarantee that players will actually take ethical, environmental, social and governance criteria on board.

We therefore propose below in Fig. 2 a map of SRI, as advocated by the foregoing debates, in other words focused on the insertion of finance within ethics.

CONCLUSION

Throughout this chapter, we have attempted to propose a critical analysis of socially responsible investing from the angle of the deconstruction of the current debates (meta-debate) and a reconstruction based on the debates to be opened up. Through our three-stage approach (ideological and philosophical debate, scientific debate and practical debate) we have observed that the concept of ethics has been lost in financial investing, contributing to the development of financial ethics centred on profitability (ESG integration). Ricoeur (1997, p. 256) asserts that 'what is at stake in any ideology is ultimately the legitimisation of a certain system of authority ...'. The

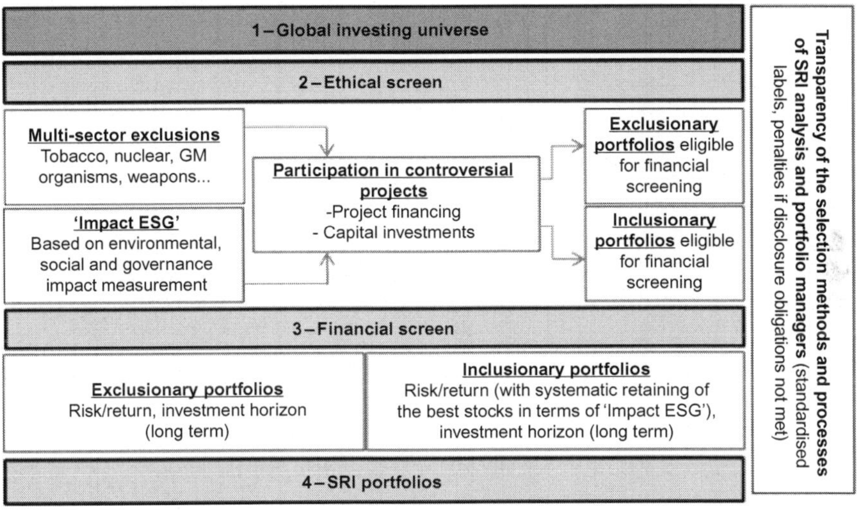

Fig. 2. SRI Screening Process within the Framework of the Insertion of Finance within Ethics.

ideological debate discussed throughout this chapter clearly shows that ethics has been integrated within financial ideology, where there is a commercial, non-cooperative approach to exchanges, resulting in shareholder power relations as defined by Gomez (2009) and Weinstein (2010). The insertion of finance within ethics may, however, steer SRI onto another course that would reposition it within a virtuous approach, with a goal of ethical 'utopia', as defined by Ricœur (1997, p. 256, 'what is at stake in any utopia is the fact of imagining another way of exercising power').

The current debates focused on the 'mainstreamisation' of SRI have supported the development of financial SRI within asset management by promoting a lack of transparency in strategies for screening and selecting companies for inclusion in portfolios. It is now urgent to stop the debate on mainstream SRI, which is preventing the concept from developing and being grounded in real ethical values. Ethics, as we have described it in the ideological debates, is defined through an individual process. This makes it pointless to try to persuade or impose a concept on all players by sacrificing the fundamental values that make ethics what it is. Investors in search of virtue must be able to recognise themselves in their investments. Attempting to propose 'quantitative ethics' rather than 'qualitative ethics' may result in SRI getting lost in the financial crowd. This leaves us with a simple choice: either we change investors' mentalities by imposing ESG restrictions and diluted ethics on them in a financial analysis context, or we actually offer them a clear alternative built on the foundations of virtuous principles. Current non-financial rating uses a static, 'binary' ('good' or 'bad' score) approach and in no way entails a relation to individual ethics based on choices made by players through the exercising of their will and their freedom, in the Spinozan sense. If SRI is really positioned within an approach that favours a search for ethical gains and impact measurement, it will capture investors who find these values genuinely appealing. They must persuade themselves and adopt an ethical process that reflects their own values and their own free will, as presented by Morin (2004). Thus, the formalisation of a model where finance is inserted within ethics, such as we propose for SRI, is aimed at restoring the primacy of individual ethical choices and the investor's free will. When guided by the moral utopia ('we all have to live together'), the investor will act according to their own preferences and predilections, so as to 'optimise' their ethical utility and cooperation with other players, or 'investor/decision-makers', as recommended in Fig. 1.

The real question is therefore whether it is really up to SRI to change the world. Is it SRI's role to try to transform players' choices and so prevent financial excesses? And do we really want to attract investors whose priority is the profitability of their investments, or investors who are more interested in, and wish to reward, the non-financial performance of companies? The real issue is therefore centred around SRI's real ideology and resides in understanding whether it is able to encourage companies to be more environmentally and socially responsible, and to refocus their strategic decisions on the consideration of stakeholders' expectations. This will depend on the willingness of governance bodies to try to modernise SRI to make it more effective and accessible, in the permanent pursuit of transparency and simplicity in selection and rating processes. But this will above all depend on the willingness of players to adopt an individual ethical process in order to contribute to the development of a fairer SRI model aligned with a social economic approach rather than a financial economic approach.

NOTES

1. Taken from *Nicomachean Ethics*.
2. Aristotle made a distinction between 'natural' chrematistics (required for human survival) and 'unnatural' chrematistics (using money to make money).

3. Thomas Aquinas (1225–1274) was a Dominican friar, theologian and philosopher, and the founder of the 'Thomist' philosophical-theological school of thought. He was canonised by the Church in 1323.

4. The *Quaker* ('Society of Friends') movement was founded in the 1650s by the Anglican Church. According to historians, George Fox (1624–1691) was the main figure behind the creation of this movement.

5. Revelli (2012) includes philanthropic finance, microfinance, shareholder engagement and Islamic finance as components of 'sustainable' finance in an SRI map.

6. Crifo and Mottis (2013) describe the principle of SRI 'mainstreamisation' as the phenomenon of the 'spreading of SRI criteria to conventional asset management'.

7. The term meta-debate may be described as the analysing of the debate or the debating of the debate (*meta* is a Greek word that means beyond or after. The prefix *meta* refers to a concept that is self-referential).

8. Paul Ricoeur, '*Éthique*', *Encyclopedia Universalis.*

9. Eric Weil, *'Morale', Encyclopedia Universalis.*

10. Lagoarde-Segot (2014) quotes Levinas when comparing enjoyment with a sensory experience. According to the author, 'a human life is filled with sensations (visual, olfactory, auditory, and so on), and 'the human being enjoys and is sustained by its environment'.

11. A contrast may be made between the neo-liberal dogma imposed, which has never proved that the maximisation of profit is an economic agent's priority, and the anthropological studies carried out by researchers including Marcel Mauss and Alain Testart (*Critique du don: Études sur la circulation non marchande*, 2007), who challenge its epistemological and theoretical foundations.

12. The CSP–CFP debate measured whether the degree of a company's CSR improves its financial performance using accounting and financial ratios as a basis for assessment (i.e. the return on assets, return on equity, return on sales, net income earnings per share and profit margin).
The debate on the financial performance of SRI was concentrated on research into the performance of socially responsible funds or ethical funds, from the viewpoint of profitability on the stock market. Researchers tried to determine whether this type of fund performs better than funds considered to be conventional.

13. Luther, Matatko, and Corner (1992, p. 57) names these costs monitoring costs.

14. Principles for Responsible Investment developed by the UN.

15. Best-in-class funds select the companies that have the best ESG ratings within their sector of activity. Best-effort funds select the companies that have made the most progress in terms of their ESG ratings. Exclusionary sector funds exclude sectors of activity that are considered to be harmful or unethical (such as tobacco, pornography and weapons). Exclusionary norm-based funds exclude companies that do not obey international norms or conventions because, for example, they violate human rights or use child labour. Shareholder engagement consists of investors demanding that companies give more consideration to ESG criteria by using their voting rights at annual general meetings or by tabling resolutions.

16. Best-in-universe funds select the best companies in ESG terms independently of their sector of activity.

17. The theory of the '100th monkey' may be an appropriate way of explaining the phenomenon of critical mass. This theory, developed by Ken Keyes Jr in *The Hundredth Monkey* (1984), explains how a critical mass phenomenon can come about. To illustrate his theory, the author uses a scientific experiment involving a species of monkey in Japan, the Japanese macaque (*macaca fuscata*), which was observed in the wild for 30 years. In 1952, on the island of *Koshima*, scientists fed monkeys with raw sweet potatoes by throwing them onto the sand. The monkeys liked the taste of the sweet potatoes, but didn't like their dirtiness. A female macaque named Imo transmitted to her fellow monkeys the practice of washing her sweet potatoes in a stream (so that she didn't have to swallow or spit out the dirt). This contagion phenomenon was observed between 1952 and 1958. After a certain number, for example 99, when the practice had spread to the 100th monkey, the whole community was washing its sweet potatoes. But the most surprising thing observed by these scientists was the fact that the habit of washing sweet potatoes was inexplicably and simultaneously transmitted to colonies of monkeys living on other islands, and to a troop of monkeys in *Takasakiyama* on the mainland, which also began to wash their sweet potatoes.

18. The hummingbird reference comes from an American Indian legend. According to the legend, there was once an enormous forest fire. All of the animals were terrified and aghast and powerlessly watched the disaster unfold. Only the little hummingbird took action, collecting drops of water with his beak to throw on the fire. After a while, the armadillo, who was irritated by this laughable agitation, said to him: 'Hummingbird! Are you mad? You're not going to put the fire out with those drops of water!' 'And the hummingbird replied: 'I know, but I'm doing my bit.'

19. According to the authors, fungibility begs the question: 'is a good action able to compensate for a bad one?' The authors add a further question: 'Can environmental, social and governance performances (whether they are good or bad) be combined?' Commensurability means comparing criteria rated on a similar, comparable basis (e.g. it is impossible to compare the volume of toxic substances released into the air by a company with its equal pay or governance policy).

20. http://iris.thegiin.org/iris-catalog/

21. http://www.thesroinetwork.org/

22. http://b-analytics.net/giirs-ratings/

23. There have been many mergers of social rating agencies in recent years: *Inrate* (2010) created from the merger between *Centre Info SA* and *Inrate SA*; *GMI Ratings* (2010) created from the merger of *The Corporate Library, Governance Metrics International* and *Audit Integrity*; *Sustainalytics* (2008) founded from the combining of former members of *SIRI Company* (*Dutch Sustainability Research, Scoris* and *Analistas Internacionales en Sosteibilidad*), followed by a merger with *Jantzi Research Inc.* (Canada) in 2010 and the takeover of *Responsible Research* in 2012; VIGEO (2002), which was created from the ARESE group and acquired *Stock at Stake* in 2005 and *Avanzi SRI Research* in 2006, to name but a few.

24. The vast majority of leading non-financial rating agencies also offer additional services to companies as a source of diversification in a highly competitive market. In addition to the ESG rating (known as 'declarative rating' as it is based on the analysis of documents transmitted by the institutions rated) of listed companies, States and supranational organisations, these agencies also offer CSR audits

(or 'requested rating') consisting of an audit and consultancy service in the social and environmental field.

25. '*Investissement socialement responsable: l'heure du tri*', a report published in 2010 and available at the address http://www.amisdelaterre.org/Investissement-socialement.html

26. Aside from the examples given above, the report published by Les Amis de la Terre in 2010 illustrates the lack of consistency in ESG rating through the case of the company BP (British Petroleum). The report points out that, just before the explosion of the drilling platform off the Gulf of Mexico on 20 April 2010, causing a catastrophic oil spill, 'the oil firm had a good enough rating to be included in some SRI funds. Out of the fifteen best-in-class funds invested in Europe, 12 contained BP shares. Some non-financial performance reports willingly noted a determination (at BP) to reduce its environmental footprint and the existence of an active safety management approach'.

27. This fund, which in 2014 had the largest market capitalisation of any sovereign wealth fund in the world, manages the surplus from oil exports.

28. Available at https://www.regjeringen.no/en/topics/the-economy/the-government-pension-fund/responsible-investments/id446948/

REFERENCES

Allouche, J., & Laroche, P. (2005). A meta-analytical investigation of the relationship between corporate social and financial performance. *Revue de Gestion des Ressources Humaines, 57*, 18–41.

Arjaliès, D. L. (2010). A social movement perspective on finance: How socially responsible investment mattered. *Journal of Business Ethics, 92*, 57–78.

Azoulay, O., & Zeller, V. (2006). ISR: Stratégie de « niche » ou « *mainstream* »? *Revue d'Économie Financière, 85*, 1–18.

Barnett, M. L., & Salomon, R. M. (2006). Beyond dichotomy: The curvilinear relationship between social responsibility and financial performance. *Strategic Management Journal, 27*(11), 1101–1122.

Benoît, J. (Eds.). (2005). *Pédagogie de l'Éthique*. Colombelles: Éditions EMS.

Bernard-Royer, M. (Eds.). (2009). *L'investissement socialement responsable, vers une nouvelle éthique*. Paris: Arnaud Franel Éditions.

Black, F., & Scholes, M. (1973). The pricing of options and corporate liabilities. *Journal of Political Economy, 81*(3), 637–654.

Capelle-Blancard, G., & Petit, A. (2013). Mesurer les performances extrafinancières. Le véritable défi de l'ISR. *Revue Française de Gestion, 236*(39), 109–126.

Chalmin, P. (2001). Le capitalisme tend-il ou non vers l'autorégulation? In P. D'Humières & A. Chauveau (Eds.), *Les pionniers de l'entreprise responsable*. Paris: Éditions d'Organisation.

Chardel, P. A. (2002). Un besoin de sens? Éthique et déontologie des cadres. *Revue Cadres – CFDT, 401–402*, 19–24.

Clow, R. (1999). Money that grows on trees. *Institutional Investor, 33*(10), 212–215.

Crifo, P., & Mottis, N. (2013). L'ISR à la recherche de nouveaux élans. *Revue Française de Gestion, 236*(39), 69–78.

De Brito, C. (2006). ISR: Comment les critères extra-financiers impactent les objectifs de gestion? *Revue d'Économie Financière*, *85*, 151–170.

De Brito, C., Desmartin, J. P., Lucas-Leclin, V., & Perrin, F. (Eds.). (2005). *L'investissement socialement responsable*. Paris: Économica.

Demont, G. (2013). L'éthique professionnelle peut-elle se penser au singulier? Le cas des formations dans le secteur de l'aide à la personne dépendante. *Recherche et pratiques pédagogiques en langues de spécialité*, *22*(2), 64–81.

Eurosif. (2012). *European SRI*. Retrieved from http://www.eurosif.org/publication/european-sri-study-2012/

Fama, E. (1970). Efficient capital markets: A review of theory and empirical work. *Journal of Finance*, *25*, 383–417.

Férone, G., D'Arcimoles, C. H., Bello, P., & Sassenou, N. (Eds.). (2001). *Le développement durable, des enjeux stratégiques pour l'entreprise*. Paris: Éditions d'Organisation.

Fischbach, F. (2009). *Sans objet: Capitalisme, subjectivité, aliénation*. Paris: Librairie Philosophique Jacques Vrin.

Friedman, M. (1970). The social responsibility of business is to increase its profits. *The New York Times Magazine*, September 13.

Glass, G. (1976). Primary, secondary, and meta-analysis of research. *Educational Researcher*, *5*, 3–8.

Gollier, C., & Leclair, A. (2006). Pourquoi l'ISR a-t-il besoin de recherche universitaire? Regards croisés. *Revue d'Économie Financière*, *85*, 11–18.

Gomez, P.-Y. (Eds.). (2001). *La République des actionnaires: Le gouvernement des entreprises entre démocratie et démagogie*. Syros: Alternatives Économiques.

Gomez, P. Y. (2009). Théorie néolibérale du gouvernement des entreprises: Critique d'un renversement critique. In D. Golsorkhi, I. Huault, & B. Leca (Eds.), *Les études critiques en management*. Québec: Presses Universitaires de Laval.

Griffin, J. J., & Mahon, J. F. (1997). The corporate social performance and corporate financial performance debate: Twenty-five years of incomparable research. *Business and Society*, *36*(1), 5–31.

Hellsten, S., & Mallin, C. (2006). Are 'ethical' or 'socially responsible' investments socially responsible? *Journal of Business Ethics*, *66*, 393–406.

Keen, S. (2014). *L'imposture économique*. Ivry sur Seine: Les Éditions de l'Atelier.

Keyes, K., Jr. (1984). *The hundredth monkey*. Coos Bay, OR: Vision Books.

Lagoarde-Segot, T. (2014). *La finance solidaire: Un humanisme économique*. Louvain-la-Neuve: Éditions De Boeck. Collection Méthodes et Recherches.

Les Amis de La Terre. (2010). *Investissement socialement responsable: L'heure du tri*. Retrieved from http://www.amisdelaterre.org/Finance-responsable-Les-Amis-de-la.html/

Lucas-Leclin, V. (2006). Qu'apporte l'analyse ISR à l'analyse financière? *Revue d'Économie Financière*, *85*, 1–24.

Luther, R. G., Matatko, J., & Corner, D. C. (1992). The investment performance of UK ethical unit trusts. *Accounting, Auditing and Accountability Journal*, *5*(4), 57–70.

Margolis, J., Elfenbein, H., & Walsh, J. (2007). Does it pay to be good? A meta-analysis and redirection of research on the relationship between corporate social and financial performance. Paper presented at the Academy of Management Conference, Philadelphia, PA.

Margolis, J., & Walsh, J. (2003). Misery loves companies: Rethinking social initiatives by business. *Administrative Science Quarterly*, *48*, 268–305.

Markowitz, H. (1952). Portfolio selection. *Journal of Finance, 7*(1), 77–99.
Mattingly, J. E., & Berman, S. L. (2006). Measurement of corporate social action: Discovering taxonomy in the Kinder, Lydenberg, Domini ratings data. *Business and Society, 45*, 20–46.
Mercier, S. (2002). Du discours à la réalité: Théorie et pratique du management éthique. *Revue Cadres – CFDT, 401–402*, 39–44.
Morin, E. (Eds.). (2004). *Éthique – La méthode 6*. Paris: Éditions Le Seuil.
Orlitzky, M., Schmidt, F. L., & Rynes, S. L. (2003). Corporate social and financial performance: A meta-analysis. *Organization Studies, 24*(3), 403–441.
Pava, M. L., & Krausz, J. (1996). The association between corporate responsibility and financial performance: The paradox of social cost. *Journal of Business Ethics, 15*(3), 321–357.
Pesqueux, Y., & Biefnot, Y. (Eds.). (2002). *L'éthique des affaires: Management par les valeurs et responsabilité sociale*. Paris: Éditions d'Organisation.
Plihon, D. (2001). *Le nouveau capitalisme*. Collection Dominos. Paris: Édition Flammarion.
Reeder, N., & Colantonio, A. (2013). *Measuring impact and non-financial returns in impact investing: A critical overview of concepts and practice*. EIBURS Working Paper 2013/01. Retrieved from http://files.lsecities.net/files/2013/10/Measuring_Impact-full-length-Oct-2013.pdf/
Renneboog, L., Ter-Horst, J., & Zhang, C. (2008). Socially responsible investments: Institutional aspects, performance and investor behaviour. *Journal of Banking and Finance, 32*, 1723–1742.
Revelli, C. (2012). La place de l'investissement socialement responsable (ISR) dans le champ de la finance durable: Proposition d'une grille de lecture. *La Revue des Sciences de Gestion, 6*(258), 43–49.
Revelli, C. (2013). L'investissement Socialement Responsable (ISR): Origines, débats et perspectives. *Revue Française de Gestion, 236*(39), 79–92.
Revelli, C., & Sentis, P. (2012). L'investissement socialement responsable diffère-t-il vraiment de l'investissement conventionnel? *La Revue des Sciences de Gestion, 3–4*(255–256), 85–95.
Revelli, C., & Viviani, J.-L. (2014). Financial performance of socially responsible investing (SRI): What have we learned? A meta-analysis. *Business Ethics: A European Review*. Retrieved from http://onlinelibrary.wiley.com/doi/10.1111/beer.12076/abstract/
Ricœur, P. (1997). *L'idéologie et l'utopie*. Paris: Seuil Essais.
Roman, R. M., Hayibor, S., & Agle, B. R. (1999). The relationship between social and financial performance: Repainting a portrait. *Business and Society, 38*(1), 109–125.
Rudd, A. (1981). Social responsibility and portfolio performance. *California Management Review, 23*, 55–61.
Sharpe, W. F. (1964). Capital asset prices: A theory of market equilibrium under conditions of risk. *Journal of Finance, 19*(3), 425–442.
Sparkes, R. (2001). Ethical investment: Whose ethics? Which investment? *Business Ethics: A European Review, 10*(3), 194–205.
Sparkes, R., & Cowton, C. J. (2004). The maturing of socially responsible investment: A review of the developing link with corporate social responsibility. *Journal of Business Ethics, 52*(1), 45–57.
Testart, A. (2007). *Critique du don, études sur la circulation non marchande*. Paris: Syllepse.
US SIF. (2012). *Report on sustainable and responsible investing trends in the United States*. Retrieved from http://www.ussif.org/files/Publications/12_Trends_Exec_Summary.pdf

Van Roey, E. (1905). La monnaie d'après saint Thomas d'Aquin. Revue néo-scolastique*, 12ème année*, *46*, 207–238.

Weinstein, O. (2010). *Pouvoir, finance et connaissance: Les transformations de l'entreprise capitaliste entre XXe et XXIe siècle*. Paris: Éditions La Découverte.

Wu, M. L. (2006). Corporate social performance, corporate financial performance, and firm size: A meta-analysis. Journal of American Academy of Business*, 8*(1), 163–171.

Zaouati, P. (Eds.). (2009). *Investir « responsable », en quête de nouvelles valeurs pour la finance*. Paris: Éditions Lignes de Repères.

SRI 2.0: MORE THAN A MAKEOVER – A FUNDAMENTAL REFORMULATION

Jacques Ninet[☆]

ABSTRACT

Purpose – *Our hypothesis about the failure of SRI as the new mainstream a series of profound misunderstandings about CSR and SRI among the various stakeholders, that is 'responsible' companies that are practitioners of CSR, academic theorists, asset management companies, SRI finance professionals, rating agencies and non-financial analysts.*

Methodology/approach – *This chapter presents a 'bottom-up' approach that reintroduces the long-term horizon in investment decisions and focus on the adaptability and innovation capacities of the firms (and States) in front of the unprecedented challenges of the century.*

Findings – *The severity of the repeated financial crises and the challenges associated with global sustainability call urgently for responsible finance. Despite praise from institutional investors, SRI is far from the*

☆With the contribution of Elisabeth Cassagnes, Sustainable Development Manager at La Française.

Finance Reconsidered: New Perspectives for a Responsible and Sustainable Finance
Critical Studies on Corporate Responsibility, Governance and Sustainability, Volume 10, 179–197

ISSN: 2043-9059/doi:10.1108/S2043-905920160000010027

norm and has met very limited success with private investors and retail networks.

Originality/value – *To truly reconcile finance and sustainability we first need to go beyond the traditional dilemma between ethics and performance which considers any non-financial criteria as a severe constraint and foster a contributive conception of sustainable prosperity, for public and private agent as well.*

Keywords: Corporate social responsibility; social and responsible investment; crise; sustainability

INTRODUCTION

SRI, a topic frequently cited in the numerous reports produced on the issue of sustainable development across a wide range of disciplines, has received much attention from market institutions (Motis, 2014). Nonetheless, the objective observer would be forced to concede that SRI has never truly 'taken off' since its promising beginnings at the turn of the century. For all the flattering figures cited in celebration of its development,[1] SRI has yet to achieve the mainstream status appealed for by its promoters, while retaining its exceptional approach. Ever since the *FRR* (French Pensions Reserve Fund) established a 'test segment' (2005) and after the creation of a *RAFP* (Civil Servants' Supplementary Retirement Fund) specifically dedicated to SRI, the approach has been met only with praise from other institutional investors in France. While the 'full' commitment of the CIES[2] to SRI has certainly had a symbolic effect, its real impact is limited by the low volume of assets currently held in employee savings plans. To see where SRI has been a complete failure, one needs look at retail and private wealth management. Upon close examination, it is apparent that the bulk of assets in 'SRI funds' are actually invested in pre-existing money market UCITS that simply have been given a 'makeover' (and have been losing steam due to near-zero returns). This proves neither the existence of real demand nor the availability of a feasible product.[3] Surveys seem to suggest that latent demand exists among individual investors, but the near-total indifference of retail networks and their lack of competence on the subject (Heinman & Pouget, 2013) prevent such demand from being met with a comprehensive solution across the full range of financial products.

As early players in this field, promoters of the first SRI-centred SICAV scheme (*Euro-Expansion Durable*, or 'Euro-Sustainable Expansion', launched in 2000) at Expertise Asset Management and pioneering managers, alongside Sarasin AM France, of the SRI funds of the *FRR* and *AGIRC ARRCO* (2006) and one of the first SRI-based bond funds (2008), we believe the time has come for us to conduct an in-depth analysis on this stagnation, especially given the universal priority being given to sustainable development and the 'ecological transition'. Underlying this analysis is an urgent need to identify the errors responsible for this stagnation, whether they lie in naive militancy or in an understanding of the topic that is as superficial as it is enthusiastic. Indeed, the severity of the repeated financial crises and the challenges associated with global sustainability call for responsible finance, both from the standpoint of its contribution to the global economy and the security of the liabilities under its watch.[4]

Our hypothesis is that this failure stems from a series of profound misunderstandings about CSR and SRI among the various stakeholders, that is 'responsible' companies that are practitioners of CSR, academic theorists, asset management companies, SRI finance professionals, rating agencies and non-financial analysts. Recently published reports (Brovelli, Drago, & Molinié, 2013; Dron, 2013) reveal, due to their compartmentalising nature, a serious lack of communication among the above-mentioned stakeholders. This largely accounts for the false starts and dysfunctions that occur when attempting to apply these solutions on the political level.

A symptom of these misunderstandings can be seen in the minimalist definition of SRI (minimalist because it is the agreed-upon definition, and vice versa) laboriously crafted by the *AFG* (French Asset Management Association) and the *FIR* (Forum for Responsible Investment): '*SRI (Socially-responsible investing) is an investment that aims to reconcile financial performance with social and environmental impact by financing companies and public entities that contribute to sustainable development across all sectors.*' Note that in this definition the French word for investment is '*placement*' which sounds more like cash trade than long-term investment.

The definition is accompanied by the following optimistic comment by the two institutions: '*This new definition highlights the objective of SRI and its relation to sustainable development. It is not solely founded on the means used by asset management companies to achieve this objective, i.e. taking into account ESG (environmental, social/societal and governance) criteria on top of the usual financial criteria. For the first time, it also emphasises the influence of SRI and the social and environmental impacts of SRI management ... This new definition, and the plans for a certification label, constitute (following the update to the AFG/FIR/Eurofi Transparency Code this past February) two major advances that will help savers better understand SRI.'*

This commentary expresses a dual aspiration: enabling the public to better understand SRI in order to garner strong public support and produce noticeable impacts on society. Hence the almost messianic virtue of a certification label, meant to finally liberate pent-up public demand. Putting aside the uncertainty that likely resides in the minds of savers due to the lack of such a label,[5] we believe it is necessary and urgent for us to focus in on the more fundamental reasons for this apparent lack of interest. In particular, we should carefully scrutinise the key points put forward in this supposedly new definition:

- Does SRI refer solely to a '*placement*' (this term implying, in economic parlance, both uniqueness and strong reversibility) rather than a general philosophy of asset management?
- What is meant by '*reconcile* financial performance and social and environmental impact'? Does this not presuppose that these objectives are mutually incompatible (without knowing whether 'investing' refers to a single investment or cash trade or an issuer company taken as a whole), unintentionally validating the argument that SRI would be (as still very often seen in the literature) *an additional constraint* that could only drag down financial performance?
- Finally, how and via what channel does SRI influence the governance and behaviour of those involved?

The section 'SRI 1.0' will decipher these ambiguities and their role in the stagnation of SRI, while the section 'SRI 2.0' will propose a solution based on a more up-to-date SRI concept that we call SRI 2.0.

SRI 1.0

A History of Confusion

Any history of SRI must inevitably begin with the Quakers and their insistence on the ethical allocation of their wealth in the logic of Max Weber's *The Protestant Ethic and the Spirit of Capitalism* (1904). This is why the first 'ethical' investments operated on the principle of excluding 'non-virtuous' issuers – a principle applied equally to bonds and equities. At the time, this represented mostly new money available to issuers. When this notion spread to European asset management in the last 25 years of the 20th century, the idea emerged that assets could be selectively chosen to redress 'economic anomalies' (cf. the 'North-South Development' SICAV managed by CDC), reflecting a fundamental misunderstanding that persists today.

The principle of incorporating non-financial criteria was imported from the English-speaking world, where investments in equities are predominant. It thus also came to be applied primarily to equities in Continental Europe, where equities accounted for only a minority of investments and where investors had a 'preference' for bonds. This transmission came with two major modifications:

- The sole criteria of 'ethics', closely linked to theoretical and practical developments in CSR, was substituted by three components: environmental, social/societal and 'governance'. The third component was a response to the managerial misconduct brought to light by the 2000–2002 crisis (Enron, Parmalat, WorldCom, etc.). This is how the acronym 'ESG' came to be.
- The practice of binary selection (inclusion/exclusion) was replaced by various forms of 'positive selection'. The most popular of these has been 'Best in Class', or selection based on the best-rated issuers according to the three above-mentioned criteria.

The next steps – incorporating ESG and excluding investments based on compliance with standards – reduced SRI to a simple hybridisation of traditional finance, no longer serving as a real constraint.[6] It brought to light the motivation of financial traders who saw SRI as constituting only a single reputational (and competitive) risk in relation to sustainable development.

This explains why, and how, SRI managers fell blindly into the trap set by the disciples of Milton Friedman and Henry Markowitz, who defined these managers' tasks exclusively in terms of the pursuit of financial returns. It also accounts for the multitude of studies, theses and dissertations published on the advantages and disadvantages of non-financial selectivity in terms of portfolio performance.[7]

It is hardly surprising that the research on the supposed causality of an unobtainable relationship between 'Financial Performance and Social Performance' and the meta-analyses summarising it could never be concluded. This indecision is exacerbated by the fact the distinction between the operating performance of firms and the market performance of their securities is a problem in itself (this point is developed in section 'SRI 2.0').

The very abundance of such research proves that the debate – which has, moreover, been silent on government debt and offered only secondary treatment of corporate debt, both of which are generally governed by a trade-off between yield to maturity and solvency risk – has retained the assumption that ethics are an impediment to profitability. Modern portfolio theory (Markowitz and Sharpe) and the underlying notions of market efficiency developed by Eugene Fama, who won a Nobel Prize in 2013, have always been formulated in the spirit of *Realpolitik*, seeing efficiency and ethics as not fully reconcilable; in other words, a portfolio incorporating SRI criteria would necessarily have lower potential for efficiency on the market.

What the Best in Class approach neglects to specify is the type of skill the portfolio manager is meant to use once the (restricted) Investment Universe has been built on the basis of ESG selectivity. Above all, the very essence of the profession of portfolio manager as opposed to a tracker – namely, alpha generation through the *relative* appreciation of equities – is simply ignored. The task then becomes to reconcile the ability to detect overvalued and undervalued securities with the application of non-financial criteria, a challenge compounded by the fact that risk premiums have fluctuated erratically in the past 15 years. Curiously, this dilemma has still not been addressed.

It is no accident that portfolio turnover was a subject of disagreement during the initial stages of label certification in a kind of a 'mirror image' of the dogmatic rigidity of the defenders of financial performance at any cost. At the same time, the ex-ante management of funds' beta through the systematic use of derivatives, while compliant with the principle of responsibility towards liabilities, was also criticised by the early certifiers, who lambasted what they saw as the nefarious nature of these products and/or the 'horribly speculative' character of such a strategy.

Ultimately, the issue of compatibility between the outlooks of evaluators of sustainability – which is, in the final analysis, the job of non-financial analysts – and those of asset managers has never truly been addressed. To begin with, does sustainability refer to the firm or the investment? We know that time, which is at the heart of all matters related to sustainability, has enormous difficulty crossing the barrier of concrete finance – at least in the world of equities, where traders deal with a time horizon that is infinite in theory but in practical terms is concerned with short-term variations.

Paradoxically, it was through the gradual spread of SRI to the other asset classes (debt and real estate) that the true nature of the problem became apparent. The publication of several studies under a single title, 'Does SRI change when applied to other asset classes?',[8] shows the extent to which the Best in Class model applied to equities, in reality the most problematic case, could take root. It is only on the basis of these developments that we can ultimately discern that it is the standard application of this imperfect methodology for equity markets that is problematic, and not the debt or real estate markets themselves (investment choices for the latter are intrinsically more sustainable).

In the real estate component, it quickly became apparent that 'value creation' had, on the one hand, been synchronised between the asset (the object of the investment) and the objective of the investor, while on the other hand it was by its very essence linked to the sustainability of the asset across all of its components: construction, energy, regional integration and the well-being of occupants. This dual 'harmony' is an important factor behind the incorporation of a non-financial, sustainable dimension in real estate investment which was immediately understood and sought out by investors.

Advances were also achieved with bonds. In 2006 and 2007, we too hastily concluded that the spread of SRI to the bond and money markets occurred out of a need for consistency in investment strategies, when in reality this offered little benefit. In a manner of speaking, an integrated management team could not 'be SRI' for one half of its product range and be indifferent to the other, lest it be accused of double standards. The real argument, according to the reverse logic to what we previously wrote, is that the negotiable debt securities (NDS) market and the majority of the bond market are above all primary markets in which portfolios – particularly those owned by employee representative bodies – have very low turnover rates. The 'I' of SRI thus takes on its full meaning, the act of management in this case effectively being both an irreversible investment and a direct contribution of liquidity to the issuer, whereas the equity market primarily deals with secondary trading amongst shareholders, creating only a small amount of net flow for companies (or none, in the case of the US market).

The Top-Down Approach: Too Ambitious and Too Vague?

Can SRI change the world? This was the topic of a round table held in 2012 as part of SRI Week. The last part of the quote alludes to this ambition: '*By influencing the governance and behaviour of participants, SRI promotes responsible economics*'.

The relation between responsible finance and sustainable development is all the more vague given the already uncertain link between macroeconomic challenges and sustainable development. Sustainable development remains resolutely absent from the standard macroeconomic approaches of financial strategies (the so-called top-down approaches), just as it is from the prevailing view of economic policy (growth = jobs = well-being). More generally, prosperity continues to be seen in the context of an unchanging and unlimited expansion of material goods (measured quantitatively by GDP), despite being recognised as incompatible in the long term with a finite ecological system. The very notion of 'sustainable development' suffers from a fundamental imbalance between its two constituents due a lack of serious prospects for development.

Furthermore, the notion of ethics, central to the origins of responsible finance, becomes confined to a secondary role. At best, it appears only on the microeconomic or individual level, supplementary to non-negotiable, conventional practices; consequently, it is stripped of the global mission accorded to it under the principles of responsibility. The suggestion that such financial leverage can 'change the world' while limiting itself to individual ethics and not financial (banking), fiscal or, more generally, political ethics sounds like a tall order, if not wholly a ruse. The lack of rating transparency, the insistence on taking criteria averages and the loss of selectivity on outliers (the weak link in the selection process) only add to the confusion.

All of this leads us to the conclusion that SRI as formulated in this manner (condemned to a process of 'reconciliation' between financial objectives and non-financial criteria Perin & Quairel-Lanoizelee, 2012) can only result in stagnation, since the investor concerned with the common good will never be convinced that it amounts to anything more than giving their investments a vaguely-defined 'human touch' – let alone trying to convince those who prioritise returns on their investments. In this forced marriage, each side fears losing some – or a lot – of itself. Refining the notion, improving rating processes, reinforcing transparency, enforcing a single label and, 'applying a sanctions principle' (Revelli, 2013) would not change anything on the fundamental level.

The aim of the analysis presented herein is to remedy these underlying inadequacies and propose an alternative approach that could avert both the potential for catastrophe if nothing is done and the certain failure of any attempt at coercion by better addressing the real challenges associated with the shifts in industrial civilisation and the globalised world.

SRI 2.0

A New Framework of Analysis

Given the contradictions and ambiguities of the top-down approach discussed above and the illusory nature of the claim that this approach can 'change the world', we believe that true reconciliation between finance and sustainability can only be achieved through a 'bottom-up' approach that reintroduces the long-term horizon in investment decisions. This long-term view is already being used in the strategies of an increasing number of economic participants, not only through the explicit incorporation of negative externalities but also, and most significantly, as a foundation of a positive vision of sustainability as a factor that creates value through innovation and adaptability. New economic paradigms such as the social economy, the circular economy and product-service systems are a response to a model that is seen to equate use with property and consumption with destruction – a model that is on its last legs given the state of resources and lack of future prospects. Jacques Attali groups all of these approaches under the banner of the 'Positive Economy', a multi-faceted view of value creation that is meant to benefit people, businesses, communities and, by extension, the entire planet.

Whereas the traditional SRI approach establishes ratings fundamentally based on the capacity to control negative externalities, taking a static (past-based) rebuke/reward outlook divorced from financial analysis, SRI 2.0 seeks to identify the factors that would contribute to long-term global entrepreneurial performance without *a priori* distinctions. This positive approach is similar to the search for 'weak signals', or rather, to borrow the terminology of Lesca and Blanco (2002), 'early warning signals'. *'The word "signal" is inadequate because it can imply the deliberate release of information by its issuer. This signal is sent intentionally to one or more target recipients who will naturally be in a position to receive it. In our definition, an Early Warning Signal is a piece of information which, in our interpretation, suggests that a highly useful event could take place ... We have termed this concept the "early warning signal", like a transformation of weak signals ... The amplification of the transformation of weak signals into early warning signals is a heuristic process on both the individual and collective levels, involving attentiveness to – and interpretation of – information.'*

This contributing process is consistent with the advent (or rather, resurgence) of a holistic vision within the real business world, one that not only coexists with the objective of creating shareholder value inspired by the dominant theory (Friedman, Van Horne, etc.) but, in the long term, is integrated within this objective. As such, the approach relies on 'field survey'; it is strictly bottom-up. It also applies equally to all types of financial instruments. Enlarging the traditional analytical framework of ESG by directing it at the search for warning signals is the first, indispensable step in giving substance to this approach. Demonstrating its suitability when it comes to identifying tomorrow's success stories and overall well-being is the second and assuredly more difficult task.

From ESG to the Magic Square of Responsibility

ESG criteria are the foundation of SRI today. These criteria, and the non-financial rating system they inspire, remain fundamentally past-oriented and focused on transparency as a guarantee of 'virtuous' investment – a modern version of the Myth of Sisyphus. By contrast, the future-oriented approach we have proposed extends this tripartite classification and directs it at the detection of early warning signals for long-term prosperity, forming what we refer to as the 'magic square' of CSR. The universal suitability of this approach is underlined by the fact that it applies both on the macro level (such as in the case of public debt) and on the micro level (the prospective valuation of companies).

The Macro Level

The application of traditional SRI to government debt is a thorny issue because the responsibility of governments is wide-reaching, multi-faceted and subject to political constraints. In other words, the habitual distinction between finance and non-finance cannot truly apply, since governments have no other objective in principle than to ensure the present and future well-being of their citizens and to maintain good relations with other peoples. This raises the issue of the inadequacy of national accounts aggregates (i.e. GDP) for measuring a country's true prosperity, both today and even more so in the future.

The solvency of government bonds, or the sustainability of public debt, is a crucial question for the owners of these securities, both individuals and institutional investors. Meanwhile, economists disagree on the notion of sustainable debt and on what constitutes an acceptable budget deficit – leading to the use of unquestioned contingent ratios and as far as the curious case of the 'golden rule'[9] – while rating agencies have repeatedly shown their inability to predict even the most violent crises (South

Korea in 1997, Iceland in 2008, etc.). An alternative means of estimating a country's potential future prosperity is thus urgently needed, not least because this would consequently resolve the debt issue itself. Based on the various models being studied today, four groups of essential factors can be identified. These constitute the four cardinal points of our magic square:

- Energy factors, including sources for long-term supply, their development and sustainability, energy efficiency (in industrial production, transport and habitat) and environmental consequences, primarily with respect to climate change. The history of industrial progress seems closely tied to this energy factor,[10] which we cover under the heading of 'Energy-Climate'.
- Innovation factors, based on education (all types), research (public and private, theoretical and applied) and the capital-related and fiscal conditions of GFCF, grouped under the heading 'Education-Research-Innovation'.
- Geographic factors, referring both to the development of regions (accessibility, development of resources and wealth) and to the deployment of human capacities (tradition and expertise, demographics, migration) in these regions, grouped under 'Human Capital and Regions'.
- Political factors, in line with our conviction of the necessity of cooperation – indispensable in the current global demographic and environmental context – for which we have borrowed the term 'Governance' but with the addendum of regional and global governance.[11]

Should we expect to succeed in building a multi-factor model that offers an accurate, quantitative prediction of future prosperity in terms of GDP and related ratios? Probably not. But could such an approach provide us with useful lessons on how to assess the quality of a sovereign issuer? We believe the answer is yes; at the very least, it would serve us better than combining a standard non-financial rating system with an even more standard financial rating system. The fact that Greece was identified as high-risk due to its high level of corruption and laxity is only a modest success when seen in light of the failure of traditional non-financial rating systems to predict the bankruptcy of Iceland and Ireland or the serious difficulties of Spain.

The Micro Level

Putting aside the topic of governments to focus on private enterprises, the good news is that the framework of analysis will be similar overall to the one we have just described, even though the energy factor is less relevant in this case. For businesses, seen here as a centre of 'profitable' cooperation among all stakeholders, the notions of regions and human capital occupy a special place (unlike traditional ESG, which relegates these to a minor role or excludes them altogether[12]). What the coupling of the financial and the non-financial is unable to recognise is the capacity of businesses to respond to major trends and the resulting appearance of an unprecedented risk/return dialectic.

The basic principle should thus be that in an investment universe marked by increasing complexity and rapid change, the true discriminating factors are hidden, thus creating alpha potential for the best-informed investors. Managerial aptitude – seen here from the angle of adaptability and innovation – ultimately becomes an early warning signal on the demarcation of firms in the long term. The four components of the magic square are thus:

- Human Capital and Regions (id)
- Environmental Sustainability (for Energy-Climate)
- Capacity for Innovation (for Education-Research-Innovation)
- Adaptability, including organisational responsiveness (for Governance)

From SRI to SAI: The La Française-IPCM Partnership

Conscious of the major societal and environmental challenges of the 21st century, in 2009 La Française launched its *Méga Trends* fund range, which aimed to obtain alpha portfolio returns on the best placed securities in view of these challenges. From 2009 to 2013, La Française also benefited from the non-financial research, carried out as part of the LFP Sarasin Joint Venture, produced by Banque Sarasin, a pioneer of SRI in Europe, using a Best in Class/Best of Class approach. This partnership concluded at the same time as the need to advance towards SRI 2.0 emerged. Consequently, La Française began developing a strategic partnership with IPCM (Inflection Point Capital Management), a research, analysis and consulting 'boutique' that bases its fundamental analysis on 'unorthodox' risk and return factors. These include environmental, social and governance risks (and performance). In reality, however, IPCM takes its analysis beyond these traditional factors by incorporating an in-depth investigation of the quality of companies' strategic management. These non-tangible factors are essential to measuring the competitiveness and performance of companies today, and even more so tomorrow.

The concept known as SAI (Strategically Aware Investing) constitutes a truly innovative approach that takes as its starting point the fact that the world is changing in a profound way and at an unprecedented pace.

The competitive environment in which major companies must operate has thus become infinitely more complex and unpredictable.

The SAI methodology is based on three fundamental premises:

1. This new world poses unprecedented challenges to companies from two directions:
   - from a physical point of view, growth in demand for energy, agriculture and natural resources (not to mention climate change);
   - from a societal point of view, companies are involved with increasingly demanding stakeholders armed with unprecedented access to information thanks to social media and instantaneous global communication channels, with implications for reputation and engagement.
2. These new challenges require companies to develop new capacities:
   - research and innovation;
   - adaptability and responsiveness to constraints, opportunities and emerging needs;
   - stakeholder management;
   - environmental sustainability;
   - the preservation and development of human capital.

   The successful companies of the future will be those that possess these capacities and characteristics. At present, they are few in number.
3. None of these critical capacities for the future can be detected using traditional financial analysis. To identify the winners of the future, we must take account of this innovative approach, developed and perfected over the past two decades, in the globalised context of demographic growth, tensions surrounding natural resources and intensifying urbanisation.

By supplementing traditional ESG factors and financial criteria with a third component – that is the analysis of major macroeconomic trends – IPCM has added the final touch to the magic square discussed above, enabling it to assume its full relevance.

SRI 2.0: A PURELY IDEALISTIC CONSTRUCT OR A TRULY EFFECTIVE NEW APPROACH?

In this section, we will make an honest assessment, in view of the severe criticisms that have been levelled against SRI 1.0 as outlined in the first section, of the effectiveness we can expect of the proposed methodology both from the standpoint of portfolio performance and of the contribution it can make to global sustainability.

Financial Performance

The *a priori* unsolvable dilemma of improving market performance through the recognition of CSR, to which we alluded in 1.1 above, may be analysed in the following manner. Suppose that at time zero, securities are equivalent from the standpoint of non-financial analysis. Suppose also that all companies having the same operating performance (instantaneous and foreseeable in the short term) are attributed the same risk premium. If one company is then recognised as strong in CSR, the hypothesis is that, all other things being equal, its risk premium would diminish and, in parallel, its share price would increase. Investors who bought shares of this company at time zero would benefit from this revaluation (capital gain) while anticipated future returns at constant operating performance would decline (also in relative terms).

In the longer term, however, the company deemed to have better performance (based on the basic premise of informed selection) would see its operating income rise. Furthermore, the decrease in its cost of capital would increase its investment capacity in developments opened up thanks to its managerial aptitude. Ultimately, and without taking into account potential positive effects from the decline in operating risks, the investor – even if led at some point to 'overpay' for the share – would, from the standpoint of traditional financial analysis, emerge a winner, independently of the sometimes erratic behaviour of equity valuation in general.

For bonds, for the same reasons and following the logic of Merton's model, there would be a decrease in the spread (specific risk premium) as the economic value of the company increased. Ultimately, we should see convergence between the traditional financial rating and SRI 2.0 as indicators of creditworthiness in the long term. Furthermore, the attention accorded by management to a fair equilibrium among its various categories of financial contributors (i.e. the renunciation of 'dangerous' dividend payments for creditors) could diminish the perceived risk on debt securities.

We have clearly strayed far from Milton Friedman's famous affirmation that maximising shareholder wealth should be the single and exclusive component of managerial responsibility. The great weakness of this lofty formula is that it completely ignores the time factor and says nothing of how to achieve this single objective. In essence, it is indifferent to the choice between 'cost killing' and 'creative accounting' on the one hand and innovation and adaptability on the other.[13] In contrast, this is precisely the issue that our proposed methodology attempts to redress.

Sustainable Development

The innovation here is that the words 'sustainable' and 'development', traditionally seen as compatible at best and antagonistic at worst, attain (or regain) their unity and inseparability. This eliminates the pseudo-duality between the economic sphere and the rest of humanity, reflected in the media by the contrast between 'serious economists' on the one hand and 'irresponsible politicians' and 'utopian ecologists' on the other. This distinction is also seen in the manner in which economics attempts to delineate itself from the other social sciences. The argument often put forward to justify this independent stance (i.e. the formalisation of the economy through the use of mathematical models) betrays a more profound belief in the *homo economicus* as a representation of human beings.

But is the bottom-up stance underlying the approach suitable? And above all, is it adequate? In other words, can we create a positive vision of the future of humanity based on a gentle but radical evolution caused by the flow of innovations? *'Throughout history, technological infrastructure has influenced economic infrastructure, which in turn has influenced sociological infrastructure, which has ultimately influenced ideology. In conclusion, I do not believe there could be an inversion of these factors, starting with an ideological revolution whereby humanity decides to "stop degrading its shared (collective, long-term, global) heritage in the name of personal (individual, short-term, local) interest." Rather, I believe there will be a chain of technological evolutions leading to economic and sociological change. Hopefully, in the age of economics and knowledge, this will turn the "experts" into "sages"'.*[14]

Herein resides the notion that all revolutions end up going full circle: royalty is replaced by Empire, aristocracy by the *grande bourgeoisie*, both of these by the *nomenklatura* and colonisers by commandeering oligarchs. As German sociologist Robert Michels wrote in 1911: '*Organisation implies the tendency to oligarchy. In every organisation ... the aristocratic tendency manifests itself very clearly'*. The bitter realisation of the failed revolutions, particularly of the communist utopian variety, goes a long way to explain the paralysis of intellectual elites at the end of the 20th century.

Thanks to the advent of ever more sophisticated technology, humanity has moved beyond the primary concern of escaping its servitude to nature. But as a result of this progress, humanity now finds itself faced with the choice of either dominating nature at the risk of human extinction through various forms of self-poisoning (particularly through the destruction of biodiversity) or building a sustainable equilibrium.[15] Whereas science and technology are ethically neutral – at least in the minds of their practitioners – their impact is no less significant; that is, they are capable of shaping reality over the course of time. Thus, the arrival of the information age (i.e. of shared immateriality) sets the stage for the ushering in of the sustainability age. By replacing property with use and commodities with connections, it would abolish Hobbes' state of nature conceived of as a winner-take-all battle and allow us to follow John Locke's prescription; namely, when humanity's survival is at stake, we should seek the common good (Locke, 1999, 1690).

This optimism is seriously dampened by the fundamentally entropic nature of human development, for two reasons. The first of these is related to demographics. Today, the acquisition of a resource (land, water, ore, etc.) by one individual limits access to that resource for other individuals. This was not the case in the 17th century (or at least, it was not perceived as such). In the context of colonial conquest, this frame of reference endured much longer. The second reason is the increase in complexity[16] resulting from the total interconnectivity of all human activity. If the idea of 'miracle solutions' imposed from above is to be rightly rejected, this leaves us with the urgent need to reformulate a political ethos to serve as a basis for a new means of living together which is appropriate for our time and which incorporates the lessons learned from the political mistakes of the 20th century. Thus, the success of Sustainable Development (as envisaged by us as proponents of a reinvigorated formulation of SRI) depends on a re-appropriation of politics, at both urban and regional levels, that reverses the centralising tendencies – coercive and dispossessing in nature – of supranational constructions such as the European Union.

CONCLUSION

From now on our world is finite and everything is interconnected. The survival of humanity is at risk if each individual strives only to maintain the conditions of their personal satisfaction. Consequently, free and undistorted competition will not be enough to build the basis for a balanced society, just as an ideological revolution could not escape being co-opted by a new minority interest. Only by starting at the 'bottom of the pyramid,'[17] combining the spirit of enterprise and innovation on the one hand with the return of political ethics on the other, will the latent potential of rapid and constant technological advancement produce true progress. The aim of SRI 2.0 and its application in the spirit of SAI as outlined here is to be transparent and active contributors to this urgently needed evolution.

NOTES

1. Reports by Eurosif and Novethic.
2. Inter-Union Committee for Employee Savings (*Comité Intersyndical de l'Epargne Salariale*).
3. Moreover, as these funds consist mainly of CDs, the selective impact of SRI is very limited.
4. In its report published in December 2013, the Responsible Finance Commission of the *Fondation pour la Croissance Responsable* (Foundation for Responsible Growth) identified three areas of responsibility: long-term financing of the economy (individuals and businesses), respect for the interest of clients and financial stability.
5. As with other 'alternative' practices (e.g. organic food), labelling will likely be indispensable to establishing the credibility of the approach, with high expectations of selectivity. See Hobeika, Ponssard, and Poret (2013).
6. Once a company is identified as having weak practices in the terms of [SRI] standards, the asset manager or institutional investor would have the choice of either excluding it from the portfolio or partaking in shareholder dialogue with the company with the aim of bringing about change. In this manner, the responsible investor is able to *impose a minimum standard of business conduct without necessarily hampering the pursuit of investment opportunities to maximise the financial performance* of the portfolio. (Eurosif Report, 2012)
7. Analysis of the Highest and Lowest-Rated Euro Stoxx 300 SRI Portfolios. *Les Dossiers de la Recherche UFG-LFP* (November 2009); Khelil, Ninet, and Rezgui (2010).
8. 'Does SRI become transformed when applied to new asset classes?' *Les Dossiers de la Recherche UFG-LFP*: *L'immobilier* (December 2009). 'The Special Case of Public Debt' (December 2009) – 'How Should Derivatives Products Be Handled?' (October 2010).
9. This is perhaps directly linked to the doctrine of ordoliberalism to which Germany has converted (nearly) all of Europe.
10. Per capita GDP growth is correlated with improvement in average energy efficiency and the increase of per capita energy consumption. (Giraud & Renouard, 2012. http://theshiftproject.org/fr/cette-page/lien-pibconsommation-denergie)
11. Faced with the challenge of sustainable development, neither national governments nor liberal globalisation seem capable of offering a satisfactory

response. This is why global governance is at the heart of progress toward sustainable development. [Building a simple governance index would involve] measuring changes in competition rules, since when these are distorted on the global level, this inevitably leads to social and environmental 'dumping', ultimately resulting in economic and environmental crises. (X. Lépine. Proposition pour un indice de gouvernance mondiale [Proposal for a Global Governance Index], November 2011)

12. Cf. The works of the *Collège des Bernardins* on the distinction that should be made between the Business itself and its legal incarnation as a commercial entity.

13. Cf. The excesses caused by stock options, direct by-products of the agency cost principle.

14. X. Lépine. *Lettre spéciale La Française* (March 15, 2014).

15. Shall we surrender to our surroundings, or shall we make our peace with nature? (R. Nixon. Annual Message to the Congress on the State of the Union, 1970)

16. Mafia-style oligarchies represent the perfect combination of complexity and egotism.

17. These unhappy times call for the building of plans that rest upon the forgotten, the unorganized but the indispensable units of economic power ... that build from the bottom up and not from the top down, that put their faith once more in the forgotten man at the bottom of the economic pyramid. (F. D. Roosevelt, 1932)

REFERENCES

Brovelli, L., Drago, X., & Molinié, E. (2013). *Responsabilité et performance des organisations*. Reports by the Stiglitz Commission and the Conseil d'analyse économique. Paris.

Dron, D. (Dir.) (2013). *White paper on financing ecological transition*. Directorate General of the Treasury and Office of the Commissioner General for Sustainable Development, Paris.

Giraud, G., & Renouard, C. (2012). *Le facteur 12*. Paris: Carnets Nord-Montparnasse éditions.

Heinman, M., & Pouget, S. (2013). La recommandation des fonds ISR. *Revue Française de Gestion*, *7*(236), 149–162.

Hobeika, S., Ponssard, J. P., & Poret, S. (2013). Le rôle stratégique d'un label dans la formation d'un Marché. Le cas de l'ISR en France. *École Polytechnique. Cahier 2013–02*.

Khelil, N., Ninet, J., & Rezgui, B. (2010). Analyse des performances de portefeuilles "best of" et "worst of" ISR. *Économies et sociétés, série KF*, *1*, 1863–1883.

Lesca, H., & Blanco, S. (2002). *Contribution à la capacité d'anticipation des entreprises par la sensibilisation aux signaux faibles*. 6° Congrès International Francophone sur la PME, October (pp. 1–18). HEC Montreal.

Locke, J. (1690). *Second treatise of civil government*. C.B.Macpherson.

Locke, J. (1999). *Second traité du gouvernement civil*. Paris: Garnier Flammarion.

Motis, N. (2014). *ISR et finance responsable*. Paris: Ellipses Marketing.

Perin, F., & Quairel-Lanoizelee, F. (2012). *L'ISR: Valeur financière – Valeur éthique?* Paris: Economica.

Revelli, C. (2013). L'investissement socialement responsable: Origines, débats et perspectives. *Revue française de gestion, 236*, 79–92.

Roosevelt, F. D. R. (1932). The forgotten man. Radio address.

Weber, M. (1904). The protestant ethic and the spirit of capitalism. [English Version], (2002) *Penguin*.

WHY HAS MICROCREDIT HAD SUCH A LIMITED IMPACT ON THE REDUCTION OF POVERTY IN SUB-SAHARAN AFRICA?

Jean-Michel Servet

ABSTRACT

Purpose – *The chapter looks for the conditions of a contribution of microcredit to poverty alleviation.*

Methodology/approach – *It uses socioeconomical hypotheses for defining a direct and fast positive effect of microcredit on the income of the poorest. The contribution raises ten issues or conditions at a micro, meso and macro level.*

Findings – *It is not often that these ten conditions are all completely met. So, the impact of microcredit is generally low as regards the alleviation of poverty. The problems to achieve them are linked to the specificities of the clients and of the prevailing institutions in various sub-Saharan Africa countries.*

Finance Reconsidered: New Perspectives for a Responsible and Sustainable Finance
Critical Studies on Corporate Responsibility, Governance and Sustainability, Volume 10, 199–227

ISSN: 2043-9059/doi:10.1108/S2043-905920160000010028

Originality/value – *The chapter clearly identifies the limits of microcredit and their reasons.*

Keywords: Debt; microcredit; micro-entrepreneurship; poverty; risk; Africa

> The vice came in always at the door of necessity, not at the door of inclination.
> – Defoe (1722/1989).

In Africa, like everywhere, the belief in the success of microcredit has mainly spread through *storytelling*, with tales of borrowers (usually female) who have improved their living standards thanks to small loans. Not only do they (especially the women) considerably increase their income and make additional small productive investments, but they also improve their living conditions, their access to water and energy, improve their children's education, get better healthcare, move away from alcoholism and violence (as far as men are concerned), and enjoy greater autonomy for action, travel and the like. The financial success of some organisations, often backed by the idea that women are more likely to pay back loans than men, is held up as proof of the undeniably positive impact of these small loans for their beneficiaries. The image of microcredit spread by the media and long-validated by academic work,[1] together with the high hopes held for it by the public powers, bilateral/multilateral cooperation organisations, foundations and non-governmental organisations, generally drew on rampant economism[2] to explain the causes of poverty. This poverty is equated with temporarily or permanently low-income levels, leading to insufficient consumption and investment; it is not viewed in terms of social and cultural discrimination. It cannot therefore be eradicated by an economic and financial tool which does not affect the deeper causes underlying poverty and inequality.

The State of the Microcredit Summit Campaign Report 2012 (Maes & Reed, 2012) refers to a number of doubts that have emerged among the main stakeholders in microcredit internationally. These reports previously acclaimed the supposed effectiveness of microcredit in considerably reducing poverty. The most radical and most publicised criticism of microcredit is undoubtedly that put forward by Milford Bateman, at the interface between appraisal, academic world and stakeholders, and summarised in *Why Doesn't Microfinance Work? The Destructive Rise of Local Neoliberalism* (2010).[3] Other scientific works (see those brought together by Lont and Hospes (2004), Fernando (2006a, 2006b), Servet (2006) and Dichter and Harper (2007) in particular) had, much earlier, questioned the illusions shared about the supposed ability of microcredit to 'put poverty in the museum', according to the expression of Grameen Bank founder M. Yunus in his speech on receiving the Nobel Peace Prize in December 2006.

Where microcredit appears successful, it is down to an exceptional local situation and rarely is it obtained without considerable support and direct or indirect subsidies to the organisations issuing the loans (Balkenhol, 2009). Success is hard to reproduce in a sustainable manner or meets with significant obstacles to duplication or durability. On a global level, the impact of microcredit alone thus often appears too low to really help reduce poverty rates. This has been demonstrated in recent studies into its impact (Banerjee, Karlan, & Zinman, 2015; Duvendack et al., 2011; Stewart et al., 2012).[4]

We can quote some of the beliefs affecting the financial services offering that are widely accepted among stakeholders to legitimise their actions, and are still applied in the form of implicit or explicit assumptions in numerous academic works. The critical need of the poorest populations (from an economic viewpoint) would be a need for formal funding for their activities and the 'poor' would prefer self-employment over salaried work or cooperative activity. Financial institutions would systematically lack the resources to satisfy the almost unending stream of loan applications from their potential client base. Given that the effects of saturation on microcredit markets would be low and because the risks of over-indebtedness would be limited, we could very quickly set up profitable microcredit institutions for the (very) 'poor' clientele, provided they are well-managed. While this kind of argument has largely disappeared in the promotion of microcredit in Latin America or Asia, making way for messages on the need to include finance at the bottom of the pyramid (Servet, 2015a) – although no analysis into the causes and forms of that need has been carried out – the legitimisation of microcredit in the fight against poverty is still widespread in sub-Saharan Africa.

Knowledge of borrowers' needs, the financial services actually available to the populations, and the actual uses and effects of microcredit, is thus biased.

Ten economic conditions are taken into consideration in this contribution, all of which are deemed necessary if microcredit is to have the hoped-for direct, rapid impact on the incomes of the 'poor' and the 'poorest'. In no way do they concern the moral or ethical operating standards of the microfinance schemes or establishments. They are approached from a socio-economic stance operating on three levels: microeconomic, mesoeconomic and macroeconomic.[5] A positive impact on poverty rates by microcredit cannot be solely dependent on the proper management of institutions and adequate regulation in the sector.

SIX CONDITIONS AT MICROECONOMIC LEVEL

The first six conditions directly concern the borrowers, their management and use of the loan received, and its impact on their budget.

> **Condition 1.** The clients of microcredit institutions have to be 'poor' or otherwise local spending on goods and services by the richest has to have a positive effect on the income of the poorest.

A primary condition for microcredit to have an impact on increasing revenues among the poorest segments of the population is that the clients of the institutions offering these services should belong to those categories of the population deemed as 'poor'. However, there are growing doubts that the poor, and especially the poorest, are actually the target of these loans. The demand for borrowing among other population categories means that financial inclusion is very limited in most developing countries. This is especially the case in sub-Saharan Africa where 29% of adults say that their only source of loans is family or friends; only 2% mention a bank. In many regions, much higher numbers refer to shopkeepers rather than banks (Demirguc-Kunt & Klapper, 2012a, p. 37).

The low profile of banks as lenders is not surprising. The percentage of the adult population with an account in a formal financial institution is 89% in so-called 'developed' countries (reaching 99% in Denmark), while it is just 24% in sub-Saharan Africa. This is more than in the Middle East and North Africa (18%), but less than in Southern Asia (33%) and Latin America (39%). In some countries, especially South-East Asia and North Africa, the low percentage of holders of an account in a formal financial institution can be explained by the discrimination experienced by women and their low level of economic independence. This is less true is sub-Saharan Africa where 22% of adult women hold an account (Demirguc-Kunt & Klapper, 2012a, p. 15; Demirguc-Kunt & Klapper, 2012b, p. 5). There are, moreover, extreme situations such as the Democratic Republic of Congo where over 95% of adults do not have an account in a formal financial institution, and likewise Niger (Demirguc-Kunt & Klapper, 2012a, p. 5).

It would be wrong to establish a close correlation between the level of per capita income and the degree of financial inclusion measured by the holding of an account in a formal financial institution. Populations in Ghana and Benin have similar levels of per capita income (equivalent to 560 dollars), yet in Ghana 29% of adults hold a formal account compared to just 10% in Benin. Likewise, we note that 62% of those belonging to the wealthiest fifth have a formal account in Nigeria, compared to just 22% in neighbouring Cameroon (Demirguc-Kunt & Klapper, 2012a, pp. 13–14). On the assumption that there is complementarity or substitution among banking services and microfinance institutions, microcredit requirements are thus different from one African country to another, depending on the percentage of the population holding a bank account.

Now let us examine access to financial services for low-income households. Across the African continent, while Morocco has a smaller 'poor' population than sub-Saharan African countries, it has the highest proportion of borrowers from microcredit institutions (17%), ahead of South Africa (10%) and Senegal (9%). In absolute terms, South Africa has the highest number of borrowers with 3.3 million poor borrowers counted by its microfinance institutions, followed by Ethiopia (1.5 million) and Morocco (1 million), far ahead of Kenya (690,000), Ghana (630,000) and Egypt (560,000) (AMAF, 2009, pp. 36–37).

A large segment of the population living above the poverty line is in a situation of financial exclusion (considerable difference with 'developed' countries where the poverty line and financial exclusion overlap). In fact, as a rule, populations that are financially excluded, but not poor provide better repayment guarantees. Investigations by Zoetelief (2004, p. 63) in the region of Dodoma in Tanzania, for example, demonstrate that the *official villages* are more often clients of external financial organisations while women are more likely to take part in informal local groups. The doctoral research carried out by Aminata Sall in Senegal (2012) shows that microcredit beneficiaries in rural areas (Kolda in Mid Casamance) and in the working-class districts of the capital are far from being 'poor' and to an even lesser extent 'very poor' and that microcredit is one of the hierarchical strategies within local groups, instrumentalised by central power. Numerous detailed field surveys come to the same conclusion after analysing the social composition of the institutions' clientele. This trend has strengthened over time while the institutions, subject to pressure on the marketing of their services and the need to function independently without subsidies, have had to abandon their initial purpose of serving the poor. As lenders strive for financial balance, the proportion of poor people served tends to fall so that the institutions are able to reach their financial goals; in fact, the very definition of the 'poor target' among clients remains vague and subject to little control. For example, a social report on the RCPB credit union network in Burkina Faso states:

> 'Discussions mainly covered the exact content of the term "working population" used during the mission. Sometimes this referred to exclusively poor populations or to people in work, but at other times, the term was applied to the entire Burkina Faso population. This debate went on throughout the entire duration of the assessment and a consensus was never reached' (Coulibaly & Kedem, 2009, p. 4).

The first *caisses populaires* or credit unions were set up as early as 1972 in the south-east area of Upper Volta (which later became Burkina Faso) and at that time were subject to the authority of a project run by the Ministry of Agriculture and mainly focused on the agricultural sector. However, after 1987, a new approach meant these unions were able to expand their activity into the urban areas of Ouahigouya and Ouagadougou. The current role of the RCPB is to serve any person that does not have access to financial services. Poverty and/or exclusion are not applied as criteria when selecting its intervention areas (Coulibaly & Kedem, 2009, pp. 7–8).

In his research into microfinance in the region of Ogou in Togo, Agbodjan (2012) shows that the turnaround of FUCEC-Togo[6] after the crisis that affected it at the turn of the century was achieved by targeting a more urban clientele. This occurred to the detriment of the rural zones. Many of its rural agencies were closed, with numbers falling from 150 in 2000 to just 50 in 2008. The prevalence of urban outlets compared to rural agencies can be seen across the continent (Beck, Maimbo Samuel, Faye, & Triki Throuraya, 2011, p. 97).

Very few institutions have up-to-date poverty tracking indicators. When a microcredit scheme, especially a subsidised one, verifies its clients' poverty levels, it is not unusual to see that its clients have borrowed the name of better-off neighbours or relatives in order to be eligible for a loan. A very wide range of financial services are viewed by the microfinance institutions as an opportunity for expansion in order to reduce their costs (with potential local saturation effects). While microcredit is targeted at clients below the poverty line, it does nothing to help reduce inequalities in income and wealth; indeed, it actually increases them. The poorest social classes may, through mimicry in terms of their needs, experience greater frustrations and thus a sense of impoverishment (Servet, 2007b). If the benefits of microcredit felt by the non-poor populations are to have a positive effect on the poorest, there needs to be a trickle-down effect. In other words, if the rich are getting richer, this should have a positive effect on the incomes of the poorest. Yet the experience of development policies since the 1950s has far from demonstrated this (Hillenkamp & Servet, 2012). Microcredit targeting non-poor, but financially excluded populations has a positive effect in terms of financial inclusion. However, this is not the same as an increase in income and capital contributions which would benefit the populations with the lowest incomes.

It is therefore necessary to have sound knowledge of the socio-economic characteristics of the microcredit clients or beneficiaries (which is unusual) to prove that the 'poor' target is actually reached by the microcredit offering, to what proportion, and to demonstrate that there is a positive effect on the local economy. Otherwise, the impact is equivalent to that of injecting money into a locality to temporarily increase spending, but with only a very limited sustainable effect. Any effect on increased incomes mainly depends on financial and monetary flights outside the zone of injection.

Condition 2. The loan has to be used by borrowers to increase their productive capacities and not for consumption.

A second condition for the effectiveness of microcredit as a development tool, in the strictest sense of an increase in income, depends on how the loan is used. To generate income, the borrowers actually need to use it to increase their productive capacities or business assets. This is the image most stakeholders in microfinance give of the system: introduced as an economic initiative, it has long been reduced to the image of loans used to finance self-employment or micro-enterprises. Its main objective would be to increase income by developing micro-enterprise (mainly through support for existing entities and in particular their working capital).

Yet not all microcredit clients are self-employed. In some countries, they include low-income employees, for example civil servants in countries such as Cameroon or miners in South Africa. The over-indebtedness of those miners led to their violently suppressed revolt in the summer of 2012. Refusing to suffer shame for not being able to pay back their debts, they did not turn against the microcredit establishments, but their employers instead; they demanded pay increases so they could pay back their debts, which were repaid via direct debit from their bank accounts (Bateman, 2012; James, 2013).

When the loan is used for income-generating activities, there is an interesting difference between the sort of investments made by men and women in production facilities. According to a study by Gifford (2004, p. 73) in Kampala (Uganda), men start out with a minimum capital ten times higher than that of women; male activities also turn out to be much more profitable than those of women. As a general rule, the effectiveness of micro-loans designed to boost the economic activities of the poorest appears limited, mainly because they are short-term loans.

In many cases, in highly informal situations, we can observe high levels of fungibility of household financial resources, which renders any attempts to control the final use of the loans within goods- and services-producing micro-units unrealistic. There are moral complications relating to the uses of monetary resources too, which have been analysed by socio-economists (Guérin, 2003; Zelizer, 2005). These may include having to agree to the microcredit institution's rules regarding use of the funds for an income-generating activity. However, the funds may end up being used within a household or by the person for other purposes. Breaching the rules on the agreed use of the loan for productive investment may, however, be legitimised by constraint and necessity.

Bateman (2010, p. 29), referring to Finoscope, a study by FinMark Trust, states that only a small proportion of loans are actually intended to boost productive activities. In Uganda and Tanzania, for example, this percentage does not exceed 15%. The study concludes that 'the main reason for borrowing is to buy food. Thereafter, funerals, school fees and medical expenses become the most pressing needs. A whole host of studies have shown exactly the same thing in most other countries' (2010, p. 29,[7] see also p. 137 for South Africa). The report *Measuring Financing Inclusion* by Demirguc-Kunt and Klapper (2012a, p. 5), which uses the same source (the 2009 FinMark Trust Survey), indicates that in Kenya, saving and credit services are mainly used to overcome 'family problems' and less often for purposes directly related to the requirements of income-generating activities. Half of the amounts lent to poor families fall within this description. These loans are mainly used to meet consumption needs.

If we look at Equity Bank, one of the main microfinance institutions in Kenya and which is listed on the stock market, its annual report states that 30.43% of the total volume of its loans are consumer loans, 9.15% are for micro-enterprises and 2.95% for agriculture; the rest of its portfolio goes to small businesses (41.88%) and to medium-sized businesses (15.55%) (Equity Bank, 2012, p. 47, 78). The weight of small and medium-sized businesses in Equity Bank's loans can be correlated with the fact that it serves almost half of all of the country's microfinance institutions' clients (715,000 clients out of a total million and a half) and that, taken as a whole, these companies account for between 15 and 20% of all loans, while in most other countries, this rate barely exceeds 5%. It is sometimes as little as 2%.

Small loans often help with better management of household and personal expenditure and resources over time, as demonstrated in *Portfolio of the Poor* (Collins, Morduch, Rutherford, & Ruthven, 2009) which devoted part of its research to South Africa. Many populations use microcredit in the same way households in 'developed' countries use their credit cards; credit cards themselves are barely used at all in sub-Saharan Africa. In the central and western areas of the continent, only 16% of adults have a debit card (64% of bank account holders), but this percentage is much lower for credit cards with only 3% of adults having one. This figure falls to 2% in Senegal (Demirguc-Kunt & Klapper, 2012a, p. 36; Demirguc-Kunt & Klapper, 2012b, p. 8, 12).

The consumerist use of micro-loans does not lead to an overall increase in the resources devoted to the acquisition of additional productive assets. They may help with better management of family budgets by spreading income and expenditure,[8] but they do not have a direct positive impact visible in the clear expansion of income-generating activities and on revenues themselves. If the loans are used to purchase medicine or cover school fees, they may have an indirect positive effect. Nonetheless, an immediate repercussion in terms of higher income still remains exceptional. The study carried out by Agbodjan (2012) in the region of Ogou in Togo shows that, in certain cases, borrowers who use loans to finance an income-generating activity make considerable efforts when it comes to working hours and the mobilisation of domestic labour, especially children, in an attempt to reduce operating costs. However, things are so difficult that the activity is not always continued with once the loan has been repaid. It would therefore be useful for all studies into support for micro-enterprise through microcredit to take into account the survival rate of those activities, beyond the period that immediately follows the loan itself.

Condition 3. Where an investment is made, there need to be outlets for the activity thus financed.

A third microeconomic condition necessary for a micro-loan to have a direct positive effect on the borrower's income is that, where an investment is made, it must be in an activity for which there are market outlets. In fact, we often observe an imitation effect among those that benefit from small loans (Bateman, 2010; Ojong, 2013, pp. 103–104; Servet, 2006,

p. 413). This entrepreneurial mimicry considerably reduces the potential effect of the loans in generating additional resources, by increasing local competition within the same area of activity. We will also see this condition on a mesoeconomic level. The failure in Senegal of public support for small business creation among young university graduates (known as *operation maitrisards* in 1982), with many of those graduates moving into the transport sector, bakery and fishing (without real knowledge of how those sectors worked) illustrates these difficulties (Baumann, 2016, chap. 6).

The inadequacy (or lack) of surpluses engendered by microcredit contributes to over-indebtedness. To conceal it, this can lead to the rescheduling of loans and to decapitalisation with regard to repayment. The interest rates on loans publicised by the organisations are often much lower than the rates actually applied, if we take into account rescheduling and loans taken out to pay back others (taking out a loan with another organisation, directly or under a borrowed name, to pay back a first, second or even third loan). If we disregard these practices, then the positive effect of microcredit on income ultimately turns out to be overestimated.

Condition 4. The financial cost of the loan must be lower than the monetary benefit of the additional income-generating activity it finances.

A fourth microeconomic condition is that the cost of the loan, in terms of the interest rate and the commissions paid,[9] has to be lower than the return from the activity in which it is invested.

To address financial exclusion, one of the main difficulties for microcredit institutions in developing countries seeking to help low-income populations is the relatively high cost, per monetary unit lent, of providing small loans.[10] This is partly due to the average salary of a credit agent (and more generally of a manager) in relation to the volume lent. This difference is greater in sub-Saharan Africa than in South Asia, for example (the average salary in the sector is three times higher in Africa than on other continents according to Beck, et al., 2011, p. 97). This can be explained by higher banking performance in Africa than in the rest of the world (Monga, 2013). With African population density being lower than in the rest of the world, there are additional costs with significant regional and national differences; Rwanda, Burundi and Uganda are densely populated in contrast to Ethiopia, Zambia and Tanzania. This explains the additional time and travel required for the distribution of financial services.[11] These extra costs, the causes of which go further than demographic issues, apply to both microfinance and retail banks (Beck, et al., 2011, pp. 51–52, 63–64; Gelbard, Gulde, & Maino, 2014, p. 28). In Uganda, to hold a bank account costs the equivalent of a quarter of the GNP per capita. It is not therefore surprising that 54% of those who do not have an account cite bank charges as the reason for not having one (Demirguc-Kunt & Klapper, 2012b, p. 7).

The cost of loan distribution explains why microcredit favours the funding of more commercial activities than the craft sector, and crafts rather than agriculture.[12] According to the summary of the average interest rates per region in 2009 established by Roodman (2012, pp. 185–186), half of all microfinance organisations in sub-Saharan Africa charge a rate (after deduction of the rate of consumer price inflation) of less than 24%.[13] While interest rates are lower in South-East Asia (rates lower than 15% for half of the organisations) and slightly lower in Eastern Europe and Central Asia (23%), they are higher in Latin America and the Caribbean (rate under 28% for half of the organisations), in Eastern Asia and in the Pacific (rate lower than 29%), the Middle East and North Africa (rate lower than 32%). Here we should note that, contrary to various statements, these differences do not reflect the large number of stakeholders or the competition on the various microcredit markets, since the main credit providers could come to an agreement on the cost of credit and competition can be created due to factors other than price. It is also worth noting the extreme rates, with 5% of organisations applying interest rates (after deduction of the rate of consumer price inflation) of over 67% per year in sub-Saharan Africa, while these rates stand at 73% for the most expensive organisations in Latin America and the Caribbean, and *only* 61% in Eastern Asia and the Pacific, 48% in Eastern Europe and Central Asia, and 44% in South East Asia, the Middle East and North Africa.

Even if the interest rates published by microfinance organisations in Africa may appear lower than those in other parts of the world, it would be useful to compare those rates to the incomes from the activities carried out by those who take out credit. According to Roodman (2012, p. 186), 80% of micro-loans in the world are subject to interest rates no higher than 20% (after deduction of the rate of consumer price inflation). He describes this rate as low. However, when the interest paid is higher than the returns on an activity[14] (it should be noted that agricultural activities rarely yield more than 15%, or even 8%), loans are applied for to fund a portion of the activity (such as the purchase of fertilizers or seeds or for one-off labour requirements) leading to underpayment of the work and of the asset and therefore a drain on the resources of the agricultural sector to the financial sector, and from the rural sector to the urban sector. This was previously the case in Rwanda in the mutualist or cooperative savings and credit organisations, for example.

This is why there is a need for public and/or private subsidies to reduce the cost of lending in agricultural and rural areas, so as to increase the margin benefiting the borrower (Morvant-Roux, 2009). In Africa, poverty is very high among rural and agricultural populations.

When the loan is used for consumption, the debit transaction may become untenable for the borrower and lead to impoverishment, since the debit largely exceeds their capacity for repayment (Dichter & Harper, 2007; Guérin, Morvant-Roux, & Villarreal, 2013).

Condition 5. The person carrying out the activity must have sufficient managerial and technical capacities to see it through successfully.

A fifth condition for the success of microcredit is that the person carrying out the activity has the necessary managerial and technical skills. Credit alone does not suffice as support for micro-enterprise. Technical, financial and managerial training of the borrowers is an additional factor key to making sure that the loan is applied effectively (while leaving the beneficiary free to manage their business as they feel fit).

Let us return to the example of the Ogou region studied by Agbodjan (2012). Here, the grain marketing business is one of the main activities backed by microfinance. While we can see that this activity appears to be very profitable due to the big price difference between times of plenty and times of scarcity, there are nonetheless high barriers to entry to the trade. To make a profit, stakeholders need in-depth knowledge of the markets, information networks, the ability to negotiate prices and so on. Many women become over-indebted as they try to break into the market. Technical support is therefore vital, for example the United States Agency for International Development (USAID) provides technical support to one of the biggest collectives of women traders in the region, Akotche Tchikossan, a collective that fell into debt with the FUCEC (*Faîtière des Unités Coopératives d'Épargne et de Crédit*-Togo).

Considerable resources have to be devoted to technical and commercial professional support for people setting up an activity. These people need to develop their access to more information, upstream regarding supplies and downstream regarding potential clients. Their living areas need to be easy to access, both in rural and urban areas, especially since marginality and exclusion are prevalent.

The fact of belonging to a group where an activity is collective and not individual *may* be a further key to success (usually, when a group has easier access to outlets than an individual). An initiative taken in March 2012 by the Nigerian government to use microfinance to modernise the country's garages by grouping them into cooperatives is one example of this. A fund of around $6.3 million was set up for this purpose to finance modernisation of garage workshops across the country. If they wanted to benefit from this, garage owners had to form cooperatives of at least 10 members. To set up this network of cooperative garages, the National Automotive Council, a government agency reporting to the Ministry of Industry, intended to call on foreign components manufacturers or sponsors in a public-private partnership approach.

However, more often than not, the wider interpretation of microfinance combining funding and training/information policies has been gradually abandoned to the benefit of a minimalist, strictly financial approach to microcredit. This has tended to do away with the non-financial activities of the credit establishments, deemed too costly, to the benefit of more specialist financial skills, also explained by the fact that it is difficult to apply strong pressure for repayment while handling the non-financial aspects of client relations. Here again, there is a need for training and support to be provided at different levels (Régnier & Song-Naba, 2004; Song-Naba, 2010 for examples of Burkina Faso and Ghana).

> **Condition 6.** The capacity for micro-entrepreneurs to bear exposure to a higher level of risk is vital.

A sixth condition, at the level of the entity receiving the loan, is that borrowers must be able to bear a higher level of risk. Studies into poverty demonstrate that, more than low incomes, insecurity and the meagre availability of resources to deal with a crisis, sickness or the like, are what hinder the most deprived sections of the populations (Sossa, 2013 for Benin and West Africa in general). This is key, especially in areas where AIDS is prevalent and where the cost of treatment is high for many families' budgets (e.g. Gifford, 2004, p. 73, 82 and Gietema, 2009 for Uganda; Sossa, 2013, pp. 126–128, 155 for Benin; Smets & Bähre, 2004, p. 226 for South Africa). The high mortality rates due to higher prevalence of the virus in sub-Saharan Africa than in other parts of the world has a negative impact on loan repayment rates and even more so on the level of trust required in economic and financial relations. The prevalence of malaria, chikungunya and river blindness can have similar effects in certain areas.

What is more, insurance is a very limited market in Africa. According to Demirguc-Kunt, Klapper (2012b, p. 12), only 3% of adults in Africa are listed as having personally taken out health insurance and 6% of those working in agriculture, forestry or fishing have taken out harvest, bad weather or livestock insurance over the past twelve months.

The populations with the highest risk exposure tend, as a means of not increasing their risks, to turn towards less hazardous activities. Yet those activities have the lowest income levels. As such, when it comes to financial support, to guard against risks, these populations are more likely to have an immediate need for low-cost, rapid transfer services for migrants and more generally, savings and insurance services rather than loans to fund productive resources. It is vital that institutionalised welfare protection is developed to reduce social pressure (assistance, protection or solidarity) on micro-entrepreneurs' resources from their close circles. This leads to a need, in a context where public welfare protection is very limited, to combine microcredit with insurance (of a different kind) and secured savings. The *Measuring Financial Inclusion* report by Demirguc-Kunt and Klapper (2012a) shows that emergency requirements, and particularly health, are the most common reasons for taking out loans in developing countries. It is the reason most frequently mentioned, accounting for 11% of responses, followed by building a house and school fees at just 5%, paying for a wedding or funeral at 3% and buying a house or flat, also at 3%. It should be noted that school fees account for 8% of responses in sub-Saharan Africa. The percentage of adults surveyed stating emergency and healthcare requirements as the primary reason for taking out a loan reaches 30% in Sudan and Madagascar. We also note that 14% of adults making up the poorest fifth of the population say they have an outstanding loan (all types of loan taken together) for emergency or healthcare reasons, while this percentage is only 8% for the richest fifth (Demirguc-Kunt & Klapper, 2012a, p. 39). However, we also see that debtors in situations of indebtedness and with health issues encounter far more difficulties paying the loan back than if in financial difficulty.

TWO CONDITIONS AT MESOECONOMIC LEVEL

Impact studies carried out only among borrowers overlook the possibility that these loans distort local-level competition among micro-entrepreneurs; people who do not benefit from a loan may lose a portion of their clientele and see their income drop. We also need to be sure that the capital injected into micro-activities generates a better return to that invested in large or medium-sized companies. This criterion taking the size of the companies into account must also be considered for each sector of activity.

Condition 7. The gains made by beneficiaries of microfinance must not be obtained to the detriment of other micro-entrepreneurs.

The increased volume of activity for beneficiaries of microcredit must not lead to any form of unfair competition, through a reduced workload for other micro-entrepreneurs who have not benefited from microcredit. If microcredit enables certain stakeholders to acquire their inputs in greater quantities and thus at lower prices, it could well lead to a drop in their sales prices; it may also increase their capacity to advance goods to their own clients or obtain credit from their suppliers. Any fall in the turnover of competitors who have not benefited from microcredit may result in a transfer of business and thus of revenues from the latter to the former, having a neutral impact on the local economy overall.[15]

Condition 8. The average return from micro-activities must be higher than that from more capitalist activities.

One other condition for the success of microcredit at mesoeconomic level is the return on the micro-activities funded must be higher than that from more capitalist activities funded otherwise. The argument in favour of small loans is based on the illusion of a decline in the marginal productivity of capital anywhere, at any time. In other words, we can assume that returns and productivity fall with the size of the unit producing goods and services, as if in a continuous mathematical function. While this may be the rule for a single production unit (excluding productive activities that these days require a large dose of knowledge where production costs are falling, Rifkin, 2014; Servet, 2015b), it is not true on a global scale. We can also suppose that there is an average productivity depending on the company type (decreasing for one type of company and increasing according to the size of the company), and thus that productivity from large or medium-sized units is higher than small units and that within each of these categories, we can see that, beyond a certain size, productivity falls.

In fact, entrepreneurship is highly promoted among the poor in sub-Saharan Africa in national strategic plans to alleviate poverty, eclipsing other production models.[16] These strategic choices may have been encouraged by certain personalities appearing frequently in the media, such as Jacques Attali.[17] On 29 October 2012 in Abidjan, at a symposium on the main strategic guidelines for making microfinance a genuine tool for social and economic development in Côte d'Ivoire, he reaffirmed that this financial service was 'sound' and was an important tool in the fight against poverty because 'it creates growth and jobs, especially for young people'.[18]

Here, Côte d'Ivoire appears to fit in with the standard picture, or indeed the romantic, sub-Saharan illusions about microcredit. Yet if we compare these African poverty reduction plans and the contribution that microfinance was supposed to make to them, with the policies applied in two countries that have driven world growth over the last two decades – namely China and India – despite the recent slowdown in those countries, it is clear that economic growth has been founded on the promotion of companies of a certain size and the take-off of salaried industrial work. Although the microfinance service offering is also encouraged in Asian countries, it is more as a means of survival for certain segments of the population rather than as the main instrument in the policy to increase their income.

TWO CONDITIONS AT MACROECONOMIC LEVEL

Lastly, there are two macroeconomic conditions key to the success of microcredit. One concerns the risk that stimulation of borrowers' demand results in the widespread acquisition of imported goods. The other is the risk of a drain on resources due to the payment of interest or dividends to external institutions funding microcredit.

> **Condition 9.** The expenditure enabled by micro-loans must not result in the import of goods and an ensuing flight of resources.

The ninth condition is that the investment made using micro-loans results in spending within the country, on locally produced goods and services, and not the import of goods from abroad. Except of course where loans are used to buy medicines produced abroad and there is (hopefully) an improvement in health, which is a positive thing. Microcredit then, is a factor in human growth and development. However, the countries exporting the goods and services acquired using these loans will benefit from the economic effects of this demand, while locally the impact will not be immediate because the effect in the value chain created is limited. We can undoubtedly transpose to a macro level the results of a study carried out at meso level in 1997 in Conjunto Palmeiras, a poor district on the edge of Fortaleza in Brazil (Meyer, 2012, p. 9). It demonstrated that the district's poverty was less the cause of low incomes among its inhabitants than the flight of available resources (through expenditure) towards the town centre. This is why it is worthwhile introducing a local complementary currency and offering microcredit[19] in that currency to ensure the money circulates internally as far as possible.[20] The hoped-for effect would not so much be a higher percentage of purchases with the local currency, but instead greater awareness among district residents of the benefits of buying locally produced goods and services. I am not aware of similar studies in sub-Saharan Africa.

> **Condition 10.** The interest paid by borrowers or the dividends paid by local microcredit banks to the security holders must not lead to the flight of resources purely to the benefit of other countries.

The tenth condition for an overall positive effect of microcredit on incomes is that the interest paid by borrowers or the dividends paid out should not lead to a flight of resources purely to the benefit of external lenders or investors.

There has to be a proven local lack of financial resources for investment and consequently a need for capital inflow. Yet a high number of the countries with the lowest levels of per capita income in the world – but not only them – encounter excess liquidity in their banking establishments. Africa in particular suffers from a reluctance among its retail banks with regard to their national credit policy, which explains the excess liquidity (Gelbard et al., 2014, pp. 27–28). According to a study by the International Monetary Fund, this was the case in 2004 for 41 of a total of 44 sub-Saharan African countries; only Gambia, Malawi and Sierra Leone remained outside this count (Doumbia, 2011; Saxegaard, 2006; Schümperli Younossian, Fino, & Servet, 2007, p. 15; Beck, et al., 2011, p. 147, 195, 209–210). This excess liquidity did not end with the global recession. This was confirmed in the 2011 annual report on the Central African Economic and Monetary Community free zone (Ojong, 2013, pp. 180–181). In microfinance, the contribution of funds from external sources often substitutes (if we disregard the savings drained by the institution) funds that could have been raised locally.

Sub-Saharan Africa, which in 2011 benefited from just 8% of microfinance investment vehicles, drew fewer external profitable investments than other regions across the world (such as Latin America and the Caribbean with 37% or Central Asia and Europe with 34%). Although on a global level, similar proportions in the breakdown of these external financial contributions have been recorded since 2006, we might consider that sub-Saharan Africa, given the crises in the sector in certain countries outside this zone (such as Nicaragua, Bosnia, Morocco and India) and the tension felt on leading markets such as Cambodia, Bolivia, Peru and Mexico, would be more attractive in the near future for this kind of investment, in order to spread the risks: in 2011, contributions from microfinance vehicles in sub-Saharan Africa grew by 79% (Ojong, 2013, pp. 38–40).

Let us take the example of Equity Bank, a stock market-listed institution in Kenya which was a 'building society' offering mortgages when it was founded in 1984. It was declared insolvent by the country's central bank in 1993 and had to be restructured. Today, its main shareholder is Helios, a pan-African investment group which holds a 24.45% stake in its capital. Helios has also invested in electronic payment, mainly in Nigeria. The second shareholding group with a 7.66% stake is Britam (British-American Investments Company – Kenya) (Equity Bank, 2012, p. 7, 82). In addition, almost thirty funds have outstanding loans with Equity Bank, including one Luxembourg fund (Dexia), two Swiss funds (Blue Orchard and ResponsAbility), two Chinese funds, plus some Ugandan and Tanzanian funds (Equity Bank, 2012, p. 78). It should be noted that this microcredit bank has 112 agencies in Kenya plus subsidiaries in South Sudan, Rwanda, Tanzania and Uganda. Owing to Equity Bank's specific nature as an institution with foreign shareholders, because the loans are made available by foreign financial groups to African microcredit institutions a portion of the interest paid by small borrowers leaves the country. However, the weight of mutualist or cooperative-type institutions in sub-Saharan Africa, especially in French-speaking countries, reduces the flight of capital through this domestic mobilisation of savings (Beck, et al., 2011, p. 95).

International guarantee funds could help address the situation of excess liquidity and drive home-grown financial dynamics (Fino & Vincent, 2007; Servet, 2007a). Similarly, instead of credit, the various forms of venture capital involvement can play a positive role when they follow a solidarity approach (such as the Africa Fund backed by Garrigue in France, operating in sub-Saharan Africa, or more recently crowdfunding with Babyloan with its first action in Benin).

The idea of pairing microcredit with local currencies also follows the logic of endogenising financial resources. However, these experiences, familiar in Brazil and Central America which are developing and emerging countries, are still largely unknown in Africa at the current time.

CONCLUSION

At micro, meso and macro levels, the success of microcredit as an effective economic and financial tool to alleviate poverty depends on a number of conditions. These conditions mainly concern the target clientele, the productive or consumerist use of the loans, the existence of a solvent demand for the extra production supposedly engendered by the loans, the cost of the credit being lower than the profitability of the activity funded (or potential impoverishment), the risks, on the one hand, of a flight of local resources out of the country due to interest or dividends paid by microfinance establishments and, on the other hand, imbalance between the international flows of goods and services thus instigated.

It is unusual to find these 10 conditions all perfectly fulfilled at once.

In a growing number of countries, as microcredit becomes more widespread, the over-indebtedness of borrowers increases (because the income earned is not enough to cover the cost of the loans, many of which are used for consumption).[21] There is also a saturation effect with demand for loans in certain areas.[22] If we look solely at the economic impact of microcredit, its supposed 'revolution' has therefore been a failure (Guérin, 2015; Servet, 2015a). Its legitimisation needs to draw on other arguments. Given the failures and the rise in unpaid debts, when the microcredit bubble bursts in one region or another, we can embark upon an unending debate on whether there is a microcredit crisis or in fact several crises.

In 2011, there was a fall in the number of microcredit clients across the world, the first since its emergence in the 1990s. According to the State of the Microcredit Summit Campaign Report 2012, on a global level, the number of clients reached 205 million in 2010, but dropped to 195 million in 2011; among those clients, the number deemed 'poor' fell from 138 million to 125 million. However, microcredit continues to grow in Sub-Saharan Africa, with the number of clients rising from 10.7 million in 2009 to 12.6 million in 2010 and 14.2 million in 2011 (highly contrasted with the Asia-Pacific zone where the number of microfinance clients fell by more than 15 million, while in Latin America and the Caribbean the number stagnated). According to the census carried out by Mix Market in 2005 (quoted by Attali, 2014, p. 244), there were 4.5 million active borrowers for a portfolio of $1.3 billion. Those numbers had almost doubled by 2012: 7.3 million active borrowers and $6.3 billion in loans. This can mainly be explained by the fact that microcredit is much less widespread in sub-Saharan Africa than it is now in Asia-Pacific and Latin America. According to a survey carried out in eighteen sub-Saharan African countries, an average 36% of the population are aware that a microfinance service offering exists in their community, while 46% say they do not have local access to these services; only 18% have never heard of it. These percentages vary considerably from one country to another. While the proportion of those who know there is an offering in their area stands at 65% in Malawi, 63% in Uganda, 57% in Kenya and 56% in Senegal,[23] the numbers are lower, with less than half the population aware in the fourteen other countries (with very low percentages in Zimbabwe (15%) where 39% of the population had never heard of it, in the Democratic Republic of the Congo (16%) where 22% were unaware and Côte d'Ivoire where 18% did not know about it (Beck, et al., 2011, p. 104)). This explains the low penetration of the microcredit sector among its target, the population living below the national poverty rate. The percentage of borrowers is 2.2% for the entire continent (4.3% in East Africa, but 1.6% in South Africa, 0.4% in Central Africa and 1.1% in West Africa; the continent's average is raised by North Africa with a rate of 7.2% (Beck, et al., 2011, p. 92)).[24] Microfinance in sub-Saharan Africa has thus not (yet) encountered the effects of saturation and (sometimes fierce) competition it meets in other parts of the world. This is what might make the continent attractive to organisations responsible for profitable investments, with a 1.4 million increase in the number of clients between 2011 and 2012. Nonetheless, the national averages may conceal the fact that the offering is sometimes highly concentrated in certain localities, a potential cause for a future crisis.

To achieve success in sub-Saharan Africa, or to reinvent itself and thus avoid the growth crises encountered in Bosnia, Andhra-Pradesh (South-East India), Morocco or Nicaragua, the growth of microcredit should go hand in hand with adequate measures to address its economic, social and cultural limitations. Here, as elsewhere, its necessary reform has not been tackled adequately, especially with the widespread commercialisation of this financial service[25] and the constraints that it brings. However, in the southern Sahara, lessons could be learned from the various failures of microcredit, so that the same mistakes are not made by the public authorities in their poverty reduction strategic plans and by those who might see investment in the African microcredit establishments as an opportunity less readily available elsewhere.

NOTES

1. See the example given in Note 5.

2. To really get a grasp of the reasons behind this economism, Pierre Bourdieu's thoughts on the issue are certainly enlightening. In *Manet une révolution symbolique* (Paris, Seuil/Raisons d'agir, 2013, p. 577), he decries: 'the persistence, in people's minds, of a washed-out form of Marxism, which is very difficult to shake off, not because it is dominant (in fact, it never was) but because it is rampant, slithering as trite common sense in pretentious discussions'. He adds: 'The current success of neoliberalism among journalists and in a section of the intelligentsia might have been boosted by the survival of the Marxist primacy granted to the economy'.

3. See also his more recent presentation on the evolution of microcredit in South Africa (Bateman, 2012), Bosnia (Bateman, 2011; Bateman, Sinkovic, & Skare, 2012). It is also interesting to read the example of the operating issues of LAPO in Nigeria, which financiers from the North refuse to acknowledge publicly (in Sinclair, 2012, p. 83 et seq.).

4. Nonetheless, certain econometricians seem to neglect recent works highlighting the failure to prove the positive effects of microcredit. They still appear incredibly gullible when it comes to microcredit. We can quote, for instance, a study published in *L'Agefi* (17 May 2013), supervised by Jean-Louis Arcand, at the request of Blue Orchard to assess the alleviation of poverty among microcredit users (Ruche, 2013). Also see the article published in *Globe* in autumn 2012 entitled 'Women's Micro-Finance as a Poverty Alleviating Strategy'. Its author, Martina Viarengo (2012), until then mainly known for econometric work on education, contributes to the Centre for Finance and Development in Geneva headed by Jean-Louis Arcand. This group of researchers is backed by Genevan financier Ivan Pictet's foundation. Pictet is one of the main shareholders in the second largest Swiss (and international) investment fund in the microcredit sector. We might ask whether this is the reason for this very complacent, indeed naïve, publication regarding the new usurers in microcredit by this young professor who, since 2012, has also featured on the World Economic Forum website in association with its Global Agenda Council on Women's Empowerment (http://www.weforum.org/global-agenda-councils/martina-viarengo). This Council is one of the main organisations rooted in a neoliberal ideology that is increasingly condemned as being the cause of the woes experienced by microcredit. The denouncement of academics' complicity with high finance and the stock market in Charles Ferguson's film *Inside Job* (2010) actually goes far beyond this sphere.

5. With regard to this method of analysing the processes of financial inclusion, see the summarised presentation in Servet (2006, pp. 26–28).

6. More than 60% of microcredit beneficiaries in Togo are clients of FUCEC-Togo (*Faîtière des Unités Coopératives d'Épargne et de Crédit*-Togo) according to CAS-IMEC (*Cellule d'appui et de suivi des institutions mutualistes ou coopératives d'épargne et de crédit*) data.

7. The overview study concludes that 'the main reason for borrowing money is to buy food. Thereafter, funerals, school fees and medical expenses become the

most pressing needs. A whole host of studies have shown exactly the same thing in most other countries.'

8. It would no doubt be useful to look at the link between a loan from a microcredit institution and the regular receipt of funds sent by family members in other countries, insofar as these transfers are seen as a loan repayment guarantee by the credit agencies. In fact, in sub-Saharan Africa, these transfers play an important role in the financial inclusion of populations. Across the world, an average 14% of bank account holders and 7% of adults use a bank account for this kind of transfer, but these percentages stand at 38% for bank account holders and 9% of adults in sub-Saharan Africa. 66% of bank account holders in Somalia resort to this, 55% in Zimbabwe and 45% in Sierra Leone (Demirguc-Kunt, & Klapper, 2012b, p. 9).

9. Concerning microfinance interest rates, see Rosenberg, Gaul, Ford, and Tomilova (2013) and the special feature in no. 26 of ADA (Hudon & Mauro, 2014). For the representation of the interest rate as a profit margin for the lender, see Baumann (1998).

10. The significant rise in money transfers via mobile phone is likely to considerably reduce the cost of financial transactions, because it can draw on the reduction in marginal costs. In June 2013, nine African countries had more Mobile Money users than holders of an account in a formal financial institution. Concerning these mobile uses in Africa, see Tchouassi (2012) and the work of Susan Johnson from the University of Bath, in particular in Kenya [http://www.bath.ac.uk/sps/staff/susan-johnson/].

11. This may explain why mutualist saving and loan systems are more common in sub-Saharan Africa, thanks to coverage by the basic contributions of a number of transactions and thus of certain costs (Périlleux, 2011). See also the greater role of savings (Beck, et al., 2011, p. 95).

12. See the comparative analysis of the situation of rural and urban saving and credit cooperatives in West Africa in Ouédraogo (Gentil, 2008, pp. 237–257) and the case of the FONGS in Senegal, an innovation for the financing of investment in family agriculture (Aminata Ndiaye in Doligez, Fall, & Oualy, 2012, pp. 141–155).

13. This is due to the relative cost of financial resources for microfinance: greater importance of savings and application of solidarity or ethical financing, etc. (Beck, et al., 2011, pp. 95–96). From this point of view, more widespread commercialisation of microcredit in sub-Saharan Africa could, if it increased the number of clients as in Latin America, all things being equal, considerably raise the cost of credit.

14. Here we can compare the perversities induced by the subprime mortgages (as analysed by Pérez in 2010) with the commercialisation of microcredit. The financialisation process of the subprimes lies downstream: the loans are granted not on the basis of the borrowers' repayment capacity but on the value of the mortgage, and then packaged together. With microcredit, the process begins upstream with the specialist institutions creating 'vehicles' or funds used to finance the microcredit institutions, which then lend out the money themselves. The anomalies induced by speculative financialisation boil down to the same thing. The microcredit institutions and credit agents are pushed to make money, and funds are thus lent to clients without much concern as to whether or not they will improve the borrowers' situation and will give them the ability to keep up their repayments; the main concern is

for incentives and repayment pressure. The race to get clients explains the collapse of certain microcredit markets and in Africa of certain microcredit institutions, especially in South Africa and Cameroon.

15. Here, we should point out that microcredit institutions very often compete with one another for the same clients; those who come across as stronger and more reliable are therefore more profitable. More loans are therefore granted to those clients, which reinforces their indebtedness. What can be seen at client level is a concentration of microfinance providers within the same regions. To minimise risks, they generally tend not to diversify their locations very far. We can often find several microfinance institutions on the same street in the same town, (Ojong, 2013, p. 208 gives the example of Bamenda in Cameroon). A social report by the RCPB in Burkina Faso notes that less than 5% of this institutions' credit unions are located in areas with no other microfinance or bank branch present (Coulibaly & Kedem, 2009, p. 8).

16. Here, we should highlight that recent performance in terms of growth in the GNP in sub-Saharan Africa, which has led to talk about 'African lions' (after the Asian 'dragons' and 'tigers' and according to the title of a study by American firm McKinsey, 'Lions on the move: The progress and potential of African economies' published in 2010), is mainly due to the boom in raw material exports and not down to local micro-entrepreneurial success.

17. In Attali (2014), it is stated that in Africa microfinance represents 'huge potential for growth and innovation' without mentioning a single impact study showing a positive effect of microcredit on populations on the continent or in a particular country. Confusion remains between the intentions expressed by the organisations and those who finance them, and the supposed results, except in cases of poor management by the organisations or the unsuitability of financial products.

18. http://news.abidjan.net/h/443914.html; http://news.abidjan.net/h/443899.html; http://www.planetfinance.org/france/FR/actualite.php?page = 3; http://microfinance.tresor.gouv.ci/index.php/programmes.

19. It should be noted that this microcredit in local currency is intended to finance consumer goods. Productive microcredit is granted in the national currency, but may be repaid in the local currency.

20. Local complementary currencies are not very well developed in sub-Saharan Africa. They are mainly found in South Africa, Senegal and Kenya (Dissaux, 2013). However, they are generally unrecognised or even suppressed, as illustrated by the arrest in Mombassa, Kenya at the end of May 2013 of five promoters of Bangla Pesa, a project headed by NGO Koru Kenya, two weeks after the introduction of these currency coupons (Benyawa, 2013; regarding this project, see: http://koru.or.ke/bangla and http://coastvibes.wordpress.com/2013/06/09/the-truth-behind-bangla-pesa/). This came after the Eco-Pesa case when coupons were circulated in 2010 in Kongewea as part of a project with environmental objectives (cleaning up the shanty town) and the goal of boosting local trade dynamics. A local parliamentarian Badi Twalib, protested against the arrests of the local currency's promoters and against accusations of currency forgery (Anonyme, 2013), and four months after the arrest of the Bangla Pesa promoters, charges were dropped and the project was allowed to continue.

21. A study of the clients' over-indebtedness as one of the main causes of the microcredit crisis in a still limited number of countries, but also the risk of crisis in a much higher number of countries forms the core of the research programme *MFI Crises*, http://www.microfinance-in-crisis.org/, backed by the European Investment Bank and headed by Isabelle Guérin (IRD), for which I have carried out field studies in Morocco, Nicaragua and in the Dominican Republic.

22. Guérin and Servet (2015) and Ojong (2013, pp. 232–233) note that in his sample of surveys in North-West Cameroon, 7.1% are not clients of any microcredit organisation because they refuse to be and they find that the financial services from the *njangis* (tontines), widespread in this region, suit them better.

23. For an analysis of the diversity of microfinance operations in Senegal, see Doligez et al. (2012).

24. With regard to savers, the percentages are 4.1 % for the entire continent (10.1% in East Africa, but 3% in South Africa, 1.2% in Central Africa, 3.3% in West Africa and 0.1% in North Africa) according to Beck, et al. (2011, p. 92).

25. Taking the example of Senegal, Baumann and Fall Mouhamedoune (2013) clearly demonstrates that the cooperative and mutualist institutions are not a sufficient safeguard. Regarding the management constraints weighing down on stakeholders in microfinance subject to pressure on the commercialisation of financial products, see La Torre and Vento (2006), and for the constraints on companies funded this way, see Guérin (2015), Mader (2015) and Servet (2015a, 2015b).

ACKNOWLEDGEMENT

I would especially like to thank the following people for their suggestions, not all of which I have been able to include here: Edoé Agbodjan (University of Ottawa), Eveline Baumann (IRD Paris), Nathanael Ojong, Yves Somé and Théophile Sossa (former PhD students at IHEID Geneva), the researchers on the Microfinance in Crisis research project backed by the European Investment Bank [http://www.microfinance-in-crisis.org/], the organisers of and participants in the session *Managing other people's money: financial services in sub-Saharan Africa after structural adjustment* at the *5th European Conference on African Studies* in Lisbon on 27 June 2013, and two anonymous readers.

REFERENCES

Agbodjan, E. D. (2012). *Déterminants monétaires de la performance sociale des institutions de microfinance: Une analyse à partir du cas de la région de l'Ogou (Togo)*. Thèse de doctorat en études du développement. IHEID, Genève.

AMAF (Africa Microfinance Action Forum)/WWB (Women's World Banking). (2009). *Diagnostic pour l'action: La microfinance en Afrique*, [s.l.], 143 pages.

Anonyme. (2013). MP supports the use of Bangla Pesa … Says it not money but just a food voucher. *The Kenyan Daily Post*, June 3. Retrieved from http://www.kenyan-post.com/2013/06/mp-supports-use-of-bangla-pesa-says-it.html.

Attali, J. (2014). Les nouveaux visages de la microfinance en Afrique. *Revue d'économie financière*, *116*, 243–258.

Balkenhol, B. (Ed.). (2009). *Microfinance et politique publique [Microfinance and public policy: Outreach, performance and efficiency]*. London: Palgrave-Macmillan/ILO.

Banerjee, A., Karlan, D., & Zinman, J. (2015). Six randomized evaluations of microcredit. Introduction and further steps. *American Economic Journal: Applied Economics*, *7*(1), 1–21.

Bateman, M. (2010). *Why doesn't microfinance work? The destructive rise of local neoliberalism*. London: Zed Books.

Bateman, M. (Ed.). (2011). *Confronting microfinance: Undermining sustainable development*. Sterling, VA: Kumarian Press.

Bateman, M. (2012). *The rise and fall of microcredit in post apartheid South Africa* (English éd.). Le Monde diplomatique. Retrieved from http://mondediplo.com/blogs/the-rise-and-fall-of-microcredit-in-post. Accessed on November 14, 2012.

Bateman, M., Sinkovic, D., Marinlko, S. (2012). *The Contribution of the microfinance model to Bosnia's post-war reconstruciton and development: How to destroy an economy and society without really trying*. ÖFSE (Österreichische Forschungsstiftung für Internationale Entwickung), Working Paper 36. Retrieved from http://www.oefse.at/Downloads/publikationen/WP36_microfinance.pdf

Baumann, E. (1998). Chez nous, c'est 10 % par mois! Coût du crédit et représentation du temps en milieu populaire au Sénégal. In L. Harding, L. Marfaing, & M. Sow (Eds.), *Les opérateurs économiques et l'État au Sénégal*. Studien zur Afrikanischen Geschichte (Vol. 19, pp. 189–202). Hamburg: LIT.

Baumann, E. (2016). *Sénégal: Le travail dans tous ses états*. Rennes. Presses universitaires de Rennes.

Baumann, E., & Fall Mouhamedoune, A. (2013). Senegal: The rise and foretold fall of microfinance? *Third European research conference on microfinance*, 10–12 June, 2013, University of Agder, Norway, 15 pages.

Beck, T., Maimbo Samuel, M., Faye, I., & Triki Throuraya, M. (2011). *Financing Africa through the crisis and beyond* (p. 303).Washington, DC: World Bank.

Benyawa, L. (2013). NGO accused of supplying illegal tender. *Standard Digital*. Retrieved from http://www.standardmedia.co.ke/?articleID=2000084855&story_title=ngo-accused-of-supplying-illegal-tender. Accessed on May 30, 2013.

Bourdieu, P. (2013). Manet.Unerévolutionsymbolique, Paris, Seuil.

Collins, D., Morduch, J., Rutherford, S., & Ruthven, O. (2009). *Portfolios of the poor: How the world's poor live on $2 a day*. Princeton, NJ: Princeton University Press.

Coulibaly, M., & Kedem, S. (2009). *Rapport social Évaluation SPI du RCPB-Burkina Faso*. Bilan social de la Confédération des Institutions Financières et de ses membres 2008–2009, 16 pages.

Defoe, D. (1722/1989). *Moll Flanders* (p. 182). Penguin Books.

Demirguc-Kunt, A., & Klapper, L. F. (2012a, April). *Measuring financial inclusion: The global findex database* (p. 61). Washington: World Bank Development Research Group, Finance and Private Sector Development Team.

Demirguc-Kunt, A., & Klapper, L. F. (2012b). *Financial inclusion in Africa: An overview*. World Bank Policy Research Working Paper No. 6088, June, 18 pages. Washington: World Bank.

Dichter, T., & Harper, M. (Eds.). (2007). *What's wrong with microfinance?* Warwickshire: Practical Action Publishing.

Dissaux, T. (2013). *Développement endogène et monnaies complémentaires sur le continent africain* (p. 6). Paris: Institut Veblen pour les réformes économiques.

Doligez, F., Fall, F. S., & Oualy, M. (Eds.). (2012). *Expériences de microfinance au Sénégal*. Paris: CRES/Karthala.

Doumbia, S. (2011). Surliquidité bancaire et "sous-financement de l'économie". Une analyse du paradoxe de l'UEMOA. *Tiers Monde, 205*, 151–170.

Duvendack, M., Palmer-Jones, R., Copestake, J. G., Hooper, L., Loke, Y., & Rao, N. (2011). *What is the evidence of the impact of microfinance on the well-being of poor people?* London: EPPI-Centre, Social Science Research Unit, Institute of Education, University of London.

Equity Bank. (2012). *Annual report and financial statements*. Nairobi: Author, p. 87. Accessed on December 31, 2012.

Ferguson, C. H. (2010). *Inside job, documentary movie*. Retrieved from http://documentary-movie.com/inside-job/

Fernando, J. L. (Ed.). (2006a). *Microfinance. Perils and prospects* (pp. XIV–242). London, New York: Routledge.

Fernando, J. L. (Ed.). (2006b). Introduction. Microcredit and empowerment of women: Blurring the boundary between development and capitalism. (pp. 1–42); Microcredit and empowerment of women: Visibility without power (pp. 187–238). *Microfinance. Perils and prospects*. London, New York: Routledge.

Fino, D., & Vincent, F. (2007). Financer le risque: Un nouveau projet pour la coopération internationale. La couverture du risque pour accéder à des ressources financières: L'expérience du Fonds international de Garantie (FIG). *Autrepart, 44*, 37–52.

Gelbard, E., Gulde, A.-M., & Maino, R. (2014). Développement financier en Afrique subsaharienne: Les enjeux pour une croissance soutenue. *Revue d'économie financière, 116*, 19–42.

Gietema, S. (2009). *Microfinance and HIV/AIDS: Who cares? A case study of Uganda* (p. 35). The Hague: Hivos, Advance Master in International Development.

Gifford, J. L. (2004). Utilizing, accumulation and protecting livelihood assets: The role of urban informal financial services in Kampala, Uganda. In H. Lont & O. Hospes (Eds.). *Livelihood and microfinance: Anthropological and sociological perspectives on savings and debt* (pp. 69–88). Delft: Eburon Academic Publishers.

Guérin, I. (2003). *Femmes et économie solidaire* (p. 234). Paris: La Découverte.

Guérin, I. (2015). *La microfinance et ses dérives: Émanciper, discipliner ou exploiter?* Paris: illustrations de Marc Roesch.

Guérin, I., Morvant-Roux, S., & Villarreal, M. (Eds.). (2013). *Over-indebtedness and financial inclusion*. London: Routledge.

Guérin, I., & Servet, J.-M. (2015). Microcredit crises and the absorption capacity of local economies. In I. Guérin, M. Labie, & J.-M. Servet (Eds.), *The crises of microcredit* (pp. 54–70). New York, NY: Zed Books.

Hillenkamp, I., & Servet, J.-M. (2012). La pauvreté, enjeu international. In C. Lequesne (Ed.), *Frontière ceriscope*. Paris: CERI, Sciences Po Paris. Retrieved from http://ceriscope.sciences-po.fr/pauvrete

Hudon, M., & Mauro, A. (Eds.). (2014). *Taux d'intérêt en microfinance: Abus ou nécessité?* Luxembourg: 26e Midi de la microfinance, ADA.

James, D. (2013, June). Regulating credit: tackling the redistribution of neoliberalism, Paper for presentation at ECAS, Lisbon, 32 pages.

La Torre, M., & Vento, G. (Eds.). (2006). *Microfinance*. Basingstoke: Palgrave Macmillan.

Lont, H., & Hospes, O. (Eds.). (2004). *Livelihood and microfinance: Anthropological and sociological perspectives on savings and Debt*. Delft: Eburon Academic Publishers.

Mader, P. (2015). *The political economy of microfinance: Financialising poverty*. London: Palgrave.

Maes, J. P., & Reed, L. R. (2012). *État de la Campagne du Sommet sur le microcrédit*. Rapport, Washington, DC.

Meyer, C. (2012). *Les finances solidaires comme biens communs durables: Étude de cas de la Banque communautaire de développement Palmas (Brésil)*. Université Libre de Bruxelles, Faculté des sciences sociales et politiques, Mémoire de master en sciences de la population et du développement sour la direction de Marek Hudon, Bruxelles.

Monga, C. (2013, June 27). Synthèse de la session managing other people's money: Financial services in sub-Saharan Africa after structural adjustment. 5th European Conference on African Studies à Lisbonne le.

Morvant-Roux, S. (Ed.). (2009). *Rapport exclusion et liens financiers 2008–2009*. Paris: Economica.

Ojong, N. D. (2013). *Microfinance, informal financial mechanisms and low-income populations: An analysis of the life-styles of low income populations in the North West Region of Cameroon*. Thèse pour le doctorat en études du développement [version provisoire], IHEID, Genève.

Ouédraogo, A., & Gentil, D. (Eds.). (2008). *La microfinance en Afrique de l'Ouest* (p. 311). Histoires et innovations. Paris: CIF/Karthala.

Pérez, R. (2010). Analyse de la crise financière ou crise de l'analyse financière? *Revue Management et avenir, 35*, 170–194.

Périlleux, A. (2011). *Governance and growth of cooperatives in microfinance*. Thèse de doctorat, Université de Mons, Bruxelles.

Régnier, P., & Song-Naba, F. (2004). Plaidoyer pour une combinaison de l'appui financier et technique aux petites entreprises dans les pays en développement africains. *Techniques financières et développement, 77*(décembre), 14–24.

Rifkin, J. (2014). *La nouvelle société du coût marginal zéro: L'internet des objets, l'émergence des communaux collaboratifs et l'éclipse du capitalisme*. Paris: Les Liens qui libèrent.

Roodman, D. (2012). *Due diligence: An impertinent inquiry into microfinance*. Washington, DC: Brookings Institution Press/Centre for Global Development.

Rosenberg, R., Gaul, S., Ford, W., & Tomilova, O. (2013). *Microcredit interest rates and their determinants*. Washington, DC: CGAP/Mix/KfW.

Ruche, S. (2013). Les enseignements post-crise. Microfinance. *L'Agefi, 17* mai, Reproduit In Revue de presse du Graduate Institute (Geneva). Retrieved from http://graduateinstitute.ch/files/live/sites/iheid/files/sites/international_economics/shared/international_economics/prof_websites/wyplosz/Media/RSR%202013.05.15.pdf

Sall, A. (2012). *Les stratégies et initiatives des femmes dans le secteur de la microfinance. Le cas du Sénégal*, Thèse pour le doctorat en sociologie sous la direction des professeurs Denys Cuche et Jean Copans soutenue à l'Université Sorbonne Paris Cité.

Saxegaard, M. (2006). *Excess Liquidity and effectiveness of monetary policy: Evidence from Sub-Saharan Africa*. IMF Working Paper, WP/06/115. Washington, IMF, 50 pages.

Schümperli Younossian, C., Fino, D., & Servet, J.-M. (2007). De l'extérieur à la mobilisation des ressources locales. In *Financer le développement par la mobilisation des ressources locales, Annuaire suisse de politique de développement* (Vol. 26, no. 2, p. 260). Genève: IUED.

Servet, J.-M. (2006). *Banquiers aux pieds nus*. Paris: Odile Jacob.

Servet, J.-M. (2007a). Les fonds de garantie, une pratique de solidarité et de mobilisation des ressources pour le développement. In *Annuaire suisse de politique de développement* (Vol. 26, no. 2, pp. 143–156). Genève: IUED.

Servet, J.-M. (2007b). Les illusions des objectifs du Millénaire. In E. Lafaye de Michaux, É. Mulot, & P. Ould-Ahmed (Eds.), *Institutions et développement: La fabrique institutionnelle et politique des trajectoires de développement* (pp. 63–88). Rennes: Presses universitaires.

Servet, J.-M. (2015a). *La vraie révolution du microcrédit*. Paris: Odile Jacob.

Servet, J.-M. (2015b). Un douteux retour du partage et de la gratuité. In C. Vershuur, I. Guérin, & I. Hillenkamp (Eds.), *Une économie solidaire peut-elle être féministe? Homo oeconomicus, mulier solidaria* (pp. 139–151). Paris: L'Harmattan.

Sinclair, H. (2012). *Confessions of a microfinance heretic: How Microfinance lost its way and betrayed the poor*. San Francisco, CA: Berett-Koehler Publishers.

Smets, P., & Bähre, E. (2004). When coercion takes over: The limits of social capital in microfinance schemes. In L. Hotze & H. Otto (Eds.), *Livelihood and microfinance: Anthropological and sociological perspectives on savings and debt* (pp. 215–236). Delft: Eburon Academic Publishers.

Song-Naba, F. (2010). *Promotion des petites entreprises de transformation agroalimentaire au Burkina Faso et au Ghana*. Thèse de doctorat en études du développement, IHEID, Genève.

Sossa, T. (2013). *La microassurance santé comme modèle alternatif de protection sociale: Cas des mutuelles de santé dans le département du Mono au Bénin*. Thèse pour le doctorat en études du développement, IHEID, Genève.

Stewart, R., van, R. C., Korth, M., Chereni, A., Rebelo Da Silva, N., & de Wet, T. (2012, September). *Do micro-credit, micro-savings serve as effective financial inclusion interventions enabling poor people, and especially women, to engage in meaningful economic opportunities in low and middle income countries: A systematic review of the evidence* (p. 216). London: UKAid/Center for Anthropological Research, University of Johannesburg, EPPI Center, Institute of Education – University of London.

Tchouassi, G. (2012). Can mobile phones really work to extend banking services to the Unbanked. Empirical lessons from selected sub-Saharan Africa countries. *International Journal of Developing societies, 1*(2), 70–81.

Viarengo, M. (2012). Women's micro-finance as a poverty alleviating strategy. *Globe: La revue de l'Institut* (Genève), (10), 16–17.
Zelizer, V. (2005). La signification sociale de l'argent, *trad.* Paris: Seuil.
Zoetelief, J. (2004). Microfinance from below: Exploring rural livelihoods in Tanzania. In H. Lont & O. Hospes (Eds.), *Livelihood and microfinance: Anthropological and sociological perspectives on savings and debt* (pp. 57–65). Delft: Eburon Academic Publishers.

LOCAL SYSTEMS OF EXCHANGE IN KABYLIA: ECONOMY OF RECIPROCITY AND CONSTRAINT OF TRADITIONS

Belaïd Abrika, Bernard Paranque and Cécile Perret

ABSTRACT

Purpose – *In a period of moral and economic crisis all the alternative solutions to finance economic activities are interesting to study, specifically those embedded in solidarity practices. The nature of the ties (bonding ties, linking ties or bridging ties) and solidarities (institutional solidarity, formal or informal solidarity, intergenerational solidarity) must then be examined.*

Methodology/approach – *The exchanges between the people are governed by three different modes: the market, the redistribution and the reciprocity which acts to maintain the relation (Lavoué, Jézequel, & Janvier, 2010, p. 34). The exchanges are not only of economic order and also participate in the symbolic world. Our main question is: can the relations of exchange become emancipated from the reification? We illustrate this chapter with the case of the Kabylian traditional society and market (Benet, 1957–1975) where the practices of exchanges are not*

Finance Reconsidered: New Perspectives for a Responsible and Sustainable Finance
Critical Studies on Corporate Responsibility, Governance and Sustainability, Volume 10, 229–243

ISSN: 2043-9059/doi:10.1108/S2043-905920160000010029

only of economic order (redistribution ...) but also matter with the symbolic world (honour).

Findings – *Even today, in Kabylia, the survival of an ancestral social organisation (tajmaat) which has anchored in tradition and rooted values (tirugza) and practices (tiwiza) sometimes allows the local populations to offer the missing public goods or the solidarity towards those who need help (elders, orphans).*

Originality/value – *In traditional Kabyle society, exchange practices are not only economic in nature (they contribute to mutual assistance, redistribution, etc.), but are also symbolic.*

Keywords: Social ties; trade and markets; embeddedness; Kabylia

INTRODUCTION

For Marx, 'man as a generic being, in his Gattungswesen, is a function of society, not of the economy' while for Weber, in traditional social orders, the lure of profit and thirst for wealth 'are limited by the ethos of reciprocity that permeates family and neighbourly relations' (Caillé & Laville, 2007, p. 80). Polanyi takes things further, deconstructing the hypothesis of the naturality of homo economicus, that calculating individual who only thinks about maximising his utility. According to him, the exchanges made on markets do not necessarily occur according to the commercial mechanism theorised by economic science: we should not confuse trade and market (Caillé & Laville, 2007, p. 80) or circulation and mercantile exchange (Testart, 2007).

Exchanges between people are governed by three distinct modes: the market, redistribution and reciprocity which act to maintain the relationship (Lavoué, Jézequel, & Janvier, 2010, p. 34). While it is noteworthy that the popularity of the social and solidarity economy rises in periods of financial crisis, and during the moral crises that go hand-in-hand with a lack of confidence in institutions, it should also be noted that solidarity-based practices are as old as humanity itself and have helped fund the economic activities of people excluded from the banking system in many countries (e.g. the tontines in sub-Saharan Africa) or have been put to work for the collective good (tiwiza in Algeria – see Perret & Paranque, 2015).

The types of social ties (bonding,[1] linking[2] or bridging;[3] Banque Mondiale, 2000) and the nature of the solidarities must therefore be scrutinised (institutional solidarity, local solidarities, formal or informal solidarity, intergenerational solidarity and so on). The contemporary period is characterised by the exhaustion of utopias and the proliferation of initiatives, indeed, the survival of practices that may seem outmoded, but that still apply in certain regions such as Kabylia; these practices fall outside the bounds of commercial trade aimed at accumulating capital.

Polanyi demonstrates that in all societies, production and distribution are covered by the various forms of socio-economic integration: reciprocity, redistribution, domestic life and exchange (Bugra, 2005). Testart (2007) also identifies five levels of relationship within a system: the gift, reciprocity, non-commercial exchange – an exchange where 'price or value considerations are not enough to trigger the exchange' (*ibid.*, p. 44) – and commercial exchange which can be subdivided to identify a specific relationship: the capitalist commercial exchange, depending on whether '[...] the trader seeks the use value of the goods provided or its exchange value (*ibid.*, p. 156).

This corresponds to three levels of connection in the action: reciprocity, which involves neither synchronicity nor obligation in the dual movement it implies; exchange, which includes a causal relationship and an obligation; and lastly the gift, where there is no obligation or right and which remains unilateral (*ibid.*, p. 221). This distinction reminds us that 'an exchange is only one particular, very particular case, among the various forms of circulation' (*ibid.*, p. 69) and that there is not only one form of exchange (Mauss, 2012, p. 65).

Exchange practices are not merely based on economic factors but also contribute to the symbolic realm. Our analysis will look at how the relationships of exchange can work outside the scope of commodification. In other words, is it possible for the use value to operate independently of the prevailing exchange value? An analysis of non-market practices occurring outside the commercial sphere is therefore necessary.

In our research, we analyse exchange practices in Kabylia, practices that are embedded in a village-based social system based on tradition and a number of values such as *lherma* (honour), *nif* (pride), *tiwiza* (mutual aid, volunteering) and *tirugza* (values associated with a man/woman of their word, someone trustworthy) which contribute to solidarity within the community and give a meaning to acts (see Perret & Abrika, 2014a, 2014b). The traditional Kabyle society is divided into segments (villages, tribes and so on), each of which has a strong awareness of its individuality and own system of solidarity, and is characterised by a lack of centralised institutions (Benet, 1957–1975, p. 195). Clearly, today, the Algerian state is a centralised body but the mountain villages nonetheless retain a specific social and political organisation, based on tradition and functioning through what we now call village committees (Perret & Abrika, 2014a, 2014b).

Trade and Markets

As mentioned in the Introduction, trade and markets should not be confused. Trading practices are not necessarily organised around a bargaining or buying/selling model, but can also follow the logic of reciprocity or redistribution, which may be financial or state-organised. 'Trade can take the form of gifts, simple trade or market trade', at pre-set prices or following the laws of supply and demand (Caillé & Laville, 2007, p. 80).

'The fact is that in non-centralised societies [such as the traditional Kabyle society], where the segments [tribes] are not connected by any power structure [...], markets exist; however, due to the lack of government, in order to maintain a peaceful market, they have to comply with the political expediency of a truce between groups. Among nomads in the desert, things are organised to ensure that these truces coincide with certain seasons, to make the most of the opportunities for trade. However, it is clear that this rhythm would not suit the sedentary mountain tribes.' (Benet, 1957–1975, p. 195). Mutual exchanges cannot remain merely occasional in mountainous areas where there are no shops. Benet (1957–1975) says that market day is often the only day that Kabyle people have meat and that no trade or commercial activity occurs outside market days and periods. The market place therefore has the 'monopoly over transactions' and even itinerant traders attend. There are, nonetheless, some exceptions to the monopoly: itinerant craftspeople, doctors who sell their medicines or peddlers who sell items to women only (fabrics, jewellery, etc.) may come to the village. They will be paid with eggs, oil or the like. Bartering is generally the rule in exchanges with women.

Traditionally, the Kabyle market is a place where items are sold and where essential foodstuffs are bought, but it is also a meeting place 'as necessary [in Kabylia] as the air we breathe', a place where the marabouts state the dates for the start and end of Ramadhan, where bans on travel, calls to arms or other news of interest to the community are notified, a place to gather political or more private news that will then be passed on, and finally the place people come to talk about the interests of the *çof,*[4] the tribe[5] or the confederation (Hanoteau & Letourneux, 1893–2003, p. 58). The market is therefore vital in forming public opinion, a real 'forum for the tribe' (to use Robin's term in Benet, 1957–1975); it is where collective feelings emerge and are demonstrated, as nineteenth-century observers noted. 'The market [ultimately] creates a sort of group individuality, often very different from the feelings of the individuals it is made up of. The egocentricity of the tribe or village *(douar)* replaces the egocentricity of individuals' (Benet, 1957–1975, p. 199). According to Benet (1957–1975), the market is ultimately a legal, social, political and often even religious institution that mainly serves economic ends. Regarding the religious aspect, Benet notes that a water source linked to a sanctuary can often be found on the site of markets and this is where statements are issued in the event of a dispute or where refuge can be found in the event of danger.

The market name refers to the owner-tribe and the day that it is held. We have, for example the '*Aït Yahia* Saturday', the '*Irdjen* Sunday', the '*Aït Ouassif* Wednesday' and so on (Hanoteau & Letourneux, 1893–2003, p. 59). Whenever a tribe wanted to set up a new market, it had to obtain consent from neighbouring tribes and select a day that would not clash with other markets.

At certain periods, Kabyle laws meant that anyone who did not attend the market, on the principle that they had nothing to buy or sell, would be required to pay a fine. In the past, in most Djurdjura tribes, only men went to market but on the right bank of the Sebaou, many women attended. They had a special pitch (*rah'ba*)[6] where they sold items like pottery, eggs and fabric. Even today, for certain village elders, going to market is something of an institution which they would not miss for anything, and the markets are highly frequented by men (this is still true since men are more easily able to travel than women in rural areas).

In the past, markets were free from fees and duties payable on the goods sold, with the exception of benefits for the *mâmera*, or the tribe's school, where there was one. *Tolba* or students were able to take pieces of meat from the animals slaughtered (two pieces from a cow, or one from a sheep or goat). Every market has its measurers (a profession deemed vile) who pay themselves with a portion of the product measured. The market therefore also plays a redistributing role.

The market is a neutral site, placed under the *anaya* (protection or patronage) of the owner-tribe, which means that two warring tribes can safely meet at the market of a third tribe (Hanoteau & Letourneux, 1893–2003, p. 60).

The market is supervised and policed by the 'market leader' (*amek k'eran-n-essouk*), who is traditionally a man belonging to a powerful family. He has moral authority and is backed by a *çof* that is powerful enough to have its decisions enforced. His powers are far-reaching (further than the village *amin*[7]): he makes sure market law (*lqanoun*) is enforced and may impose an instant fine on offenders because offences at market are deemed to go against the village *anaya*. The large *souks* always have historical origins; repeated exchanges occurring randomly within a site do not automatically give that place market status. A place can only become a market after a declaration has been made and 'market law' and the related fines have been notified at a specific location (Benet, 1957–1975).

Theft is severely reprimanded. The sentence is implemented by people from outside the tribe so as not to discredit the market and can go as far as death by stoning. Even today, dissuasive lynching can occur in the event of theft at market: theft in a society where major transactions still take place in cash can cause the victim's financial ruin. In cases where the security forces come along, we were recently told that villagers will ask them to arrest them all because they are all guilty of lynching – and in the end, no one is arrested.

While the 'market leader' is responsible for crimes and offences concerning public order and the freedom of transactions, all civil and commercial disputes are referred to the tribe's marabout who serves as judge: the *âlem* (wise man) of the market. The market leader enforces the *âlem*'s rulings and, to ensure market upkeep, he can make use of income from fines and the measurers' pitch revenues.

Market and Embeddedness

Polanyi's approach shows that the market is neither spontaneous nor self-regulating. Economic institutions, including the market, have to be seen as social constructs. 'The human economy is [...] embedded and enmeshed in economic and non-economic institutions. The inclusion of the non-economic is vital. For religion or government may be as important to the structure and functioning of the economy as monetary institutions or the availability of the tools and machines themselves that lighten the toil of labour' (Polanyi, 1957 republished in 2008, p. 59).

In The Great Transformation, Polanyi explains that until the nineteenth century, human societies were characterised by an embedded economy where the ultimate aim was not to make profit for profit's sake but to allow society to reproduce itself. Although markets existed, they were governed by political, cultural, social and symbolic demands. Conversely, in his view, from the nineteenth century onwards, the economy became disembedded from society. The relationship between society and economy was turned around: the quest for profit and the fear of hunger formed the foundations on which social relationships were built, with the economy governed by market prices alone, despite attempts to introduce non-commercial regulations. However, this was untenable and the 'market society' collapsed in the twentieth century in the face of totalitarianism. Now in the twenty-first century, will the 'financial market society', which has seen a weakening in public regulations, buckle again in the face of the inequalities engendered by extremism?

In the case of the traditional Kabyle market as described above, thanks to Benet's work (1957–1975), the economic activities are clearly not fully independent of non-economic constraints: the importance of the village *anaya* and the fact that the 'market leader' is a man from a powerful family, with moral authority and backing from a powerful *çof,* are primary examples of this.

On the other hand, every traditional market belongs to a tribe and each tribe is part of a 'headless' socio-political system made up of a series of nested collectivities that can be illustrated as a series of concentric circles of loyalty, each with their own name, possessions and honour (Bourdieu, 1958–2012; Gahlouz, 2010; Perret & Abrika, 2014a). Bourdieu (1958–2012) pointed that traditional socio-political structure could be presented as a succession of concentric circles (i.e. Fig. 1).

Every economic process is unique and comprises a system of social relations, shared rules and common beliefs that remain stable over time and generate opportunities and constraints (Maucourant and Plociniczak, 2011). What is remarkable in Kabylia is, as pointed out by Hanoteau and Letourneux as early as 1893, that 'The entire social organisation, [...] all Kabyle institutions (political, administrative and civil) work towards this single goal: maintaining and developing solidarity between members [of the community], to give the 'group' as much strength as possible' (Bourdieu, 1958–2012, p. 16). This 'art of association' is anchored in a society characterised by a certain number of underlying practices and values. Thus, the notion of 'word' is very important: 'it is through his words and metaphors, loyalty, courage, science, knowledge and the value of sermon and his word that a man can claim to be rich' (Adli, 2010, p. 18). It is immaterial values (*tirugza*) that define the *argaz* (*tabargazt* in its feminine form), a term we could translate by a man/woman of their word, of courage, of trust or

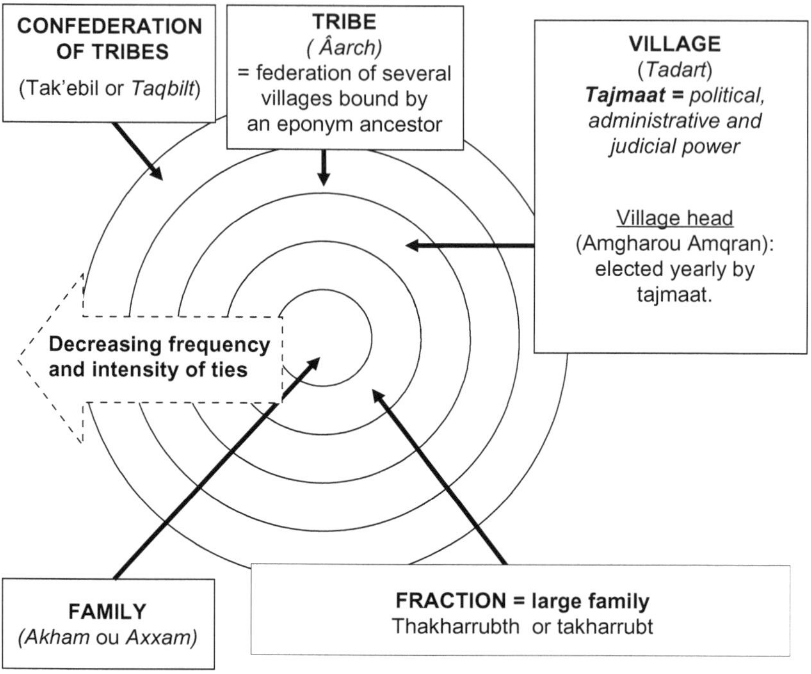

Fig. 1. Traditional Kabyle Socio-Political Structure.
Source: Perret and Abrika (2014a).

an honest man. This ethic governs the rules of exchange and of trust between people who do not know one another, but belong to the same community. The notions of *tirugza* and *lherma* (male honour aimed at protecting women) are determined by that of the woman. '[…] To say that women [are] weak or do not [count] would be to misunderstand the standards that [govern] society. Women [are] so important that the entire system (mythical or real) [cannot] operate without them' in Malikam, 2013, p. 7.

Exchange Practices in Kabylia

Gifts, Reciprocity and Exchanges

As mentioned in the chapter "Finance Reconsidered: New Perspectives for a Responsible and Sustainable Finance," Testart (2007) distinguishes

Table 1. Forms of Circulation.

Level of Relationship	Testart (2007)
Gifts	Gifts are disinterested and not bound by time. They do not imply any obligation or right, either for the giver or the beneficiary. They are unilateral.
Reciprocity	There is no synchronicity or obligation implied in the dual movement this involves.
Exchanges	They involve a causal relationship and an obligation.
Non-commercial exchange	Price or value considerations are not enough to trigger the exchange.
Non-capitalist commercial exchange	The trader seeks the use value of the goods provided in exchange.
Capitalist commercial exchange	The trader seeks the exchange value of the goods provided in exchange.

between different levels of relationship within a system, as shown in Table 1.

Among Kabyle people, 'offering a gift is not only a way of showing your good intentions or a wish to please, but is also a binding way of making the recipient a potential debtor'.[8] There are different types of gift: those received at certain everyday events, those received during celebrations or family events, those received at the time of a bereavement and those received at the time of a visit. Gifts brought when visiting friends or family (*tarzeft*), and those at the time of a celebration (*lkhir* and *lehna*) are seen as an obligation committing the family's honour. No one can avoid it, and it is preferable to cancel a visit rather than arrive empty-handed (Table 1). Hence, even today, when a woman goes to visit an acquaintance, (friend, family, neighbour, etc.), she never goes empty-handed. She will take a bag containing confectionery, coffee, soda, cakes or something similar, and will never leave without a small gift at the end of the visit. A guest will never leave with an empty bag. It would even be preferable to leave the bag behind, pretending to have forgotten it, if nothing was offered (in which case, the return gift will be given at a later date), but this is unlikely to happen (Table 2).

The Women's Market

While traditionally men went to market to trade, in Aïn El Hammam, a women's market (*Rahba n'Tlawin*), specific to the region, is held every

Table 2. Type of Gifts in Kabylia.

	Name of the Gift	Occasion	Gift Given	Recipient of the Gift	Return Gift
Family or everyday events	*Tunt'ict*	Small family events: conclusion of a marriage, baby's first steps, return of an absent family member, etc.	Cooked dish, usually couscous	Parents, neighbours, friends	The container will not be returned empty; wheat, semolina, but not barley 'as a good omen (*i lfal*)'. If it is a birth: dried vegetables to express a wish for the child to grow fine and strong, to 'flourish (*ad yedjudjeg llufan*)' and be as fruitful as these plants.
		The first milk from a cow that has just given birth to a calf.	Cheese on a dish of couscous		Return the container with water in it, at the very least.
		When preparing a dish that is out of the ordinary.	Crepes or fritters		Dish returned empty: no return gift.
Celebrations known as *timeɣriwin:* Weddings, births and circumcisions	*Lkhir*	The celebrating family receives the gift.	Money or eggs or both	Celebrating family	Tradition has it that you give more than you received in similar circumstances in the past. Anyone who wants to bring an end to this seemingly unending competition can forewarn that they have sworn not to accept anything: they are then seen as released from obligation and only a very small gift is given.
	Lehna	The celebrating family receives the gift.	Semolina, eggs, meat, oil, sometimes in large quantities		

Bereavement		Burial	Figs, couscous, cakes	Friends of the family offer the couscous to the bereaved family to serve to the guests they will receive at the wake	Mutual assistance.
Visits	*Tarzeft*	Visits to friends, parents, the sick, etc.	Dish of couscous with meat, crepes, fruit, raw vegetables and the like, and nowadays, sodas and confectionery	People visited	Return gift: you never leave empty-handed.

Sources: Personal information and François et al. (1992).

Sunday.[9] The goods sold there range from fabrics and Ath Yenni jewellery to households goods. The women's market is located in Ahechad Bouakouir, near Aïn El Hammam hospital. While it is difficult to establish exactly when it was founded, some sources date it back to the war of independence because, at that time, visits to hospital patients were only authorised twice a week, on Tuesdays and Saturdays. Female visitors gathered early in front of the hospital gates as they waited for it to open. Older women started to 'offer rabbits, squash or other garden produce, "under the counter".'[10] After independence, the number of sellers increased although the 'official' market did not yet become established because the authorities had the area evacuated if there was too much agitation near the hospital.

Over time, the women decided to move their informal market to Ahechad Bouakouir, a bit further away from the hospital. To start with, only older women from poor backgrounds presented their wares. More recently, men have started to sell goods. However, the customers are still women only.

Three criteria that address three questions can be identified in order to assess the degree of embeddedness/insertion of a market (Bohnnan & Dalton, 1965 in Le Velly, 2007):

- are the prices the outcome of unrestricted confrontation between supply and demand?
- does material survival require participation in the market?
- and are economic decisions guided by remuneration coming from market prices?

We are now considering conducting an applied study into current practices at this women's market (now it is a formal one). This would let us take a deeper look at these questions to see how embedded the market is. What is sure is that even today, small-scale exchanges between women do not necessarily comply with purely economic logic. For example, a woman who makes her own *kohl* at home may (informally) sell tubes of her powder at a loss to a neighbour, on the grounds that she is experiencing financial difficulties or going through a difficult period.

CONCLUSION

In the traditional Kabyle market, as described above, mainly thanks to the founding work of Benet (1957–1975), economic activity is clearly not independent from non-economic constraints. This traditional market is not only a place to sell one's wares and buy essential foodstuffs, but also a forum for meeting, exchange and information, an institution that could be qualified as symbolic and diplomatic (the market is under the *anaya* of the owner-tribe and other warring tribes can meet there safely). Market supervision and security are entrusted to a man who has moral authority and the backing of a *çof* that is powerful enough to have its decisions enforced: he represents an institution. Even though things have of course evolved, even today men still make sure they go to market, which is a forum for exchange.

In traditional Kabyle society, exchange practices are not only economic in nature (they contribute to mutual assistance, redistribution, etc.), but are also symbolic. As such, gifts given on visits to friends or family, or at the time of celebrations, commit the family's honour and no one can avoid this. These practices are embedded within a system of social relations that emphasises horizontal links (family, village or tribe), shared rules and common beliefs.

While village committees, a spin-off of the *tajmaat*, still exist today, many of them are now associations, which could also explain why they are now less independent and accept State subsidies. Reinforcement of the Algerian state redistribution system also reduces de facto the forms of and need for traditional solidarity.

NOTES

1. The bonding ties unite individuals of identical status (horizontal ties). They characterise community relations, that is people adhering to the same representation system, but aim towards a 'relational closure' (Coleman, 1988).

2. The linking ties characterise interactions between agents across a cleavage that typically divides society (vertical ties between social classes). They are require to be reaffirmed and are characterised by reciprocity transactions. Their frequency tends to result in the convergence of representations.

3. The bridging ties link distant agents; this distance can be geographical (an emigrated from the village) or the tie is not permanently activated. The bridging network is a virtual one. The relations can be punctual, intermittent and the respected rules are similar to 'an agreement without mutual commitment' (Angeon, Caron, & Lardon, 2006, p. 10).

4. A *çof* is an 'association for mutual assistance in cases of defence and attack, in all areas of life'. Its purpose can be summed up well by the old saying: *ouinek aïnoun ith idhelem ner medhloum*, 'help your own, whether they are right or wrong" (Hanoteau and Letourneux, 2003, Vol. 2, p. 14). The quality of the links forged by

the *çof* is all the more important when it concerns the *çof* of a single village or of a single tribe.

5. Depending on the size of the village and the links formed across its territory, a village may join up with other villages to form a tribe (*âarch*), which itself may join up with others in a tribal confederation that defines the rules of reciprocity, solidarity and protection in the event of external attack.

6. Different foodstuffs are sold at different areas within the market, areas known as *rah'ba*: there is a *rah'ba* for oils, another for fabrics, one for cereals and another for chickens, etc. (Hanoteau & Letourneux, 1893/2003, Vol. 2, p. 59).

7. The *amin*'s role is to implement the decisions of the *tajmaat* (village assembly where the elders and family leaders have their say), which holds political, administrative and legal power (see Perret & Abrika, 2014a, 2014b or Perret & Paranque, 2015).

8. François, Dornier, Louis, and Pandolfi (1992).

9. Slimane (2011).

10. Nacer (2006).

REFERENCES

Adli, Y. (2010). *Les efforts de préservation de la pensée kabyle aux XVIIe et XIXe siècles*, éditions L'Odyssée.

Angeon, V., Caron, P., & Lardon, S. (2006). Des liens sociaux à la construction d'un développement territorial durable: quel rôle de la proximité dans ce processus? *Développement durable et territoire*, Dossier 7 Proximité et environnement, 1–21.

Banque Mondiale. (2000). *Combattre la pauvreté. Rapport sur le développement dans le monde*. Washington, DC: Banque Mondiale.

Benet, F. (1957–1975). Les marchés explosifs dans les montagnes berbères. In K. Polanyi & C. Arensberg (Eds.), *Les systèmes économiques dans l'histoire et dans la théorie* (pp. 195–216). (Sciences humaines et sociales, 1975). Paris: Larousse, coll.

Bourdieu, P. (1958–2012). *Sociologie de l'Algérie*. Paris: PUF.

Bugra, A. (2005). Karl Polanyi et la séparation institutionnelle entre politique et économie. *Raisons Politiques*, 4/2005 *20*, 37–56.

Caillé, A., & Laville, , J.-L. (2007). Actualité de Karl Polanyi. *Revue du MAUSS*, 1/2007, *29*, 80.

Coleman, J. S. (1988). Social capital in the creation of human capital. *The American Journal of Sociology*, *94*, S95–S120.

François, E. B. S. M., Dornier, P., Louis, A., & Pandolfi, P. "Cadeaux", in *Encyclopédie berbère, 11 | Bracelets – Caprarienses* [En ligne], mis en ligne le 01 avril 2013, consulté le 17 juin 2016. URL. Retrieved from http://encyclopedieberbere.revues.org/1892

Gahlouz, M. (2010). Droit coutumier et régulation dans la société kabyle de la fin du XIXe siècle. *Droit et cultures* [online], 60, 2010-2, Online since March 29, 2011. Accessed on June 6, 2014. Retrieved from http://droitcultures.revues.org/2359

Hanoteau, A., & Letourneux, A. (1893–2003). *La Kabylie et les coutumes kabyles*. Tome 2. Saint-Denis: Éditions Bouchène.

Lavoué, J., Jézequel, M., & Janvier, R. (2010). *La ressource des organisations de l'économie sociale et solidaire face à la crise du lien social.* Crise du collectif et intervention, Érès, no. 94/2010-2, pp. 29–47.
Le Velly, R. (2007). Le problème du désencastrement. *Revue du MAUSS*, 2007/1,*29*, 241–256.
Malikam. (2013). *La magie des femmes kabyles et l'unicité de la société traditionnelle.* L'Harmattan. Histoire et Perspectives Méditerranéennes.
Maucourant, J., & Plociniczak, S. (2011). Penser l'institution et le marché avec Karl Polanyi. *Revue de la régulation* [online], 10, 2e semestre/Autumn 2011. Accessed on June 2, 2014. Retrieved from http://regulation.revues.org/9439
Mauss, M. (2012). *Essai sur le don.* Paris: PUF, Quadridge.
Nacer, B. (2006, July 24). Le marché des femmes prend de l'ampleur. *La Dépêche de Kabylie.*
Perret, C., & Abrika, B. (2014a, May 29–31). Capital social, confiance et développement territorial. Une étude appliquée en Kabylie. *XXXes Journées du développement ATM 2014, Éthique, entrepreneuriat et développement*, Université Cadi Ayyad, Marrakech.
Perret, C., & Abrika, B. (2014b). Les systèmes de gouvernance traditionnels en Kabylie à la lumière du concept de capital social. *Mondes en développement*, 42-2014/2 *166*, 131–144.
Perret, C., & Paranque, B. (2015). L'organisation sociopolitique des villages kabyles : une gestion spécifique des ressources naturelles. *ROR – Revue de l'Organisation Responsable*, *7*(2), 69–82.
Polanyi, K. (2008). La sémantique des usages de la monnaie. In M. Cangiani & J. Maucourant (Eds.), *Essais de Karl Polanyi* (pp. 221–243). Seuil: Editions du seuil.
Slimane, B. A. (2011, September 15). Aïn El Hammam: Il se tient chaque dimanche. Le marché des femmes, un carrefour à valoriser. *La Dépêche de Kabylie.*
Testart, A. (2007). *Critique du don, études sur la circulation non marchande.* Paris: Syllepse.

BRAND VALUE CREATION VERSUS DESTRUCTION: THE RELATIONSHIP BETWEEN CONSUMERS, MARKETERS, AND FINANCIERS☆

Bernard Paranque and Bernard Cova

ABSTRACT

Purpose – *The aim of the chapter is to focus on the connections between three types of actors who build the new world of brands – consumers, marketers, and financier – by focusing on the co-creation of value between the brand community and the company owning the brand.*

Methodology/approach – *The chapter use three case vignettes to highlight the dual process at play when a community of consumers co-create brand value.*

Findings – *The chapter not only highlights a value-creating trajectory for companies but also shows how a reverse process can destroy value for*

☆Published in Cova and Paranque (2012) with authorisation of the review.

Finance Reconsidered: New Perspectives for a Responsible and Sustainable Finance
Critical Studies on Corporate Responsibility, Governance and Sustainability, Volume 10, 245–261

ISSN: 2043-9059/doi:10.1108/S2043-905920160000010030

the very same companies. It suggests that marketers' desire to maximize the value co-created between the company and the community in order to answer the financial requirement of brand valuation could damage the value co-creation process. According to our case vignettes' results, these marketers are exposing themselves to the risk that consumers/fans will rebel as a result of this branding maximization, leading in return to the creation of a competitor in the form of a community brand.

Research limitations/implications – *Future research will have to investigate how by cutting across organizational boundaries and functional areas, brand communities would reshape the marketing–finance interface.*

Practical implications – *The chapter stresses the need for companies to manage carefully the triadic relationship community/marketing/finance in order to avoid the development of a reverse brand value destruction process. In addition, the chapter contributes to research on the marketing–finance interface by highlighting the need to look beyond this level of interaction when it comes to branding.*

Originality/value – *Starting with the principle that consumers grouped into communities are increasingly responsible for making brands through their value-creating practices, the chapter highlights the problems raised by the company's will to transform them into value for shareholders.*

Keywords: Brand community; brand valuation; financialization; marketing–finance interface; value creation

INTRODUCTION

This chapter focuses on the connections between three types of actors who make brands: consumers, marketers, and financiers.

Starting with the principle that consumers grouped into communities are increasingly responsible for making brands through their value-creating practices (Schau, Muniz, & Arnould, 2009), the chapter highlights how value created in this way is captured by companies as a result of the efforts of marketers or brand managers to generate and develop value co-creation practices (Hatch & Schultz, 2010). It also indicates how such co-creation translates into an evaluation of immaterial assets on the part of financiers and consultants (Salinas & Ambler, 2009).

The chapter not only highlights this value-creating trajectory for companies but also shows how a reverse process can destroy value for the very same companies. To improve the bottom line, increase share prices or negotiate a company takeover or sale, financial analysts need to evaluate assets, particularly intangible ones such as brands. As part of this process, they may have cause to pressure marketers to increase brand strength, since this is part of the calculation of a company's future potential. By so doing, they are trying to capture all potential from the value emanating from consumer practices. Consumers, on the other hand, are often quite aware of such maneuvers (Cova & Dalli, 2009) and might protect themselves by leaving the brand community (and sometimes even by generating a new community focusing on a new brand that competes with the original one). Through these efforts to continually increase their firm's financial performance, financiers (and in their wake, marketers) are modifying the subtle balance that rules over the value co-creation process. The result is that they run a risk of triggering a reverse process that will lead to the destruction of brand value.

We begin our chapter with a look at the virtuous process of creating value for a brand which aligns brand communities, brand management, and brand valuation. Next, through three case studies, we explore the possibility of a reverse brand value destruction process. These exploratory cases reveal the basic shape of a process that reverses the virtuous circle, sparking a destructive process generated by the virtuous process's very existence.

A VIRTUOUS PROCESS OF CREATING VALUE FOR BRAND

What people do with brands has always been considered a source of value for them (Arvidsson, 2006). Moreover, this phenomenon has accelerated over the past decade due to the rising power of consumer communities (Cova, Kozinets, & Shankar, 2007) backed by the development of the internet and social media. It has been shown (Veloutsou & Moutinho, 2009) that the success of a brand increasingly relies on the existence of a community of totally captive and loyal fans who co-create the value of that brand through their many different practices (Schau et al., 2009).

The following section will detail the virtuous process of brand value creation/monetization by ascertaining the connections between three worlds that remain rather unknown to each other: the world of the *brand communities* (Muniz & O'Guinn, 2001); the world of *brand management* (Sawhney, Verona, & Prandelli, 2005); and the world of *brand valuation* (Salinas & Ambler, 2009).

Consumer Perspective and Brand Communities

There has been a notable change in attitudes toward consumption, which used to be mainly considered as an activity that destroys goods and services but has now been conceptualized (Arnould & Thompson, 2005; Firat & Dholakia, 1998) as one that produces experiences by mobilizing resources found in the marketplace. As a result, consumers are perceived less and less as targets and increasingly as partners for a company. This is particularly true when the consumers in question are united by a similar passion and grouped into a dedicated brand community. These impassioned and empowered consumer collectives assert greater channel power and make claims on core competencies formerly reserved for the marketer (O'Guinn & Muñiz, 2005). The point here is that a new ethos of brand participation is emerging. The shared passion of certain consumers for a cult brand translates, via various collective learning systems, into expertise and competencies, thereby according online communities increasing amounts of production and marketing legitimacy. Examples abound in modern marketing literature: Ducati, Harley-Davidson, Lego, Mercedes, Mini, Saab, Star Trek, Star Wars, etc.

Schau et al. (2009) have used social practice theory to reveal the process of collective value creation within brand communities. Their research supports three emerging perspectives in branding: value is manifest in the collective enactment of practices, which favor investments in networks rather than company–consumer dyads; ceding control to consumers enhances consumer engagement and builds brand equity; and companies derive added brand value by creatively using willing consumers as resources. All of the practices highlighted by Schau et al. (2009) are rooted in the construction and expansion of a brand's linking value, which represents the value of the brand and its related products and services during the construction, development or maintenance of an interpersonal link – however ephemeral – between consumers. According to Kates (2006, p. 96), "the linking value reaches its most organized expressions in brand configurations such as brand communities, subcultures of consumption and cultures of consumption." Muniz and O'Guinn's (2001) study of brand communities provides evidence of this sort of linking value. The research conducted in the Fairlawn neighborhood in Bloomingdale, a small Midwestern town in the United States, revealed (among other things) the informal, assumed, and symbolic linking value of the Saab brand for Saab drivers, and of the Bronco brand for Bronco drivers. Linking value must be produced, and companies currently invest significant resources in this. They cannot, however, produce linking value without the support of consumers who work at producing it (Cova & Dalli, 2009). Communities of consumers are both creators and users of linking value – the crowd is the most important resource in offline and online gatherings. The more people participate, the greater the opportunity to interact and develop relationships. Consumers create communities through their participation and generate the kind of linking value that will then be attached to a brand and its products or services, which are subsequently perceived as being more valuable.

Marketing Perspective and Brand Management

Marketing management theory has advanced the understanding that value is embedded in products and produced by firms in isolation from consumers (Bagozzi, 1975). This understanding has been challenged by new marketing approaches, which hold that value is co-created by producers and consumers through their activities and interactions.

When in the early 2000s management scholars Prahalad and Ramaswamy (2000, 2004) began to write a series of essays suggesting that the locus of economic value creation is shifting from the firm's research and development department to the interaction between the firm and the consumer, they gave birth to an area of research that is now, a decade later, commonly referred to as value co-creation. The term denotes that the production of value that takes place increasingly via the interaction between firm and consumer is the outcome of both collaborating in manufacturing products and services. As Foster (2007, p. 715) points out, "this engagement has been identified as a trend, dubbed 'Customer-Made' and defined as 'the phenomenon of corporations creating goods, services and experiences in close cooperation with experienced and creative consumers, tapping into their intellectual capital, and in exchange giving them a direct say (and rewarding them for) what actually gets produced, manufactured, developed, designed, serviced, or processed'".

This co-creation concept has been introduced in marketing theory by the new Service Dominant Logic (SDL) theory (Lusch & Vargo, 2006;

Vargo & Lusch, 2004). The point is no longer to "market to" consumers but to "market with" consumers. Fundamental to SDL are the foundational premises (FPs) that elaborate the nature of the logic. The original eight premises proposed in 2004 have now been modified and extended to 10 (Vargo & Lusch, 2008). Of these, one is core to our investigation (FP6): The customer is always a co-creator of value! Customers integrate the resources offered by companies and combine them with their own to co-create and co-extract value from a consumption experience. Thus, the consumer is said to assume the guise of an integrator of resources (Vargo & Lusch, 2008).

Within this logic, the brand becomes the pivotal hinge that allows producers, consumers and other stakeholders to interact (Merz, He, & Vargo, 2009). "*The brand becomes the concept that relates externally focused brand communities and internally organized cultures*" (Kornberger, 2010, p. 131). Brand communities are said to be particularly relevant contexts for "marketing with" consumers (Hatch & Schultz, 2010). With a brand community, the concept of value co-creation is pushed to the limit insofar as brands are transformed into virtual platforms (Arvidsson, 2006) used to stage the aggregation of staff members and consumers united by the same passion. In the field of brand management, alongside the case of the US brand Harley-Davidson – which has hypnotized marketers everywhere (Schouten & McAlexander, 1995) – there is in Europe the famous example of Ducati (Sawhney et al., 2005). The brand management model that Ducati created has had great success, and today Ducati is not only the darling of the European motorcycle industry but also a cult brand with a growing number of followers called Ducatists. In this branding model, staff members and consumers have the same status in relation to their brand community, that is, they are indistinguishable because they belong to the same community. On one hand, staff members consume brand products. On the other, consumers can be transformed into producers of events, ideas, and even brand accessories. Thus, Ducati and the Ducatists represent a classic example of how brand communities provide a favorable context for the emergence of consumers who can become true partners of the company.

On the basis of their observation of how the *Lego* Group interacts with its brand community (LUGNET, Lego User Group Network), Hatch and Schultz (2010) have asserted that the more consumers gain access to (and interact closely with) a company, the more important it becomes for the *Lego* Group to redraw organizational boundaries in a way that includes such consumers. This does not mean that the community is part of the company and must be managed as such. The trend toward increasing consumer/company engagement and organizational self-disclosure brings attendant risks, one of which is companies' loss of control over their brands and ultimately their organizations (Hatch & Schultz, 2010).

Financial Perspective and Brand Valuation

The active role that brand communities play in the marketing-driven value co-creation process has modified the relationship that used to exist within companies between the marketing and finance functions. As long as consumers were passive (and even destructive) in nature, the issue of value creation could only be apprehended in financial terms and on a company-internal basis at such times as the firm in question would engage in budgetary allocation decisions. As soon as usages started to develop outside of the structures of a company and its market (best illustrated by peer-to-peer processes) – leading in turn to the emergence of a potential for new exchanges (specifically commercial ones) – it became necessary to source such value; capture and internalize it; and ultimately translate it into monetary terms (Willmott, 2010). In turn, this brought financiers into the equation, specifically because of the brand evaluation processes they pursue. We must insist here on the term "financier." Finance is a function of the company dedicated to manage wealth created by the firm, but also to answer the expectations of present and future/potential shareholders. The financier is at the crossroads between the search for value creation for the company, the search for value maximization for existing shareholders and the search for new opportunities for potential investors (Jensen, 2001; Jensen & Meckling, 1976). Financiers thus have to manage, from a financial point of view, the coherence between all these expectations and desires.

According to Salinas and Ambler (2009), three methods reign in this area: a cost approach, where the brand is valued on the basis of the historical cost of its creation or the cost of its replacement; a market approach, by reference to open market values; and an approach that is primarily income-oriented, based on the premise that future cash flow attributable to a brand dictates its value for its owner, our potential investor. Not surprisingly, they note that the latter *"is the most popular approach"* (Salinas & Ambler, 2009, p. 44), thus confirming that the main issue in the debate about brands, from companies' point of view, is in actual fact the creation of shareholder value, an exchange value that involves not only developing a company's productivity but also ensuring that it is capable of tapping and appropriating the potential value that is likely to emerge from the production process.

The measure of brand value is based on three key aspects according to Interbrand:[1]

- "*the financial performance of the branded products or services*" is measured from financial analysts' standpoint via a concept (Brealey, Myers, & Allen, 2008) that is akin to Economic Value Added (EVA) to determine the profitability of the organization as a whole;
- "*the role of brand in the purchase decision process*" which according to Interbrand "*measures the portion of the decision to purchase that is attributable to brand*";
- and the brand strength which "*measures the ability of the brand to secure the delivery of expected future earnings.*"

Interbrand has developed an understanding and measurement of "connector brands" (Isakovich & Johnston, 2009) capable of gathering consumers into a group. Their brand strength can be determined by the brands' ability to ensure strong future connections. These metrics include a customer's: (1) Brand loyalty; (2) Interactivity with the brand; (3) Engagement with the community; and (4) Perception of brand uniqueness. Interbrand (Isakovich & Johnston, 2009, p. 3) defines the third metric "Engagement with community" in the following terms: "*The stronger the community that a brand creates for its customers, the more they will rely on the brand to create and sustain the community. This connection can refer to an actual community or a sense of community.*" Thus, some brands – cult brands – are able to foster a sense of zealous appeal. The ensuing loyalty is very valuable for the companies that own these brands.

A virtuous brand process therefore involves:

- On one hand, a definition of modes transforming community practices (Schau et al., 2009) into brand value that is acceptable to the community while encouraging the community to engage in brand assemblages that generate the valuable feedback that keeps the brand evolving (Arvidsson, 2006) as well as any identity-related projects (Arnould & Thompson, 2005). In such a way, companies derive added brand value by creatively using willing consumer resources (Vargo & Lusch, 2004);
- On the other hand, an increase in shareholder value (translation of brand value creation in brand valuation) based on the practices bearing/underlying/qualifying the brand (see the Coca-Cola case; Foster, 2011) in

an attempt to respond to shareholder expectations and/or attract new shareholders.

This virtuous brand process shows the connections between three types of actors who make brands: consumers gathered into communities; marketers; and financiers (Fig. 1). As such it takes part to the emerging discussion on the marketing–finance interface. The marketing–finance interface approach is a relatively new research stream (Hyman & Mathur, 2005) that, broadly speaking, examines the relationship between firm level marketing spending and firm level financial performance (especially shareholder value). Interest in the marketing–finance interface emerged with the issue of assessing immaterial assets, such as brands, which are of paramount importance for the growth of financial markets and the strategies of merger and acquisition (Haigh & Knowles, 2004; Salinas & Ambler, 2009). It (re)surged after publication of global brands rankings such as the Interbrand one in the 2000s. Today, brands are at the heart of the marketing–finance interface because "brands (what marketers build) have been shown to be associated with the market value of the firm, which signals the generation of future benefits" (Sidhu & Roberts, 2008, p. 676). As marketing activities can influence financial performance, financial activities can also impact marketing operations and this for the good – the virtuous

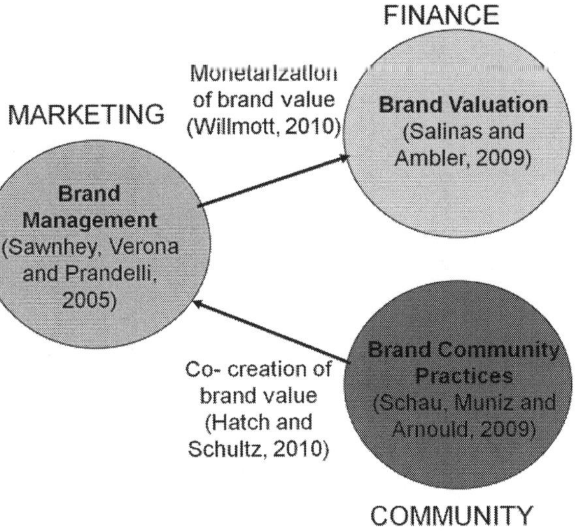

Fig. 1. A Virtuous Brand Process.

brand process described above – as for the bad – the reverse brand process described here under. However, the focus on the sole marketing–finance interface results in a kind of myopia: what is a play now is not a dyad (marketing–finance) but a triad (community–marketing–finance).

THE REVERSE BRAND VALUE DESTRUCTION PROCESS

Academics and professionals have both noted the existence of a virtuous process transforming brand community practices into brand exchange values following a co-creation approach (Hatch & Schultz, 2010), with such value subsequently being monetized by the firm via brand valuation methods (Willmott, 2010). Two types of strategic maneuvers for companies derive from this new awareness:

- The first involves creating brand consumer-fan communities in an attempt to initiate a virtuous process. As *Business Week* already noted in 2004 following the publication of the Interbrand ranking of global brands (which highlighted for the first time the role of communities), *"Analyzing the shifts in this year's ranking, though, it's clear something else is in the air: Consumers are changing how they view and even relate to brands. They remain purchasers of products, true, but through the power of the Internet and as a result of cultural and demographic shifts, many consumers now actively form larger communities around their favourite brands. Creating this new sense of belonging is what the most successful marketers are striving for"* (Dowling, 2004, p. 1). The idea here is to use all of the potentialities offered by Web 2.0 to create and nurture a brand community
- The second maneuver involves maximizing existing virtuous processes for those companies that are lucky enough to already possess a brand community of impassioned consumers. The idea here is to maximize the potential for value represented by this community.

Following many failures that companies have experienced while pursuing their Promethean dream of creating a community – some of which can even be virtual in nature (Cova & Pace, 2006; Wipperfürth, 2005) – this second strategic maneuver has concentrated companies' entire attention in recent years and hence our decision to examine this phenomenon so as to highlight its limitations and even potential dangers. This will be based on a reconsideration of case studies that have been published previously (Cova & White, 2010; Ladstätter, 2011) or else that are accessible on the communities' own websites.

We can start with the oldest case involving Afri-Cola Premium (Ladstätter, 2011). Afri-Cola is a cola soft drink produced in Germany, with a trademark first registered in 1931 by the company F. Blumhoffer Nachfolger GmbH. Over the years, Afri-Cola Premium became a cult brand for its consumer population in Hamburg, North Germany. The product was purchased by Mineralbrunnen Überkingen-Teinach AG in 1999, which then secretly changed the recipe and dropped "Premium" from its name. A collective of brand fans ("Interessengruppe Premium") then ran protest campaign lasting more than two years (1999–2001) opposing changes in Afri-Cola's recipe. These protests raised public awareness but remained unsuccessful as far as Afri-Cola was concerned – explaining why in November 2001 the group took the initiative of producing the original recipe cola. Baptized Premium-Cola, the new product started as a small collective but quickly grew into a medium-sized entity that seeks to link economics and ethics in a way that is unique yet seems logical to all of its members. There is no office, no salaries, and no actual boss. Members of the collective choose what percentage of their time they are going to work for the brand. For some, Premium is sort of a hobby alongside their real work or studies, whereas for others, it is a full-time job. Instead of expanding or selling at any price, the collective puts much thought into "appropriate" brand leadership and ethical economic behavior. Premium-Cola is sold in selected outlets only, ones whose philosophy must be similar to the brand's (Ladstätter, 2011). In parallel to this, Mineralbrunnen Überkingen-Teinach AG encountered some problems with Afri-Cola due to the unpopularity of the new recipe. The mixture was therefore changed again so that it tasted more like the original variant, with the caffeine content being increased in 2005 to ca. 200 mg/L and caffeine again being listed as an ingredient on the label. This new mixture also failed to spark great enthusiasm and on April 1, 2006 the company changed back to the original recipe, with a caffeine content of 250 mg/L.

What we have in this case is a company, Mineralbrunnen Überkingen-Teinach AG, that has tried to maximize its gains from a brand that it acquired, one that had been supported by a fan community. By not recognizing the community's preferences – despite two years of protests – the company not only alienated any support it might otherwise have received from the community but caused it to create its own brand, one that replicated some of the original brand name and ingredients. In this way, it created a rival who would take market share in the bars of North Germany while destroying the value potential of the original brand, which was no longer being supported in the community. The company's desperate and unsuccessful attempts to turn things around demonstrated that once a process reversing a virtuous value creation process has been triggered, the company in question will enter a value construction process. This example is relatively similar to another one from the same sector involving the historical Snapple drinks brand in the United States (Deighton, 2002).

A notorious example of a similar reversal process involves the football club FC United of Manchester in the United Kingdom, which was set up by a community of 2,000 ex-Manchester United fans in protest at Malcolm Glazer's takeover of Manchester United. While there is no doubt that FC United would not have happened without this American invasion, it is also clear that this action was the catalyst or the final straw in a long process but not the sole explanation for the final outcome. "*The material theft of a Manchester institution, forcibly taken from the people of Manchester, was the tip of a pyramid of destruction, with changing kick off times for the benefit of television, soulless all-seater stadia full of 'new' supporters intent to sit back and watch rather than partake in the occasion, heavy handed stewarding and ridiculously priced tickets propping it all up*" (http://www.fc-utd.co.uk/history.php). By May 2005, some supporters had had enough. A group of individuals determined to continue the fight formed a steering committee and FC United of Manchester was born. "*They wanted Our Club, Our Rules and they got just that, a member owned democratic, not-for-profit organisation created by Manchester United fans*" (http://www.fc-utd.co.uk/history.php). June 2011: the club is ranked 4th in the Premier Division (level 7 of the National League System) with an average attendance of 2,000 people.

In this example, Manchester United and its owner Malcolm Glazer seem to have forced some of the traditional community of fans to rebel against what they viewed as an over-evaluation and over-monetization of the club, processes they themselves deemed to destroy value. Rather than continuing to participate in a virtuous value creation process, they embarked upon a process that would destroy value for Manchester United by defecting from the community and creating a rival club. Clearly, the numbers may appear minimal and insignificant for Manchester United, but this is exactly what Mineralbrunnen Überkingen-Teinach AG thought at the beginning of its Afri-Cola Premium saga. Note that the same thing happened when fans protested against the new owners of Liverpool FC, resulting in the creation of a football club called AFC Liverpool (http://afcliverpool.org.uk/go/) and set up by 1000 Liverpool football club fans. This new club had a difference, however. Whereas "*it draws its support base from Liverpool fans, AFC*

Liverpool fans still support Liverpool and those who can afford to will still go to Anfield to support the Reds. The club is meant as a grassroots addition to Liverpool FC, not to be a replacement for it."

The last case is the well-known one of Warhammer (Cova & White, 2010), a strategic battle game played with various miniatures on a battlefield. Launched in 1983, Warhammer belongs to Games Workshop, the largest and the most successful tabletop wargames company in the world. Warhammer is a friendly social activity loved by millions of gamers, who altogether form a powerful brand community. However, a decade ago, some Warhammer fans harbored serious doubts about Games Workshop's role, accusing it of making exorbitant profits from players. This criticism was embodied in many players' joke that Games Workshop's acronym G.W. actually stands for Great Weasel. Two players created a game that was less complicated and onerous than Warhammer: "Confrontation!" This new game became successful immediately and a community of ex-Warhammer fans sprang up to support it, mainly motivated by the desire to escape from what they perceived as Games Workshop's outrageous commercial exploitation of players.

This case has become emblematic of what is now referred to as "*counter-brand communities*" (Cova & White, 2010), where part of a brand community totally or partially abandons the brand to go off and create and consume another brand that becomes a direct rival of the first one. The destructive process at this level is twofold, characterized by the loss of loyal consumers and the creation of a new competitor.

These three exploratory cases reveal the basic shape of a process that reverses the virtuous circle of which managers like to dream, sparking a destructive process generated by the virtuous process's very existence (Fig. 2):

- Pressure from actual shareholders, potential ones (investors) and financial decision-makers to over-estimate brand value (Mineralbrunnen Überkingen-Teinach AG for Afri-Cola Premium; Malcom Glazer for Manchester United; Games Workshop for Warhammer);
- This pressure can be translated at the brand management level by increasing prices for these products and services and/or by an undesired change in their characteristics – actions that are both resented as forms of consumer exploitation;
- Pressure and growth of this nature is considered unacceptable by part of the brand community, which then decides to defect and create a rival product and brand.

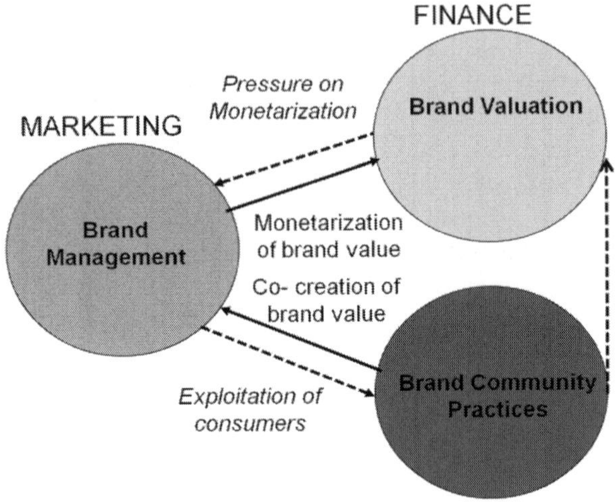

Fig. 2. A Destructive Brand Process.

The attempt to increase brand valuation puts pressure on brand managers. In turn, they over-exploit community practices, thereby undermining the brand in question.

CONCLUSION

The chapter suggests that marketers' desire to maximize the value co-created between the company and the community in order to answer the financial requirement of brand strengthening could damage the value co-creation process. According to our case studies' results, these marketers are exposing themselves to the risk that consumers/fans will rebel as a result of this branding maximization, leading in return to the creation of a competitor in the form of a "community brand" (Füller, Lüdicke, & Jawecki, 2007). The chapter thus contributes to identifying the need for companies to manage carefully the triadic relationship community/marketing/finance in order to avoid the development of a reverse brand value destruction process. In addition, the chapter contributes to research on the marketing–finance interface by highlighting the need to look beyond this level of interaction when it comes to branding.

Organizational cultures and brand communities while different are compatible provided that the dangers of the financialization of branding are avoided. "*The brand equity produced by user-consumers becomes a target of valorization as the monetary value attributed to branded goods, such as Lego bricks or Virgin broadband, is factored into the stock price of the companies owning the intellectually property vested in the brand*" (Willmott, 2010, p. 521). One of the challenges at this level is to avoid creating adverse effects by injecting excessive shareholder pressure into the company–consumer relationship, while ensuring that the exchange value being created is distributed appropriately and sufficiently to shareholders and not siphoned off toward other ends, such as shared knowledge or reputation (Jensen & Meckling, 1976). At the same time, there is also a need to ensure that shareholder and financial demands do not jeopardize the means deployed to achieve brand orchestration, based as they are on the acquisition of practices that are likely to convey exchange value benefiting the brand.

Brands are said to be a new way of organizing production and managing consumption: they become the intellectual, social, and cultural medium connecting inside and outside of the company in a "brand society" (Kornberger, 2010). Future research will have to investigate how by cutting across organizational boundaries and functional areas, brand communities would reshape the marketing–finance interface.

NOTE

1. http://www.interbrand.com/en/best-global-brands/best-global-brands-methodology/Overview.aspx on the 03/09/2011

REFERENCES

Arnould, E. J., & Thompson, C. J. (2005). Consumer Culture Theory (CCT) – Twenty years of research. *Journal of Consumer Research*, *31*(1), 868–882.

Arvidsson, A. (2006). *Brands: Meaning and value in media culture*. London: Routledge.

Bagozzi, R. P. (1975). Marketing as exchange. *Journal of Marketing*, *39*(October), 32–39.

Brealey, R. A., Myers, S. C., & Allen, F. (2008). *Principles of corporate finance* (9th ed.). New York, NY: McGraw-Hill.

Cova, B., & Dalli, D. (2009). Working consumers – The next step in marketing theory? *Marketing Theory*, *9*(3), 315–339.

Cova, B., Kozinets, R. V., & Shankar, A. (Eds.). (2007). *Consumer tribes*. Burlington, MA: Elsevier/Butterworth-Heinemann.

Cova, B., & Pace, S. (2006). Brand community of convenience products: New forms of customer empowerment – The case 'My Nutella, The Community. *European Journal of Marketing*, *40*(9/10), 1087–1105.

Cova, B., & Paranque, B. (2012). Value creation versus destruction: The relationship between consumers, marketers and financiers. *Journal of Brand Management*, *20*(2), 147–158.
Cova, B., & White, T. (2010). Counter-brand and alter-brand communities – The impact of Web 2.0 on tribal marketing approaches. *Journal of Marketing Management*, *26*(3), 256–270.
Deighton, J. A. (2002). How Snapple got its juice back. *Harvard Business Review*, *80*(1), 47–53.
Dowling, R. (2004). Rise of the cult brand. *Business Week*, August 9, p. 1.
Firat, A. F., & Dholakia, N. (1998). *Consuming people: From political economy to theaters of consumption*. London: Sage.
Foster, R. J. (2007). The work of the "new economy" – Consumers, brands, and value creation. *Cultural Anthropology*, *22*(4), 707–731.
Foster, R. J. (2011). The uses of use value: Marketing, value creation and the exigencies of consumption work. In J. Cayla & D. Zwick (Eds.), *Inside marketing* (pp. 42–57). Oxford: Oxford University Press.
Füller, J., Lüdicke, M. K., & Jawecki, G. (2007). How brands enchant – Insights from observing community driven brand creation. In *Proceedings of the Annual North American Conference*. Association for Consumer Research, Memphis, TN (pp. 359–366).
Haigh, D., & Knowles, J. (2004). Brand valuation – What it means and why it matters. *Intellectual Asset Management*, *6*, 18–21.
Hatch, J. H., & Schultz, M. (2010). Toward a theory of brand co-creation with implication for brand governance. *Journal of Brand Management*, *17*(8), 590–604.
Hyman, M. R., & Mathur, I. (2005). Retrospective and prospective views on the marketing/finance interface. *Journal of the Academy of Marketing Science*, *33*(4), 390–400.
Isakovich, H., & Johnston, L. (2009). *Strength of connection – How brands that act as social glue ensure a stronger future*. Interbrand Working Paper. Retrieved from http://www.interbrand.com/images/papers/10_IP-Strength-of-Connection.pdf
Jensen, M. C. (2001). Value maximization, stakeholder theory, and the corporate objective function. *Journal of Applied Corporate Finance*, *14*(3), 8–21.
Jensen, M. C., & Meckling, W. H. (1976). Theory of the firm – Managerial behavior, agency costs and ownership structure. *The Journal of Financial Economics*, *3*(4), 305–360.
Kates, S. (2006). Researching brands ethnologically – An interpretive community approach. In R. Belk (Ed.) *Handbook of qualitative research methods in marketing* (pp. 94–105). Cheltenham: Edward Elgar.
Kornberger, M. (2010). *Brand society: How brands transform management and lifestyle*. Cambridge, UK: Cambridge University Press.
Ladstätter, F. (2011, February 27–March 2). *FMCG community brands – The Premium Cola case*. 1st Brand Camp, University of Innsbruck, Obergurgl.
Lusch, R. F., & Vargo, S. L. (Eds.). (2006). *The service-dominant logic of marketing: Dialog, debate, and directions*. Armonk, NY: M.E. Sharpe.
Merz, M. A., He, Y., & Vargo, S. L. (2009). The evolving brand logic – A service-dominant logic perspective. *Journal of the Academy of Marketing Science*, *37*(3), 328–344.
Muniz, A. M., Jr., & O'Guinn, T. C. (2001). Brand community. *Journal of Consumer Research*, *27*(4), 412–432.
O'Guinn, T. C., & Muñiz, A. M. (2005). Communal consumption and the brand. In S. Ratneshwar & D. G. Mick (Eds.), *Inside consumption: Frontiers of research on consumer motives* (pp. 252–272). London: Routledge.

Prahalad, C. K., & Ramaswamy, V. (2000). Co-opting customer competence. *Harvard Business Review*, *78*(January–February), 79–87.

Prahalad, C. K., & Ramaswamy, V. (2004). *The future of competition: Co-creating unique value with customers*. Harvard: HBS Press.

Salinas, G., & Ambler, T. (2009). A taxonomy of brand valuation practice – Methodologies and purposes. *Journal of Brand Management*, *17*(1), 39–61.

Sawhney, M., Verona, G., & Prandelli, E. (2005). Collaborating to create – The internet as a platform for customer engagement in product innovation. *Journal of Interactive Marketing*, *19*(4), 4–17.

Schau, H. J., Muniz, A. M., Jr., & Arnould, E. J. (2009). How brand community practices create value. *Journal of Marketing*, *73*(5), 30–51.

Schouten, J. W., & McAlexander, J. H. (1995). Subcultures of consumption – An ethnography of the New Bikers. *Journal of Consumer Research*, *22*(1), 43–61.

Sidhu, B., & Roberts, J. (2008). The marketing accounting interface – Lessons and limitations. *Journal of Marketing Management*, *24*(7–8), 669–686.

Vargo, S. L., & Lusch, R. F. (2004). Evolving to a new dominant logic for marketing. *Journal of Marketing*, *68*(1), 1–18.

Vargo, S. L., & Lusch, R. F. (2008). Service-dominant logic – Continuing the evolution. *Journal of the Academy of Marketing Science*, *36*(1), 1–10.

Veloutsou, C., & Moutinho, L. (2009). Brand relationships through brand reputation and brand tribalism. *Journal of Business Research*, *62*(3), 314–322.

Willmott, H. (2010). Creating value beyond the point of production – Branding, financialization and market capitalization. *Organization*, *17*(5), 517–542.

Wipperfürth, A. (2005). *Brand hijack: Marketing without marketing*. New York, NY: Portfolio.

COOPERATIVES – AN ALTERNATIVE TO CAPITALISM? THE CASE OF THE JOHN LEWIS PARTNERSHIP☆

Bernard Paranque and Hugh Willmott

ABSTRACT

Purpose – *From a perspective of 'critical performativity', John Lewis is of special interest since it is celebrated as a successful organization and heralded as an alternative to more typical forms of capitalist enterprise.*

Methodology/approach – *Our analysis uses secondary empirical material (e.g. JLP documents in the public domain, histories of John Lewis and recent empirical research). Our assumption is that engagement and interrogation of existing empirical work can be at least as illuminating and challenging as undertaking new studies. In addition to generating fresh insights, stimulating reflection and fostering debate, our analysis is intended to contribute to an appreciation of how structures of ownership*

☆Chapter previously published in Organization: Paranque and Willmott (2014). The online version of this article can be found at http://org.sagepub.com/content/21/5/604

Finance Reconsidered: New Perspectives for a Responsible and Sustainable Finance
Critical Studies on Corporate Responsibility, Governance and Sustainability, Volume 10, 263–296

ISSN: 2043-9059/doi:10.1108/S2043-905920160000010031

and governance are significant in enabling and constraining practices of organizing and managing.

Findings – *The structures of ownership and governance at John Lewis, a major UK employee-owned retailer, have been commended by those who wish to recuperate capitalism and by those who seek to transform it.*

Research limitations/implications – *JLP can be read as a 'subversive intervention' insofar as it denies absentee investors access to, and control of, its assets. Currently, however, even the critical performative potential of the Partnership model is impeded by its paternalist structures. Exclusion of Partners' participation in the market for corporate control is reflected in, and compounded by, a weak form of 'democratic' governance, where managers are accountable to Partners but not controlled by them.*

Practical implications – *Our contention is that JLP's ownership and governance structures offer a practical demonstration, albeit flawed, of how an alternative form of organization is sufficiently 'efficient' and durable to be able to 'compete' against joint-stock companies.*

Originality/value – *By examining the cooperative elements of the John Lewis structures of ownership and governance, we illuminate a number of issues faced in realizing the principles ascribed to employee-owned cooperatives – notably, with regard to 'democratic member control', 'member economic participation' and 'autonomy and independence'.*

Keywords: Capitalism; cooperatives; employee-owned organization; governance; responsibility

> ... it is a powerful thing to have a model which focuses on Partners, secures their experience and commitment and fosters a desire to perform, for their teams, for their customers, and ultimately through the Partnership, for themselves. We call it the Partner-Customer-Profit circle. Many businesses have something similar—the employees, customer, profit chain—but there's a key difference. There's a break at the end of their chain where the profit flows mainly to external shareholders. In our business it flows to our Partners and so the circle starts all over again. That's a powerful differentiator.
>
> – Mayfield (2008), Chairman of John Lewis Partnership

INTRODUCTION

During his Party Conference in March 2012, UK Deputy Prime Minister Nick Clegg commended the retailer, *John Lewis*, as a model of *responsible capitalism*.[1] This begs a number of questions. Is *John Lewis* – or, to be formally precise, the John Lewis *Partnership* – a beacon of 'responsible *capitalism*'? Or is it a *cooperative* organized as a Partnership? Larger questions are also invited: What degree of responsibility can be exercised in a company owned by its employees where managers are accountable to their fellow Partners but which operates in an economy dominated by capitalist priorities and practices? Does the 'responsible capitalism' ascribed to *John Lewis* affirm or transgress 'capitalist' principles? And what is 'responsible capitalism' responsible to or for? These questions speak to the perennial concerns of commentators and practitioners in search of alternatives to the capitalist corporation (Hutton, 2012), and they are especially salient in the context of multiple crises associated with modern capitalist development (Gamble, 2009).

The John Lewis Partnership (JLP) is a public limited company[2] that embraces many of the values and principles of the International Cooperatives Alliance (ICA)[3] which defines cooperatives as 'businesses owned and run by and for their members [who] have an equal say in what the business does and a share in the profits'.[4] Defined in more rigorous terms by Webb and Cheney (2014), JLP complies, formally at least, with what these authors identify as 'four key pillars of the cooperative business model' with regard to 'an internationally accepted framework of values and principles and a founding ethic of economic fairness or justice' as well as share equity (Warhurst, 1996; Webb & Cheney, 2014, p. 67).[5]

Many commentators on JLP, as reviewed by Cathcart (2009, 2013a, 2013b), concentrate upon specific limited aspects of its operation. Our interest, in contrast, is in whether JLP structures of ownership and governance offer a 'critically performative' alternative to capitalist enterprise (Spicer, Alvesson, & Kärreman, 2009). This possibility is suggested by how, as an example of an employee-owned cooperative, JLP Partners (permanent staff[6]) are the primary beneficiaries of income derived from assets held in trust through the vehicle of the John Lewis Partnership Trust Limited (JLPT).[7] With regard to governance, Partners are legally empowered by the JLP Constitution to participate in a range of fora and media, which includes the Partnership Council, elected predominantly (80%) by Partners, that is formally empowered to remove the Chairman and Chief Executive.

In common with many other cooperatives, JLP structures of ownership and governance do not meet the most demanding of criteria used to identify cooperatives. The Trust structure does not allow Partners, individually or collectively, to exercise ultimate control of JLP by selling their shares and, equally, there is no threat of acquisition by distant investors. JLP is a type of employee-owned cooperative (Gios & Santuari, 2002; Huertas-Noble, 2010). It is not a 'labour managed firm' in which 'ultimate control rests with workers and their representatives' (Schwartz, 2011, p. 14), and JLP managers are not directly elected or appointed by the Partners. Nonetheless, and unlike most organizations in which employees own some or even all of the shares (Carberry, 2011), the Constitution of the Partnership ensures that a surplus is distributed to its Partners through a common percentage increase in salary and it requires that JLP managers are accountable to the Partners. So, despite important limitations, might there not be something at least mildly 'critically performative' about JLP's ownership and governance structures?

This question is prompted by how JLP's democratic governance structures actively invite Partners' 'interven[tion] in managerial discourse and practice' (Spicer et al., 2009, p. 544) as a means of curbing managerial autocracy in addition to how the device of the Trust closes JLP to ownership by absentee investors. Albeit imperfectly, in these respects JLP structures are designed and operate 'to subordinate the maintenance of capital to the interests of labour and human values' (Cheney, 1999, p. 39). Accordingly, scrutiny of JLP can help illuminate and interrogate issues and challenges of establishing and sustaining a post-capitalist form of organization with regard to 'democratic member control', 'member economic participation' and 'autonomy and independence' (principles of the ICA). In this regard, we share Hartmann's (2014) assessment that 'the examination of alternative organizations ... counteracts a tendency in CMS (critical management studies) research to "refrain from studying alternatives" [when they] might be a better and more efficient choice or even be able compete [with capitalist enterprise]' (pp. 13–14).

Our contention is that JLP's ownership and governance structures offer a practical demonstration, albeit flawed, of how an alternative form of organization is sufficiently 'efficient' and durable to be able to 'compete' against joint-stock companies. These structures also suggest how the Partnership form can act to check some grosser social inequalities with regard to political domination through processes of corporate decision-making and economic exploitation arising from the separation of ownership from value-producing activity. This proposition is unfashionable and contentious as many scholarly accounts and commentaries on JLP are antagonistic to, if not dismissive of, such claims.[8] Without denying the limitations and ambivalences of JLP structures, including a pervasive paternalism and incipient managerialism, we contend, nonetheless, that, in principle, and to a degree in practice, JLP exemplifies a comparatively 'responsible' kind of enterprise, at least with regard to its employees and its customers. Such 'responsibility' is significant, if hardly earthshattering, we argue, *even* when it is acknowledged that the 'alternative' character of JLP's structures of ownership and governance is compromised by an instrumentalism directed at more typically 'capitalist' performance measures (Cathcart, 2009, 2013a, 2013b) than, say to, community well-being or ecological sustainability.

Our analysis uses secondary empirical material (e.g. JLP documents in the public domain, histories of *John Lewis* and recent empirical research). Our assumption is that engagement and interrogation of existing empirical work can be at least as illuminating and challenging as undertaking new studies (Moore, 2007). In addition to generating fresh insights, stimulating reflection and fostering debate, our analysis is intended to contribute to an appreciation of how structures of ownership and governance are significant in enabling and constraining practices of organizing and managing.

We begin by providing a brief history of the formation of JLP in which we address the rationale for its creation and intended operation. We then present the contours of the formal design of JLP by considering its ownership and governance structures. This fills out the relevant background and orientation for our assessment of JLP in relation to the complex practices associated with capitalist and cooperative principles of organization, and its relevance to critical performativity.

JOHN LEWIS: IN PURSUIT OF HAPPINESS

Business, Objective and Structure

Established in 1864, the family drapery store, *John Lewis*, was converted, in 1929, into a Partnership with a formal Constitution that distributed its profits to the Partners. After 25 years, the property of the Partnership was assigned to the Partners through a second Trust settlement (O'Regan & Ghobadia, 2012). At the time of writing (2013), the JLP has around 84,700 Partners (Annual Report, 2013) working across the United Kingdom in 39 *John Lewis* stores and 290 *Waitrose* supermarkets. With annual gross sales of over £9.5 billion in 2013, JLP was the fourth largest non-publicly owned company in the United Kingdom measured by sales.[9]

A household name in the United Kingdom, JLP is widely acclaimed for being financially and commercially successful. It is highly trusted by its loyal and generally affluent customers.[10] The 'ultimate purpose' of JLP, as stated in its Constitution, is

> the *happiness of all its members*, through their *worthwhile and satisfying employment in a successful business*. Because the Partnership is owned in trust by its members, they share the responsibilities of ownership as well as its rewards—*profit, knowledge and power*. (Cox, 2010, p. 272, emphasis added)

This overarching purpose is one to which all JLP Partners are held accountable, and to which all Partners are able to make direct appeal, as do JLP Registrars (see later) who are appointed to act as the guardians of the company Constitution.

The architect of JLP, who was John Spedan Lewis (J.S.L.), one of the sons of the firm's founder, who bequeathed the company to its employees. In a British Broadcasting Corporation (BBC) poll, in 2002, J.S.L. was voted Britain's top business leader, ahead of Andrew Carnegie, Joseph Rowntree and William Lever.[11] J.S.L.'s bequest followed his disenchantment[12] with a more conventional and deeply entrenched philosophy and operation of capitalist enterprise, as exemplified by the business practices of his father. J.S.L. voiced his disillusionment in a talk aired by the BBC in April 1957, where he recalls how his father 'seemed to have all that anyone could want', and yet spent 'no more than a small fraction of his income' (Lewis, 1957). For his father's staff, in contrast, 'any saving worth mentioning was impossible. They were getting hardly more than a bare living' (Lewis, 1957). Commenting upon the impact of capitalism upon working people, J.S.L. first remarks that 'capitalism ... has done enormous good and suits human nature far too well to be given up as long as human nature remains the same' (Lewis, 1957). But he immediately adds that it is 'all wrong to have millionaires before you have ceased to have slums' (Lewis, 1957) – a state of affairs that he describes as 'a perversion of capitalism' (Cox, 2010).

In J.S.L.'s eyes, the 'perversion' was widespread in business practices, and especially in the treatment of employees, that were unjustifiably inegalitarian, socially divisive and ultimately self-destructive. J.S.L. set himself the challenge of (re)constructing the family business in a form compatible with his conception of 'human nature' and consistent with retaining the capacity of capitalism to do 'enormous good' so that its (performative) effect is to reduce unnecessary suffering rather than needlessly producing or perpetuating it. Conveyed in the subtitle of his book *Fairer Shares* (Lewis, 1954), J.S. L. regarded the model enacted in the Partnership as 'a possible advance in civilization and perhaps the only alternative to Communism'.

Commentary

Whether intended or not, the formation and maintenance of the Partnership is simultaneously a direct and practical intervention in debates around 'alternative forms of organization' – alternatives which have been defined primarily in relation to the expansion and domination of the joint-stock company. The slump of the late 1920s (Schwartz, 2011) re-ignited discussion of the relevance of ideas about collective and cooperative, rather than capitalist, organization 'as the best way to create a better society' that continued into the early 20th century (Cathcart, 2009, pp. 96–97; Goglio & Leonardi, 2010, p. 12). It also fuelled moral concern about the damaging and degrading consequences of unbridled capitalist expansion in which, established institutions (e.g. family and state) were becoming progressively harnessed to, and reshaped by, its priorities.

J.S.L.'s vision of a Partnership, governed by a Constitution setting out very detailed rules for its day-to-day operation, was apparently inspired primarily by an offended morality tinged with a philanthropic paternalism than it was animated by any political allegiance or agenda. Considered from a more contemporary vantage point, the creation and longevity of JLP may be seen as a practical demonstration of how

> the economy [does] not have to be thought as a bounded and unified space with a fixed capitalist identity. Perhaps the totality of the economic could be seen as a site of multiple forms of economy whose relations to each other are only partially fixed and always *under subversion*. (Gibson-Graham, 1996, p. 12, emphasis added)

Capitalist relations are 'under subversion' (Gibson-Graham, 1996) in diverse ways. The accumulation of capital by entrepreneurs and/or their family members affords them the option of becoming absentee shareholders in joint-stock companies in which, unlike the Partnership form, their liability for losses is legally limited to their share holdings. In such companies, salaried managers are hired to act as custodians of the assets of the company as the ex-owners spread their risks and smooth their returns within diversified investment portfolios. It is the rise of the joint-stock company that Marx (1981) describes as a 'negative' (p. 572) form of transition within capitalism (to be discussed later). And it was this (joint-stock) trajectory of capitalist development that J.S.L. sought to escape, and perhaps also to forestall, by establishing and demonstrating the viability of an alternative 'form of economy' (Gibson-Graham, 1996, p. 12) involving the use of a Trust to convert the family business into a Partnership.

OWNERSHIP AND GOVERNANCE

Structures of ownership and governance define the broad parameters of the operation of companies. These structures are of critical importance as they facilitate but also restrict the practices that comprise corporate activity (see Appendices A and B).

JLT Ownership: Voting Rights and Types of Shares

The locking down of JLP assets in a Trust (JLPT) prevents the dilution of equity, as it forbids its acquisition by non-Partners.[13] The device of the Trust frustrates the attentions of 'carpetbaggers' and thereby protects the benefits (e.g. employment) enjoyed by future as well as present Partners.[14]

JLP is organized around two main structures: a Trust and a Partnership (John Lewis Partnership Plc – JLPplc), with cross-holding. This cross-holding is organized with the support of different kind of shares.

At the Trust level, there are three types of share, but only one share, owned by the Chairman, has full voting rights. JLPplc owns the majority of the shares but with no voting rights, just dividend rights, called Deferred Ordinary Shares (DOS).

At the Partnership level, there are also three kinds of shares but only one, owned by JLPT, has full rights attached (DOS – which are different to those of the Trust). The Cumulative Preference Stocks (CPS)[15] have priority on dividends and are owned by the employees (the Partners). JLPT also owns Share Incentive Plan (SIP) shares that have only dividend rights. The position is summarized in Fig. 1.

Commentary

The salient points are as follows:

- Partners have the benefit of dividends paid by the CPS. But they have no other rights with regard to voting, and so on, and they cannot sell CPS.

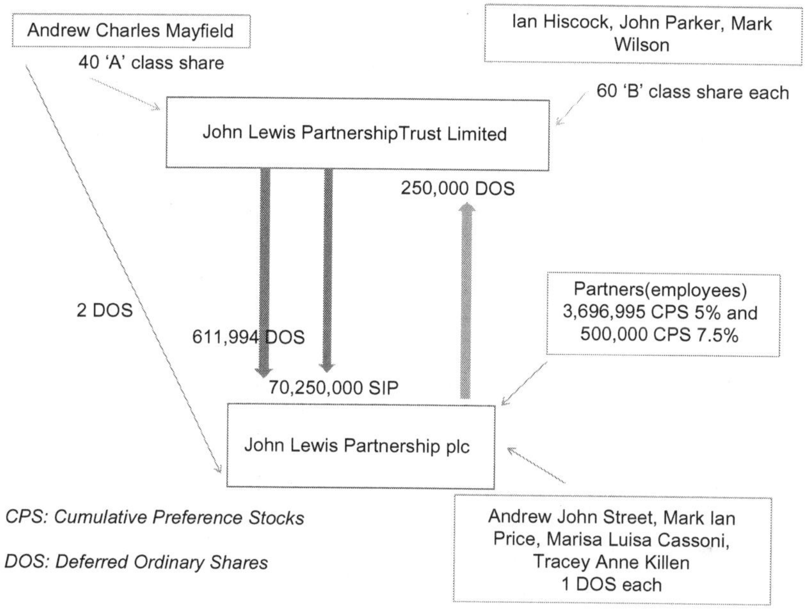

Fig. 1. Overall Ownership Structure.

This stock simply underwrites giving priority to a minimal level of annual bonus paid to Partners.

- The Trust (JLPT), and not individual partners *except Directors*, owns DOS and the SIP. Only the former have full voting rights and neither can be sold.
- It is a cross-holding organization linking JLPT and JLPplc.

JLP is a wholly employee-owned cooperative Partnership. Since the financial beneficiaries of the Trust are solely JLP employees, it is relevant to consider how this structure differs from that of *non-cooperative* organizations where (a) there is some employee ownership but neither extensive ownership and/or control (Ben-Ner and Jones, 1995; Doucouliagos, 1995) and (b) *cooperatives* are founded by their members. A typology devised by Pendleton (2011) distinguishes (a) 'worker cooperatives', (b) firms with minority share plans and (c) 'firms that are substantially or wholly worker owned' (p. 315). Applying this typology, JLP is a 'business succession firm'[16] in which the motive ascribed to the divesting owner is 'to protect the firm they have built up' (Pendleton, 2011, p. 323), presumably from external investors who might seek to control or acquire it, and 'a paternalist desire to protect the interests of their workforce' (Pendleton, 2001, p. 323, 2011). Indeed, Pendleton explicitly refers to JLP which he includes among employee-owned firms that 'adopt cooperative principles of equality of ownership, even though they do not register as fully fledged cooperatives' (Pendleton, 2011, p. 320) with regard to *direct* ownership by employees accompanied by full voting rights. JLP is, in very many respects, close to Pendleton's 'worker cooperative' but, notably, in the Partnership, *at the Trust level*, the ownership of shares with full voting rights is limited to the Chairman.[17]

JLT Governance: Constitution, 'Critical Side', Board and Council

Three key elements characterize the governance structure of JLP: The 'Critical Side', the Partnership Board and the Partnership Council.

The *Critical Side* is a novel and significant feature of the JLP governance structure included within its Constitution. Its purpose is to counterbalance and check the 'Executive Side', and thereby, in J.S.L.'s memorable formulation, 'safeguard the Executive from inadvertence' (Lewis, 1948, p. 425). The 'Critical Side' comprises 'independent' advocates of the JLP Constitution – and of Partners' rights within it and obligations to it – who are found across branches of the Partnership. Called *Registrars*, their role is to ensure that all forums and committees comply with the employee input and representation functions, as set out in the Constitution. A Chief Registrar, who is often elected by Partners to the Board (considered later), oversees the 'Critical Side'. Additionally, there are 'independent' Partners' *counsellors* at HQ who engage with the Registrars across the branches whose responsibility is to ensure that employment and work practices are consistent with Partnership values (e.g. the 'happiness' of Partners). The most senior within this intricate governance structure, the councillors provide a further constitutional counterweight to the 'Executive Side' in relation to complaints of, and grievances between, Partners.

The *Partnership Board* is the body ultimately responsible for fulfilling the purpose of the Partnership. In addition to the Chairman, the membership of this Board comprises three non-executive directors, five directors elected by the Partnership Council and a further five directors appointed by the Chairman. Members of the Partnership Board are responsible for managing JLP strategy, the quality of its financial statements, and the direction and reputation of its commercial activity (John Lewis Constitution, 2012, article 38).[18]

In the organization and work of the Partnership Board, the role of the Chairman – a position first occupied by J.S.L. – is pivotal. Not only is he or she responsible for deciding who should be admitted and retained in the Partnership, and for maintaining the Constitution to the satisfaction of the Partnership Council (considered later), but the Chairman has sole responsibility for the appointment of his or her successor (Constitution, article 41), and as noted earlier, he or she has full voting rights (Appendix A). Additionally, the Chairman is charged with ultimate responsibility for reconciling conflicting pressures between, for example, (a) re-investment of surpluses to develop the business, (b) Partners' desire for a good quality of working life but also the receipt of a substantial bonus and other benefits and (c) the competitiveness of JLP with regard, for example, to staffing costs and increasing employee productivity. When drawing up the Constitution, J.S.L. reports that he agonized over the contradictions between his advocacy of industrial democracy (e.g. election of 80% of the Partnership Council, see next paragraph) and the autocracy vested in the role of the Chairman. Whether his motivations were self-interested (recall that he appointed himself as the first Chairman) or more altruistic, J.S.L. justified this structural design by reference to fear of the 'disastrous' consequences that might result from its abolition (Cathcart, 2009, p. 46).

The *Partnership Council* is the third element of the governance structure which, in effect, is the General Assembly of JLP. In all, 80% of Council members are elected by the Partners on the basis of one person-one-vote, with the remaining 20% of the Partnership Council being appointed by the Partnership Board. Members of the Partnership Council are required to 'represent Partners as a whole and reflect their opinion' (John Lewis Constitution, 2012, article 7). The Partnership Council discusses and makes recommendations on the development of policy, and it shares responsibility with the Board and the Chairman for making decisions about the governance of the Partnership.

The Partnership Council can ask for explanations from the Board; it can propose strategy, and the Board and its Chairman are obliged to respond to such proposals and requests. However, the Board is not required to respond if this would, in the Board's opinion, damage the Partnership's interests. The relationships between the Constitution, the Board and the Council are summarized in Fig. 2.

We now introduce a comparative framework in which we contrast, capitalist with cooperative structures of ownership and governance before

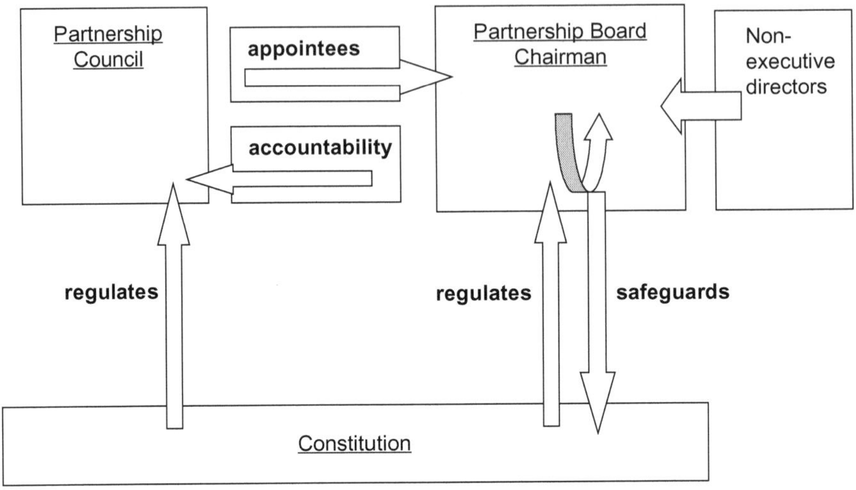

Fig. 2. Constitution, Council and Board.

applying this framework to illuminate and interrogate those of the Partnership, as sketched earlier. A key question is whether JLP can be credibly regarded as a critically performative alternative to capitalist enterprise.

ENTERPRISES: CAPITALIST AND COOPERATIVE

Conditions of Possibility

To explicate the organization of work within different (e.g. tendentially) 'capitalist' or 'cooperative' structures of ownership and governance, it is important to appreciate that structures per se are impotent: the catalyst of human agency is required to enact their reproduction or transformation. Attentiveness to agency serves to recall how, for example, 'efficient markets' and organizational hierarchies are, on the whole, forged and protected by emergent or entrenched elites and then are reproduced (and transformed) by the masses. Agency is obfuscated when, for example, the determination of prices, including the terms and conditions of labour, are abstracted from the political (re)construction of seemingly impersonal market forces. But, equally, the 'agency' of organizational members is conditioned by their situatedness and participation in 'structure(s)', even if their 'agency' is not reducible to, or determined by, the 'structure(s)' in which it is embedded.

In work organizations, structures of ownership and control are maintained or transformed through day-to-day struggles wherein agents (e.g. employees) introduce, absorb, question, reject, moderate or reproduce those structures. J.S.L., for example, reflected upon structures and associated employment practices typical of his day, and he determined to establish an alternative, Partnership structure capable of fostering and sustaining substantially different practices. In JLP today, governance bodies, including the Partnership Council,[19] are arenas of day-to-day struggle where, by virtue of the Constitution and its guardians (the Registrars), the exercise agential powers of governance is facilitated but also restricted, resulting in the preservation, or the alteration, of work practices and benefits (e.g. pensions provision).[20] In this context, it is salutary to recall Marx's (1981) observation that:

> Capitalist joint-stock companies as much as cooperative factories should be viewed as transition forms from the capitalist mode of production to the associated one, simply that in the one case the opposition is abolished in a negative way, and in the other in a positive way. (p. 572)

Marx's reflections suggest that, as a 'transition form', cooperatives are on the margins of an opposition between capital and labour. It is an assessment echoed by Pendleton (2005) when commenting upon employee share ownership which, he notes, modifies the ownership relationship but '*does so by making the worker a capitalist* rather than by changing the capital-labour relationship fundamentally' (Pendleton, 2005, p. 77, emphasis added). In effect, without more radical, extensive politico-economic change, employees in cooperatives become mini-capitalists who, it may be said, participate in their own 'self-exploitation'.[21]

It is unsurprising to find that the historical and on-going processes of 'positive transition' (Marx, 1981, p. 572) – from a family-owned capitalist enterprise into an employee-owned cooperative enterprise – are permeated by constraints, contradictions and compromises with regard to issues and processes of governance as well as ownership. There are, nonetheless, structural differences of ownership and governance between JLP and its earlier form as a family business. Of greater contemporary relevance, there are differences between the structures of JLP and the joint-stock form of enterprise. They facilitate but also restrict distinctive complexes of practices that articulate an embeddedness in dynamic and, to a degree, open historical and cultural contexts. This dynamism and openness is symptomatic not only of the volatility and instability arising from the capitalist 'imperative' of creative destruction but also of the dependence of this imperative upon the catalyst of human agency. As the formation of JLP demonstrates, what is accepted and apparently enduring today may be challenged and overturned tomorrow.

Capitalist Enterprise: The Joint-Stock Company and Disempowering Governance

Capitalist enterprise, in its joint-stock variant, is here conceived as tendentially organized to prioritize and safeguard the concerns of investors. This predilection is accomplished by the *exclusion of* sellers of labour power and other stakeholders from direct ownership of assets (e.g. buildings, raw materials, tools). Sale of goods generates a surplus which, in the form of dividends or capital gains, is privately appropriated by investors. With the exception of senior managers, who may also possess substantial stock options, wage labour has no significant, formal involvement in determining or reforming the structures of ownership or governance.[22] The accountability of senior executives (e.g. through audit and analysts' reports) is primarily to financial institutions through financial markets.

Understood in these terms, capitalist enterprise is considered to be *systematically* exploitative and oppressive (Weeks, 2010). Economic exploitation and political oppression exist irrespective of claims about the 'progressive' or 'enlightened' character of particular practices – with regard, for example, to employee involvement and employee share ownership schemes, or even token worker directors. Capitalist practices are, however, rarely represented, or even consciously experienced, as either exploitative or oppressive since, commonsensically, the terms 'exploitation' and 'oppression' are reserved for their most extreme and abhorrent forms – such as slavery, child labour or trafficking. Sanctified by bourgeois economics, economic exploitation and oppression are normalized in value-orientations that many employees learn to accept and defend. In common with J.S.L., poverty and misery are considered to harboured or engendered by capitalism *only* in their (most) 'perverted' forms. Everyday contractual exchanges between purchasers and sellers of labour power are deemed to be *fair*, not exploitative. That is because 'prices' – which include the prices in labour and capital as well product markets – are regarded as a result of impersonal and impartial forces rather than the outcome of relations of power and domination through which elites make markets and maintain hierarchies (Böhm & Land, 2012; Orleans, 2011). In financial markets that have been spawned by the rise of the joint-stock form of capitalism, shares and indeed companies are traded speculatively, as commodities, by absentee investors who often have only a short-term interest in maximizing the value of their holdings. Investors' preference is to finance companies in which they, and not other parties such as employees, can collectively exert a majority, controlling grip. Their concerns are then prioritized through the disciplining operation of capital markets.

Cooperative Enterprise: Employee Ownership and Collective Governance

Employee-owned cooperatives are here conceived to be tendentially organized to prioritize and safeguard the concerns of employees – notably by establishing and maintaining majority ownership and by democratizing governance. In employee-owned cooperatives, where its members are majority shareholders, there can be no *systematic* exploitation of labour by a different group, or class. Ownership of the assets of cooperative enterprise is normally through the investment of members or supporters in enterprise shares supplemented by other sources of finance, such as grants and loans. Cooperative members are either directly responsible for enterprise governance, including strategic and operational decision-making, or managers are appointed by and/or held accountable to the membership. Labour is no longer commodified even if the domination of exchange value persists in the economy as a whole (Weeks, 2010). In cooperatives, there are no dividends distributions, so the surplus value is dedicated to improving wages and conditions in addition to re-investment and creating reserves, and there is no opportunity to speculate on their future value as this is fixed.

When operating in an economy dominated by joint-stock companies and financial markets established to serve them, cooperative work organizations are financially disadvantaged so that their members struggle to achieve competitive economies of scale or scope. Nonetheless, their members opt to create or join such organizations where they are able to exercise a greater degree of autonomy and independence with regard to their governance. Notably, they are able to exercise democratic control over the goods or services that they produce and also over how they are produced. In employee-owned cooperatives, governance is not confined to the activities of an elite of board members but extends to decision-making across the organization in a way that assumes trust and commitment, and so also risks its abuse. In principle, decisions are either directly determined by cooperative members or they are scrutinized through mechanisms of accountability where managerial decisions are subject to challenge and potential reversal (Paranque, 2014).

Commentary

Our presentation of capitalist and cooperative enterprise, as comprising tendentially distinct practices, has served to highlight the significance of structures of ownership and governance in conditioning employment relations and the organization of work. But those structures are impotent without the catalyst of agency. The presence of agency accounts for why, in their day-to-day operation, practices of organizing and managing rarely mirror the structural features ascribed to them. Members of cooperatives, for example, may turn a blind eye to 'free-riding' by members whose commitment to principles of working together and inclusiveness is, at best, partial. It is to such recalcitrance that J.S.L. may have been alluding when, reluctantly,[23] he concludes that reducing the power of the Chairman 'would open the door to troubles that might be disastrous' (Lewis, 1948, p. 369).

As anticipated by Marx (1981), the formation of cooperatives may signal 'the first examples of the emergence of a new form' (p. 571), but they also 'naturally reproduce in all cases, *in their present organization*, all the defects of the existing system, and must reproduce them' – by which we understand Marx to refer inter alia to forms of self-interested behaviour as well as self-exploitation and work degradation. Marx conceives of cooperatives as foreshadowing a 'new' form of work organization in which the opposition between capital and labour is abolished 'even if at first only in the form that the workers in association become their own capitalist, that is they use the means of production to valorize their own labour power' (Jossa, 2005, p. 5, citing Marx, 1981, p. 571).[24] Here, Marx might be describing the situation at JLP where the social division between capital and labour is abolished, at least with regard to external owners. Cathcart's (2009) study of JLP echoes Warhurst's (1996) observation that 'management as an occupational group [within the kibbutz system] is becoming more coherent and consistent' (p. 434), and in this sense, it comprises a fraction within the Partnership that is in some tension with the more unified spirit of the JLP Constitution. In this light, 'economic sites' (Gibson-Graham, 1996, p. 18) that are widely represented as 'homogeneously [cooperative] may be re-envisioned as sites of economic difference where a variety of [cooperative and non cooperative] class processes interact' (Gibson-Graham, 1996, p. 18).

An exclusive focus upon the *political economy* of enterprise courts the danger of reducing relationships to ones of economic ownership versus economic non-ownership. While political economy is vital – we have stressed the importance of structures of ownership – this emphasis can overlook the heterogeneity of corporate practices. It may fail to appreciate how, for example, even within joint-stock enterprises, relations may be pervaded by, and depend upon, other (e.g. cultural) relationships, including friendship, family and community (Grey & Sturdy, 2007). Those 'informal' relations may, of course, be more or less purposefully harnessed by management to smoothing or intensifying the capital-labour relationship, but they are rarely reducible to that single objective. Analysis which considers only the expansive tendencies of capitalism to colonize and commodify ever wider areas of social life risks conveying an indefensibly totalizing picture in which the economy is left 'theoretically untouched' (Gibson-Graham, 1996, p. 38), or, at least, the abstraction of the economic from the cultural is inadequately interrogated and problematized so that sites are (mis)represented as homogeneously capitalist or cooperative.

DISCUSSION

We now assess JLP as an example of critical performativity with respect to its structures of ownership and governance and its relevance for moving 'beyond capitalism'.

Ownership and JLP

When employees are the shareholders, the systematic exploitation of one class by another is, by definition, excluded *within* the company. If this logic is accepted, then in employee-owned cooperatives there is no logical justification for a distinctive, potentially oppositional, employee voice. And yet, even where, as in the case of JLP, the opposition of capital and labour is formally abolished, and a comparatively democratic structure of governance is established, its day-to-day operation may be conditioned or even dominated by other (e.g. financial) considerations.

Unlike many employee-owned cooperatives, JLP is in an enviable position of being minimally reliant upon external sources of capital. Even so, the 'professionalization' of JLP management has been accompanied by the importation of financial performance conventions and by a managerially encouraged emphasis upon running the business to deliver the annual bonus paid to Partners. These considerations inform decision-making within the Partnership, including discussion of governance reforms and proposals to change the terms and conditions (e.g. extension of trading hours) of Partners.

The absence of a directly oppositional employee voice, which JLP shares with certain cooperatives (e.g. Mondragón), may be taken to reflect the abolition of the social division between capital and labour. But it may also indicate the latent influence of a shareholder ideology and associated discourse of shareholder value creation (Pendleton, 2005, p. 76). JLP staff may then identify themselves primarily as recipients of dividends rather than as Partners committed to the 'happiness' of all members, where 'happiness' is not conflated with the 'self-exploitation' required to deliver a substantial bonus. The dividend paid to shareholders and the Partners' bonus may function in a similar way when each encourages, or induces, the generation of a surplus in a manner that does not, and perhaps cannot, readily countenance, accommodate or fulfil other, non-financial objectives (e.g. sustainability), except perhaps by promoting higher margin 'green' products in its stores, thereby improving financial returns. If Partners' identification with the ethos of Partnership is shallow or eclipsed by other priorities, their relationship to (fellow members of) the cooperative becomes less distinguishable from the alienated labour found more typically in capitalist enterprises.

In capitalist enterprise, it is the concern of investors rather than other stakeholders that are prioritized. This follows, in substantial part, from (mis)ascribing to shareholders ownership of residual rights (claimants) on the assets of the enterprise when, legally, they own no more than the shares traded on financial markets. This (mis)ascription leads to an agency-theoretic (mis)representation of executives as 'agents' of the 'principals' (i.e. shareholders). For, legally, executives are guardians of the assets of the enterprise, not of the 'principals' of a going-concern in which diverse parties, including shareholders, make a contribution and have a stake. In JLP, the (mis)ascription of ownership of the assets is avoided. It is clear that the Partners derive a share of the surplus produced from the productive use of those assets. The role of managers is, however, less well defined beyond a rather vague notion of their responsibility for 'the happiness of all [the Partnership's] members, through their worthwhile and satisfying employment in a successful business' (Cox, 2010, p. 272). The question begged is the meaning of 'happiness', 'satisfaction' and 'successful' and whether, managerially, it might be framed in relation to service to the community, for example, or to the size of the bonus.

Even allowing for how, in Marx's (1981) words, the formation of cooperatives may reproduce 'the defects of the existing system, and must reproduce them' (p. 571) (as illustrated earlier), if JLP structures of ownership and governance were to be widely adopted, there would be far-reaching consequences. Capital/labour divisions would be very considerably eroded and the conditions of possibility of the (mis)ascription of asset ownership to shareholders, and the associated mantra of shareholder value maximization, would be silenced. Private wealth could still be accumulated by loaning capital without voting rights, but external shareholders could not engage in trading their shares or entire companies without regard to those who create the assets from which capital is privately accumulated.

Given the radical implications of any widespread adoption of the JLP model, as commended by the UK Deputy Prime Minister, it is surprising that *John Lewis* is routinely presented, and indeed is celebrated, as an icon, and perhaps a saviour, of 'true' capitalism – that is, 'responsible capitalism'. On the other hand, and in common with employee-owned cooperatives, such as Mondragón, JLP poses no direct threat to the 'free market' principles of capitalism, and it offers no succour for the nationalization of enterprises. Indeed, the inspiration for establishing the Partnership lay in demonstrating the viability of 'responsible' capitalism, and not in engineering a replacement for it. Even the aspiration to counteract and reduce the *pathological* effects of 'free markets' can prove difficult to fulfil – as is evident from how members of the Mondragón cooperative reportedly regard their relation to it 'less as citizens and more as consumers'.[25] This consumerist orientation, which finds echoes among the Partners of JLP has been interpreted as an effect of how 'the cooperatives themselves [have] imported managerial regimes that privilege constant orientation towards the customer/client' (Asparagus, Cheney, & Udaondo, 2012, p. 79). Had a survey equivalent to that administered at Mondragón been undertaken in JLP, it would probably elicit similar responses. That said, it is undoubtedly easier for a retailer to preserve such principles than it is for a producer cooperative that faces intense international competitive pressures.

Governance and JLP

Partners do not own JLP, only a specific right to a minimal level of dividend, and so they are prevented from exerting direct pressure upon JLP managers through the market for corporate control. Instead, Partners are obliged to control managerial decision-making through an elaborate governance structure. Their capacity to resist managerialism flows from the powers of governance bestowed upon them by the Constitution, and not from their property rights as shareholders. It is Partners' election of a majority (80%) of the Partnership Council that, ultimately, empowers them to influence strategy as well as operational decisions,[26] and even to remove the Chairman.

In direct contrast to joint-stock enterprise, JLP institutionalizes a recognition of the productive engagement of labour in the creation of assets and guards this in its Constitution. That said, and as Pendleton (2011) has noted of 'post-conversion governance structures' similar to JLP, they are 'likely to be especially influenced by [the ex-owner(s)]' (p. 332). Bequeathing the assets of a company to employees, as J.S.L. did, tends to place them in the position of passive beneficiaries, rather than active advocates and practitioners, of a cooperative ethos. An indicator of such passivity is the way 'employee involvement in governance is typically kept clearly distinct from day-to-day management' (Pendleton, 2011, p. 332). The JLP governance structure is extensive in its design and scope, but it can prove difficult to operate effectively on a day-to-day basis. Historically, the various channels of representation have tended to be disproportionately populated by managers and time-serving, institutionalized staff (Cathcart, 2009; Erdal, 2011). The governance structure may, consequently, deliver only a weak, and perhaps ritualistic, form of accountability. Participants may be complicit in managerial decision-making rather than watchful and questioning of it (Cathcart, 2009, 2013a) – a posture that reflects Partners' exclusion from share ownership and, more specifically, their powerlessness to exert pressure upon JLP managers through the market for corporate control in the form of their collective divestment.

Managers' accountability to Partners is indirect and collective through the Partnership Council and its associated bodies. The day-to-day approach to managing JLP tends to be predominantly technocratic, with decisions being rationalized post hoc by justifying their compliance with Partnership principles, and thereby minimizing the risk of challenge by the Partnership Council or its sub-committees (Cathcart, 2009). Managerial authority is thus exercised by virtue of specialist knowledge and/or previous experience, and not primarily through a democratic mandate. *Qua* managers, rather than Partners, their status and expertise provides them with a platform for articulating and influencing the 'interests' of the Partners in a way that is congruent with a managerialist agenda.[27]

JLP and 'beyond Capitalism'?

Finally, we relate our discussion of JLP's structures of ownership and governance to the question of how capitalism might be transformed into a less divisive and destructive political economy.

Directly pertinent to this issue is Wolff's (2009) thesis that the prospects of such transformation are impeded by structures of ownership and governance that are entrenched, though not immutable. Wolff argues that capitalist structures bestow monopoly power upon boards of directors, drawn from a narrow elite, whose decision-making has increasingly become exclusively geared to maximizing shareholder value, and so intensifies the economic exploitation and political oppression of labour by capital. The broad-brush remedy proposed by Wolff (2009) is for

> workers inside enterprises to displace their boards and become their own collective boards of directors … As people once dethroned kings in favour of universal suffrage, workers can abolish boards of directors in favour of receiving and distributing the surpluses/profits themselves … [In this process, employees are understood to become] their own surplus/profit appropriators … [and are] … more personally invested in the quality of their work. (pp. 14, 15)

Wolff (2009) is silent on the question of how boards are to be 'dethroned', except to say that it will somehow be accomplished by workers. JLP offers an alternative kind of 'dethronement' in the form of abdication. Relinquishing ownership by gifting the assets of the company to present and future employees does, however, present significant challenges in terms of worker/Partner 'investment' in post-capitalist, *cooperative* enterprise. Wolff's 'new strategy of "reform plus"' is, nonetheless, *to a degree* foreshadowed in the Constitution and structures of JLP. JLP admittedly falls short of Wolff's vision,[28] but it is important to recall, once again, that few cooperatives fully exemplify cooperative principles and/or wholly embrace all aspect(s) of Wolff's 'reform plus'. Taking this into account, Wolff's ideas are relevant for conducting a thought experiment where a transition occurs in which enterprises are incentivized, or required, to adopt JLP structures of ownership and governance.[29] With this change, as Wolff (2009) anticipates, 'capitalist boards of directors' would be deprived of the resources and incentives to 'shape political processes … to secure their situations' (Wolff, 2009, p. 16). There would, as he anticipates, be a major politico-economic shift as 'the absence of economic democracy inside enterprises [would no longer] systematically undermine political democracy outside them' (Wolff, 2009, p. 16). Such a possibility connects to wider debates. Those debates include discussions circling around the notion of critical performativity within CMS. Their focus is upon on how a transition towards a less divisive and destructive post-capitalist political economy might develop that is *not* premised upon abolition of capitalist privately owned means of production (assets) and/or planning and command by the state. We have seen how, in the JLP model, the assets of the organization are held in Trust for the benefit of its present and future employees/ Partners. And we have shown how, despite lacking the ultimate means of sanctioning managers by selling their shares, the JLP governance structure permits, but does not compel, Partners to exercise some control of management as vouchsafed by the Constitution.

Wolff's 'reform plus' proposal invites further reflection on the critical performativity of JLP. *If* Partners' 'happiness' is framed primarily in terms of self-centred concerns, such as working conditions, it displaces any more extensive concern for diverse stakeholders and the natural environment. *When* the 'happiness' of Partners and a 'successful' business is defined in terms of financial performance and increasing the annual bonus, there is a more tenuous basis for 'shar[ing] common interests with surrounding communities', let alone for paying greater attention to 'air, water, ground and other pollution by the enterprise' (Wolff, 2009, p. 15). JLP structures of ownership and governance are currently myopic with respect to stakeholders other than Partners, and to wider considerations – such as sustainability. While this myopia could be ascribed to the timing of JLP's formation, and its history as a business succession firm, it is also evident in more recently established cooperatives where employees directly own the shares, such as Mondragón. The primary and overriding aim of Mondragón is confined to serving the people and culture of the Basque region. In common with Mondragón, JLP structures of ownership, and especially governance, require radical revision if their current emphasis on financial performance for the benefit of an inner circle of Partners is to be re-oriented to facilitate participation by a wider constituency of stakeholders, deep commitment to sustainability and/or respect for the commons.

SUMMARY AND CONCLUSION

Our examination of the ownership and governance structures of *John Lewis* is intended to advance and deepen reflection and debate upon possibilities for a 'critically performative' transformation of capitalism, and not just its recuperation. We have noted that the ownership structure of JLP protects future as well as current Partners from the attentions of distant investors. We have also shown how the JLP governance structure makes managers formally accountable to Partners through a range of channels. Endorsement of these progressive, putatively post-capitalist features of JLP has been qualified by reference, respectively, to the infantilizing and managerially colonizing effects of its structures.

The very existence of JLP is, nonetheless, significant as it presents a direct challenge to the *necessity* of what has become normalized as the joint-stock form of capitalist enterprise. Since 1928, JLP has delivered comparatively secure employment, good working conditions and generous fringe benefits to its Partners. The vitality and longevity of the Partnership is attributable, at least in part, to its transgression of Marx's dictum that 'co-operative societies … are of value only insofar as they are the independent creations of workers and not protégés either of governments or of the bourgeoisie' (Jossa, 2005, p. 8, citing Marx, 1875, p. 94). JLP demonstrates that it is possible to develop and sustain a highly successful business without recourse to the ownership and governance structure of the joint-stock form of capitalist enterprise. Yet, JLP's philanthropic formation and its paternalistic structures of ownership and governance also make its cooperative status, and its emulation as an alternative model of enterprise, somewhat problematical, but without rendering its claim to offer an alternative, even a critically performative one, wholly indefensible or irrelevant. JLP is not an 'independent creation of workers' (Marx, 1875). Indeed, and in common with most cooperatives, it does not comply with the more idealized principles ascribed to them. But, in a market context, dominated by joint-stock enterprises, JLP's limitations may also be a source of strength or at least of durability.

What, then, are the 'critically performative' credentials of JLP? JLP scores comparatively highly on the cooperative principles of 'member economic participation' (e.g. through bonuses and benefits) and 'autonomy and independence' (JLP operates independently of external shareholders). The JLP Constitution confers considerable formal powers on Partners and protects them from the control of JLP assets by distant investors. But its Constitution also assumes, or at least leaves unquestioned, the legitimacy and continuation of capitalism as a politico-economic system. There is an assumption that the JLP Constitution can be faithfully enacted in an economy dominated by joint-stock enterprises. But whether or not that supposition is supportable, the very existence of the Trust form tacitly challenges and frustrates the development and expansion of capitalism by ruling out the control of JLP assets by external shareholders.

Turning to the question of how JLP incorporates 'democratic member control', its scope has been circumscribed from the outset. Managerial decision-making is accountable to Partners through a range of mechanisms and media, but, crucially, managers are not appointed or elected by the Partners: J.S.L.'s vision of the Partnership was not one of collective self-determination. Symptomatic of this deficit, the most influential person in JLP – the Chairman – nominates his or her successor subject to the approval of the Partnership Board but without any formal consultation with Partners. Within the JLP governance structures, there is also vulnerability to over-prioritizing conventional commercial objectives, such as retaining or expanding market share, without equivalent or greater regard to their democratic determination or endorsement. Those pressures are especially difficult to resist when strong financial performance is a prerequisite of meeting Partners' expectations, including receipt of a substantial annual bonus on top of funding an exceptionally generous package of fringe benefits. For those committed to the cooperative values of the Partnership, the challenge is not 'simply' to demonstrate the viability as its business model but, above all, to nurture and strengthen a strong counter-ideology capable of resisting pressures to circumvent or compromise 'democratic member control' and thereby translate formal accountability into its substantive operation.

Despite its Partnership Council and the 'Critical Side', the JLP governance structure operates, with an occasional challenge, to facilitate and legitimate Partners' loyal and largely passive participation in the pursuit of a managerial elite's (benevolent) priorities, which this elite represents as imperative to ensuring the future 'happiness' of the Partners (Cathcart, 2009, 2013a). Since Partners have no direct power to shape the financial strategy of the firm through the market for corporate control, they can only endeavour to convince different boards and committees to heed and adopt their preferences. JLP Partners are, in principle, collectively sovereign but, in practice, JLP's structures of ownership and governance co-opt and colonize, as well as facilitate, Partners' powers of self-determination.

These observations signal our ambivalence about JLP as an example of 'critical performativity' (Spicer et al., 2009). JLP can be read as a 'subversive intervention' (Spicer et al., 2009, p. 538) insofar as it denies absentee investors access to, and control of, its assets. If the UK's Deputy Prime Minister's advocacy of a '*John Lewis* economy' was to be realized, then opportunities for the reproduction and further enrichment of the capitalist class would be significantly curtailed. Currently, however, even the critical performative potential of the Partnership model is impeded by its paternalist structures. Exclusion of Partners' participation in the market for corporate control is reflected in, and compounded by, a weak form of 'democratic' governance, where managers are accountable to Partners but not controlled by them.

For these reasons, it is implausible to characterize JLP as an unequivocally progressive or emancipatory form of organization. It is deeply infused with paternalism and the narcissistic spirit of contemporary capitalism. Its ownership and governance structures are dedicated primarily to mitigating needless 'perversions' of capitalism, rather than their eradication. Moreover, such mitigation is pursued without regard to the inclusion of other stakeholders, such as suppliers, and to the consideration of socially responsible objectives, such as sustainability. For variety of reasons, it is doubtful that the JLP model 'offer(s) a powerful response to today's and tomorrow's economic, social, and environmental needs' (Webb & Cheney, 2014, p. 24). Framed within a Constitution that pays little regard to other stakeholders, let alone to the natural environment, JLP presents a 'response' to 'environmental needs' that is highly partial, rather than 'powerful'.

What, then, might be done to tackle these and other structural limitations of the JLP model? Empirical research is undeniably helpful in generating findings with which to probe and challenge received understandings (Cathcart, 2013a, 2013b). Yet, as such evidence is inescapably theory dependent, generating additional data will not resolve interpretive differences except disingenuously through evidence-based fiat. Indeed, focussing scholarly effort primarily on conducting further empirical studies may inadvertently (or perhaps intentionally) displace or obscure the structural conditions of possibility of the practices being investigated. Such conditions include the *structures of ownership and governance* which support but also circumscribe those practices.

Returning to the question of whether JLP offers an example of 'critical performativity', our answer is, with many reservations, cautiously affirmative. Crucially, the Trust, unlike the join-tstock enterprise, safeguards the assets created by employees among other contributors, and makes them, rather than absent shareholders, the primary beneficiaries. It also makes Partners the custodians of JLP assets through a comparatively democratic form of governance. The ownership and governance structures designed by John Spedan Lewis have proved remarkably practical and resilient. They have provided some restraint upon tendencies towards 'perversion', whether those arise from the avarice of owners or the unchecked power of managers. And, it may just be that areas of deficit, especially with regard to democratic member control, have facilitated the survival of JLP in a context where it faces intense competition from joint-stock enterprises that are not 'hampered' by the restrictions upon access to capital and upon managerial prerogative faced by JLP.

Finally, it is relevant to recall that JLP was bequeathed to its Partners, and that the conversion of joint-stock enterprises into equivalents of JLP would require a comparable and rather improbable act of philanthropic generosity on the part of their shareholders, perhaps facilitated by appropriate tax breaks. With regard to governance, it has been noted how its structures tend to infantilize its Partners and co-opt them, as passive participants, within practices that accommodate managerialism even if they also curb its worst excesses. So, would disestablishing the Trust better instantiate or advance 'critical performativity'? It is by no means self-evident that its dismantlement would be advantageous for future employees or for other stakeholders (customers, suppliers, the wider community or natural environment). Its dissolution would risk distant investors gaining control of *John Lewis* which, in turn, would likely result in its governance structures being weakened or even dismantled rather than strengthened and extended. If, instead, the Partnership structure were somehow to replace *every* joint-stock company, there would be a substantial reduction in the external pressures which currently frustrate the democratization of work organizations. There would, of course, remain concerns about the infantilizing effects of the Trust and the coherence of its governance model (e.g. the role of the Chairman and the exclusion of Partners from the process of hiring managers). But latent potentials within the JLP Constitution and its structure of governance might be leveraged to build a more radical, outward-looking, 21st-century company[30] in which a revised Constitution could ensure not only that managerial appointments are collectively determined by Partners but that other stakeholders and ecological considerations become central, rather than peripheral, to JLP's strategy and operations. Whether the retention of JLP's existing structures of ownership and governance, or a push for their radical reform, would save capitalism, or bury it, is question to which we have offered no unequivocal answer. By leaving the question open, our intention is to stimulate further reflection and debate on the possibilities of 'critical performativity' and the degree to which the JLP model does, or could potentially, advance it.

NOTES

1. Closing speech at Liberal Party Conference, 11 March 2012. See http://www.politics.co.uk/commentanalysis/2012/03/11/cegg-conference-speech-in-fulll. It is a description echoed by other commentators, including the left-leaning think-tank *Demos*. See also Cathcart (2013a).

2. Plc indicates a company with shares. It is not necessarily a public company with shares tradable on the stock market.

3. See http://ica.coop/en/whats-co-op/co-operative-identity-values-principles (accessed on 2 June 2014).

4. http://ica.coop/en/whats-co-op (accessed on 17 July 2013).

5. The Constitution is available at http://www.johnlewispartnership.co.uk/content/dam/cws/pdfs/about%20us/our%20constitution/john-lewis-partnership-constitution.pdf

6. John Lewis Partnership (JLP) also employs many temporary, part-time staff, especially in its Waitrose supermarket chain, who are not eligible to become Partners. It is necessary to be a Partner for three years before becoming enroled in the final salary scheme.

7. Instead of being distributed to external, absentee shareholders, the equivalent of a dividend is paid to its Partners through an annual bonus (currently around 15% of salary). This is in addition to a range of other generous fringe benefits (e.g. pension scheme, heavily subsidized leisure activities, store discounts).

8. For example, even though he acknowledges that the elected Council of JLP 'has consultation and veto rights on all capital decisions', Ramsay (1980, p. 51) declares that *only* 'apathy and triviality' are the outcome of the scheme (Ramsay, 1980, p. 52), and that 'if anyone gains it is management' (Ramsay, 1980, p. 51). Our analysis places in question such zero-sum thinking. For some reflections on this 'culture of thinking', see Gibson-Graham (2006, p. 2 et seq.).

9. For an overview, see O'Regan and Ghobadia (2012).

10. These include a substantial number who have shifted their affections from joint-stock companies, notably *Marks and Spencer*, where the short-term pursuit of shareholder value has become a perennial preoccupation. See http://www.theguardian.com/education/2009/feb/03/access-university (accessed on 4 August 2013).

11. See http://news.bbc.co.uk/1/hi/business/2526147.stm (accessed on 21 October 2013).

12. It has been speculated that a very serious riding accident in 1909, which prevented John Spedan Lewis from working, forced upon him to take a period of extended leisure and contemplation during which he devised the idea of a Partnership (see Macpherson, 1985).

13. Partners are not legally allowed to trade their equity, even among themselves, and are required to surrender their equity stake when they leave the Partnership.

14. In principle, Partners may vote collectively, through the Partnership Council, to sell the company, but this would require testing in the Courts and ultimately in Parliament as the Trust is designed to frustrate such a move.

15. See Brealey, Myers, and Allen (2011, p. 378) for definitions.

16. The other two categories are 'human capital firms', which are dependent upon highly knowledgeable and skilled personnel, and management–employee buy-outs.

17. The extensive powers vested in the Chairman clearly excludes JLP from full 'worker cooperative' status, even though in some cooperatives, only a minority of employee-owned shares carry full voting rights.

18. John Lewis Partnership Annual report and accounts (2011, p. 29). All information comes from http://www.johnlewispartnership.co.uk/about/the-partnership/governing-authorities/partnership-council.html; http://www.johnlewispartnership.co.uk/about/the-partnership/governingauthorities/partnership-board/all-directors.html; http://www.johnlewispartnership.co.uk/about/thepartnership/management-bodies.html

19. In addition to the Partnership Council, there are three other arenas of formal democratic engagement: Divisional Council, Forum and Partner Voice. Divisional Councils are elected every three years by and from their Forums, where no Forum is established, representatives are elected by all Partners in the constituency. These representative bodies meet whenever they wish, but at least four times a year, and when asked by the Trustees of the Constitution. All representatives formally commit to fulfil their role to the best of their ability and with the best interests of the Partnership in mind. Adapted from the John Lewis Constitution (2012, pp. 7, 14). See note 5.

20. See http://www.telegraph.co.uk/finance/newsbysector/retailandconsumer/10607636/John-Lewis-to-cutback-gold-plated-pension-scheme.html (accessed on 26 February 2014).

21. It is difficult to find a term that adequately expresses the point, hence the scare quotes. What is described here as 'self-exploitation' results from the struggle (e.g. of cooperative members) to subsist by cost-cutting, including reducing the cost of labour, in order to be competitive.

22. Treated as a *commodity* equivalent to other factors of production, labour is a target, and not an agent, of supervision and regulation. Nonetheless, structures of ownership and governance in joint-stock enterprises inescapably depend upon the catalyst of agency, and so invariably accommodate or incorporate forms of 'indulgency' (Gouldner, 1954). 'Participation' and performance-related inducements hat lubricate the smooth generation of a surplus sufficient to sustain the involvement of investors.

23. He writes, 'I wish very much indeed that I had been able to devise something more democratic' (Lewis, 1948, p. 368).

24. In this regard, reference to the kibbutz form of organization is pertinent as 'many kibbutz branches operate on use value alone' (Warhurst, 1996, p. 423), and thereby endeavour to escape 'exploitation' (the capture of surplus value by external investors from the exchange value derived from goods and services).

25. The expansion of Mondragón, pursued 'primarily to protect cooperative employment and operations in the Basque country' (Gibson-Graham, 2006, p. 121), has largely resulted from joint-ventures, acquisitions and start-ups outside of the region where 'workforces are wholly or partly composed of contract-based or non-owning employees', which are reported to comprise 'approximately 50 per cent' of the workforce (Durance, 2011; Gibson-Graham, 2006, p. 123).

26. Cathcart (2009, pp. 296–97) gives two recent examples of how the Partnership Council rejected recommendations for quite radical changes proposed by management.

27. Such measures include cost-cutting to increase competitiveness and/or increase turnover, and thereby justify an expansion of activity which is especially beneficial to the pursuit of managerial careers.

28. A key difference, discussed earlier, is that ownership was bequeathed to John Lewis employees through the vehicle of a Trust. Other significant features include the split election/appointment of the Partnership Council, the minority of elected Partners on the Board and the 'Godfather' status of the Chairman.

29. Perhaps by offering tax incentives for owners progressively to bequeath businesses to their stakeholders using the vehicle of a Trust.

30. This would require the Partners to mobilize two-thirds of their membership to revise the JLP Constitution.

ACKNOWLEDGMENTS

Many thanks to Abby Cathcart, Peter Cox, Richard MacVie, Ewan McGaughey and Peter Smith (Partner Constantin) as well as to participants in the 'Cooperatives' UMASS-Boston CMS Paper Development Workshop held in August 2012, for their very useful help and comments in the preparation of this article. All errors remain ours.

REFERENCES

Asparagus, J., Cheney, G., & Udaondo, A. (2012). Worker's participation in a globalized market: Reflections on and from Mondragon. In M. Atzeni (Ed.), *Alternative work organizations* (pp. 76–102). London: Palgrave.

Ben-Ner, A., & Jones, D. (1995). Employee participation, ownership, and productivity: A theoretical framework. *Industrial Relations*, *34*, 532–553.

Böhm, S., & Land, C. (2012). The new "hidden abode": Reflections on value and labour in the new economy. *The Sociological Review*, *60*(2), 217–240.

Brealey, R. A., Myers, S. C., & Allen, F. (2011). *Principles of corporate finance*. New York, NY: McGraw-Hill/Irwinn, Global Edition.

Carberry, E. J. (2011). Employee ownership and shared capitalism: Assessing the experience, research, and policy implications. In E. J. Carberry (Ed.), *Employee ownership and shared capitalism: New directions in research* (pp. 1–26). Champaign, IL: Labor and Employment Relations Association.

Cathcart, A. (2009). *Directing democracy: The case of the John Lewis partnership*. School of Management, University of Leicester. Retrieved from http://eprints.qut.edu.au/44149/1/CathcartThesis.pdf. Accessed on June 20, 2012.

Cathcart, A. (2013a). Directing democracy: Competing interests and contested terrain in the John Lewis partnership. *Journal of Industrial Relations*, *55*(4), 601–620.

Cathcart, A. (2013b). Paradoxes of participation: Non-union workplace partnership in John Lewis. *International Journal of Human Resource Management*, *25*(6), 762–780.

Cheney, G. (1999). *Values at work: Employee participation meets market pressure at Mondragon* (Updated ed.). New York, NY: Cornell University Press.

Cox, P. (2010). *Spedan's partnership: The story of John Lewis and Waitrose*. London: Labatie Books.

Doucouliagos, C. (1995). Worker participation and productivity in labor-managed and participatory capitalist firms: A meta-analysis. *Industrial & Labor Relations Review*, *49*(1), 58–77.

Durance, P. (2011). La coopérative est elle un modèle d'avenir pour le capitalisme? Retour sur le cas Mondragon. *Gérer et Comprendre*, *December*(106), 69–79.

Erdal, D. (2011). *Beyond the corporation humanity at work*. London: The Bodley Head.

Gamble, A. (2009). *The spectre at the feast: Capitalist crisis and the politics of recession*. London: Palgrave.

Gibson-Graham, J. K. (1996). *The end of capitalism (as we know it): A feminist critique of political economy*. Oxford: Blackwell.

Gibson-Graham, J. K. (2006). *A post-capitalist politics*. Minneapolis, MN: University of Minnesota Press.

Gios, G., & Santuari, A. (2002). Agricultural cooperatives in the county of Trento (Italy): Economic, organizational and legal perspectives. *Journal of Rural Cooperation*, *30*(1), 3–12.

Goglio, S., & Leonardi, A. (2010). *The roots of cooperative credit from a theoretical and historical perspective*. Euricse Working Paper No. 011-10. Retrieved from http://ssrn.com/abstract=1698611

Gouldner, A. (1954). *Patterns of industrial bureaucracy*. Chicago, IL: Labor and Employment Relations Association, Free Press.

Grey, C., & Sturdy, A. (2007). Friendship and organizational analysis: Toward a research agenda. *Journal of Management Inquiry*, *16*(2), 157–172.

Hartmann, R. K. (2014). Subversive functionalism: For a less canonical critique in critical management studies. *Human Relations*, *67*(5), 611–632.

Huertas-Noble, C. (2010). Promoting worker-owned cooperatives as a CED empowerment strategy: A case study of colors and lawyering in support of participatory decision-making and meaningful social change. *Clinical Law Review*, *17*(1). Retrieved from http://ssrn.com/abstract=1761669

Hutton, W. (2012). *Plurality, stewardship and engagement: The report of the ownership commission*. London: Mutuo. Retrieved from http://ownershipcomm.org/files/ownership_commission_2012.pdf. Accessed on June 6, 2014.

John Lewis Constitution. (2012). Retrieved from http://www.johnlewispartnership.co.uk/content/dam/cws/pdfs/about%20us/our%20constitution/john-lewis-partnership-constitution.pdf

John Lewis Partnership Annual report and accounts. (2011). *John Lewis website*. Retrieved from http://www.johnlewispartnership.co.uk/about.html. Accessed on July 3, 2012.

Jossa, B. (2005). Marx, Marxism and the cooperative movement. *Cambridge Journal of Economics*, *29*(1), 3–18.

Lewis, J. (2013). Partnership Annual report and accounts. John Lewis website. Retrieved from http://www.johnlewispartnership.co.uk/financials/financial-reports/annual-reports.html. Accessed on July 3, 2014.

Lewis, J. S. (1948). *Partnership for all: A thirty four year old experiment in industrial democracy*. London: Kerr-Cross Publishing.

Lewis, J. S. (1954). *Fairer shares: A possible advance in civilization and perhaps the only alternative to communism*. London: Staples Press.

Lewis, J. S. (1957). Talk aired by the BBC.

Macpherson, H. (Ed.) (1985). *John Spedan Lewis 1885–1963: Remembered by some of his contemporaries in the centenary year of his birth*. London: John Lewis Partnership.

Marx, K. (1875). *Critique of the Gotha programme* (Vol. 24) (Marx-Engels Collected Works). Moscow: Progress Publishers.

Marx, K. (1981). *Capital* (E. Mandel, Trans.) (Vol. 3). Harmondsworth: Penguin.

Mayfield, C. (2008). *Building a culture of ownership*. Retrieved from http://www.johnlewispartnership.co.uk/media/speeches/building-a-culture-of-ownership.html. Accessed on June 22, 2012.

Moore, N. (2007). Re-using qualitative data. *Sociological Research Online*, *12*(3). Retrieved from http://www.socresonline.org.uk/12/3/1.html. Accessed on February 14, 2014.

O'Regan, N., & Ghobadia, A. (2012). John Lewis partnership lessons in logical incrementalism and organic growth: A case study and interview with the chairman, Mr Charlie Mayfield. *Journal of Strategy and Management*, *5*(1), 103–112.

Orleans, A. (2011). *L'empire de la valeur* (Points, Economie). Paris: Seuil.

Paranque, B. (2014). Private property and collective action: Co-operation instead of competition. *Euromed Journal of Business*, *9*(1), 37–59.

Paranque, B., & Willmott, H. (2014). Cooperatives – Saviours or gravediggers of capitalism? The ambivalent case of the John Lewis partnership. *Organization*, *21*(5), 604–625. doi:10.1177/1350508414537622

Pendleton, A. (2001). *Employee ownership, participation and governance*. London: Routledge.

Pendleton, A. (2005). Employee share ownership, employment relationships and corporate governance. In B. Harley, J. Hyman, & P. Thompson (Eds.), *Participation and democracy at work: Essays in honour of Harvie Ramsay* (pp. 75–93). London: Palgrave Macmillan.

Pendleton, A. (2011). Employee ownership in Britain: Diverse forms, diverse antecedents. In E. J. Carberry (Ed.), *Employee ownership and shared capitalism: New directions in research* (pp. 311–340). Champaign, IL: Labor and Employment Relations Association.

Ramsay, H. (1980). Phantom participation: Patterns of power and conflict. *Industrial Relations Journal*, *11*(3), 46–59.

Schwartz, J. (2011). *Where did mill go wrong? Why the capital managed firm rather than the labor managed enterprise is the predominant organizational form in market economies*. Retrieved from http://ssrn.com/abstract=1886024

Spicer, A., Alvesson, M., & Kärreman, D. (2009). Critical performativity: The unfinished business of critical management studies. *Human Relations*, *62*(4), 537–560.

Warhurst, C. (1996). The management of production and the changing character of the kibbutz as a mode of production. *Economic and Industrial Democracy*, *17*, 419–445.

Webb, J. T., & Cheney, G. (2014). Worker-owned-and-governed cooperatives and the wider cooperative movement: Challenges and opportunities within and beyond the global economic crisis. In M. Parker, G. Cheney, V. Fournier, & C. Land (Eds.), *The Routledge companion to alternative organization* (pp. 47–63). London: Routledge.

Weeks, J. (2010). *Capital, exploitation and economic crisis*. London: Routledge.

Wolff, R. (2009). Economic crisis from a socialist perspective. *Socialism and Democracy*, *23*(2), 3–20.

APPENDIX A

Table A1. Ownership of John Lewis Partnership Trust Limited.

Shares	Voting Right	Capital and Dividend Distribution Rights	Other Rights	Comments	Nominal Value	Number	Total Value
A class	Yes	Yes	No right of redemption	Owned by C Mayfield	1	40	£40
B class	No	Yes	No right of redemption		1	60	£60
DOS	No	After other shares capital rights	No	Owned by JLPplc	1	250,000	£250,000
Total						250,100	£250,100

Source: Companies House, ARO1, Annual Return, 27 July 2011.
Note: DOS: Deferred Ordinary Shares.

APPENDIX B

Table B1. Ownership of John Lewis Partnership plc.

Shares	Voting right	Capital and Dividend Distribution Rights	Rank for Dividends	Other Rights	Comments	Nominal Value	Number	Total Value
CPS 5%	No	Dividend 5%	Priority on DOS	No	Owned by employees (partners)	1	3,696,995	£3,696,995
CPS 7.5%	No	Dividend 7.5%	Priority on DOS	No	Owned by employees (partners)	1	500,000	£500,000
DOS	Full	Capital and distribution rights	Behind CPS	No right of redemption	Owned by JLP Trust ltd (611,994) and directors (1 each)	1	612,000	£612,000
SIP	No	Dividend	Relation with DOS	No	Owned by JLP Trust ltd (70,250,000)	1	70,250,000	£70,250,000
Total							75,058,995	£75,058,995

Source: Companies House, ARO1, Annual Return, 20 July 2011.
Note: CPS: Cumulative Preference Stocks; DOS: Deferred Ordinary Shares; SIP: Share Incentive Plan.

PART IV
FINANCE, ETHICS, AND SOCIETY

APPLYING MINDFULNESS AND COMPASSION IN FINANCE

Christophe Faugère

ABSTRACT

Purpose – *I investigate the efficacy of adopting two mental aptitudes in the financial industry: mindfulness and compassion.*

Methodology/approach – *A conceptual link is drawn between the powerful mental acuteness obtained from practicing Mindfulness (defined by Jon Kabat-Zinn) and Ruthless Compassion (defined by Chögyam Trungpa Rinpoché) and the pursuit of a noble purpose for finance, which is to channel resources into the most deserving social and/or economic activities that raise community and societal welfare.*

Findings – *These techniques allow decision-makers to reach new levels of awareness, giving them a competitive advantage for instance in terms of avoiding behavioral traps. Making money remains an important by-product of financial services, but not the overriding or sole criterion. An interview of Solomon Halpern, longstanding disciple of Chögyam Trungpa Rinpoché, expert in Buddhist meditation, and president of Highlander Wealth Services, illustrates how these mental tools are applied for running a small US equity fund.*

Finance Reconsidered: New Perspectives for a Responsible and Sustainable Finance
Critical Studies on Corporate Responsibility, Governance and Sustainability, Volume 10, 299–319

ISSN: 2043-9059/doi:10.1108/S2043-905920160000010032

Research limitations/implications – *The present study provides a starting point for further survey research on how these practices are becoming adopted in the industry.*

Originality/value – *This chapter is the first to analyze the impact of both ruthless compassion and mindfulness in the business of finance not only in terms of raised morality but also as an added tool to resolve informational asymetries proper to the finance business.*

Keywords: Ruthless compassion; mindfulness; information asymetry; noble purpose

MINDFULNESS AND COMPASSION: TRADITIONS AND EVIDENCE OF BENEFITS FOR FINANCE?

The formalized concept of mindfulness has its roots in the Buddhist tradition. It is most commonly defined as the state of being attentive to and aware of what is taking place in the present. In the Satipatthana Sutta (The Foundation of Mindfulness Discourse), one of the key Buddhist discourses on mindfulness, Gautama Buddha recommends to maintain mindfulness of one's bodily functions, sensations, feelings, consciousness, and content of consciousness while observing clearly the impermanent nature of these objects. Nyanaponika (1972) called mindfulness "the clear and single-minded awareness of what actually happens to us and in us at the successive moments of perception." Hanh (1976) defines mindfulness as "keeping one's consciousness alive to the present reality." The popularized version of the concept comes from the best-selling book *Wherever you Go There you Are* by Kabat-Zinn (1994) who defines mindfulness as "paying attention in a particular way; on purpose, in the present moment, and nonjudgmentally."

Davis and Hayes (2011) survey psychotherapy-related research on mindfulness. They document a huge range of benefits from mindfulness meditation including fewer depressive symptoms, stress reduction, boosts to working memory, ability to focus attention and suppressing distracting information, less emotional reactivity, more cognitive flexibility such as enabling present-moment input to be integrated in a new way. Mindfulness has been shown to enhance self-insight, morality, intuition, and fear modulation. In addition, mindfulness meditation practice appears to increase information processing speed as well as decrease task effort and less distracting thoughts from the task at hand. Mindfulness seems to promote empathy. One study, for example, looked at premedical and medical students who participated in an eight-week mindfulness stress reduction training. It found that the mindfulness group had significantly higher self-reported empathy than a control group. Mindfulness-based stress reduction training has also been found to enhance self-compassion among health-care professionals.

As it relates to money and Finance, it would appear that the list of stated psychological benefits along the lines of stress reduction, ability to focus on flows of information and process information faster would be very valuable to finance professionals. Without developing a full-blown mindfulness meditation practice, one may wonder whether the ability to be self-aware and attuned to one's own intuition and feelings while being concentrated on a financial task could simply do the trick?

Fenton-O'Creevy, Soane, Nicholson, and Willman (2011) interviewed 118 professional traders and 10 senior managers at four City of London investment banks. The most successful traders (whose annual income averaged £500,000) relied on a blend of analytics and feelings/intuition. They focused on a full range of emotions, which they used to judge the value of their intuition. When they suffered losses, they acknowledged their anxiety, became more cautious, and took fewer risks. The least successful traders (whose income averaged only £100,000) tended to ignore their anxiety and kept going with their initial gut intuition. *One may infer that because they failed to listen to these additional internal signals, they did not make the proper decisions.*

To a certain extent, it seems that mindfulness might become part of an arsenal of performance-inducing "tools" and raise financial professionals' effectiveness in their activities, even though the moral consequences of these actions may be in question. Indeed, could mindfulness be exploited for purely egotistic reasons and be turned into an instrument that further unleashes greedy behavior?

The extant literature more or less directly sides against that concern. Brown and Kasser (2005) find that mindfulness correlates with stronger intrinsic values and more ecologically responsible behavior. Lakey, Campbell, Brown, and Goodie (2007) find, after controlling for potential moderating variables, that mindfulness correlates with lower levels of gambling pathology, which relates to some behavioral patterns among rogue traders (DeCovny, 2012). In a second study, they find evidence to suggest that mindfulness reduces gambling pathology because more mindful participants are less concerned about financial payoffs and better assess bet outcomes.

In the March 28, 2014 online edition of *The Guardian*, Thich Nhat Hanh, the 87-year-old Zen Buddhist master considered by many to be the father of mindfulness in the West, stated as long as business leaders practice "true" mindfulness, *it does not matter if the original intention is triggered by wanting to be more effective at work or to make bigger profits. That is because the practice will fundamentally change their perspective on life as it naturally opens hearts to greater compassion and develops the desire to end the suffering of others (emphasis added).*

Recently in 2014, there was a relatively quiet meeting in the London financial center. The meeting was attended by some of the city's financial bigwigs. Chade-Meng Tan, a people development expert who works at Google, was addressing the group about the benefits of mindfulness and its relationship to compassionate leadership. Participants included founder of Pimco, Bill Gross, and Lord Myners, senior independent board director of UK's Co-operative Group. Both Myners and Gross have talked publicly about how meditation clears their mind, making it easier to set priorities. The CFA Institute for investment professionals is considering launching a meditation program. KPMG, Goldman Sachs, and the Bank of England have also introduced mindfulness in well-being seminars to their staff.

Blackrock is the world's largest asset management firm with over $4.3 trillion in assets under management. In 2013, Golbie Kamarei who is Global Program Manager for Blackrock, founded the BlackRock Meditation Program which now offers mindfulness and meditation training and resources to over 1,300 employees in 17 countries. As a result of the program, employees testified for example that they were more able to observe when their thoughts were wandering away from their tasks and in some cases sleeping patterns were improved … Later results were quantified. 91% of the participants believe the program positively adds to Blackrock's culture. 88% would recommend the program to a colleague. 60% testified that they were more effective and productive in their work as a result of the program. 8% testified that they were more effective by at least 50% … 60% noticed increased focus and mental resilience in decision making.

Hence mindfulness appears to be not only a mental tool that enhances productivity on the job and mental capacities, it fortunately enhances self-awareness and the ability to gauge one's behavior and actions against an internal moral compass, which the masters of Buddhism believe is present in any human being, even dimly. The interview with Solomon Halpern in a later section below will add some evidence for these effects.

Let's now move on to compassion. Compassion comes from the Latin cum patior, which means "suffering with" and the greek sym patheia, or empathy. Compassion is empathy followed by action. Current neuroscience research has found that a special category of neurons called mirror neurons may be involved in sourcing the feeling of empathy. The findings are still embryonic to adduce a direct link, but Iacoboni (2009) for instance reports evidence of mirror neurons coding facial actions of others. Communicative actions appear to be also coded by mirror neurons (Ferrari, Gallese, Rizzolatti, & Fogassi, 2003). This is especially important for the hypothesis that mirror neurons facilitate our perception of the emotions of other people, because the face is the key organ used to express our own emotions. It is still early to tell what the latitude is for us humans to freely choose to be compassionate or not, given the workings of mirror neurons.

For a disciple of Buddhism, compassion is a quality through which she empathizes with other beings because she understands that these beings are caught in a physical reality (Samsara) in which the experience of suffering (Dukkha) prevails. As a result, she is moved to help alleviate that suffering.

In his book, *Cutting Through Spiritual Materialism*, Trungpa Rinpoché (2002) (CTR) introduces the concept of *Ruthless* Compassion. He states on page 210:

> "To the conventional way of thinking, compassion simply means being kind and warm. This sort of compassion is described in the scriptures as 'grandmother's love'. You would expect the practitioner of this type of compassion to be extremely kind and gentle; he would not harm a flea. If you need another mask, another blanket to warm yourself, he will provide it. But true compassion is ruthless," (emphasis added here) "from ego's point of view, because it does not consider ego's drive to maintain itself. It is 'crazy wisdom'. It is totally wise, but it is crazy as well, because it does not relate to ego's literal and simple-minded attempts to secure its own comfort."

CTR's view of compassion is that it is not soft, it is ruthless. CTR purposefully uses the juxtaposition of two apparently antinomical words to stir our mind out of the numbness and comfort of mental prejudices. The same mind-opening effect is produced for example by the related expression "tough love." Why would compassion need to be ruthless? Beyond the word game, CTR wants us to have a realization.

Compassion alone implies a limited focus on suffering. Allying kindness with compassion produces a more balanced outlook, but under these influences, a person can be overrun by powerful emotions. A lack of discernment may ensue regarding our position relative to the other person in need. Kindness mixed with compassion may trigger responses that are inappropriate. Acting toward our friends and customers out of a "grandmother's" type of love will indubitably look strange.

CTR's allegory warns of the danger of getting swept by compassion and creating a harmful co-dependency between people. Hence, it is important to keep a certain emotional neutrality or equanimity while practicing kindness and compassion. *Ruthlessness is a form of equanimity or clear and penetrating vision. Ruthlessness is what keeps our minds sharp, and helps preserve each other's integrity when we act out of kindness and compassion.*

CTR teaches us that the ego is responsible for corrupting the pure intentions of kindness and compassion. The reason is that the ego craves control; control of circumstances, people, and things, in order to secure its own comfort. In a relationship originating from a compassionate intent, the voice of the ego may influence the giver to exert power and control on the receiver, who appears defenseless. The receiver may be tempted by his ego to use the giver's compassion as a means of securing resources, and thus prolong his/her dependency.

Crazy wisdom is only "crazy" because it opposes the tendencies of the ego, which most of us find normal and are used to obey in this day and age. Such tendencies are expressed as the need, for example, to be liked by others and never have anyone upset at us. People you are trying to help will sometimes become annoyed with you if you demonstrate Ruthless Compassion toward them, as you do not fall in these egoistic traps. Overall, the presence of equanimity allows the ego to be put in check and frees the practitioners to fully express their intended kindness and compassion.

I assert in Faugère (2014) that Ruthless Compassion is a hitherto unrecognized natural and valuable ingredient in the personality profile of a good banker and financier. Ruthless Compassion is not to be confused with ruthless behavior, which is indeed the opposite of compassion. Ruthless behavior such as the use of excessive leverage and risk by many Wall-Street financiers at the heart of the 2008 crisis is more akin to psychopathology (Washington, 2012).

The financier (or banker) who is compassionate uses a very important sensory apparatus. Compassion can help the decision-maker tune in to a very important informational dimension of the capital commitment, which is *the quality of the person* who will use this capital and the *quality of purpose*. In other words, if the banker shuts off his ability to be compassionate, he removes from the equation a powerful sensory perception, which can help him discover several clues that may not be detectable by other means; for example whether the "story" told by the borrower holds water or not, that is, whether the borrower is honest or not. Compassion is firstly driven by an empathetic attunement to another person's need and secondly by the desire and impulse to help.

An analogy for Ruthless Compassion as an instrument is a radar. A radar sends waves out, these waves bounce back and bring information on what is truly out there. Ruthless Compassion is a tool that can mitigate the costs of information asymmetry that are typical in the finance business. In particular, when the person in need of capital has no quantifiable financial track record, the banker can use Ruthless Compassion to send out feelers and get a sense of how trustworthy the person is. However, it is important to emphasize that Ruthless Compassion must be heartfelt, and not a manipulative strategy, otherwise it won't work.

In a path-breaking research in Neuroeconomics, Zak (2012) makes a strong claim that empathy has a chemical component: "In the last five years, we have discovered this molecule called oxytocin that lives in the human brain and is particularly potent in making us care about the outcomes of others. When someone trusts you with their money intentionally, the brain releases this molecule." However, when the brain is under stress, it can stop releasing this chemical.

One reason bankers and financiers often shut down their sense of compassion, is that they feel stressed or afraid of making a decision based mostly on emotions and not logic. In other words, they are afraid of being taken advantage of. The combination of compassion and ruthlessness gives the right chemistry. Ruthlessness adds the penetrating vision of what is right and fair to do. As previously explained, Ruthless Compassion is what keeps the integrity of all parties in the transaction.

On the other hand, bankers need to also be compassionate toward their depositors, so that the clients trust that their capital will be in good hands, and well taken care of. This is the custodian's responsibility or so-called fiduciary responsibility. This trait is illustrated in the interview of Solomon Halpern presented below.

In 2011, Dr. Chakrabarty, Deputy Governor of the Reserve Bank of India, gave a speech about what he called the Ten Commandments for a successful banking career, in his address to a group of young graduates from a banking program (ICICI Manipal Academy, in Bangalore). These are:

1. Thou shalt manage the people with empathy: clients, co-workers, etc.
2. Thou shalt strive to become a knowledge worker: become a sensitive banker, that is, a banker who is sensitive to the needs of a growing economy.
3. Thou shalt be accountable for all your work.
4. Thou shalt do hard work.
5. Thou shalt develop the right attitude: Try to extend fair services to all customers of the bank irrespective of their background.

6. Thou shalt attempt to become a pioneer.
7. Thou shalt develop a professional approach.
8. Thou shalt be analytical: Banking business, essentially, involves managing risk. This job of managing risk cannot be done efficiently without having sharp analytical capability.
9. Thou shalt be information literate: A good banker should continuously innovate and update themselves with the latest technological advancements to make banking further easier and convenient to customers.
10. Thou shalt avoid complacency during good times and not lose hope during bad times.

Commandments 2, 3, 4, 6, 8, and 9 are necessary hard skills. These are specific job skills that can be quantified. The other points are soft skills or relational or value-based skills. In particular, points 1, 5, 7, and 10 are related to Ruthless Compassion. Dr. Chakrabarty adds the following about being professional: "*You can be passionate about the needs and grievances of customers, but do not compromise on your logic. During the course of your careers, you might, at times, be faced with various pressures which seek to influence your decisions. Develop the ability to objectively evaluate situations, regardless of external pressures, and take the right decision – always. Do not allow your personal problems and relationships to influence your decision making process. Be objective and be efficient. One cannot become a true professional in any area unless he/she remains committed to the core principles of the profession even under the most adverse circumstances.*" This quote directly brings to bear the idea of not letting oneself been carried away by compassion, in the sense of being influenced by friendships for example, and always keep a discerning mind and the integrity of the situation and roles.

ETHICAL FIGURES OF THE WORLD OF FINANCE: EXERCISING MINDFULNESS AND COMPASSION?

Finance professionals often do spark envy because of the publicized lavish lifestyles of many Wall-Street top executives. However, this profession is among the lowest ranked in US public polls in terms of perceived ethical values. Financial professionals are ranked just above lawyers and still quite ahead of car salespeople and members of congress! (Gallup Poll, December 2014). It is nevertheless clear that not all financiers deserve to be judged thus harshly. Financial occupations are diverse enough so that many top executives (e.g., those working in community banks) are "reasonably" paid by comparison to other industries. Many of these individuals champion a professional ethics that is completely at odds with the values demonstrated by real-life impersonators of Gordon Gekko, the icon of greed in Oliver Stone's classic movie "Wall Street."

One of the great role models of the investing world is Warren Buffett. Not only Mr. Buffett has the record of being the most successful long-term investor of the second half of the 20th and beginning of 21st centuries, the wealthiest business man alive along with Bill Gates for most of the late 1990s and 2000s, but he also has the reputation of being a man of great personal and professional integrity.

Buffett's writings and actions have been scrutinized, studied, and analyzed for many years (Hagstrom, 2005). Buffett often repeats "*what [I] do is not beyond anybody else's competence*." His methodology is easy to understand and applicable by any individuals.

One of Warren Buffett's least publicized accomplishments is his role as a "reluctant" savior of Wall-Street. He has volunteered in several major instances to help restore integrity to the system, when misbehaviors went too far.

In 1991, the U.S. government brought legal action against Wall-Street iconic firm Salomon Brothers and its executives for their using a scheme of illegal bidding in treasury auctions and for insider trading. Salomon Brothers was soon placed under Buffett's stewardship and a managerial shake-up followed.

Buffett helped redefine how the organization would behave in the future by implementing a new compliance system that would help "make Salomon a leader in setting new standards in regulatory behavior in the financial services industry" (Paine & Santoro, 1994). Compliance officers enforced these processes and employees' ethical behavior was indirectly reinforced via training programs.

Another tactic Buffett implemented to drive ethics in the organization was a shift in executive compensation. This shift aligned compensation more with the long-term success of the firm. While many did not like the new system, Buffett believed it kept onboard the people who shared the firm's values and vision. "*Were an abnormal number of people to leave the firm, the results would not necessarily be bad. Other men and women who share our thinking and values would then be given added responsibilities and opportunities, because in the end, we must have people to match our principles, not the reverse*" (Paine & Santoro, 1994).

Buffett is uncompromising when an organization demonstrates a lack of integrity, as exemplified by his offer to rescue the hedge fund Long-Term

Capital Management (LTCM), under the clear condition that management would have to go. LTCM had failed in 1998 and was eventually rescued by other Walls-Street firms without letting go of management. Buffett has stated in other contexts that "*We do not wish to join with managers who lack admirable qualities*," he says, "*no matter how attractive the prospects of their business. We've never succeeded in making a good deal with a bad person.*"

In the midst of the financial crisis, Buffett publicly took an "ethical" position by investing to support corporate America's stocks against a downward spiral, communicating his confidence in the US economy's ability to return to normal after this huge market drop. Upbeat about America's future, he stated in 2008: "*Our economic system has worked extraordinarily well over time. It has unleashed human potential as no other system has, and it will continue to do so.*" Buffett bought US stocks at low prices and also sold 15 to 20-years maturity put options on the S&P 500, which was consistent with his bullishness about the future. While he initially lost money, most of his positions were profitable after 2010.

So, while Buffett intends to profit as a result of his investments, he is also principled and sticks to a professional ethics. He generally shares these values and stances publicly, which sometimes leads to the perception that he is trying to "talk" the market into following him, so as to profit from the crowd driving-up prices. It is however clear that, when he proceeds that way, he also opens himself up to counter-speculators, so that the criticisms of "manipulative intentions" that he faces are not necessarily valid.

Throughout his career Buffett has demonstrated focus and discipline by staying true to values centered on integrity, honesty, and business acumen. His status in the industry is that of a savvy and incorruptible financier. That way, "The sage of Omaha" has earned the respect of an entire industry. Ruthless compassion is also exemplified by Warren Buffett's dealings with Salomon Brothers (Sims & Brinkman, 2002) and the choice he makes to associate with companies having good products and good management.

Another example of unusual (and publicly displayed) ethical behavior among financiers is found in the story of banker Fabrizio Cerina. In a *Financial Times* magazine article dated July 19, 2013, M. Cerina recounts his experience as an investment banker as he "repaid" his "clients fraud losses out of my own pocket." He states "*One morning in 1991 ... We discovered that the head of private banking, who was managing client assets, had bought securities in various Nasdaq companies whose prices had collapsed. To hide the losses he got this American broker, who later was also arrested with him, to send him fake prices by telex. We had over 1,000 clients and he screwed up 163 of them. The losses came to $46m. These clients were people I'd known for* *years. I had three options. One was to jump from the window. Another was to run away. The third was to accept a kind of Swiss Chapter 11 called concordato moratorio, where you can pay less than 20 per cent. My lawyers were saying, 'Put up $10m and we'll use $7m to pay off the creditors'. The rest would have gone to lawyers, advisers and accountants. I flew to London to speak to one of the banks that was a victim of the fraud and I remember hoping that the plane would crash. It would have been a liberation for me. Instead I came back and announced that I would pay everybody back out of my own money. All $46m plus $800,000 in interest ....Looking back, I decided to reimburse my clients because of my father. He taught me that if you want to be in a business that implies a special degree of trust from customers, you cannot be motivated purely by self-interest; you have to be accountable. These are the old ways of investment banking. I don't want to come across as someone who is trying to teach morality. But for me it was more about building a relationship, building an enterprise. That takes 10 to 20 years. The system today puts too much pressure on young bankers to deliver immediate profits and that is wrong. It leads to disasters big and small every day.*"

This is a much different story than that of Warren Buffett and it gives a good sense of the Fabrizio Cerina's focus to act out of compassion. Clearly, he did not get swayed by a purely self-interested rational calculus, which would have had him preserve his wealth. Fabrizio Cerina's moral fiber was tested by this event. He came out on top. By taking on his company's liabilities personally, Fabrizio did something that is similar in philosophy to our next example.

The case of the London-based C. Hoare & Co. bank also stands out. The bank was founded in 1672 by Richard Hoare, and is still in existence today. C. Hoare & Co is a small private bank with about £2 billion in assets. They have nearly 10,000 customers, a number they have kept constant for five decades. They are sustainably more profitable and have better capital ratios than their competitors. In 2008, they were voted Private Bank of the Year in the Citi Wealth Magic Circle. Without turning this presentation into an advertising billboard, we may ask how they achieved this lasting performance.

First, while they provide the same retail banking services, they search to differentiate their services over dimensions like relationship, flexibility, care, independence, and speed of service. The bank is owned by seven descendants of the founder, and their mission is to perpetuate a profitable family business.

Shareholders are partners in an *unlimited liability partnership*, which is quite unique in the modern corporate world. They also pride themselves in having a strong independent board. When they die or retire, their shares of ownership return to the bank, so they are in effect trustees with a life interest. The ex-CEO Alexander Hoare states that they "will never get super rich this way – but that they work hard and are happy!"

Their stated goal is *not* to maximize profits. Instead, they try to optimize quality and minimize risk while making a living in banking. They only deal in products and services they fully understand with people they know and trust, which has kept them away from the toxic products sold before the 2008 crisis.

Values appear to play a prominent part in the bank. Generally speaking, they adhere to Christian values. They apply the golden rule and treat customers as they would wish to be treated. They are loyal to their employees and vice versa, with a very low turnover. They maintain a philanthropic tradition. They are involved in all sorts of charity work, community enhancement projects, and do microfinance in the developing world. The most recent impetus is to provide training for their clients on whether they should invest capital for social impact. They never invite their customers to do anything with their money which the partners won't do with theirs.

The main requirement of prospective customers is that they must share their values. Their values remain absolutely constant, and are in demand. Ex-CEO Hoare (2012) makes the following stunning statement: "*We do this by remaining small and true to our philosophy, which is not far from Buddhist Economics – the whole system has proven sustainable over the last 3 centuries, and if we continue to harmonize the interests of profit, people and planet, it should work for much longer. I have often been known to say to other businessmen 'my aim is to keep our business small', or to entrepreneurs 'my aim is to keep our family poor'!*"

The C. Hoare & Co. bank is also another instance where Ruthless Compassion is applied by the managers, as a way to preserve a value system based on integrity. They function in a similar way to ethical banks, as their investment choices reflect moral values that are espoused by clients and aligned with their values.

Looking eastward, the cultural divide between standard western banking and the approach followed by some institutions in Asia can be almost incomprehensible. Gait (2012) who is a senior portfolio manager at First State Stewart gives this mind-bending account of a visit to the CEO of one of India's largest banks. He says "*We are … struggling to make ourselves heard. Just to the right of the sofa we are sitting on is a large statue of Lord Vishnu, enclosed in a glass case. Every ten seconds he comes alive, glows bright red and broadcasts a loud mantra across the room. Om Namo*

Narayana. We quickly learn to time our questions between chants. To our left is an equally large TV screen, where the Business Anchor of the hour is shouting at us above the flashing stock prices. The CEO seems unfazed. 'Here, we do not work for pay'. This is a bank which was founded four years before Partition. It remains extremely proud that during Partition, it honored all deposits on both sides of the dividing line, unlike some of its counterparts at the time. The CEO returns to his theme. 'Our duty is banking. My mission is to create lots of vibrations, to touch the hearts and spread the smiles'. We leave dazed and confused."

Each of the above "leading" characters in these stories showcases a strong personal and professional ethical system. These individuals demonstrate a capacity to make cool and rational decisions even in the face of extremely stressful environments. These qualities of focus and alignment between core values and actions, through clear intent and vision in the moment, are akin to the principle of mindfulness. The rationality of their decision does also take into account fairness and global ethics. To the extent that these individuals appeal to empathy and care is akin to ruthless compassion in the sense that it is not exploitative of another person's weaknesses and they view their financial business still subordinated to considering the other person's humanity and the greater good.

APPLYING MINDFULNESS AND COMPASSION TO FINANCE: THE SOLOMON HALPERN INTERVIEW

Solomon Halpern is President of Highlander Wealth Services described on the company's website as "a mindful finance company dedicated to creating a better world." Highlander is a small fund with about $50m in managed assets that was founded in 2008 by Solomon and a partner. Solomon has accumulated over 14 years of experience on financial markets and managing businesses. His broad investment background includes creating proprietary equity and bond investment strategies, managing outside managers, and structuring and analyzing private investments – with a specialty in private credit. Solomon also brings 25 years of mindfulness practice to his professional life as well.

I contacted Solomon, following a random online search and found that the investment philosophy stated on the fund's website closely matched the theme of this chapter. The interview took place by phone on November 14, 2014, and lasted about 45 minutes. I began the interview by *asking*

Solomon to describe his background as a Buddhist. He stated that he was born a Buddhist and spent his childhood being trained in the Shambhala community located in Boulder Colorado. This community was founded by Chögyam Trunga Rinpoché in the early 1970s.

Solomon was introduced to meditation and mindfulness practices from a very young age. He participated in his first retreat at age 12, which was led by Pema Chödrön, the famed Buddhist nun. He did multiple week-end retreats at various levels and then graduated to two-week retreats and eventually a three-month seminary by age 18. He ran the summer camp for young people, and became a teacher of meditation practices, and still is. Solomon thought about becoming a monk, but was attracted instead to act in the business world as a "householder-yogi," which is encouraged in the Shambhala tradition. In Shambhala Buddhism, the path is designed to help society, to be in the world and engage with the world. Solomon was always fascinated by money and power.

Did he feel a sort of a conflict/contrast between finance and the spiritual path? Specifically, what was the path that led him into finance and did that resonate with him as a Buddhist? Solomon always felt compelled to ask himself "how can I be of use?" The key to him was to identify the most influencing factors, which in his view are money, power, and politics. He never saw a problem with pursuing his spiritual path, discovering the "truth" as a Buddhist and doing finance. On the Shambhala path, everything is workable. "Negative emotions" can arise in any field. The problem is how to work with them. Finance is not inherently "evil" it's just that it has a tendency to cause confusion probably as much as any other area because of power, and the key issue is how to work with that.

Solomon shared that it is in 2012 that he and his partners really began emphasizing and making explicit mindful investing in Highlander's stated approach. He says that people's finances can be a source of sanity for them. There are really a lot of opportunities to use mindfulness to create sanity in the world of finance.

The next question was regarding the size of assets under management and the historical performance of the fund. Solomon answered that the historical returns of its longest running fund Market + was based on smart alphas and multiple betas strategies using the S&P500. In terms of risk-adjusted returns, over a 9 years period, this strategy yielded more than the S&P500 (about 10%/year) with about 85% of the standard deviation; that is 85% less risk.

How do you define mindfulness, and what does it mean for you? Solomon and his associates use Jon Kabat-Zinn's definition "paying attention in a particular way, on purpose, and non-judgmentally." For him, mindfulness is the practice of creating space around something in the mind. It is a mental experience of clarity with an ability to divorce oneself from the emotions and seeing things in a simpler way.

Is mindfulness a key component of the way you do business? And does it give you a competitive advantage? Solomon answered that they have two main businesses: (1) Client acquisition and servicing and (2) investment decision making. Mindfulness as a business tool gives Highlander a clear competitive advantage in the first area of business. Solomon believes that through mindfulness practices you can't help but develop a sense of compassion (emphasis added). As a result, you can be more authentic and empathetic in your understanding of what your clients are going through. Because of your ability to care for your client, you become a better service-provider for them.

On the investment side, Solomon has witnessed plenty of people who are *not* mindfulness practitioners, via his experience of visiting and interviewing many hedge fund managers and investment professionals, when Solomon was a fund of hedge funds manager. The advantage is simple. The emotional pitfalls, the discipline traps, the gut-wrenching experiences that come with managing other peoples' money are much easier to work with and understand and maintain some sense of perspective around, when you have mindfulness training, you develop an ability to observe emotional states as they arrive and realize that they are not permanent, and may not even be accurate or intelligent. When the market is going against you and your strategy, it can be difficult to have a little bit of clarity, perspective, remain non-judgmental, or have the strength of mind in the face of these experiences, and make decisions. Finance is an incredible training ground and place to apply mindfulness practices (emphasis added).

Do you think that the states of mind of traders (heightened states alertness/ intense focus and adrenaline, aggressiveness) could serve a positive purpose or could be an impediment to trading or making decisions? This sounds like a description of what in sports is referred to as "the zone" or hyper-awareness or concentration. That kind of state of mind is very useful to accomplish whatever you're trying to accomplish. Can that be beneficial? Yes, to accomplishing whatever task you're trying to accomplish. But Solomon is not entirely convinced that people who enter in that state of mind do it for an ultimate purpose that is all that beneficial. Just turning someone's money onto more money, regardless of any awareness of the other factors that can be at play, leads to the question, whom is this beneficial to? It is beneficial for the trader and person whose account it is. So yes, it is beneficial if their goal is to turn money into more money.

Overall, where does that fit in with respect to beneficial for Society or these people's states of mind, in their regular life and in the way that they manifest in the world, outside of their work environment? This is why mindfulness is important to Solomon, because if people have greater self-awareness, if they have strength and then train their mind, then they'll have more awareness of what's happening around that situation, and they'll find meaning in what they do or they may see some kind of emptiness in it (emphasis added). As a result they may make other life decisions as they go forward.

Let's go back to the compassion aspect. *Do you believe compassion should be part of asset management? And do you think there is potentially a trade-off between financial performance and exercising compassion?* Solomon answers that yes compassion is an important part piece to include in the business. Two reasons for that: the first reason is that it is the right thing to do from a long-term perspective. For example, if we knew that something was bad for the Earth, all cost-benefit analysis being equal, and make money off of it, it would make sense to avoid it. The other reason is that it is a competitive advantage in today's marketplace. More of the world today, the Millennial generation and next ones they'll influence, are interested in equal part in what they're investing and what their returns are (emphasis added). This is a simple business perspective; you'll have more clients and provide some investment returns that people are satisfied with.

With respect to the second part of the question does a manager have to sacrifice return? Solomon does not think so, but this depends on how you define what you're trying to accomplish in terms of having compassion be in your portfolio. Compassion is sort of a proxy for using *impact* in your portfolio. A very important aspect for Solomon is the notion of putting humanity back into finance. He says: if I want an S&P500 tracking fund, in an ideal world, I would find one that's with a company with values that are similar to mine, such as more women on board or fair treatment of employees, etc. ... I see that as putting compassion in the portfolio and you haven't changed the underlying investment one iota.

If you were to go too far, for example 10–12 years ago, Solomon was trying to put ISR into portfolios ... ISR is a term that is totally outdated nowadays ... People rather talk about impact investing ... (emphasis added). This would lead to a totally uninspiring portfolio, containing mostly small cap and often foreign stocks, mostly belonging to the retail consumer sector. That just doesn't build a portfolio that you could tell to the client is OK for you.

So now, I believe you can, and it's about taking the definition to a point that you understand what it is and the limitations of it. There is no perfect solution right now. Solomon believes that anyone can incorporate compassion into their portfolio without having to suffer from performance degradation. You will have to work harder to do that. You have to go meet investment managers, see who they are, and have a relationship with them.

Do you think that this notion of impact investment fund is more flexible than ISR and avoids picking from a small and too-restrictive universe of stocks? Not entirely, Solomon answers this is an evolutionary process and we are at the beginning of it, both from the number of products that are supplied and the amount of assets invested. I think there will be a massive inflow over time. People will invest where their values are. That just makes sense. Once a company has become publicly traded and it is joined with the world in a pretty big way. It has become complex and interdependent from the system it exists within. As a result is always a matter of "shades and green."

Investment managers with an ISR mandate may find themselves in a corner with too few options, when they have chosen too narrowly. The way to expand that is to look at different aspects of the company's performance and their job as a company's stockholder, so that a mutual fund with certain ISR values may choose to focus on certain activities of the company they invest into and if enough investors join up as shareholders via this fund, they can become stronger advocates of these values. Thus, shareholder advocacy is the key to impact socially responsible behavior of corporation and is the next evolution of ISR. If you need to raise pay standards in poor countries or have more women on the board, it would just happen.

Do you hire analysts and do you have partners based on this congruency of values and do you have a compensation system that rewards these values? We are a small outfit. The short answer is yes, we want people to have some sort of openness toward these processes, but you don't have to be someone with a long history of meditating or trying to develop compassion in a formal way to be someone with these kinds of values. In fact, Solomon does not think it is very rare anymore to have these kinds of values, especially with the Techies and Millennials generation. It's the new cool. There would not be any formal requirement, in that respect. They would however need to understand the culture of our company and be excited to be engaging with respect to that. From there, their path would be their own.

How would you go about designing a training program for business students who would want to go in asset management and at the same time have a desire to develop a deeper awareness practice? Solomon shared his enthusiasm at the idea of doing this. The best way to do that (Solomon talked to Naropa Institute located in Colorado about that).... There is some room for some kind of partnership with a university like Naropa, which would develop a curriculum around mindfulness, maybe a quarter of the total curriculum .... It is not the quantity that you do, it is something about consistency of the practice, which creates new habits, new neurological connections, and grow your brain capacity and pathways that are believed shut down when you are 18. Solomon emphasized having academic legitimacy from both sides, the mindfulness side and the finance side of the curriculum.

Would there be a way of treating mindfulness and financial activities in a more integrative fashion; that is, for example people who make financial decisions would be trained to adopt a meditative frame of mind when making these decisions? Solomon answered from his own personal experience and how he would like it to grow overtime in his own self-awareness. Solomon offered his own definition of "mindful finance": it is the joining of matters relating to money and matters relating to personal experiences (emphasis added). When one makes a financial decision, a lot of times we can be tempted to run over the physical feelings or the mental questions that arise in our minds, because we feel like we need to act like we know something or come across as decisive. But we need to train ourselves, it is not that we have to admit anything externally or socially, or fall apart or any of that crap, in fact we are much stronger for doing this.

We want to create true resiliency not brittleness. True resiliency can see those things when they arise and just not push them away, in the sense of forget about that, I don't want to see this or feel that or hear that. OK, there is some information there, and I need to pay attention to that. Internally, what was that? Why was there something that was bothering me? Because that is very valuable information (emphasis added). What this would do is possibly change the whole financial industry and world. It would be a natural antidote to greed and self-possession. This is because nobody really feels good when they cheat somebody else. But if you make excuses for it, and you gloss over it enough and you get used to it enough, you can get used to anything. But if you allow for a little bit of openness around the experience, leave self-judgments aside, and wonder what was that and become curious about it, all of a sudden the whole world of information opens up that you were denying before. How do you train for that? Mindfulness can really speak to that.

A GLOBAL ETHICAL CRISIS AND THE NOBLE MISSION OF FINANCE

In hindsight, the 2008 financial crisis may arguably best be characterized as an ethical crisis. It is now well understood that much of the crisis was spurred by unscrupulous subprime lending practices, which hooked householders with little income, induced them to take on sizable mortgage loans, without checking or worrying about these people's capacity to repay. Borrowers clearly bore their share of responsibility in the crisis by willingly entering into these contracts, knowing that in all likelihood that they could not afford their mortgage payments, once interest rates did reset on their adjustable rate mortgages (Tavakoli, 2011).

The so-called originate-to-distribute model of lending insured that these practices could go on almost indefinitely, as long as the *true underlying* risk of these securities remained opaque (Ashcraft & Schuermann, 2008). This risk-opacity was sustained for two reasons: (1) the market-wide belief in continually rising real estate prices and (2) the securitization process underwritten by Wall Street investment banks with the help of rating agencies, which *artificially* created *riskless* mortgaged backed securities issues (aka tranches) that found their way in the hands of institutional investors, school districts and pension funds and whose value later collapsed. On the eve of the subprime crisis in 2007, Chuck Prince CEO of Citigroup shared his "zombic" vision of the necessity for any major industry player to try to make money even if it meant using these dangerous products: "When the music stops, in terms of liquidity, things will be complicated. But as long as the music is playing, you've got to get up and dance. We're still dancing." Greed really was (and probably still is) the name of the game on Wall Street.

However, yielding moral and regulatory sledgehammers to reign in unethical behaviors in the finance industry has repeatedly failed to curtail abuses throughout modern history. The latest failure is apparent in the wake of the 2008 crisis. Calls for tough regulations and convictions of unethical practices have gone unheeded, due to lack of political will in the United States and Europe. For instance, the Dodd Frank act of 2010 has been constantly under attack and undermined by financial industry lobbyists. One of U.S. Congress's last acts of 2014 was to pass a measure largely repealing a Dodd-Frank provision that required banks to push the trading of exotic financial instruments known as derivatives into subsidiaries that are *not* eligible for deposit insurance and other forms of government support.

Regarding the purpose of banking and finance, Juan Samavia, Director-General of the International Labor Organization at the UN has asserted that: "We have to come back to the basic legitimate function of finance which is to promote the real economy – to lend so that entrepreneurs can invest, innovate, produce jobs and products" and create "public policies and smart regulation that rewards hard work and enterprise once again."

In Faugère (2014), I articulate a vision of the noble purpose of banking and finance that takes root in Samavia's view. I am slightly modifying the definition here. In my view, the noble purpose of finance is to:

Implement wise lending and investing practices that support the greatest achievements of human potential (and creativity) to facilitate the uplifting of individuals and communities and the spread of real wealth in the economy, in harmony with the ecosystem. This is achieved by

1. Cultivating *mindfulness* practices so that bankers and financiers become aware that they are stewards of idle or future key resources and must learn the rules and skills of governing the process of moving resources from lesser uses to ones holding the promise of a greater future for members of society and the environment.
2. Cultivating (Ruthless) *Compassion* bringing human relationships and the commonality of noble goals at the core of the business.
3. Allocating capital under two conditions:
   a. That financed activities only have beneficial effects on humans and society at large.
   b. That these activities do not spiral out of control to only make money for the sake of making money.

By training bankers and financiers to develop compassion and mindfulness, our societies can altogether avoid crises of excessive greed and regulatory ineptitude. We can create a financial culture that will serve a greater purpose than just making money for its own sake. In this chapter, I have documented many examples of these new behaviors and promising initiatives. A full-blown institutionalized training program for business students wanting to go in the finance field still remains to be articulated and implemented along these lines (Faugère, 2014).

REFERENCES

Ashcraft, A. B., & T. Schuermann. (2008). Understanding the securitization of subprime mortgage credit. Federal Reserve Bank of New York Staff Reports No. 318.

Brown, K. W., & Kasser, T. (2005). Are psychological and ecological well-being compatible? The role of values, mindfulness, and lifestyle. *Social Indicators Research*, *74*, 349–368.

Davis, D. M., & Hayes, J. A. (2011). What are the benefits of mindfulness? A practice review of psychotherapy-related research. *Psychotherapy*, *48*(2), 198–208.

DeCovny, S. (2012). The financial psychopaths next door. CFA Magazine, March–April, pp. 34–35.

Faugère, C. (2014). Ruthless compassion in banking and finance. *Research in International Business and Finance*, *32*, 106–121.

Fenton-O'Creevy, M., Soane, E., Nicholson, N., & Willman, P. (2011). Thinking, feeling and deciding: The influence of emotions on the decision making and performance of traders. *Journal of Organizational Behavior*, *32*(8), 1044–1061.

Ferrari, P. F., Gallese, V., Rizzolatti, G., & Fogassi, L. (2003). Mirror neurons responding to the observation of ingestive and communicative mouth actions in the monkey ventral premotor cortex. *European Journal of Neuroscience*, *17*, 1703–1714.

Gait, D. (2012). How finance has lost its dharma? ESG Asia 2012 Special Report, 16–17.

Hagstrom, R. G. (2005). *The Warren Buffett way*. Hoboken, NJ: Wiley.

Hanh, T. N. (1976). *Miracle of mindfulness*. Boston, MA: Beacon.

Hoare, A. (2012). Banking on Buddhist economics: How enduring values underpin a 300-year-old family bank. The Brewery, p. 4.

Iacoboni, M. (2009). Imitation, empathy, and mirror neurons. *Annual Review of Psychology*, *60*, 653–670.

Kabat-Zinn, J. (1994). *Wherever you go there you are: Mindfulness meditation in everyday life*. New York, NY: Hyperion.

Lakey, C. E., Campbell, W. K., Brown, K. W., & Goodie, A. S. (2007). Dispositional mindfulness as a predictor of the severity of gambling outcomes. *Personality and Individual Differences*, *43*(7), 1698–1710.

Nyanaponika, T. (1972). *The power of mindfulness*. San Francisco, CA: Unity Press.

Paine, L. S., & Santoro, M. (1994). Forging the new Salomon. Harvard Business School case No. 9-395-046.

Sims, R. R., & Brinkman, J. (2002). Leaders as moral role models: The case of John Gutfreund at Salomon Brothers. *Journal of Business Ethics*, *35*(4), 327–339.

Tavakoli, J. (2011). Blame the victims and enrich the perpetrators. *Huffington Post*, January 13. Retrieved from http://www.huffingtonpost.com/janet-tavakoli/third-world-america-blame_b_808592.html

Trungpa Rinpoché, C. (2002). *Cutting through spiritual materialism*. Boston, MA: Shambhala Publications Inc., Horticultural Hall.

Washington, G. (2012). Psychopaths caused the financial crisis ... And they will do it again unless they are removed from power. *ZeroHedge Blog Guest Post*, January 3. Retrieved from http://www.zerohedge.com/contributed/psychopaths-caused-financial-crisis-%E2%80%A6-and-they-will-do-it-again-and-again-unless-they-ar

Zak, P. J. (2012). *The moral molecule*. New York, NY: Penguin/Dutton.

FROM FINANCIAL TO ECONOMIC INTERMEDIATION: ISLAMIC BANKING'S UNHEARD MESSAGE

Abdel-Maoula Chaar

ABSTRACT

Purpose – *This chapter uses Islamic finance to question the universality of contemporary finance leading principles. It establishes the existence of different financial paradigms and attempts to determine the form that might take operations in a non-profit maximising context.*

Methodology/approach – *This chapter uses Thomas Kuhn's notion of paradigm to demonstrate that Islamic finance has its own dominant logic and, hence, cannot be reduced to a subset of contemporary finance. It describes how the former has been infused by the leading principles of the latter following the adoption by the Islamic financial field of an accounting system using a conventional referential as a point of reference. Finally, the chapter elaborates on the form that might take financing if profit maximisation is not the operation's main purpose.*

Findings – *If the condition of profit maximisation is relaxed, the utilisation of Islamic finance instruments might lead to the creation of*

Finance Reconsidered: New Perspectives for a Responsible and Sustainable Finance
Critical Studies on Corporate Responsibility, Governance and Sustainability, Volume 10, 321–353

ISSN: 2043-9059/doi:10.1108/S2043-905920160000010033

economical microcycles able to enlarge the socio-economic reach of financing operation.

Originality/value – *The notion of economic intermediation is introduced to describe the operations of Islamic banks using their instruments in a non-maximising context. This approach should not be restricted to Islamic finance but viewed as the result of a case study advocating for an alternative view of finance favouring socio-economic development.*

Keywords: Financial paradigm; Islamic finance; sharia; social business; sustainable development

INTRODUCTION

The contemporary world's development is punctuated with regular crises, where economic downturns with often dramatic effects alternate with upswings in activity. This cycle has gone on since the mid-nineteenth century, despite the radical transformation of economies and the learning effect of states which, repeatedly confronted with this type of situation, should know how to overcome it by now. But are they really able to? Some believe that these upheavals are an integral part of the system. For more than a century and a half, they have been part of '… some central mechanism of capitalism' (Sewell, 2008, p. 522) accompanying (supporting?) the endless expansion of the system and the gradual commodification of every sphere of society. Somewhat paradoxically, the history of capitalism has also seen the emergence of thinking focused on corporate social responsibility and business ethics. This started to appear in the United States at the end of the 19th century, with a mixture of good intentions among businessmen (Acquier & Aggeri, 2008) that later developed and structured around a number of currents and movements that all sought, at varying levels, to force businesses to internalise some, if not all, of their externalities.

From a strictly financial point of view, this debate led to the emergence of the notion of ethical finance in the 1920s (Bayard & Pannier-Runacher, 2002), the gradual development of the concept of financial solidarity and the appearance in Egypt in the 1960s of a financial model that complies with the principles of 'Islamic law' (*sharia*). Since then, this so-called Islamic finance has become widespread and some sources now even refer to a Catholic finance and 'catho-compatible' financial institutions (Cuny de la Verryère, 2013) that apply the principles and values of the Catholic religion.

These various approaches are often presented as a way of correcting the excesses of the current financial system (ethical, solidarity or Catholic finance) or of overcoming certain shortfalls by enabling, for example, certain categories of consumers to access contemporary financial services (Islamic finance). They therefore challenge certain contemporary finance practices without really questioning the overall relevance of the system. However, in spite of their clear differences, these ethical, solidarity, Catholic and Islamic forms of finance share a very similar concept of currency, which is seen as a means and not an end, and the same desire to foster general well-being by putting a 'tamed' sustainable economy to the service of society. As such, they come across as highly revolutionary with regard to a now-globalised system that places profit at the top of its priorities, that uses a phenomenon of perpetual dynamic imbalance (Beckert, 2009) to renew the sources of profit that ensure its growth and with the intent of subjecting social matters to market laws; a market where the main thing, as Foucault pointed out, lies not in trade but in '(competition which) is akin to formal interplay between inequalities' (Foucault, 2004, p. 124).

The divergence in the institutional logic (Friedland & Alford, 1991; Thornton & Ocasio, 2008) structuring these various forms of finance seems obvious, thus placing them within distinct paradigms. If that is indeed that case, the emergence of alternative modes of finance would be an indicator of the 'paradigmatic flaw' originating from the growing incapacity of the dominant financial system to address the issues raised by the socio-economic realities of the contemporary world.

This chapter explores the possibility of the existence of an alternative financial paradigm and attempts to measure the potential impact of its use. In order to do so, it analyses the case of Islamic finance. This finds its roots in the religious realm and is 'reinvigorating' the world of contemporary finance despite the fact that the latter lays claim to strict secular rationalism. Some people believe that this characteristic is the only basic difference between 'finance for Muslims' and the practices of contemporary finance. Others consider that the similarities and differences between these two forms of finance challenge the notion of the universality of the contemporary finance paradigm and therefore the pervasiveness of the notions of material profit and balance by the markets.

The first part of this chapter looks at the expansion of Islamic finance and more especially a decisive episode in its young history – the creation of the Accounting and Auditing Organisation for Islamic Financial Institutions (AAOIF). It then provides a brief description of the mechanisms that enable transactions deemed lawful in the eyes of devout Muslims and highlights the dominant role played by *sharia* (Islamic law). The second part explores the essence and the connections within this corpus. Our analysis will let us put forward the structure for a paradigm of Islamic finance. As a counterpoint, 'The Protestant Ethic and the Spirit of Capitalism' by Weber (1991 [1904–1905]) is analysed to present the structure of a 'paradigm of capitalism' that embeds the dominant mode of contemporary finance. Analysis of these constructs will emphasise the differences in essence and logic found in the two systems. The third part of our study focuses on the consequences of this finding and attempts to measure the consequences. It adapts the Yunus Social Business fund to Islamic finance and analyses this new structure to look at a concept of economic intermediation that would allow for the re-embedding of finance in a dynamic of socio-economic development which would not, of course, be restricted to Islamic finance or the Islamic markets and populations.

ISLAMIC FINANCE PUT TO THE ACCOUNTING TEST

In early 2014, Islamic financial institutions controlled assets worth almost \$1.8 trillion. While this sum might appear substantial, it only represents a tiny fraction of the total value of world financial assets. So why refer to this amount?

In fact, the significance of this figure only becomes apparent when it is compared with the history of Islamic finance. It then serves as an indicator and attests to the vigorous growth seen in the sector. Islamic finance is in fact a very recent phenomenon. It emerged in the 1960s almost simultaneously in Egypt and Malaysia. It therefore took little more than 50 years to break the symbolic trillion dollar mark. This incredible growth is far greater than that seen in conventional finance. For example, the average growth rate accumulated over the last decade (2000–2011) is 20% for Islamic finance compared to growth of just 10% for so-called conventional finance (Bain and Company, 2012). The comparison of the performance in both sectors following the 2008 crisis is even more revealing: conventional finance saw growth of 4% in 2009, a decline of 1% in 2010 and growth of 6% in 2011, whereas Islamic finance grew, respectively by 9%, 10%, and 22% over the same period.

In light of all this, it comes as no surprise that Islamic finance is attracting the interest of all financial operators. The interest it is garnering is further strengthened by the quantity of liquidities available in the Arabian Gulf where stakeholders increasingly demand the use of *sharia*-compatible financial instruments when investing funds. The myth of a captive market of 1.6 billion Muslims, of a young and dynamic population group who are just waiting for the right product range to send them flocking to institutions offering Islamic finance products also adds to this interest.

These contextual factors highlight the nature of the role often assigned to the Islamic financial institutions: giving Muslims access to modern financial services that comply with their beliefs. It is therefore only natural that conventional banks are now setting up their own special schemes (Islamic windows, branches or subsidiaries) to exploit this bountiful market segment. All the main international banks have therefore developed a capacity for *sharia*-compatible operations. The appearance of these financial institutions in the field of Islamic finance tends to prove that *sharia*-compatible finance is just a variant of modern finance. This finding quite naturally leads the operators of 'genetically' Islamic institutions to endeavour to imitate the operations of so-called conventional financial institutions in a way that complies with *sharia*. This quite singular approach fits in with the image that Islamic banks have of themselves. In fact, an analysis of their visions and missions tends to demonstrate that most of these institutions consider their functions to be similar to those of their conventional counterparts (Chaar, 2011).

Islamic finance's role of taking contemporary financial operations and making them *sharia*-compatible was no doubt confirmed with the creation of the Accounting and Auditing Organisation for Islamic Financial Institutions (AAOIFI) in 1991. This organisation was and is still tasked with preparing standards for accounting, auditing, governance, ethics and *sharia*. In 2014, it had 200 members, representing 40 nations.

The creation of the AAOIFI was of extreme importance for Islamic finance. Indeed, for a profession to have ties with an abstract body of knowledge (in this case, accounting standards) is one of the key factors underpinning its professional credibility (Abbott, 1988). What is more, the setting up of an association is, for a profession, a specific way of formalising its identity, asserting its professional status and contributing to the governance of the field in which it operates (Lounsbury, 2002).

On a more operational level, the existence of uniform public standards has enabled Islamic finance practices to be transferred to a variety of regulatory contexts and to appear 'transparent' to foreign observers. The AAOIFI has thus helped remove any possible doubts as to legality and to strengthen trust in the sector (Maurer, 2002). The regulation of financial relations in Islamic banks has also helped them compare their performance and to improve the perception of their credibility (Karim, 1990). By applying the benchmark, these establishments enter a comparative process with respect to their performance which lets them cognitively endorse their existence in the eyes of their stakeholders.

In reference to this process, Rao (1994) talks about 'certification contests' and to illustrate his point, he quotes the ratings applied in several industries by specialist organisations which score and rate products or organisations. The AAA, A +, BBB – and other such scores littering the rating agencies' reports naturally come to mind. Clearly, a good rating endorses an establishment's action. It also consolidates its reputation on the premise that a competition is a rational test and a winner is 'better' than a loser. For Islamic banks, participation in these certification contests comes with an additional challenge: the very fact of taking part in the contests positions them within a clearly defined professional field in the eyes of stakeholders (consumers, financiers, investors, etc.) and also helps legitimise their existence while giving them a much more serious aura.

With issues such as legitimisation, transparency, transferability, credibility and performance comparison, the development of an accounting standard is of crucial importance to the field of Islamic finance and its stakeholders. We might think that, to establish rules designed to structure the financial reports of Islamic establishments, the experts from the AAOIFI started out with a brand-new system based on the precepts of *sharia*. This assumption seems all the more credible since *sharia* comprises a system that can be used to formulate rules: a kind of a meta-grammar that determines the conditions that make it possible to practice Islamic virtues in a morally organised universe (Maurer, 2002). However, so as not to find themselves 'reinventing the wheel', these experts preferred to take the rules of the American Financial Accounting Standard Board (FASB) as their basis and modify them when necessary to make them compatible with *sharia*. This would appear to be an extremely rational choice but has one major flaw: it fails to account for the fact that accounting issues are not purely technical. Accounting is in fact seen as a convention; here the term is understood as '… a collective procedure that can be identified by its conformation' (Amblard, 2000, p. 1). As such, it is made up of a set of socially constructed markers (*ibid.*) which forms part of a higher-level constituent convention (Eymard-Duvernay, Favereau, Orléan, Salais, & Thévenot, 2003) that defines cognitive frameworks (Gadrey, 2003) and sets a common framework for action (Eymard-Duvernay et al., 1989; Raveaud, 2005). Hence, the conventions of wealth, which according to Gadrey (2003) are central to the national accounting systems, establish a relationship between accounting wealth and well-being. The definition of the wealth to be recorded obviously depends on the definition of well-being and in this respect, Gadrey points out that requests to revise the French national general accounting framework were formulated with regard to a certain idea of well-being. Accounting systems therefore tend to record those elements that are in tune with their purpose.

By deciding to adopt the American FASB standards, experts from the AAOIFI thus 'imported' the convention of wealth that provides the framework for the accounting standards in contemporary finance and applied them to Islamic financial institutions. This paradoxical decision can be explained by the status claimed by modern finance and which it has largely succeeded in institutionalising: that of a science inspired by positivism (Frankfurter & McGoun, 1999) conveying the reality of the situation. Hence, for the vast majority of stakeholders, including those of Islamic finance and, clearly, the experts from the AAOIFI, there can only be one Finance, a single legitimate objective for financial transactions and a single way of controlling them.

So, is this a social convention or a reflection of reality? Looking beyond the epistemological debate, these differing approaches have some far-reaching consequences for Islamic finance: either accounting is actually based on unchanging standards that define the proper functioning of Finance and any other form of finance is condemned to the fringes unless it fits into the mould and thus loses its specific nature, or accounting schemes are defined by socio-cultural values and alternative frameworks and alternative forms of finance are thus possible.

FINANCES AND PARADIGMS

These contradictions and divergences in logic suggest it is possible that cultural entrenchment has an impact on financial mechanisms, thus paving the way for reflection on the universality of the financial act.

Here, the notion of paradigm (Kuhn, 1970 [1962]) has special importance through the link that it forges between the dominant logics, values and practices found within given systems. In this respect, Kuhn explains that the scientific models are made up of laws, theories, applications and technologies (Kuhn, 1970 [1962], p. 10) tied to bodies of theoretical and methodological beliefs (idem, p. 16), determined by specific metaphysical convictions (*ibid.*, p. 12). Kuhn used this approach to explain the dynamics of scientific fields. However, it was rapidly diverted from its initial function (explaining the development of sciences) by various authors who adapted it to different fields including the study of organisations and their development.

The use of the term 'paradigm' also became more widespread and is now currently used as a learned (pedantic?) synonym of the word 'system'. Hence, studying the paradigms of conventional and Islamic forms of finance comes down to comparing the components of two different systems. However, more widespread familiarity with the concept of paradigm is flawed in that it conceals its originality and value as:

(a) an integrated vision of the phenomena studied combining metaphysics and theory with action. This approach enables the analysis of a given reality while looking into the nature and coherence of its structural levels,
(b) highlighting the existence and co-existence of alternative scientific realities (Morgan, 1983).

In the context of management sciences, the complexity of the notion of paradigm was conveyed quite faithfully by Litterer and Young (1984). They refer to systems comprised of (i) a metaphysical level that defines the basic premises of human reality, (ii) a philosophical level that provides the meaning and coherence of the system by defining the principles that regulate the composition and interaction of the fundamental entities governing the social world and (iii) a final level that defines the values, the distribution of those values and the moral systems of the system (standard-setting function) as well as the legitimate objectives to be achieved and the methodologies making that possible (descriptive function).

We will apply this model to Islamic finance to determine its dominant logic and compare it to that of so-called conventional finance. More specifically, as recommended by Morgan (1983), we will highlight the basic premises that characterise and define the world vision shared by advocates of both systems to determine whether they are two distinct paradigms or if they are simply two sides of a single phenomenon. This approach seems all the more relevant since, for Litterer and Young (1984, pp. 249–250), 'every method of wealth distribution is underpinned by beliefs and a moral system that determine how value should be distributed'.

The Paradigm of Islamic Finance

Islamic finance is most often defined by what it forbids and especially the prohibition of interest (*riba*[1]). In fact, operators in Islamic finance define themselves on the basis of their compliance with this prohibition in contrast to the so-called conventional finance sector, which is known as *ribawi* (practising *riba*). Nonetheless, this definition of Islamic finance is extremely simplistic. This prohibition is in fact part of a set of rules, standards and values that all devout Muslims are required to follow if they are to attain eternal salvation. Under these conditions, it is not surprising that *sharia* takes its main inspiration from the Koran and prophetic tradition (*sunna*), the principles of which it 'operationalises' to enable followers to live their lives consistent with their religion.

With the Koran, *sunna* and *sharia*, the nature of the components at the metaphysical level of the Islamic finance paradigm does not give rise to any controversy since the premises of the Koran and the prophetic tradition (*sunna*) are recognised by all specialists. The basic premise structuring this level is *tawhid* (Ata al Sid', 1998, p. 44). This is the affirmation that God is unique, absolute, transcendent, the creator, master and lord of all things. This very strict monotheistic approach constitutes the Koran's fundamental message (Thomas, Cox, & Kraty, 2005) as shown by the fact that half of a Muslim's act of faith (*shahada*) is devoted to the affirmation of the oneness of God.

The link between this metaphysical level and secular activities is made on the basis of a principle of regency, or *istikhlaf*. This is a divine delegation that enables humankind[2] to manage the earth and its copious resources for the benefit of the community. For DeLorenzo, things are clear: 'When the earth and everything in it belong to the Almighty, the role of humankind is no more than that of caretakers ... The terms of the stewardship are simple and unambiguous: the Almighty allows humankind the use of the physical universe, and in return humankind agrees to be accountable for how the physical universe is used' (DeLorenzo, 2004, p. 11). Against this backdrop, humankind must '... be able to provide for (their) own good and that of the animate and inanimate world that surrounds it' (Sellami, 1994, p. 86).

This principle of regency means Muslims are able to ensure 'the coherence, meaning and purpose of their life', a function which, according to Litterer and Young (1984), forms the primary objective at the philosophical level of the paradigms. This regency principle could even form the very basis of an economic system whose main objective is socio-economic justice (Chapra, 1996). In any event, on a practical level, it results in principles of action that put the focus on the stakeholders' interest by giving humankind both an individual and collective responsibility[3] (Naqvi, 2001). In this respect, Pomeranz (1997) considers that a parallel can be drawn between

Islamic ethics and the Western (Kantian) model of stakeholders, based on the principle whereby every person benefits from basic rights in a moral universe.

The practical applications of the regency concept are governed by the principle of public interest (*maslaha*) that provides the basis for the main guidelines of *sharia* (*maqasid al-sharia*); '... all texts revealed or laws passed (have) the sole objective of seeking the public interest (*maslaha*)...' (Hassan, 1995, p. 13), making it possible to determine whether an economic activity may be carried out or not (Khan, 2002).

Hence, the Islamic finance paradigm has a metaphysical level dominated by the notion of *tawhid*, a philosophical level that explains social dynamics by the need to serve all stakeholders (principle of vice-regency), where the term 'stakeholders' is understood in its broadest sense, and an epistemological and methodological 'footing' aimed at optimising economic performance to the benefit of those same stakeholders (theory of *maslaha*).

The Paradigm of So-Called Conventional Finance

To analyse the structure of a paradigm of capitalism within which the dominant practices of contemporary finance are entrenched, we decided to refer to 'The Protestant Ethic and the Spirit of Capitalism' by Weber (1991 [1904–1905]). In this key work, the sociologist affirms that modern capitalism, as expressed in Western Europe and the United States, is characterised by an ethos structured by Calvinist ethics.

It is not a question of reducing the explanation of the emergence of capitalism to the affirmation of specific traits of religious origin, but instead of using an assertion that has '... become a canonical text in social science and the sociology of religions' (Grossein, 1996, p. 52) to be able to compare the constructs of comparable antecedents and apply this 'art' that is of use to the researcher in '... being able to show their partners the similarities between similar things and the dissimilarities between dissimilar things' (Pellissier-Tanon, 2001, p. 63).

For Weber, Calvinist ethics are based on the concepts of 'original sin' and the absolute liberty of God. The first of these notions is reflected in the principle of 'total depravity'[4] whereby, after their Fall, humankind, enslaved by its sinful nature, found itself (and still finds itself) incapable of choosing between good and evil without the grace of God.[5] Hence, 'every creature was separated from God by an unbridgeable gulf and deserved only eternal death, except in so far as he, for the greater glory of his majesty, had willed differently' (Weber, 1991 [1904–1905], p. 114).

The notion of God's absolute liberty results in the principle of double predestination, which is particularly associated with the name of Calvin: God chose certain individuals before the creation of the world for eternal salvation (principle of conditional election), while the rest of humankind is foreordained to eternal damnation. There is no point in trying to understand the reasons for this choice since the fate of humankind is shrouded in mystery. Similarly, it would be presumptuous to think that individual behaviour can influence God's will. That '... would be to think of God's absolutely free decrees, which have been settled from eternity, as subject to change by human influence, an impossible contradiction' (idem).

Man is thus '... forced to follow his path alone to meet a destiny which had been decreed for him from eternity. No one could help him'. (*ibid.*). Against this backdrop, the only concern of the faithful puritan is his personal salvation and the money earned from his work can serve as an indicator as to the divine blessing he has been granted. This is why accumulating capital becomes a duty and Weber specifies that money 'is thought of so purely as an end in itself, that from the point of view of the happiness of, or utility to, the single individual, it appears entirely transcendental and absolutely irrational' (Weber, 1991 [1904–1905], p. 50).

Another outcome of the theory of double predestination is an attitude of contempt and hate among those who have been 'chosen' towards those they see as the enemy of God and condemned to eternal damnation. If access to wealth is one of the signs of divine salvation, it seems pretty clear that the 'enemies of God' are in a state of destitution and no help should be given to them. This concept undermines the basis of any notion of social solidarity.

As such, a paradigm of capitalism forming part of so-called conventional finance would have its metaphysical level structured by the premises of an almighty God and 'original sin', with its philosophical level governed by the concept of double predestination and its descriptive and standard-setting aspects marked by the principal of maximising the utility function of individuals as an indicator of potential Eternal Salvation.

The Paradigms of Contemporary Finance

Webster's approach has definitely been challenged by a number of specialists, but we have to admit that the basic principles of Calvinism, as set out in 'The Protestant Ethic and the Spirit of Capitalism' can be seen in contemporary expressions of capitalism, and in particular in its so-called Anglo-Saxon model and its embodiment in neoliberalism. Hence all variants of neoliberalism, including the left-leaning version that advocates equal opportunities, legitimise individual competition and call into question the existence of collective structures (Amable, 2011). As such, neoliberals have seemingly introduced a programme to methodically destroy collective organisations, seeking to establish a system that organises the Darwinist struggle of all against all (Bourdieu, 1998) to create a society regulated by markets and subject to competitive dynamics (Foucault, 2004).

This desire to free the system from its socio-economic entrenchments and institute the superiority of individual competition via the markets over all other forms of organisation (Mudge, 2008) is the main divergence between the logic of the dominant contemporary economic system and that governed by *sharia*. This contrasting approach shows there is a fundamental difference between conventional and Islamic forms of finance and emphasises the main contradiction between the two systems, which lies not at the level of the disenchantment/re-enchantment of the world but in the juncture/disjuncture of operations with imperatives that goes beyond purely technical dimensions.

ISLAMIC FINANCE IN ACTION

Concrete examples of the Islamic finance paradigm are characterised by the application of 10 or so rules providing a framework for financial and commercial transactions that aim to be compatible with *sharia*. These include the prohibition of *riba*, a term generally translated by 'interest', *gharar* (deception/ambiguity), *mayssir* (speculation), interference in third-party transactions, the trading of articles banned by *sharia*, hoarding, and the exploitation of a person's unfortunate circumstances for financial gain. These same rules imply honesty, fair commercial practices, sale on public markets, the requirement to reveal all flaws and offer goods as they are.

These rules form the standard-setting 'footing' of the paradigm and are determined by its dominant logic of socio-economic enhancement. This link is clear in most cases (hoarding, exploitation of a person's unfortunate circumstances, fair commercial practices, honesty, etc.) and actually explains the ban on *riba* and *gharar*.

The Ban on Gharar

The term *gharar*, which is generally replaced in this chapter, by the expression 'ambiguity', is extremely complex to translate. Its Arabic root *taghreer* means 'placing oneself or placing one's property in danger without knowing it' (Al Dhareer, 1997). The word itself has connotations of 'uncertainty', 'risk', 'errors' and 'deception'. There is *gharar* in a commercial transaction when the consequences are concealed or are unclear. This generally becomes apparent when there is a doubt or uncertainty about the reality of a transaction or where one of the parameters of a transaction is unknown.[6]

While it is quite easy to determine cases of *gharar* when the cause is obvious (specifications, price or delivery date omitted in a contract), in most cases the complexity of the concept can make such a decision extremely problematic. To overcome this issue, Al Suwailem (2000) recommends the use of game theory. Briefly, this means that stakeholders can either commit to interaction in a 'win-win situation', the term used in modern management glossaries, so that they simultaneously record gains or losses, or opt for a 'win-lose situation' where one person's gains lead to the other person's losses, and vice versa. In the latter case, the fact that one party wins at the expense of the other can only be explained by information asymmetry. For Al Suwaillem, this is where *gharar* applies and it is simply a question of determining the type of game in which the players are engaged to identify potential cases.

This approach does away with all notions of semantics in the assessment of cases of prohibition and 'scientificates' the approach to *gharar*, which is the clear aim of the author given the title of his work: 'Towards an objective measure of *gharar* in exchange'. It is therefore logical that Al Suwailem ends his analysis after noting the correspondence between *gharar* and a 'win-lose situation' with the intervening information asymmetry. In doing so, the author neglects another characteristic of win-lose situations: the fact that no additional resource is created during the interaction between players. As such, the ban on *gharar* automatically blocks 'sterile' transactions, making increased munificence in the players' operating environment one of the factors of the prohibition. The first condition enabling players in a win-win situation to register profit is the setting up of an operation that responds to demand on the market on which they operate. The ban on *gharar* therefore responds to the development imperatives stipulated in the concept of vice-regency governing the philosophical level of the Islamic finance paradigm.

The Ban on Riba

The same economic concern completed by social considerations can be seen in the ban on *riba*. This is one of the major prohibitions in Islamic finance. The principle is set out in the Koran (Koran, 2, pp. 275–280; 3, p. 130; 4, p. 161; 30, p. 39) and in prophetic tradition (*sunna*), and it has always been acknowledged as valid by Muslims. However, what actually constitutes *riba* has been the subject of debate and controversy for centuries (Siddiqi, 2004). The most common explanation restricted *riba* to the use '... of a loan generating excessively high interest, or doubled and redoubled according to the Koran' (Saleh, 1979, p. 66). However, most legal advisers have concluded that bank interest should be likened to *riba*, a position that was endorsed by the consensus (*ijma'*) of the Fiqh Academy (Al-Jarhi, 1996) and which thus acquired '... legal force ...' (Kamali, 1996).

These specialists link *riba* to bank interest but do not believe it is a true equivalent. The distinction lies in the fact that *riba* goes beyond the financial aspect of transactions under the name *riba al-hadith* (riba of the hadith)[7] to ban not only the payment of 'bonuses' linked to the duration of financial loans, but also, within the context of a direct exchange of goods, any material compensation that is not related to a specific activity or a potential economic risk. In both cases, the prohibition results from the same principle: a return on an investment must be linked to an economic activity. Islamic finance thus assigns capital with a cost linked to its actual value in use rather than to a theoretical value in use defined solely on the basis of the time value of that capital. For specialists, this characteristic denotes the main difference between interest rates and mark-up, which recompense the financing operations of Islamic banks.

To really appreciate the significance of this distinction, it should be noted that the Islamic vision of the economy gives the financial sector the role of serving the development of the 'real' economy. However, current events prove daily that the self-replicating mechanisms of interest often lead to a reversal of the situation where global economic growth is disrupted by a 'real' economic activity that feeds the financial sector.

An unjustified increment (*riba*) also comes with clear social issues and legal advisers consider that the act of drawing 'rent' from money loaned perpetrates a double injustice. On the one hand, the lender ought to give money to the person in need rather than lending it, in line with the principle of social solidarity advocated by the Koran.[8] Asking for a fee for the provision of the loan increases the injustice and challenges social harmony by accentuating the differences between the different components of the population.

By disrupting economic well-being and upsetting social harmony and solidarity, *riba* partially challenges the principle of vice-regency which advocates the management of earthly goods for the well-being of the community. It is therefore directly linked to the philosophical level of the paradigm.

THE INSTRUMENTS OF ISLAMIC FINANCE

The condemnation of an unjustified increment (*riba*) and ambiguity (*gharar*), together with the ban on speculation (*maysir*), form the basic rules of Islamic finance. The reason for these prohibitions lies in a desire to see the outcome of financial and commercial operations carried out by Islamic institutions optimised for all stakeholders (social harmony and solidarity for *riba*, economic growth for *riba* and *gharar*) on the basis of the general interest (*maslaha*), in line with the principle of vice-regency. There is no need to spend time demonstrating that the ban on speculation (*mayssir*) follows the same logic, since there are plenty of examples in the news of operations carried out by players triggering economic crises affecting the well-being of large segments of the population.

In this respect, the instruments of Islamic finance also have some specific characteristics. One distinctive technique is an uncertain return on investment through a profit-sharing structure (sponsorship/*mudaraba*) or the sharing of profit and loss (partnership/*musharakah*). Another set of instruments allows for more predictable gains by enabling the financing of various types of operation under the names of *murabaha* (commercial financing), *salam* (financing tradeable goods), *istisna'* (financing projects), *ijarah* (rental) and *ijarah mountahia bi istimlak* (hire-purchase). The originality of these latter operations lies in the mechanisms that allow for profit: this is theoretically indexed on the performance of the underlying assets that are financed; assets that the financiers have to appropriate temporarily, the length of time varying according to the type of operation, to be able to claim the profit.

The difference between these techniques and those used by so-called conventional finance is clear. As you would expect, these instruments structure the methodological element of the paradigms in which they are embedded and have to be in line with the dominant logic structuring those constructs. For Islamic finance with its socio-economic bias, there is the question of the role of the banks (although should we still call them banks?) and/or of the logic of the financial operations in non-maximising contexts. In other words, are Islamic banks still banks like any other and do they do the same thing as other banks?

Despite the theoretical demonstration provided above, it has to be noted that the Islamic financial institutions endeavour to imitate the structures, strategies and operations of conventional banks as closely as possible. They therefore conduct some extremely complex arrangements to reproduce the operations and/or performance of these conventional banks. The most characteristic example of this type of arrangement is undoubtedly the case of Islamic bonds, the renowned *sukuks*.

To sum up very briefly, bonds are debt securities issued on financial markets which enable companies or states to fund certain operations. Subscribers receive annual interest until they recover the full amount of their loan. As such, this type of operation contravenes two prohibitions under *sharia*: the ban on *riba* (interest) and the ban on making a profit without risk[9] insofar as collection of the principal is guaranteed. Islamic finance specialists have nonetheless managed to devise an Islamic equivalent to bonds, known as *sukuks*. In this context, the funds the originator requires will be generated by the sale of shares of an ad-hoc legal entity (SPV – special purpose vehicle) set-up for the purpose. This SPV will form a partnership with the entity initiating the operation to develop a project that will generate profits which will be used to pay for the coupons. The initiating entity will also undertake to buy the SPV's shares in the operation on maturity, to pay back the subscribers' initial investment.

The financial arrangements implemented to meet with the imperatives of the various stakeholders can be extremely complex. In 2004, for example, German federal state Saxe-Anhalt decided to raise $100 million on markets in the Arabian Gulf region. To this end, a *sukuks* issue, the first of its kind in Europe, was organised: (i) An SPV was formed, (ii) it sold securities and (iii) used the sum raised to buy from the federal state the right of usufruct over a number of administrative buildings, for which it paid US$100 million. The SPV paid the sum in question to the federal state, thus satisfying the first goal of the operation. In return, the federal state (vi) undertook to buy back the right of usufruct on maturity of the securities. To be able to pay coupons to the subscribers, (v) the SPV then rented out these buildings to the federal state and on maturity of the securities (v) the latter bought back the right of usufruct so that it could pay back the initial investment to the subscribers. This special operation applies rental contracts (*ijara*) as its main mechanism, but all the instruments of Islamic finance can serve as the basis for *sukuks*, depending on the stakeholders' requirements.

The success of these Islamic bonds has been confirmed year after year, with an average annual growth rate of almost 48% between 2008 and 2012. Nonetheless, the efficiency of this type of operation can be questioned when the complexity of their structure is held up against the simplicity of conventional bond issues. The same can be said when all Islamic banking transactions are analysed. They overlap contracts in order to reproduce conventional banking operations that remain compatible with *sharia*. So what is the difference between a so-called conventional bank and an Islamic institution? When we put this question to him, the former credit manager of the Arab Finance House, an Islamic bank operating out of Lebanon, answered: 'The difference between Islamic banks and conventional banks lies in the interaction with the customer and the transparency of operations'.

From Financial to Economic Intermediation

One of the most remarkable results of the 'Islamic translation' of so-called conventional banking transactions is a clear lack of efficiency and not least the multiplication of costs linked to the Research and Development activities required to put together increasingly complex structures, plus the omnipresent '*sharia* risk', as can be seen in the number of legal proceedings initiated by stakeholders who claim to have discovered that the operations they entered into turned out not to be *sharia*-compatible, or simply the intrinsic costs of each contract used.

Analysed in light of the paradigm theory, this lack of operational efficiency is quite logical. By simulating the transactions of so-called conventional finance, the Islamic banks use instruments with a socio-economic vocation to reach the goals set by a paradigm with a maximising logic. The tension between the two dominant systems explains the lack of operational efficiency of the arrangements based on principles such as *murabaha*, *ijara* and *salam*. If this is actually the case, the same instruments should retain all their power when used in a context that is consistent with the dominant logic of the paradigm to which they belong.

The Case of Social Businesses

As we explore this question, a case study of social bushiness will be highly useful. These structures were set up by Nobel Peace Prize winner Mohammed Yunus. Their stated goal is to combine the efficiency of for-profit businesses with the objectives of non-governmental or charitable organisations to find a solution to one or more problems (education, health, access to technology, environment, etc.) threatening people or society. This is how Yunus launched Grameen-Danone in 2005 to help address the issue of malnutrition in Bangladesh by providing local children with yoghurts at affordable prices containing all the nutrients they require for growth (Yunus & Weber, 2007). The Nobel Prize winner also founded Grameen-Veolia to provide purified water to populations in regions of Bangladesh where water is contaminated with arsenic, and Basf-Grameen to provide insecticide-treated mosquito nets to populations threatened with malaria or other diseases transmitted by insects (Yunus Social Business, 2013). Over 30 years, Yunus founded some 40 social businesses in Bangladesh. In fact, he claims to have set up a social business every time he tried to solve a social issue (Yunus, 2013).

In 2011, Yunus launched the Yunus Social Business Global Initiative (YSB) to share his experience on the international stage. To reach its goals, YSB oversees the creation of social accelerator schemes that incubate and fund social businesses. To this end, a fund provisioned by charitable donations or social investors' investments is paired with an incubator that identifies, structures and selects projects. The sums collected by the fund are loaned or invested in these projects after a thorough investigation and the amounts paid back are used to pay back the social investors and invest in new operations. The social accelerators take the following form (Fig. 1):

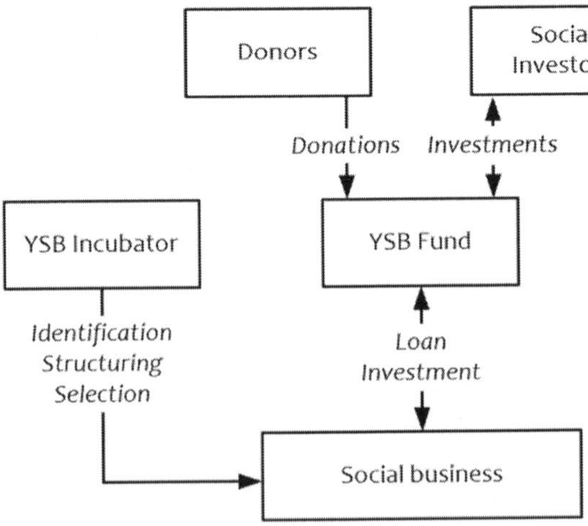

Fig. 1. Structure of a Social Accelerator (So-Called Conventional Finance). *Source*: According to Yunus (2013).

The social businesses funded by the accelerator funds can take one of two forms: The first (type 1) is a non-profit business where the main goal is to produce and/or provide a service with a social, ethical or environmental purpose. All the structures created by Grameen in association with large international corporations are examples of this type of social business. They do not distribute the profits they make. Instead, the sums are used to refund social investors and ensure the sustainability of operations on the basis of Yunus' now-famous formula: 'Non-loss, non-dividend company with a social objective' (Yunus, 2007, p. 108). Type 2 social businesses are for-profit organisations. They are owned by underprivileged people and provide them with an income.

Over three years, 20 social businesses employing 800 people have been set up in seven countries: Albania, Uganda, India, Haiti, Colombia, Brazil and Tunisia. The case of this latter country is especially interesting. Tunisia is the only country among those in which YSB operates that is largely populated by Muslims[10] and with a risk of heightened religiosity; poverty and religiosity appear to be positively correlated (Crabtree, 2010). If this is actually the case, the religious acceptability of social businesses is clearly critical. The people behind IBDA, the social accelerator scheme created in Tunisia by YSB and the African Development Bank, clearly understood this. In 2013, the structure's director contacted us to talk about the possibility of making all of the operations he oversees compatible with *sharia*.

A 'Sharia-*Compatible' Version of the Accelerator Fund Structures*

On a conceptual level, the guiding principles applied to the creation of social businesses, as set out by Yunus (2007),[11] are perfectly in line with the *sharia* ethos which stipulates that one of the basic responsibilities of humankind is to ensure the harmonious development of creativity (*i3mar al ard*) while protecting life (*nafs*), faith (*din*), property (*mal*), lineage (*nasl*) and intellect (*akl*).[12]

At an operational level, however, the use of social accelerators by devout Muslims comes up against the obstacle of *riba*. Indeed, YSB funds lend money to social businesses that pay them back with interest. In addition, during our discussions the director of IBDA said that he was considering increasing the sums paid back to certain investors to account for inflation. The *sharia*-compatibility of accelerator operations therefore depends on the alignment of both the relationship between the fund and the social business it funds (downstream relationship) and the ties between the fund and the parties that fund it (upstream relationship) with *sharia* rules. The array of contracts that Islamic finance can put to use means that it can adapt without too much difficulty (Fig. 2).

Relationships Upstream of the Fund. The fund benefits from different sources of finance and its relationships with each source are governed by different financial agreements:

- *Social donors* are philanthropists who do not seek to recover the sums they donate to the fund. The contractual agreement used in this case in known as (1) *HIBA* (donation).
- *Social creditors* want to recover their funds but do not seek profit. Their contribution takes the form of an interest-free loan. The Islamic terminology for this type of operation is (1′) *QARD HASSAN.*
- *Social investors* seek to recover their investments, increased by a sum that at least neutralises inflation. In a conventional finance context, the fund and investors would negotiate the payment of interest at a rate that fulfils this objective. In a *sharia*-compatible structure, the use of

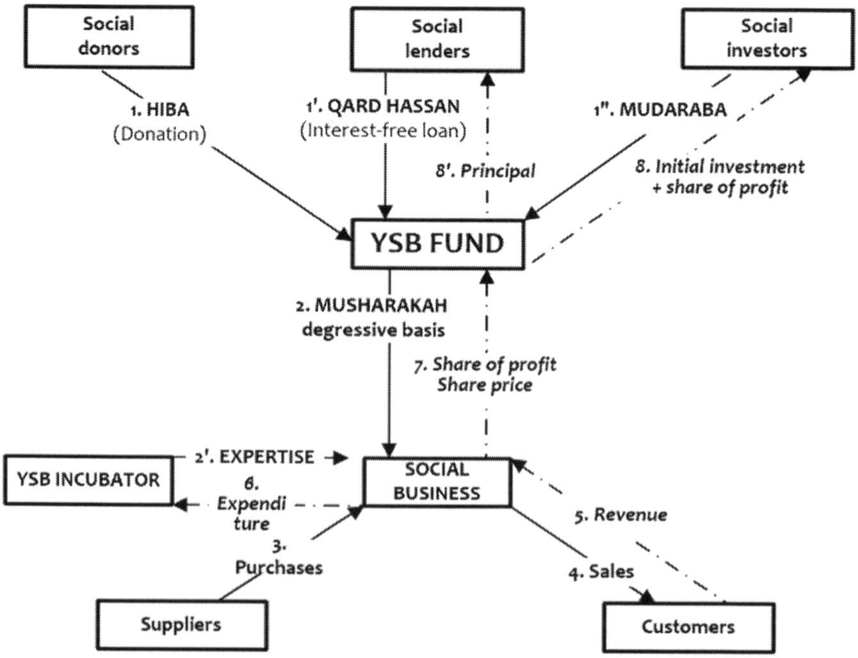

Fig. 2. Proposal Structure of a Social Accelerator (Islamic Finance).

interest is prohibited. To overcome this problem, a form of sponsorship is used, known as (1″) *MUDARABA* (Fig. 3).

Here, social investors, known as *RAB al-MAL*, entrust the fund with the management of their investment (1) in their capacity of an expert (2) (*MUDARIB*) and receive a share of the profits generated by their contribution. This type of contract is commonly used by Islamic banks to generate a return on their clients' deposits. In this case, the financier receives the largest portion of the profits (80%) but the partners can negotiate the distribution of profit as they see fit (3). The only obstacle to the use of this contract is the rule that states that the financier bears any losses alone. To alleviate this risk, the fund can, in the same way as banks, create a hedging reserve in which all the profits that exceed an amount agreed on by the partners are deposited (4). In the event of poor performance, this reserve can compensate the investor for their losses (5) and at the end of the operation, the balance of the reserve is paid to the fund as a performance bonus (6).

Relationships Downstream of the Fund. In its conventional form, the fund contributes to the capital or provides funding in the form an interest-bearing loan to a social business which has been identified, structured and selected by the fund's incubator (2′). While nothing opposes the incubation phase, as Islamic finance allows for the payment of fees for a service

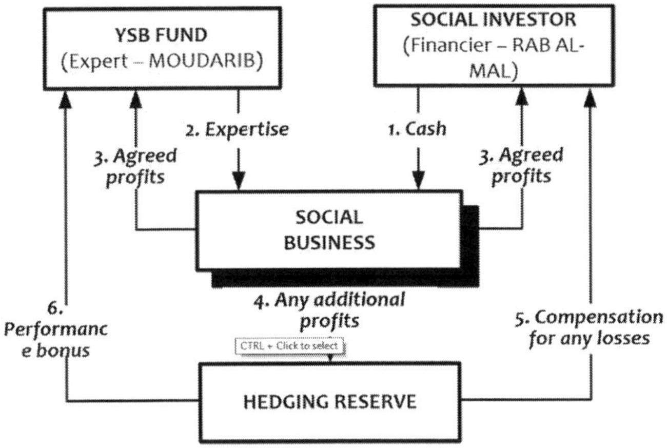

Fig. 3. Structure of a Mudaraba Paired with a Hedging Reserve.

rendered (6), again the issue of *riba* arises in terms of the funding, because of the interest-bearing loan. To overcome this problem, the YSB fund could limit its funding to a stakeholding via an association contract (*musharakah*). The advantage of this solution is that:

- it automatically secures the funding;
- it means YSB can directly supervise the operation, assuming responsibility for the oversight functions;
- insofar as the income of each party depends on the stake they own in the operation and on the operation's performance, it means YSB may receive more profit than expected;
- it frees the social entrepreneur from the pressure of regular payments (interest) unrelated to the operation's performance.

Since the goal of social accelerators is to multiply the creation of social businesses and not to own the specific structures, the contract to be used in this case would be a variant of *musharakah*, namely (2) *musharakah mutanaqisah* (on a degressive basis) which allows YSB to sell its shares in the business progressively to its partner(s). In a case like this, the profit on the sale of YSB's shares (7) will be used to reconstitute the fund's initial capital and to pay back the initial contributions to investors (8) and creditors (8′). The share of the operations' profits (7) due to YSB will be used by it to pay for the incubator's services (6), to fund the profit rate promised to social investors as part of *mudaraba* – the sponsorship agreement that ties them to the fund, and to increase the size of the fund.

The use of *musharakah mutanaqisah* comes with a major drawback, however, in that it involves a risk of loss for the fund. The contract is in fact an instrument for sharing profit and loss. To mitigate this risk, the funds using this option can implement an array of financing agreements that are commonly used by banks. These agreements have the benefit of generating predictable cash flows and, more importantly, of separating performance payments from the operations they fund. However, as demonstrated with the *sukuks*, the main drawback of these instruments is the cost of the complexity of the operations requiring overlapping contracts.

Let us take the example of a cheese factory (Alter Prenga) founded by a social accelerator in Albania. This social business was set up in an underprivileged area of the country with the goal of producing high-quality cheese using milk from a hundred or so farmers. To do so, the factory employed seven people directly and ensured regular income for these farmers so they could envisage an expansion of their respective operations. To facilitate the set-up of this operation, the accelerator fund granted the factory a loan of US$190,000 repayable over six years. The money was used to fund the factory's construction, the purchase of equipment and the operating costs over the start-up period. In a *sharia*-compatible structure, the following contracts would have been required to reach the same goals:

- *Factory construction*: YSB directly funds construction of the factory using an *istisna'* contract (project funding). YSB then rents out the building to the social business before transferring ownership at the end of the rental period negotiated within the framework of an *ijara wa iktina* contract (lease agreement).
- *Purchase of equipment*:
  - YSB buys the equipment on its own account and leases it to the social business before transferring ownership under a *ijara wa iktina* contract (lease agreement).
  - Or YSB buys the equipment and sells it on hire-purchase to the social business, making a profit (*murabaha*).
- *Funding the operating costs*: YSB buys and pays up front for the factory's production (*salam*) and gives it proxy (*wakala*) to sell the production on its own account since YSB does not have a network via which the goods could be sold.

Relationships of the Social Business with its Environment. The social business has normal market relationships with its partners, buying raw materials and equipment from suppliers (3) and selling goods to customers (4). These operations are no different to the regular transactions of any company, on condition that the social business does not use financial facilities that are incompatible with *sharia*.

From Socially Responsible Financing to Economic Intermediation

The transformation of the Alter Prenga structure to make it *sharia*-compatible and all other contract arrangements that can be considered to make social accelerator operations compatible with *sharia* are part of an 'Islamic translation' strategy for operations founded on the methodologies of so-called conventional finance. Hence, the thinking behind the theoretical 'Islamisation' of the Albanian cheese factory's financing structure was guided by a desire to replicate the performance of the initial loan, that is financing the construction of the factory, buying the equipment and providing working capital, generating a predictable profit and recovering the initial capital.

Islamic banks are used to this kind of process: they identify the goal of the 'conventional' operation to be replicated and, to achieve this, they assemble the necessary Islamic financing agreements. The socially responsible Islamic finance industry, and especially microfinance, does the same thing. Hence, 70% of the operations carried out by microfinance institutions in the Middle East and North Africa are based on *murabaha* (Pearce, 2011), an agreement used in place of an interest-bearing loan. It lets the financial institution buy the assets the beneficiary requires (1, 1′) and sell them to the beneficiary on credit (2), applying a margin (2′) (Fig. 4).

The similarity between this type of contract and an interest-bearing loan is clear and explains why many people, including Muslims, state that Islamic finance is hypocritical. However, it is worth pointing out that the aspect of *sharia* devoted to social interaction[13] permits anything that is not expressly forbidden and rules on the letter of contracts and not their underlying intention. *Murabaha* complies with the rules of *sharia* and is therefore perfectly acceptable. This is an important detail. The vast majority of Muslims are located in regions (sub-Saharan Africa and the Asia-Pacific zone) where poverty and extreme poverty levels exceed the international average. While 22% of the world's population lives on an income less than or equal to US$1.25 a day and 34% have an income less than or equal to $2[14] (Phelps & Crabtree, 2013), the level of extreme poverty in the regions under consideration varies between 54% and 18%[15] while poverty oscillates between 78% and 45%[16] (PovcalNet, 2014). Religiosity levels are extremely high in these regions; between 90% and 99% of people consider religion an important part of their life[17] (Crabtree, 2010), so any system that strives to ensure the well-being of these populations and accommodates for their beliefs is welcome. On a completely different level, it should also be noted that the fact that *murabaha* allows for purchase of the sought-after asset is a significant advantage. It means that the funds provided are actually used for their stated purpose. It means, for example, that loans for production purposes are not used as 'sterile' consumer loans that the beneficiary is then unable to pay back.

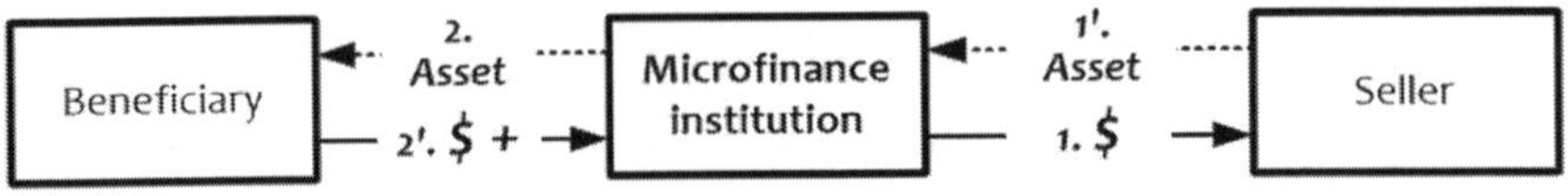

Fig. 4. Structure of a *Murabaha*.

In spite of these benefits, the *sharia*-compatible 'translation' of loans and all operations designed to 'Islamise' so-called conventional finance transactions come with a serious conceptual problem. Let us look again at social businesses: Yunus explains the emergence of the concept by a shortcoming in the capitalist system in that market use is restricted to people who are merely looking to make a profit (Yunus, 2008). In a paper written with Moingeon and Lehmann-Ortega, the Nobel Prize winner specifies that maximising shareholders' value is still the rule in the capitalist regime and that reconciling this system with social goals remains fraught with issues. They explain that while advocates of CSR suggest company performance should be measured using three key indicators relating to financial, social and environmental performance, only a single indicator really counts: financial profit (Yunus, Moingeon, & Lehmann-Ortega, 2010, p. 309). In other words, the dominant logic of the present system is omnipresent. Testimony to this is the fact that certain practitioners and authors have distorted the initial concept of development aid to the benefit of the discovery of new sources of profit, as illustrated by the idea of a 'base-of-pyramid' fortune (BOP) in Prahalad and Stuart (2002) or that of 'shared valued' in Porter and Kramer (2006, p. 2011).

Due to socio-economic development issues, the dominant paradigm is subject to the same tensions affecting the Islamic finance paradigm when it comes up against the need for maximisation. It is thus paradoxical to see Islamic finance institutions imitating the *modus operandi* of so-called conventional finance when it develops socially responsible operations. The obvious alternative would be to seek to maximise the socio-economic utility of operations directly, instead of trying to increase it by creating structures that let stakeholders express their altruism by relinquishing their right to a profit from time to time. Quite logically, Islamic finance, which is embedded in a paradigm with a socio-economic vocation, should be able to achieve this goal through the synergies it enables between its financial contracts.

The Hodeidah Microfinance Programme (HMFP)

The microfinance programme launched in Hodeidah in Yemen in 1997 is a structure that seeks to imitate, in a *sharia*-compatible manner, an operation originally implemented using conventional finance instruments.

Hodeidah is a port town with half a million inhabitants who work in trade, fishing, the food industry, light industry, transport and crafts. As elsewhere in the country, this population is poor[18] and has strong Islamic religious convictions. To accommodate these beliefs, the HMFP uses *murabaha* to meet the financing requirements of its customers. As such, when a person expresses a need, the agent examining their application looks at the feasibility of the operation, checks the solvency of the group to which the beneficiary belongs (HMFP only lends to groups), identifies the suppliers of the asset sought after, buys the asset and sells it on credit to the beneficiary. Funding is on average for an amount of US$240. Loans are granted to the poor, mainly women, who are or have been in work. During these operations, the HMFP makes a profit of around 35% on the funds granted. Clearly, the programme's initiators have only used *murabaha* in response to a wish expressed by the population in a survey that preceded the fund's set-up. As proof, in the interim report published on behalf of the project's initiators, the 'Global Microenterprise Initiative' (GMI) only refers to operations in terms of loans, even stating that: 'given the cost structure of Hodeidah, the organisation is far from covering all its costs through the *revenues generated by interest*[19] and fees' (GMI, 2005, p. 41).

This bias conceals all other uses of Islamic financial contracts. An interest-bearing loan is only granted to a single party who uses the funds to meet their needs before repaying the sum lent plus a profit. The simplest instrument to fulfil this function is therefore *murabaha* and the wish to reproduce the structure of an interest-bearing loan strictly governs its implementation. However, the socio-economic efficiency of this same operation could easily be increased by developing synergy between *murabaha* and other contracts. HMFP could therefore remunerate the construction of the asset it wishes to transfer under *mudaraba* to its initial customer, which would amount to using the same sum to fund the activity of two stakeholders instead of one. It could thus fund the construction of the boat a fisherman needs to do his job (1, 1′) before selling it to him on credit (2, 2′) (Fig. 5).

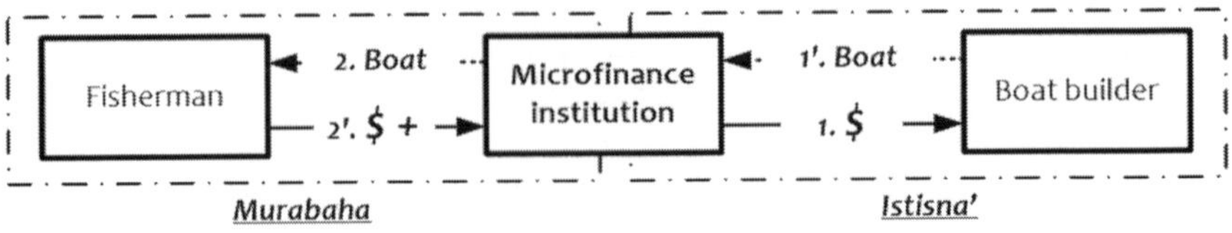

Fig. 5. Istisna'/Murabaha Structure.

One solution more in line with the spirit of *sharia*, which links profit to the risk incurred in an operation and advocates the sharing of risks and profits between partners in an operation, would be to see the relationship between the fisherman and the institute governed by *musharakah* (partnership) which allows for the sharing of profit and loss. In this context, the microfinance institute would fund, as above, the construction of the boat under *istisna'* (1, 1′) and would take part in *musharakah* by providing the fisherman with his equipment (2). The latter would contribute to the operation through his work (2′). The partners would share the profits on the basis of a predefined agreement and the losses would be shared proportionally to the share each partner has in the operation (3, 3′). Since the institute's vocation is not to serve as a fishing operator, the partners would plan for the repurchase of the institute's shares in the operation by the fisherman (4, 4′) under *musharakah mutanaqisah* (Fig. 6).

This type of funding automatically creates economic microcycles, maximising the socio-economic scope of the sums committed by multiplying the number of beneficiaries.

The increased use of this type of financing ought to lead to a rise in the quantities fished and, in order to protect its profits, the institute would be required to help the fishermen seek out new markets, create a transport network, set up storage facilities, and so on. As such, the institute would end up financing and supervising the entire value chain in order to recover its investment. It is clear that a financial institution is not prepared to handle this type of situation and that a special social

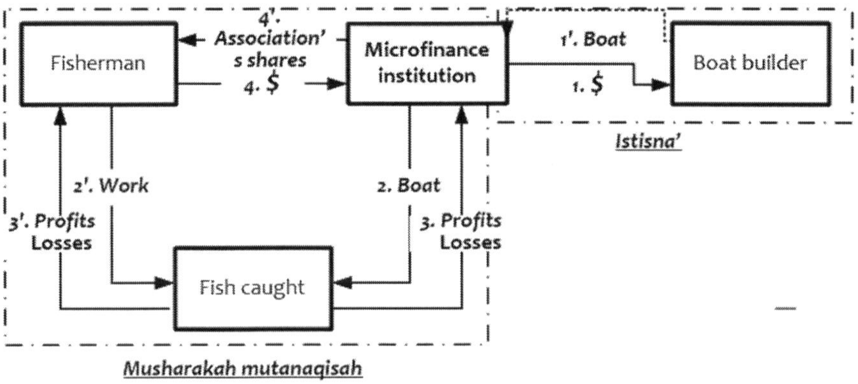

Fig. 6. Istisna'/Musharakah Mutanaqisah Structure.

business aimed at developing fishing in the Hodeidah region would no doubt be better armed for this type of task. We could thus imagine a type 1 non-profit social business financing, organising and coordinating a network of type 2 social businesses belonging to underprivileged people looking to secure an income.

CONCLUSION

The task assigned to these hypothetical social businesses in Hodeidah reminds us, as Bourdieu (1997) did, that markets are complex, that they are not limited to purely financial aspects and imply that any operation with a socio-economic vocation has to operate at the level of the various components if it is to be effective. These social businesses create, organise and manage a network of type 2 businesses with what we imagine to be complementary activities. This is the main characteristic of the array of firms linked through strategic alliances described by Gomes-Casseres (1997). Against this backdrop, the institutions that finance the operations play the role of a kind of economic hub, which raises a number of questions about the role of banks in non-maximising ventures. Why the banks? The financial arrangements and the creation of economic micro-cycles described in the Hodeidah example apply above all to microfinance and the funding of very small businesses, but we could envisage the expansion of this type of operation which would then be seen as a kind of economic intermediation. But how can we define the concept precisely? What would be the role of the financial institutions, which do not appear to be properly equipped in their current form to manage this type of situation? How do we measure and compare performance? The notion of economic footprint, corresponding to the socio-economic impact of operations is one avenue worth exploring. What indicators would be used?

The answers to these questions do not concern the field of Islamic finance alone. The use of the notion of paradigm, separating conventional finance and Islamic finance, means we are able to look at the dynamics at work between these two forms of finance. They might be able to adopt different relationship configurations, including a form of complementarity which would see the ethical values of Islamic finance form synergies with the technical excellence of conventional finance and create what we could describe as contemporary finance. This approach would make it possible to free Islamic finance from its religious foundations and let it be viewed as a case study for alternative finance able to serve different sectors of the market in an inclusive manner.

NOTES

1. We should point out that while all legal advisers associate banking interest with *riba*, they do not restrict the latter to this prohibition. In fact, *riba* prohibition goes beyond the financial aspect of transactions under the name *riba al-hadith* (*riba* of the *hadith*) to ban not only the payment of 'bonuses' linked to the duration of financial loans, but also any material compensation that is not related to a specific activity or a potential economic risk. In both cases, the prohibition stems from the same principle: a return on an investment must be linked to an economic activity and its inherent risk.
2. We use the expression 'humankind' to overcome any ambiguity that could be created with the use of the terms 'man' or 'mankind'.
3. The latter is exemplified by the sacred character of the alms tax (*zakat*) that forms one of the five pillars of Islam and by the Koranic recommendation to make donations.
4. The principle of 'total depravity' is one of the five basic principles of Calvinism. The others are 'conditional election', 'limited atonement', 'irresistible grace' and the 'perseverance the saints'. They were formulated by the Synod of Dordt (1618–1619).
5. This grace is expressed by faith which, from the Calvinistic viewpoint, is not the fisherman's gift to God but God's gift to the fisherman, giving him a new nature.
6. ... which explains our preference for the term 'ambiguity'.
7. As such, *sharia* distinguishes between two kinds of *riba*: the first, which is called *riba al-quran*, standardises monetary loans while the second, known as *riba al-hadith*, forbids any unjustified compensation in a direct exchange.
8. Here, we should point out that the alms tax, *zakat*, which every Muslim is required to pay to the community on the basis of what they own, is one of the five pillars of Islam.
9. According to the saying '*al-ghorm bil ghonm*', there is 'no reward without risk'.
10. 99.5% of the 10.5 million people in Tunisia are Muslim (Pew Research Center's Forum on Religion & Public Life, 2012).
11. Finding a solution to one or more problems threatening people and/or society instead of maximising profits.
12. The importance of this task is such that the rules of *sharia* may be undermined to protect one of those domains (principle of *darura*).
13. *Sharia* can be divided into two chapters: *ibadat* devoted to the rules on interaction between humankind and God and *muamalat* which covers social interaction.
14. The World Bank sets the extreme poverty threshold at US$1.25 and the poverty threshold at US$2.

15. Indonesia: 18.06%, Pakistan: 21.04%, India: 32.68%, Bangladesh: 43.25%, Nigeria: 54.37%.

16. Indonesia: 45.22%, Pakistan: 59.10%, India: 67.87%, Bangladesh: 75.80 %, Nigeria: 77.90 %.

17. India: 90%, Pakistan: 92%, Nigeria: 96%, Indonesia: 99%, Bangladesh: 99%.

18. 17.5% of the 24 million Yemenites live in a state of extreme poverty (less than US$1.25 per day) and 33.5% live on less than US$2 per day.

19. Emphasis added.

REFERENCES

Abbott, A. (1988). *The system of professions: An essay on the division of expert labor.* Chicago, IL: The University of Chicago Press.

Acquier, A., & Aggeri, F. (2008). Une généalogie de la pensée managériale sur la RSE. *Revue Française de Gestion,* (180), 131–157.

Al Dhareer, S. M. (1997). *Al-Gharar in contracts and its effects on contemporary transactions.* Kingdom of Saudi Arabia: Islamic Development Bank – Islamic Research and Training Institute.

Al-Jarhi, M. A. (1996). Préface, in islamic development bank. In *Introduction aux techniques islamiques de financement.* Kingdom of Saudi Arabia: Islamic Development Bank – Islamic Research and Training Institute.

Al Suwailem, S. (2000). Towards an objective measure of Gharar in exchange. *Islamic Economic Studies, 7*(1&2), 61–102.

Amable, B. (2011). Morals and politics in the ideology of neo-liberalism. *Socio-Economic Review, 9,* 3–30.

Amblard, M. (2000). Le changement des règles comptables: une interprétation de la théorie des conventions. *Actes de l'Association Française de Comptabilité, Mai.*

Ata al Sid', M. (1998). General objectives of Islamic Shari'ah: The reality of the divine. In M. Kahf (Ed.), *Lessons in Islamic economics.* Jeddah: Banque Islamique de Développement – Centre de Recherche et de Formation Islamique.

Bain and Company. (2012). *Islamic finance market: Overview and key challenges going forward – Key findings.* Paris: Bain and Company.

Bayard, S., & Pannier-Runacher, A. (2002). *Rapport d'enquête sur la finance socialement responsable.* Inspection Générale des Finance. Paris: La Documentation Française.

Beckert, J. (2009). The social order of markets. *Theory and Society, 38*(3), 245–269.

Bourdieu, P. (1997). Le champ économique. *Actes de la recherche en sciences sociales, 119,* 28–66.

Bourdieu, P. (1998). L'essence du néolibéralisme. *Le Monde Diplomatique.*

Chaar, A. M. (2011). *La structuration des stratégies au sein des champs en voies d'institutionnalisation: Le cas de la finance islamique au Liban.* Thèse de Doctorat. Paris: Université Paris-Est.

Chapra, M. (1996). *Qu'est-ce que l'économie islamique?* Jeddah: IDB – IRTI.

Crabtree, S. (2010). *Religiosity highest in world's poorest nations.* Washington, DC: Gallup, Inc.

Cuny de la Verryère, A. R. (2013). *Finance catholique – Au fondement de la finance éthique et solidaire*. Paris: Editions EMS.

DeLorenzo, Y. (2004). The religious foundations of Islamic finance. In S. Archer & R. Abdel-Karim (Eds.), *Islamic finance – Innovation and growth*. London: Euromoney Books & AAOFI.

Eymard-Duvernay, F., Favereau, O., Orléan, A., Salais, R., & Thévenot, L. (2003). *Valeurs, coordination et rationalité. L'économie des conventions ou le temps de la réunification dans les sciences économiques, sociales et politiques*. PSE Working Paper, October.

Eymard-Duvernay, F., Orléan, A., Dupuy, J.-P., Thévenot, L., Favereau, O., & Salais, R. (1989). Introduction. *Revue Economique*, *40*(2), 141–146.

Foucault, M. (2004). *Naissance de la biopolitique – Cours au Collège de France (1978–1979)*. Paris: Gallimard – Seuil.

Frankfurter, G. M., & McGoun, E. G. (1999). Ideology and the theory of financial economics. *Journal of Economic Behavior and Organization*, *39*(2), 159–177.

Friedland, R., & Alford, R. R. (1991). Bringing society back in: Symbols, practices, and institutional contradictions. In W. W. Powell & P. J. DiMaggio (Eds.), *The new institutionalism in organizational analysis*. Chicago, IL: The University of Chicago Press.

Gadrey, J. (2003, December 11–13). *Les conventions de richesse au cœur de la comptabilité nationale, anciennes et nouvelles controverses*. Paris X – Nanterre: Colloque conventions et institutions.

GMI. (2005). *Microstart midterm evaluation*. New York, NY: Global Microenterprise Initiative.

Gomes-Casseres, B. (1997). Alliance strategies of small firms. *Small Business Economics*, *9*(1), 33–44.

Grossein, J.-P. (1996). Présentation. In M. Weber (Ed.), *Sociologie des religions*. Paris: Gallimard.

Hassan, H. (1995). *Jurisprudence de la Maslahah et ses applications contemporaines*. Jeddah: IDB – IRTI.

Kamali, M. H. (1996). Methodological issues in islamic jurisprudence. *Arab Law Quarterly*, *11*(1), 3–33.

Karim, R. A. (1990). Standard setting for the financial reporting of religious business organizations: The case of Islamic banks. *Accounting and Business Research*, *20*(80), 299–305.

Khan, F. (2002). Fiqh foundations of the theory of Islamic economics: A survey of selected contemporary writings on economics relevant subject of Fikh. In H. Ahmed (Ed.), *Theoretical foundations of Islamic economics*. Jeddah: IDB – IRTI.

Kuhn, T. (1970 [1962]). *The structure of scientific revolution* (2nd ed.). Chicago, IL: The University of Chicago Press.

Litterer, J. A., & Young, S. (1984). Organizational paradigm as a tool in analyzing organizations and their problems. *Academy of Management Proceeding*, *1*, 249–253.

Lounsbury, M. (2002). Institutional transformation and status mobility: The professionalization of the field of finance. *Academy of Management Journal*, *45*(1), 255–266.

Maurer, B. (2002). Anthropological and accounting knowledge in Islamic banking and finance: Rethinking critical account. *Journal of the Royal Anthropological Institute (N.S.)*, *8*, 645–667.

Morgan, G. (1983). Paradigms, metaphors, and puzzle solving in organization theory. *Administrative Science Quarterly*, *28*(4), 601–614.

Mudge, S. L. (2008). What is neo-liberalism? *Socio-Economic Review*, *6*, 703–731.

Naqvi, N. (2001). The Islamic ethical system. In K. Ahmad & A. Sadeq (Eds.), *Ethics in business and management*. London: ASEAN Academic Press.

Pearce, D. (2011). *Financial inclusion in the Middle East and North Africa: Analysis and roadmap recommendations*. World Bank Policy Research Working Paper Series.

Pellissier-Tanon, A. (2001). L'induction, au coeur du dilemme des savoirs en sciences de gestion. In A. C. Martinet & R. A. Thiétart (Eds.), *Stratégies: Actualité et futurs de la recherche*. Paris: Vuibert – FNEGE.

Pew Research Center's Forum on Religion & Public Life. (2012). *The global religious landscape – A report on the size and distribution of the world's major religious groups as of 2010*. Washington, DC: Pew Research Center.

Phelps, G., & Crabtree, S. (2013). *More than one in five worldwide living in extreme poverty*. Washington, DC: Gallup, Inc.

Pomeranz, F. (1997). The accounting and auditing organization for Islamic financial institutions: An important regulatory debut. *Journal of International Accounting & Taxation*, *6*(1), 123–131.

Porter, M. E., & Kramer, M. R. (2006). Strategy & society. *Harvard Business Review*, *84*(12), 78–92.

PovcalNet. (2014). *PovcalNet: The on-line tool for poverty measurement developed by the development research group of the World bank*. Retrieved from http://iresearch.worldbank.org/PovcalNet/index.htm?3

Prahalad, C. K., & Stuart, H. L. (2002). The fortune at the bottom of the pyramid. *Strategy + Business*, *26*(first quarter), 1–14.

Rao, H. (1994). The social construction of reputation: Certification contests, legitimation, and the survival of organizations in the American automobile industry: 1895–1912. *Strategic Management Journal*, *15*, 29–44.

Raveaud, G. (2005). *L'économie des conventions: Théorie pragmatique ou méthode radicale?* France: Document de travail – Série règles, institutions. Unité mixte de recherche No. 8533 du CNRS – Convention No. 05-03.

Saleh, S. (1979). *Réponse de l'Islam aux défis de notre temps*. Lebanon: Editions Arabelle.

Sellami, M. (1994). *Le Qiyas et ses applications contemporaines*. Jeddah: IDB – IRTI.

Sewell, W. H. (2008). The temporalities of capitalism. *Socio-Economic Review*, *6*, 517–537.

Siddiqi, N. M. (2004). *Riba, bank interest and the rational of prohibition*. Kingdom of Saudi Arabia: Islamic Development Bank – Islamic Research and Training Institute.

Thomas, A., Cox, S., & Kraty, B. (2005). *Structuring Islamic finance transactions*. Londres: Euromoney Books.

Thornton, P. H., & Ocasio, W. (2008). Institutional logic. In R. Greenwood, C. Oliver, K. Sahlin, & R. Suddaby (Eds.), *The Sage handbook of organizational institutionalism*. London: Sage.

Weber, M. (1991 [1904–1905]). *L'éthique protestante et l'esprit du capitalisme*. Paris: Presses Pocket.

Yunus, M. (2007). Social enterprise: Doing well by doing good. *The Journal of Business, Entrepreneurship & the Law*, *1*(1), 99–109.

Yunus, M. (2008). *Social business for a new global economic architecture. Adam Smith Lecture* (Vol. 1). Glasgow University.

Yunus, M. (2013). *Investing for social benefit – Yunus social business incubator fund*. Germany: Yunus Social Business.

Yunus, M., Moingeon, B., & Lehmann-Ortega, L. (2010). Building social business models: Lessons from the grameen experience. *Long Range Planning*, *43*, 308–325.

Yunus, M., & Weber, K. (2007). *Creating a world without poverty: Social business and the future of capitalism*. New York, NY: PublicAffairs.

Yunus Social Business. (2013). Social Business & YSB. *CAIA Germany Social Business Symposium*.

ISLAMIC INVESTMENT VERSUS SOCIALLY RESPONSIBLE INVESTMENT: LESSONS FROM COMPARISON

Bernard Paranque and Elias Erragragui

ABSTRACT

Purpose – *The objective of this chapter is twofold. It first explores the complementarities of Islamic investment with Socially Responsible Investment. Secondly, it examines the financial price, for investors, of being both shariah-compliant and socially responsible.*

Methodology/approach – *Using a value-weighted approach, we experiment the construction of a set of sharia-compliant stock portfolios with different Environmental, Social, and Governance (ESG) performance. We use the KLD ratings of 238 companies listed in U.S. stock market from 2007 to 2011. We measure and compare their performance using the model developed by Fama and French (1993) and extended by Carhart (1997).*

Findings – *The results indicate no adverse effect on returns due to the application of a double screening, Islamic and SRI, and show a*

Finance Reconsidered: New Perspectives for a Responsible and Sustainable Finance
Critical Studies on Corporate Responsibility, Governance and Sustainability, Volume 10, 355–383

ISSN: 2043-9059/doi:10.1108/S2043-905920160000010034

substantially higher performance for positive governance screen during 2008–2011 periods. This outperformance cannot be explained by differences in investment style. Though, we observe significant outperformance for some 'irresponsible' portfolios involved in community and human rights controversies.

Research limitations/implications – *The study only focuses on U.S. market. Future works should extend the experimentation to other markets.*

Practical implications – *This study provides a venue for Islamic funds managers to consider SRI screening as fully in line with shariah-compliance requirements, while preserving the performance of their portfolios.*

Social implications – *Potentially, the reconciliation of Islamic investment with positive SRI practices may foster the implementation of CSR policies by firms' manager willing to attract Islamic investors.*

Originality/value – *With reference to the many studies emphasising the compatibility between CSR criteria and Islamic principles, this experimental study is the first to investigate the integration of a positive screening process designed to select companies based on their ESG performance in addition to a traditional shariah-compliant screening.*

Keywords: Islamic investment; corporate social responsibility; *sharia-compliance*

INTRODUCTION[1]

In 2013, a report from NGO Human Rights Watch condemned the 'ethnic cleansing' carried out by a fringe of Burma's population against its Muslim minority, the Rohingyas. The report criticised the massive breaches of human rights perpetrated by Burma's military regime over the last decade. Certain multinationals in the oil industry, such as Chevron, were taken to court for their involvement in these crimes of state. In response to these revelations, some fund managers and socially responsible index providers decided to exclude the Chevron group from their investment universe. Paradoxically, Chevron is included in most American Islamic indexes, even though the managers of those Islamic indexes affirm that their portfolios comply with Islamic ethics. The diversity of methods used by investors in their ethical screening processes shows just how complex it is to take ethics into consideration when making financial choices. The 'Chevron' case is symptomatic and calls into question the relevance of Islamic screening methods when it comes to corporate social responsibility (CSR).

Contrary to traditional investment, Socially Responsible Investment (SRI) applies a series of screens to select or exclude companies on the basis of their Environmental, Social and Governance (ESG) performance alongside other positivist practices such as shareholder activism (Renneboog, Ter Horst, & Zhang, 2008). The practices of *sharia*-compliant investment (SCI) also endeavour to exclude companies on the basis of ethical principles inspired by Islamic law, or *sharia* (Forte & Miglietta, 2007). Mainly taking the Koran[2] and *sunna*[3] as its source, *sharia* lays down the founding principles that broadly underpin Islamic finance. Aside from a concern to remain consistent with a certain set of principles or values, there are various reasons why some people consider Islamic investment an integral part of the SRI market. Firstly, just as the theological framework provides the boundaries for Islamic investment practices, the history of SRI is also marked by a religious influence. Secondly, like SRI fund managers, Islamic fund managers apply non-financial criteria as they put together their portfolios. In addition, some studies have shown that Islamic ethics are compatible with the business ethics that provide the theoretical underpinnings of CSR practices (Beekun & Badawi, 2005; Brammer, Williams, & Zinkin, 2007; Dusuki, 2008; Dusuki & Abdullah, 2007; Rice, 1999; Williams & Zinkin, 2010). Their conclusions suggest that a strategy that focuses merely on excluding prohibited or *haram*[4] activities is not enough to ensure compliance with the ethical and social principles prescribed by Islamic sources. These authors agree on the need to include a positive dimension in the Islamic investment process. Islamic finance and SRI give rise to the same expectations among their advocates, that is being more ethical than conventional finance. They also come up against similar criticism over their inability to fully accomplish that goal. This criticism is evident in the debate on the prevalence of form over substance in Islamic financial practices and accusations of 'cosmetic cover-up' or 'greenwashing' in the case of SRI. A survey among Islamic finance professionals revealed that 98.8% of respondents thought that acting in a socially responsible manner would create value for Islamic financial institutions (IFI) (Sairally, 2007). The author concludes that 'the IFIs could learn more from the positive commitment practices of SRI funds that encourage companies to be more attentive to society's needs'.

Despite their philosophical and conceptual similarities, no serious attempt has been made to identify the complementarities between these two ethical investment paradigms. Many reasons have been put forward to explain this, for example their different geographical concentrations, their different market targets, their respective growth concerns, reputational risks, the cultural barrier, the lack of practical innovations, and so on (Hayat, 2013). By looking at the social goals underlying Islamic ethics alongside the positivist approach of SRI, we will try to enrich this debate. More specifically, we will examine empirically whether a combination of Islamic and SRI investment practices could emerge as a new financially viable form of investment. We might be led to believe that, to strengthen their position in a market dominated by conventional finance, these forms of investment should share strategies in an attempt for diversification. However, despite the initiative by index provider Dow Jones,[5] this avenue so far remains unexplored. As a result, our study aims to enrich the literature on ethical finance from both theoretical and practical point of view. In this empirical work, we will investigate the financial impact of the inclusion of ESG criteria in the Islamic investment process.

From a practical point of view, this study will spotlight innovative investment strategies for ethical investors. This research puts forward a twofold argument – both ethical and financial – for the adoption of an SRI approach by Islamic investors. This kind of approach could influence the development of more environmentally aware conduct among companies in the oil and gas industries, which still generates high levels of pollution and remains one of the largest components in Islamic portfolios today. This chapter will first describe the origins and practices of SRI and Islamic investment. The section 'Fundamentals and Practices of Islamic Investment and SRI' will first describe the origins and practices of SRI and Islamic investment. The section 'Review of the Literature' will then look at the existing empirical contributions. The section 'Method and Data' will describe the methodology applied for our empirical study. We will then analyse the main findings in the section 'Results'. Lastly, in the conclusion, we will sum up the main contributions.

FUNDAMENTALS AND PRACTICES OF ISLAMIC INVESTMENT AND SRI

Historical Background

In the same way that the theological framework provides the boundaries for Islamic investment practices (see Chapter 12), the history of SRI is also marked by a religious influence. Traditionally, the roots of SRI have been traced back to the 17th century when the Quakers in the United States refused to make a profit from the slave and arms trade (Renneboog et al., 2008). However, the first investment fund applying ethical screening criteria, the *Pioneer Fund*, was only set up in 1928, on the initiative of the Methodist church. This entity was reserved exclusively to a restricted religious community and prohibited investments in so-called 'sinful' (in the biblical sense) companies, that is those involved in activities such brewing, tobacco, weapons and gambling. While SRI has its roots in religion, the increase in social, environmental and governance considerations among individual and institutional investors saw it expand the scope of its objectives beyond compliance with theological beliefs (Sparkes, 2003). First of all, against the backdrop of the Vietnam War and the emergence of pacifist movements, the first socially responsible mutual fund, the Pax World Fund, opened to the public in 1971. As well as excluding 'sin stock', the fund also sanctions companies that make a profit from war. Lastly, the repeated ecological[6] crises of the 1980s and the recurring financial scandals of the 2000s (Worldcom, Enron, Parmalat and the like) have given rise to a new generation of SRI funds concerned with the environmental impact and governance practices of companies that might be included in the socially responsible portfolio. Although the very close link between ethics and Christian religion has long provided the driving force behind the growth of SRI, this form of investment has gradually been freed from its religious footing. SRI has become a well-rooted sector in the conventional finance industry, where it now accounts for 10–20% of assets under management in industrialised countries (Eurosif, 2012). In 2012, the European and American markets, the two biggest SRI markets, accounted for more than $10.4 billion of assets under management (Eurosif, 2012).

The history of Islamic investment is much more recent and continues to operate under a religious influence. Although the first official Islamic fund, *Daina Al-Aiman*, was founded in Malaysia in 1968, it was only in the 1990s that investment in shares was permitted by the *Sharia Scholars*, on condition that it could be certified compliant with Islamic law. In this respect, the role of the *Sharia Scholars* is similar to that of the Church Commissioners in the Anglican or Methodist churches. Since then, like SRI, the assets managed by Islamic funds have grown at a spectacular rate; in fact, having the highest annual growth rate of all sectors in the financial industry.[7] In 2005, there were just under 400 Islamic funds managing $34 billion, but the figures rose to over 800 funds in 2010, managing some $60 billion (Ernst & Young, 2011). Although most *sharia*-compliant funds are marketed by local stakeholders, especially in Saudi Arabia and Malaysia, powerful international financial institutions such as HSBC, Citigroup and BNP Paribas have now moved into this area of business.

Objectives

SRI could be described as the financial application of the concept of sustainable development, which the Brundtland Commission defined in 1987 as 'development which meets the needs of current generations without compromising the ability of future generations to meet their own needs' (Brundtland, 1987). According to the Brundtland Commission, the ultimate goal is to combine long-term economic and social performance while protecting the environment. SRI fund managers therefore have the duty to adapt the concept of 'Triple Bottom Line' (Clarke, 2001) or the 3P rule – People, Planet and Profit – to the financial sphere. This means that financial considerations (Profit) are on an equal footing with social preoccupations (People) and environmental concerns (Planet).[8] In the definition of SRI put forward by Eurosif in 2012, we can see the importance of reconciling these financial and non-financial objectives: 'SRI is any type of investment process that combines investors' financial objectives with their concerns about Environmental, Social and Governance (ESG) issues'.

Contrary to the management of so-called 'SRI' assets, the goal of maximising financial and social performance is not pursued in the same way by Islamic fund managers. For them, the financial performance goal is subject to the imperatives of *sharia* compliance (Forte & Miglietta, 2011). There are four main prohibitions: interest (*riba*), contractual uncertainty or deceit (*gharar*), speculation (*maysir*) and unlawful activity (sale of alcohol, tobacco, pork, weapons, pornography, traditional banking, etc.). These principles which must be applied by Islamic portfolio managers may explain several discrepancies with the rules that govern SRI. For example, Islamic investment does not seem to have a direct interest in ESG aspects, which form the core of SRI as it stands today. Nonetheless, looking beyond compliance with these legal prescriptions, the philosophy of Islamic law is rooted in the principles of social justice and fairness between the various stakeholders in the economy (Hassan & Kayed, 2009). In this respect, Islamic investment draws on a kind of 'social responsibility'. The reduction of excessive risk-taking, combined with an obligation to match transactions with a tangible asset as advocated by Islamic finance, automatically implies a number of other objectives for Islamic investment, including greater responsibility of the financial system and its role as an intermediary serving the real economy. The application of regulating principles like these would help reduce the frequency and severity of the financial crises that are symptomatic of the social irresponsibility of the financial markets (Ahmed, 2010). The next section of this chapter will look at how the main precepts of sustainable development and of Islamic finance are applied to portfolio management.

Practices Observed

SRI practices are marked by the plurality of objectives to be reached and are more heterogeneous than those applied in Islamic investment. We can categorise the screening methods employed by ethical portfolio managers into two groups: negative screening and positive screening. Of these two groups, negative screening is the most basic and oldest strategy used by ethical funds. It is based on the exclusion of companies according to ethical criteria and comes in three different forms: sectoral exclusion, normative exclusion and accounting exclusion. Sectoral exclusion rejects companies on the basis of their area of business.

Within the framework of SRI, the reasons for sectoral exclusion are not systematically normative and may evolve in line with social issues.[9] In contrast, Islamic investment is based on timeless, universally shared normative values and has therefore standardised the sectors for exclusion. While certain sectors of business such as alcohol, weapons, gambling, pornography and tobacco are excluded from both SRI and *Sharia*-compliance portfolios, others remain specific to one sphere or the other. For example, the financial sector, due to its interest-earning financial system, is only excluded from Islamic portfolios.[10] On the other hand, Islamic investment does not have any qualms with other controversial sectors such as oil, chemistry, nuclear and genetic engineering. Lastly, some Islamic indexes (mainly in Malaysia) have a tolerance threshold with regard to 'forbidden' revenue, for example only companies whose share of 'prohibited' business exceeds a certain level[11] of total revenue are excluded. This notion of tolerance does not exist in SRI. Islamic portfolio managers are then required to 'purify' that portion of 'forbidden' revenue included in the portfolio by donating it to charities.[12] Normative exclusion means rejecting issuers that do not comply with international conventions such as the Global Compact,[13] the Universal Declaration of Human Rights, the International Labour Organisation or the United Nations Convention against Corruption; SRI managers thus boycott countries that breach these international standards. As those countries are often Muslim (Angola, Egypt, Iran, Saudi Arabia, Syria or Zimbabwe), it is highly unlikely that this type of exclusion would be included in the Islamic screening process. Lastly, accounting exclusion, which is only applied by Islamic portfolio managers, consists in excluding companies on the basis of accounting or financial ratios, where their debt burden is too high or they are deemed to be too highly exposed to interest. Although these financial ratios may marginally vary from one Islamic index provider to another, there is a consensus over the accounting screens to be applied. The most frequent are:

- Debt/(Market Capitalisation or Total Assets[14]) <33%[15]
- (Cash Assets + Accounts Receivable)/(Market Capitalisation or Total Assets) <33%
- Interest-Earning Assets/(Market Capitalisation or Total Assets) <33%

Control of the debt level, interest-earning assets and cash assets (which may be invested) is justified by the prohibition on earnings from *riba* (Khatkhatay & Nisar, 2007).[16] Empirical studies estimate that the Islamic sectoral and accounting screening processes exclude between 65% and 90% of the conventional securities universe (Peillex & Ureche-Rangau, 2012; Rahman, Yahya, & Nasir, 2010).

Parallel to the sectoral and accounting exclusions, one of the specific features of Islamic investment is its ban on certain financial instruments deemed non-compliant with Islamic ethics. In fact, managers may not use certain asset categories seen as speculative and thus falling within the scope of the ban on *maysir* (e.g. derivatives) or which could be likened to interest or *ribaoui* (e.g. bonds).

Positive screening can be combined with negative sectoral and/or normative screening and is exclusively used by SRI managers. Contrary to negative screening which is based on a logic of enforcement, it aims to reward the best issuers (states or companies) on the basis of ESG criteria. These criteria usually take the form of non-financial ratings that are either the outcome of an internal analysis by a dedicated team or an external analysis by specialist rating agencies, or even a combination of both. These ratings are then used differently, depending on the manager's selected approach. The *Best in Class* approach aims to select or give extra weighting to companies with the best non-financial ratings in portfolios. According to Eurosif (2010), *Best in Class* screening reduces the initial investment universe by between 40% and 60%. The 'themed' SRI funds focus their screening process on a specific theme.[17] Shareholder activism, a common practice in SRI funds, emerged during the segregationist events in South Africa in the 1980s and meant pressurising fund managers so that they did not include companies (South African or Western) present in South Africa in their portfolios. This type of shareholder involvement, intended to influence or promote certain forms of conduct, is not part of the Islamic fund managers' remit. More generally, the lack of positivist integration practices is more likely explained by the lower level of maturity among Islamic funds than by fundamental ethical differences. In actual fact, *sharia* provides a framework for reflection that is conducive to the inclusion of ecological concerns in the investment process. The Islamic legal system refers to the need to anchor any jurisprudential process within an overarching normative framework known as *maqasid al-sharia*, which can be translated as the fundamental goals of Islamic law. Al Shâtibi,[18] pioneer in this school of thought, laid down the bases as follows: '*the Legislator's overall goal, in the requirements of the law, is to protect the interests of humankind*'. Through this concept of social benefit, we can integrate the preservation of ecological (*hifdh al bi'a*) and social (*hifdh al ijtimari*)[19] matters. As such, practitioners of Islamic finance have a special responsibility in putting this theological thinking into practice, as they take the social benefit into consideration in the investment process.

REVIEW OF THE LITERATURE

Islamic Investment Performance

The Islamic finance market turned out to be relatively resilient during the subprime crisis, something that caught the interest of a number of researchers, who have since been striving to understand how it works. Nonetheless, contrary to SRI, there is only a scattering of papers devoted to Islamic investment. Among the pioneering works, we can quote Wilson (2001) and Ahmed (2001) who were the first to empirically demonstrate the viability of Islamic funds. They were followed by Hakim and Rashidian (2004) who used co-integration techniques to compare the performance of the Dow Jones Islamic Market (DJIM) Index with the Wilshire 5000 Index between 1999 and 2002. Their results show that, on the basis of risk-adjusted yield, there is no performance loss stemming from the screening process used by the DJIM and that, as a result, Islamic investors are not financially penalised by their ethical constraints.[20] Similarly, the studies that followed these first works also concluded that there is no significant statistical difference in terms of risk-adjusted performance between Islamic funds and their reference indices (Abderrezak, 2008; Elfakhani & Hassan, 2005; Hayat & Kraeussl, 2011). The work conducted by Hoepner, Rammal, and Rezec (2011) is, however, more measured in its conclusions. While the authors confirm that Islamic funds do not suffer from any overall under-performance compared to their conventional equivalents, they also state that this is only true in countries where the Islamic financial market is relatively well developed (e.g. Malaysia, UAE or Bahrain). They noted that in non-Muslim countries, Islamic funds tend to under-perform their reference indexes. Hussein and Omran (2005) observed abnormal positive yields for Islamic indexes from January 1996 to March 2003. They affirmed that the Islamic indexes outperformed their conventional equivalents in bullish markets (January 1996 to March 2000) but underperform them in bearish markets (April 2000 to July 2003). The authors link the positive performance of Islamic indexes to their over-exposure in certain sectors (new technologies, cyclical consumption, industry, telecommunications) and explain their poor performance in bearish conditions by the exclusion of the alcohol sector, which performs well at such times. They conclude that screening processes that exclude entire sectors from the investment universe have negative effects on portfolio performance. On the other hand, accounting screening has proven to be especially profitable thanks to the exclusion of over-indebted companies such as Enron and Worldcom that went into bankruptcy sometime after their exclusion. Contrary to the observations of Hussein and Omran (2005) for the period from January 1996 to March 2003, other recent studies have shown that Islamic indexes outperform their conventional counterparts during financial crises (Alam & Rajjaque, 2010; Peillex & Ureche-Rangau, 2012), mainly due to the exclusion of the financial sector. As such, Islamic accounting screening can be an effective method for investors looking to avoid the repercussions of financial crises (Arouri, Ben Ameur, Jawadi, Jawadi, & Louhichi, 2013).

SRI Performance

For SRI, the search for performance has strengthened over the last two decades, resulting in some heterogeneous outcomes. Certain meta-analyses show a lack of consensus on the question of SRI performance due to the wide variety of methodologies applied. This is particularly clear in the meta-analysis produced by Revelli and Sentis (2012). The empirical results on SRI performance lead to some very different, even contradictory conclusions, and vary according to country, method and period under consideration (Renneboog et al., 2008). However, these studies seem to indicate that, contrary to what the financial orthodoxy stipulates, there is no statistically significant difference between the financial performance of SRI and conventional portfolios suggesting a negative impact of the ESG screens (Bauer, Derwall, & Otten, 2007; Kreander, Gray, Power, & Sinclair, 2005; Statman, 2006). The conventional theoretical assumption suggests that reducing the investment universe affects the optimisation of the yield/risk pairing of ethical portfolios (Markowitz, 1952), but this does not seem to be confirmed empirically. Some researchers shed additional light on the relationship between the type and strength of screening and the profitability of the SRI funds. Barnett and Salomon (2006) point to a curvilinear association as performance first appears to be negatively correlated to the strength of screening, before the trend is reversed to reveal a positive link between performance and strength of screening above and beyond a minimum number of screens. Similar conclusions were put forward by Capelle-Blancard and Monjon (2012) who suggest that the strategic distinction of SRI funds, based on strong screening, is positively linked to their performance. Their study, along with that by Humphrey and Lee (2011), revealed that transversal, non-sectoral screens are less damaging to the financial performance of SRI portfolios. Lastly, Statman and Glushkov (2009) demonstrate that ethical investors obtain the best yields by selecting companies with high ESG sores. However, they state that these positive returns are counterbalanced by lower profitability attributable to the exclusion of forbidden sectors.[21]

The above empirical contributions provide a theoretical basis for the assumptions of a higher yield for the Islamic portfolios with the best social performance. As such, we can put forward the following two assumptions:

A1. Socially responsible Islamic portfolios outperform their conventional benchmark index.

A2. Socially responsible Islamic portfolios outperform non-socially responsible Islamic portfolios.

METHOD AND DATA

Social Performance and Portfolio Composition

Our database is made up of financial and ESG data from 238 American companies listed on the stock markets from 2007 to 2011. We use the social ratings provided by the agency Kinder Lynderberg and Domini (KLD) Research & Analytics STATS.[22] The financial data is extracted from Datastream. Thanks to complimentary assistance from the MSCI index provider, we were able to reconstruct the MSCI USA Islamic Index, which served as the benchmark index for this study. 2007 is the year that Islamic indexes were launched by MSCI.[23] KLD assesses company ESG performance on the basis of indicators split into seven areas of ESG[24]: Community, Governance, Diversity, Labour Relations, Environment, Human Rights and Products. For each area, KLD evaluates several indicators which are given a binary score (0 or 1). For each family of indicators, KLD looks at two dimensions: one positive (*strengths*) sanctioning virtuous behaviour[25] and the other negative (*concerns*) representing ESG controversies.[26] In line with the recommendations expressed by Sharfman (1996), we opted to use disaggregated measurements of ESG performance. Hence, for each company, we successively set out each of the seven areas of ESG then each dimension (positive and negative). The scores obtained are then categorised into three classes corresponding to different levels of performance.[27] Using these disaggregated scores, we put together our panel of portfolios. We obtained a series of non-mutually exclusive portfolios[28] built according to (1) different families of ESG indicator, (2) the two dimensions of ESG rating (positive and negative) and (3) the three levels of ESG performance. Given the small range of ratings for certain indicator families, we achieved a panel of 34 portfolios out of a hypothetical 42 portfolios.[29] Table 1 shows the structure of the portfolio panel.

Since our objective is to measure the effect produced solely by screening, without taking into account the managers' selection qualities, our portfolios are built and weighted on market capitalisation, taking a passive approach. Passive selection works as shown: at the end of year Y−1, KLD issues the ESG ratings for each company. We then build our portfolio for year Y on the basis of the ratings obtained in Y−1 and keep our portfolios unchanged until new ratings are issued at the end of year Y, which we then use to reshape our portfolios for year Y + 1. We thus obtain a series of monthly observations for the period running from January 2008 to December 2011.[30]

Performance Measurement

We used two types of performance measurement. The first measures the return on the portfolios, estimated using the performance of their

Table 1. Construction of Islamic SRI Portfolios using ESG Ratings from KLD.

	Socially Responsible			Socially Irresponsible		
	No	Partially	Significantly	No	Partially	Significantly
Community	✓	✓	×	✓	✓	×
Governance	✓	✓	×	✓	✓	✓
Diversity	✓	✓	✓	✓	✓	×
Labour relations	✓	✓	✓	✓	✓	✓
Environment	✓	✓	✓	✓	✓	✓
Human rights	✓	✓	×	✓	✓	×
Products	✓	✓	×	✓	✓	×

Note: × indicates that the portfolio concerned could not be put together as no rating was available. The terms 'No', 'Partially' and 'Significantly' refer to the score levels '0', '1' and 'over 1'. The 'Socially responsible' and 'Socially irresponsible' portfolios are respectively built according to their positive (*strengths*) and negative (*concerns*) dimensions.

benchmark index. The second measures the relative performance of the portfolios, estimated using the performance gap between two portfolios with distinct responsibility profiles.

Portfolio Returns

We use the method developed by Fama and French (1993) then Carhart (1997), which consists in measuring performance (alpha) adjusted to portfolio risk by neutralising its exposure to market return (beta) taken from MEDAF (RM – RF) and the different investment styles represented by the factors of: company size (SMB), the ratio of net book value to market value (HML) and 'momentum' (MOM). The model is formally represented in the following equation:

$$R(i,t) - \mathrm{RF}(t) = \alpha i + \beta i[\mathrm{RM}(t) - \mathrm{RF}(t)] + si\mathrm{SMB}(t) + hi\mathrm{HML}(t) + mi\mathrm{MOM}(t) + \varepsilon(i,t) \quad (1)$$

where $R(i,t)$ describes the return on portfolio i for month t; RM(t) describes the return on the reference index (beta); RF(t) describes the return on the risk-free asset[31]; SMB(t) is the difference in monthly return between the small and large caps; HML(t) is the difference in return between 'growth' stocks (ratio of net book value to high market value) and 'value' stocks (net book value/low market value); and MOM(t) is the difference in the monthly profitability of a portfolio with a long position for growth stocks and a short position for falling stocks[32] (Jegadeesh & Titman, 1993). SRI portfolio performance studies recommend controlling the effects related to investment style (Bauer, Koedijk, & Otten, 2005).

Relative Performance of Portfolios

To measure the relative performance of portfolios, we measured two types of gap describing two socially responsible strategies: (*i*) a commitment benefiting socially responsible companies, and (*ii*) disinvestment from socially irresponsible companies. To do so, we adopted the method used by Derwall, Guenster, Bauer, and Koedijk (2005) then Galema, Plantinga, and Scholtens (2008). For each family of indicators, we first measured the performance gap between responsible portfolios[33] and portfolios that are neutral in responsibility terms, and then the gap between neutral portfolios (in responsibility terms) and their irresponsible equivalents.[34] The equation that describes this model is thus:

$$R(i,t,p) - R(i,t,n) = \alpha i + \beta i[\mathrm{RM}(t) - \mathrm{RF}(t)] + si\mathrm{SMB}(t) + hi\mathrm{HML}(t) + mi\mathrm{MOM}(t) + \varepsilon(i,t) \quad (2)$$

$R(i,t,p)$ represents the profitability of portfolio i with a positive social impact (responsible or non-irresponsible portfolio) and $R(i,t,n)$ is the profitability of portfolio i with a negative social impact (non-responsible or irresponsible portfolio). With the exception of the alpha factor, which here represents the profitability gap between two distinct portfolios, the factors used as explanatory variables remain the same as those used in the model first described in Eq. (1).

RESULTS

Portfolio Returns

Table 2 comprises a summary[35] of the results of the linear regression describing the four-factor model from Fama and French (1993) and Carhart (1997). In our observations, we have excluded the extreme results shown by the partially responsible portfolio in the area of human rights, due to its over-exposure to variations in a single security.[36] Out of the 34 portfolios that make up our panel, only five of them have a statistically significant alpha. The results do not show any overall trend, either in

Table 2. Summary of the Significant Performances.

	Difference in Profitability	Market Risk	Investment Style
Partially responsible portfolios			
Governance	Positive	Under-exposure	
Partially irresponsible portfolios			
Community	Positive	Over-exposure	
Human rights	Positive	Over-exposure	Small caps
Significantly responsible portfolios			
Diversity	Positive	Under-exposure	High accounting value
Significantly irresponsible portfolios			
Governance	Positive	Under-exposure	Small caps

the fields of ESG or ESG performance levels. As a result, we are unable to confirm absolute validation of assumption A1. Indeed, the wide variety of performances observed would appear to be the outcome of the multi-dimensional aspect of ESG performance and the varying financial impact of the different ESG criteria. We can note, for example, that the portfolios that are partially responsible in the field of *governance* and significantly responsible in the field of *diversity* obtain a higher score than their benchmark index (respectively 4.91% at the threshold of 5% and 4.41% at the threshold of 10%). Paradoxically, we also see clear outperformance for the portfolios that are partially irresponsible in the fields of *community* and *human rights* (respectively 6.04% and 5.54% at the threshold of 5%) and for the significantly irresponsible portfolio in the field of *governance* (7.06% at the threshold of 5%). These results suggest that the effects (positive or negative) of SRI screening depend both on the SRI field and the level of social performance considered. Specifically, the results for governance suggest that the *sharia*-compliant companies that are positively committed to a good governance approach, even those that are not the most committed, attain higher market yields than their counterparts. On the other hand, the results indicate that only those companies significantly committed to diversity achieve higher yields. Moreover, the results obtained by certain 'irresponsible' portfolios shed light on the nature of ESG controversies that are positively correlated with market performance. In particular, they indicate that *sharia*-compliant companies that are controversial in their treatment towards local communities and in human rights achieve better performance. These results suggest that the best-performing companies in financial terms tend to neglect certain human rights[37] and the negative impacts[38] of their operations on local communities. Lastly, when it comes to governance, the good results attained by the significantly irresponsible and partially responsible businesses reveal a paradox. By examining the indicators taken into account by KLD to assess a company's governance performance, we see that good governance is measured by the support companies show for public policies on social issues[39] and by the quality of their social *reporting*.[40] In addition to these two aspects, bad governance is measured by the severity of the controversies surrounding executives' remuneration, governance structure and unlawful practices (corruption, tax evasion, insider trading, accounting irregularities, etc.). As such, these contradictory performances suggest that the best-performing companies in terms of the market would be more exposed to poor governance practices and that consequently, they would tend to conceal these bad practices via a CSR communication strategy.[41]

Relative Performance

The results shown in Table A3 give us a view of the relative performance of responsible portfolios (strategy A) and non-irresponsible portfolios (strategy B) compared to their non-responsible and irresponsible counterparts. In line with the previous results, the estimates included in Table A3 do not allow us to come to a conclusion on the clear outperformance of SRI portfolios compared to their non-SRI equivalents. We can therefore reject assumption A2 and put forward a more measured conclusion. On the one hand, our results show that only the performance gap between responsible and non-responsible portfolios with regard to governance is significantly positive, confirming the result attained in our first measurement.

On the other hand, we can see that the initial results are also confirmed for irresponsible portfolios in the area of *human rights* and *community*. In these two areas, we observe a significant performance gap between the non-irresponsible and irresponsible portfolios. Conversely, our initial results are not confirmed for responsible portfolios in the area of *diversity* or for irresponsible portfolios in the field of *governance*. This final outcome indicates that the effects observed when we differentiate two levels of responsibility (or irresponsibility) vanish when we only consider one level. This subtlety provides ex post justification for our choice to differentiate between several levels of social performance when putting together our initial portfolios and confirms that the level of social performance is one factor explaining SRI performance.

CONCLUSION

The Islamic investment process is ready to step up its development. Negative screening by Islamic funds no longer appears to be enough to promote the responsible practices of large business and turns out to be incapable of fully addressing the principle of social benefit as advocated by *sharia*. With reference to the many studies emphasising the compatibility between CSR criteria and Islamic principles, it would seem relevant to envisage the integration of a positive screening process designed to select virtuous companies. This study looks at the appropriateness of reconciling Islamic investment with the positive screening practices of Socially Responsible Investment. To do so, we have empirically measured the performance of Islamic portfolios with different social responsibility profiles. The results of our study, which is based on the four-factor model first introduced by Fama and French (1993) and Carhart (1997), reveal heterogeneous effects that may be explained by the multi-dimensional character of social performance (type of indicators, ESG field or scoring level). In spite of this heterogeneity, the results still indicate that promoting good CSR practices does not affect the performance of *sharia*-compliant portfolios. Lastly, this study provides some strategic insight for Islamic investors keen on integrating social considerations into their investment choices.

NOTES

1. Chapter taken from the article of the same name, La Revue du Financier, Issue 204–205 – Volume 35–36, November 2013 to February 2014.
2. Important Islamic scriptural text.
3. Set of traditions and lessons from the prophet Muhammad (pbuh), the main figure in the Islamic faith.
4. The word *haram*, which means 'forbidden', is the opposite of *halal* which means 'permitted'.
5. In 2006, Dow Jones launched its *Dow Jones Islamic Market Sustainability Index*, the first of its kind to combine Islamic constraints and sustainability within the same index.
6. The ecological crises of the 1980s include the industrial disaster in Bhopal (India) in 1984, which counted thousands of victims, the Chernobyl nuclear disaster in 1986 leading to thousands of cancer cases and the grounding of American oil tanker Exxon Valdez in 1989, causing the spillage of 40,000 tons of crude oil along the coasts of Alaska.

7. An average 15% per year according to a report by Ernst and Young (2011).

8. The question remains as to the compatibility of these goals with financial performance influenced by 'short-termist' financial markets.

9. For example, French SRI managers do not exclude the nuclear sector while that same sector may be included in the exclusion criteria in other countries.

10. Likewise the hotel, music and entertainment, pork and non-halal meat sectors.

11. This threshold, usually set at 5% after a consensus among Muslim legal experts, is related to the interest received by companies on their bank deposits. It is seen as an unavoidable prohibited revenue by the scholars and is subject to the principle of purification.

12. Not included in SRI, this philanthropic dimension is found in certain sharing funds where the goal is to redistribute the capital gains made by the funds to charities.

13. Launched in 2000 on the initiative of the United Nations, the Global Compact is based on a series of principles concerned with human rights, labour standards, the environment and the fight against corruption.

14. The choice of denominator varies from one Islamic index provider to another. For example, while the Dow Jones Islamic Market range and the S&P Shariah Indices use market capitalisation, the MSCI Islamic Index and the FTSE Shariah apply total assets.

15. This 1/3 rule seems quite arbitrary. Derigs and Marzban (2008) stated that it came from a *hadith* or prophetic text according to which donations of more than one-third of one's wealth are discouraged. The lack of a direct connection between the *hadith* in question and the use of a financial ratio seems to suggest that the religious reference was used ex post as a way of justifying the ratio to be applied.

16. Some funds integrate a ratio measuring the level of tangible (current) assets to total assets to guarantee the tangible nature of the economic activity and thus avoid investing in purely speculative businesses.

17. For example, clean energy funds or renewable energy funds.

18. Renowned Muslim theologian who first introduced the concept in his reference work 'Al Mouwafaqâte' published in the 14th century.

19. One of the contemporary precursors of this initiative is Doctor Abdel-Majid Najar who set out the ecological issue as a distinct goal (which in Arabic he called *maqsad moustaqil*) in his book 'Les finalités de la Voie islamique avec de nouvelles perspectives'.

20. We should, however, note the dominance of the financial paradigm that has made financial performance the ultimate indicator of personal interest.

21. That are seen to be more profitable (!!! INVALID CITATION !!!).

22. KLD Research & Analytics STATS has recently changed its name to MSCI ESG STATS (Statistical Tool for the Analysis of Trends in Social and Environmental Performance). The ESG rating method used by KLD is described in its 'User Guide' for 2011.

23. Out of the 270 securities making up the MSCI USA Islamic Index in 2007, only 238 were rated by KLD.

24. Defined as qualitative screens by KLD.

25. For example, the introduction of a waste recycling process, measures to prevent discrimination against minorities and improved working conditions.

26. For example, conviction for ecological disasters, failure to comply with labour laws or human rights.

27. The first category groups together companies with a zero score (for the indicator family and dimension concerned), the second groups all scores equal to 1 and the third scores of over 1.

28. A same company can be included in several portfolios.

29. 7 families $\times$ 2 dimensions $\times$ 3 score levels = 42 portfolios.

30. A table showing the descriptive statistics for our portfolio panel is provided in the appendix to this chapter.

31. We opted for the one-month American treasury bill taken from the Kenneth French online data library: http://mba.tuck.dartmouth.edu/pages/faculty/ken.french/

32. This factor measures the managers' tendency to select securities on the basis of their previous good performance.

33. Grouping together partially and significantly responsible portfolios (strengths >0).

34. Grouping together partially and significantly irresponsible portfolios (concerns >0).

35. Details in the appendix.

36. Explained by the low number of components in this portfolio (less than 20 securities) resulting in strong weighting of the security.

37. Societal analysts take into account the history of a firm's involvement in legal proceedings related to human rights in certain controversial countries (Sudan, Burma, etc.).

38. These impacts are measured based on NGO criticism or complaints lodged by independent observers (see source documentation at MSCI ESG STATS, new name of KLD).

39. These regulations concern compliance with standards on climate change, labour rights, shareholders' rights and consumer protection.

40. Established on the basis of the Global Reporting Initiative.

41. To counter this phenomenon of 'greenwashing', some authors such as Parguel, Benoît-Moreau, and Larceneux (2011) suggest a review of social rating practices.

REFERENCES

Abderrezak, F. (2008). The performance of Islamic equity funds: A comparison to conventional, Islamic and ethical benchmarks. *Failaka*. Retrieved from www.failaka.com/downloads/AbderrezakF_Perf_IslamicEquityFunds.pdf. Accessed on September, 2013.

Ahmed, A. (2010). Global financial crisis: An Islamic finance perspective. *International Journal of Islamic and Middle Eastern Finance and Management*, *3*(4), 306–320.

Ahmed, O. B. (2001). *Islamic equity funds: The mode of resource mobilization and placement*. Jeddah: Islamic Research and Training Institute, Islamic Development Bank.

Alam, N., & Rajjaque, M. S. (2010). Shariah-compliant equities: Empirical evaluation of performance in the European market during credit crunch. *Journal of Financial Services Marketing*, *15*(3), 228–240.

Arouri, M. E., Ben Ameur, H., Jawadi, N., Jawadi, F., & Louhichi, W. (2013). Are Islamic finance innovations enough for investors to escape from a financial downturn? Further evidence from portfolio simulations. *Applied Economics*, *45*(24), 3412–3420.

Barnett, M. L., & Salomon, R. M. (2006). Beyond dichotomy: The curvilinear relationship between social responsibility and financial performance. *Strategic Management Journal*, *27*(11), 1101–1122.

Bauer, R., Derwall, J., & Otten, R. (2007). The ethical mutual fund performance debate: New evidence from Canada. *Journal of Business Ethics*, *70*(2), 111–124.

Bauer, R., Koedijk, K., & Otten, R. (2005). International evidence on ethical mutual fund performance and investment style. *Journal of Banking and Finance*, *29*(7), 1751–1767.

Beekun, R. I., & Badawi, J. A. (2005). Balancing ethical responsibility among multiple organizational stakeholders: The Islamic perspective. *Journal of Business Ethics*, *60*(2), 131–145.

Brammer, S., Williams, G., & Zinkin, J. (2007). Religion and attitudes to corporate social responsibility in a large cross-country sample. *Journal of Business Ethics*, *71*(3), 229–243.

Brundtland, G. (1987). *Our common future: The world commission on environment and development*. Oxford: Oxford University Press.

Capelle-Blancard, G., & Monjon, S. (2012). Trends in the literature on socially responsible investment: Looking for the keys under the lamppost. *Business Ethics: A European Review*, *21*(3), 239–250.

Carhart, M. M. (1997). On persistence in mutual fund performance. *Journal of Finance*, *52*(1), 57–82.

Clarke, T. (2001). Balancing the triple bottom line: Financial, social and environmental performance. *Journal of General Management*, *26*(4), 16–27.

Derigs, U., & Marzban, S. (2008). Review and analysis of current Shariah-compliant equity screening practices. *International Journal of Islamic and Middle Eastern Finance and Management*, *1*(4), 285–303.

Derwall, J., Guenster, N., Bauer, R., & Koedijk, K. (2005). The eco-efficiency premium puzzle. *Financial Analysts Journal*, *61*(2), 51–63.

Dusuki, A. W. (2008). What does Islam say about corporate social responsibility? *Review of Islamic Economics*, *12*(1), 5–28.

Dusuki, A. W., & Abdullah, N. I. (2007). Maqasid al-shariah, maslahah and corporate social responsibility. *The American Journal of Islamic Social Sciences*, *24*(1), 25–45.

Elfakhani, S., & Hassan, M. K. (2005). Performance of Islamic mutual funds. Paper presented at the Economic Research Forum, 12th Annual Conference.

Ernst & Young. (2011). Islamic Funds and Investments Report. *Achieving growth in challenging times*. Dubai, UAE: Ernst & Young.

Eurosif (2010). *Eurosif's 2010 European SRI study. Eurosif.*

Eurosif. (2012). Étude sur le marché européen de l'ISR 2012: Eurosif.

Fama, E., & French, K. R. (1993). Common risk factors in the returns on stock and bonds. *Journal of Financial Economics*, *33*(1), 3–56.

Forte, G., & Miglietta, F. (2007). *Islamic mutual funds as a faith-based funds in a socially responsible context*. Working Paper, Bocconi University, Milan.

Forte, G., & Miglietta, F. (2011). A comparison of socially responsible and Islamic equity investments. *Journal of Money, Investment and Banking*, *21*, 116–132.

Galema, R., Plantinga, A., & Scholtens, B. (2008). The stocks at stake: Return and risk in socially responsible investment. *Journal of Banking and Finance*, *32*(12), 2646–2654.

Hakim, S., & Rashidian, M. (2004). Risk and return of Islamic stock market indexes. Paper presented at the International Seminar of Non-Bank Financial Institutions: Islamic Alternatives, Kuala Lumpur, Malaysia.

Hassan, M. K., & Kayed, R. N. (2009). The global financial crisis, risk management and social justice in Islamic finance. *ISRA International Journal of Islamic Finance*, *1*(1), 33–58.

Hayat, R., & Kraeussl, R. (2011). Risk and return characteristics of Islamic equity funds. *Emerging Markets Review*, *12*(2), 189–203.

Hayat, U. (2013). Islamic finance and socially responsible investing. *CFA Institute Magazine* March–April, p. 8.

Hoepner, A. G. F., Rammal, H. G., & Rezec, M. (2011). Islamic mutual funds' financial performance and international investment style: Evidence from 20 countries. *European Journal of Finance*, *17*(9–10), 829–850.

Humphrey, J., & Lee, D. (2011). Australian socially responsible funds: Performance, risk and screening intensity. *Journal of Business Ethics*, *102*(4), 519–535.

Hussein, K., & Omran, M. (2005). Ethical investment revisited: Evidence from Dow Jones Islamic indexes. *The Journal of Investing*, *14*(3), 105–126.

Jegadeesh, N., & Titman, S. (1993). Returns to buying winners and selling losers: Implications for stock market efficiency. *Journal of Finance*, *48*(1), 65–91.

Khatkhatay, M. H., & Nisar, S. (2007). Shariah compliant equity investments: An assessment of current screening norms. *Islamic Economic Studies*, *15*(1), 47–76.

Kreander, N., Gray, R. H., Power, D. M., & Sinclair, C. D. (2005). Evaluating the performance of ethical and non-ethical funds: A matched pair analysis. *Journal of Business Finance & Accounting*, *32*(7–8), 1465–1493.

Markowitz, H. (1952). Portfolio selection. *The Journal of Finance*, *7*(1), 77–91.

Parguel, B., Benoît-Moreau, F., & Larceneux, F. (2011). How sustainability ratings might deter 'Greenwashing': A closer look at ethical corporate communication. *Journal of Business Ethics*, *102*(1), 15–28. doi:10.1007/s10551-011-0901-2

Peillex, J., & Ureche-Rangau, L. (2012). Création d'un indice boursier islamique sur la place financière de Paris: Méthodologie et performance. *Revue d'économie financière*, *3*(107), 289–314.

Rahman, A. A., Yahya, M. A., & Nasir, M. H. M. (2010). Islamic norms for stock screening: A comparison between the Kuala Lumpur stock exchange Islamic index and the Dow Jones Islamic market index. *International Journal of Islamic and Middle Eastern Finance and Management*, *3*(3), 228–240.

Revelli, C., & Sentis, P. (2012). L'investissement socialement responsable differe-t-il vraiment de l'investissement conventionnel? [Is socially responsible investment significantly different from conventional investment? With English summary.] *La Revue des Sciences de Gestion*, *47*(255–256), 85–95.

Renneboog, L., Ter Horst, J., & Zhang, C. (2008). Socially responsible investments: Institutional aspects, performance, and investor behavior. *Journal of Banking & Finance*, *32*(9), 1723–1742.

Rice, G. (1999). Islamic ethics and the implications for business. *Journal of Business Ethics*, *18*(4), 345–358.

Sairally, S. (2007). Evaluating the 'social responsibility' of Islamic finance: Learning from the experiences of socially responsible investment funds. Paper presented at Advances in Islamic Economics and Finance: Proceeding of the 6th International Conference on Islamic Economics and Finance.

Sharfman, M. (1996). The construct validity of the Kinder, Lydenberg & Domini social performance ratings data. *Journal of Business Ethics*, *15*(3), 287–296.

Sparkes, R. (2003). *Socially responsible investment: A global revolution*. Wiley.com.

Statman, M. (2006). Socially responsible indexes: Composition, performance, and tracking error. *Journal of Portfolio Management*, *32*(3), 100–109.

Statman, M., & Glushkov, D. (2009). The wages of social responsibility. *Financial Analysts Journal*, *65*(4), 33–46.

Williams, G., & Zinkin, J. (2010). Islam and CSR: A study of the compatibility between the tenets of Islam and the UN global compact. *Journal of Business Ethics*, *91*(4), 519–533.

Wilson, R. (2001). The economics of mutual funds: An Islamic approach. *University of Durham*, *1*(1), 1–25.

APPENDIX

Table A1. Descriptive Statistics of the Monthly Profitability of Islamic SRI Portfolios.

	Average Profitability	Standard Deviation	Sharpe Ratio	Min. Average Profitability	Max. Average Profitability	Pr (Skewness)	Pr (Kurtosis)
				Group 1: Neutral portfolios			
Panel A: Non-responsible (strengths = 0)							
Community	1.11	22	0.05	−16.47	17.58	0.32	0.17
Governance	−0.31	23.35	−0.01	−18.95	17.07	0.17	0.19
Diversity	1.99	26.22	0.08	−19.48	18.11	0.19	0.54
Labour relations	2.67	20.59	0.13	−19.29	13.95	0.04	0.05
Environment	2.68	21.16	0.13	−18.46	15.48	0.1	0.09
Human rights	0.34	17.76	0.02	−15.06	11.04	0.08	0.26
Products	−0.67	18.95	−0.04	−15.25	13.68	0.19	0.27
Panel B: Non-irresponsible (concerns = 0)							
Community	1.12	18.74	0.06	−15.58	12.02	0.1	0.27
Governance	2.54	23.91	0.1	−21.33	15.52	0.04	0.1
Diversity	3.53	18.99	0.18	−17.45	10	0.02	0.12
Labour relations	0.55	17.78	0.03	−15.28	10.91	0.16	0.29
Environment	0.94	18.88	0.05	−17.7	10.58	0.03	0.09
Human rights	−0.43	18.19	−0.02	−14.63	11.74	0.12	0.32
Products	0.67	21.88	0.03	−18.91	14.56	0.07	0.22

Table A1. *(Continued)*

	Average Profitability	Standard Deviation	Sharpe Ratio	Min. Average Profitability	Max. Average Profitability	Pr (Skewness)	Pr (Kurtosis)
Group 2: Partially responsible or irresponsible portfolios							
Panel C: Partially responsible (strengths = 1)							
Community	1.6	16.29	0.1	−14.17	9.25	0.05	0.21
Governance	3.08	15.24	0.2	−12.88	8.12	0.03	0.2
Diversity	−1.87	25.55	−0.07	−25.8	18.58	0.01	0.01
Labour relations	0.06	22.1	0	−17.96	13.62	0.14	0.38
Environment	−3.54	19.9	−0.18	−14.3	16.01	0.4	0.16
Human rights	−8.92	35.44	−0.26	−57.45	12.48	0	0
Products	6.01	17.43	0.34	−15.22	10.56	0.04	0.14
Panel D: Partially irresponsible (concerns = 1)							
Community	2.64	17.92	0.15	−14.94	8.89	0.06	0.45
Governance	2.64	18.91	0.14	−15.99	10.37	0.07	0.37
Diversity	−0.65	17.54	−0.04	−11.16	14.13	0.52	0.31
Labour relations	0.68	19.36	0.03	−15.38	13.78	0.15	0.29
Environment	2.11	18.6	0.11	−16.4	11.21	0.04	0.2
Human rights	2.59	18.55	0.14	−15.97	10.76	0.08	0.33
Products	1.56	15.38	0.1	−12.16	8.31	0.14	0.52

Group 3: Significantly responsible or irresponsible portfolios							
Panel E: Significantly responsible (strengths > 1)							
Diversity	3.34	15.39	0.21	−11.86	8.66	0.1	0.53
Labour relations	0.76	17.46	0.04	−12.27	14.56	0.55	0.17
Environment	2.72	16.68	0.16	−13.35	10.69	0.21	0.35
Panel F: Significantly irresponsible (concerns > 1)							
Governance	4.37	16.19	0.26	−12.6	8.39	0.09	0.45
Labour relations	0.94	17.31	0.05	−15.08	9.06	0.06	0.26
Environment	0.43	18.1	0.02	−13.24	12.33	0.32	0.63

Note: This table shows the descriptive statistics for Islamic portfolios created using ESG ratings. The Sharpe ratio is the ratio between average monthly profitability and standard deviation. Average profitability, standard deviation and the Sharpe ratio are annualised. The last two columns show the skewness and kurtosis for each series. Group 3 contains six portfolios containing the only companies that obtained scores of over 1. The observation period ran from January 2008 to December 2011.

Table A2. Absolute Performance of Islamic SRI Portfolios.

Empirical Results for Four-Factor Regression on the MSCI USA Islamic Index											
	A	*t*-Stat.	RM – RF	*t*-Stat.	SMB	*t*-Stat.	HML	*t*-Stat.	MOM	*t*-Stat.	Adj. R^2
Group 1: Neutral portfolios											
Panel A: Non-responsible (strengths = 0)											
Community	0.96	0.36	1.17***	15	0.15	1.3	0.06	0.55	0.01	0.27	0.93
Governance	–2.02	–0.68	1.23***	19.7	0.30***	3.44	–0.08	–0.68	–0.06	–2.42	0.94
Diversity	–0.12	–0.02	1.32***	13.3	0.40**	1.69	–0.09	–0.59	–0.01	–0.24	0.86
Labour relations	0	–0.01	1.04***	16.8	0.41***	2.73	–0.13	–1.05	–0.06	–1.33	0.92
Environment	0.96	0.33	1.12***	18.7	0.29***	4.05	–0.11	–1.09	–0.05	–2.7	0.94
Human rights	1.21	0.69	0.99***	117	–0.03	–0.89	0.05	0.87	0	0.44	0.98
Products	0.36	0.18	1.06***	32.4	–0.04	–0.74	0.02	0.24	0.03	2.3	0.95
Panel B: Non-irresponsible (concerns = 0)											
Community	–1.07	–0.51	0.92***	30.9	0.41***	3.3	0.02	0.27	–0.03	–0.68	0.92
Governance	0.36	0.1	1.22***	14.3	0.35***	2.04	–0.07	–0.62	–0.08	–1.8	0.91
Diversity	3.29	1.25	1.00***	17	0.13	0.88	0.05	0.63	–0.02	–0.79	0.92
Labour relations	–0.48	–0.18	0.91***	20.8	0.17	1.31	–0.04	–0.56	–0.05	–0.94	0.89
Environment	–1.31	–0.59	0.93***	16.8	0.37***	4.75	0.01	0.13	–0.08**	–3.16	0.94
Human rights	–1.19	–0.88	0.94***	40	0.21***	4.08	0.08	1.32	–0.03	–1.15	0.96
Products	1.09	0.4	1.18***	24	0.04	0.64	0.08	0.9	–0.03	–0.87	0.94

Group 2: Partially responsible or irresponsible portfolios											
Panel C: Partially responsible (strengths = 1)											
Community	1.94	1.14	0.89***	30.2	0.05	0.44	0.01	0.31	0.01	0.45	0.94
Governance	4.91**	2.54	0.84***	24.9	−0.1	−1	0.13	1.86	0.05	1.83	0.93
Diversity	−4.24	−1.22	1.34***	12.5	0.38**	2.6	−0.25*	−1.72	−0.04	−1.02	0.9
Labour relations	−0.48	−0.16	1.16***	19.4	0.22*	1.27	0.01	0.06	0.03	1.01	0.9
Environment	−1.79	−0.53	1.12***	15.4	−0.15	−1.18	−0.07	−0.64	0.06	2.13	0.88
Human rights	−11.04	−0.61	1.07***	10.8	0.19	0.75	−0.53	−0.86	−0.06	−0.73	0.21
Products	5.03	1.68	0.78***	9.61	0.19	1.36	0.14	1.31	−0.09*	−1.48	0.8
Panel D: Partially irresponsible (concerns = 1)											
Community	6.04**	1.99	1.03***	23.8	−0.33	−4.96	0.11	1.47	0.04	1.55	0.94
Governance	1.81	0.63	0.94***	20.6	0.27***	2.16	0.15*	2.12	−0.01	−0.2	0.92
Diversity	0.12	0.04	0.95***	12.3	0.06	0.52	0.04	0.51	0.09**	2.75	0.9
Labour relations	1.57	0.84	1.05***	26.7	0.02	0.38	0.15***	1.94	0.02	0.92	0.97
Environment	2.43	1.01	1.00***	31.7	0.06	0.75	0.06	0.86	−0.01	−0.6	0.94
Human rights	5.54**	1.61	1.07***	38.4	−0.30***	−4.75	0.02	0.25	0.04	1.81	0.93
Products	2.67	1.15	0.84***	22.9	−0.06	−1.16	0.07	1.1	0.01	0.42	0.92
Group 3: Significantly responsible or irresponsible portfolios											
Panel E: Significantly responsible (strengths > 1)											
Diversity	4.41*	2.06	0.82***	25.2	−0.01	−0.09	0.14*	2.15	0.03	0.87	0.91
Labour relations	1.57	0.54	0.96***	11.5	0	−0.01	0.04	0.4	0.03	1.68	0.92
Environment	3.29	1.83	0.87***	19.7	0.04	0.55	0.16**	2.09	−0.02	−0.46	0.93

Table A2. *(Continued)*

Empirical Results for Four-Factor Regression on the MSCI USA Islamic Index

	A	*t*-Stat.	RM – RF	*t*-Stat.	SMB	*t*-Stat.	HML	*t*-Stat.	MOM	*t*-Stat.	Adj. R^2
Panel F: Significantly irresponsible (concerns > 1)											
Governance	7.06**	1.98	0.90***	20.5	−0.24**	−1.49	0.07	0.81	0.05	2.22	0.88
Labour relations	2.43	0.9	0.98***	20.1	−0.14	−1.64	−0.03	−0.5	0.01	0.43	0.91
Environment	3.04	1.1	1.04***	28.2	−0.23***	−4.14	0.06	0.85	0.05	3.42	0.94

Note: This table shows the statistical estimates for linear regression for the return on each portfolio compared to a benchmark index put together using the MSCI USA Islamic Index. The regressions are described in the following equation: $R(t) - \mathrm{RF}(t) = \alpha + \beta[\mathrm{RM}(t) - \mathrm{RF}(t)] + s\mathrm{SMB}(t) + h\mathrm{HML}(t) + m\mathrm{MOM}(t) + \varepsilon(t)$. For each regression, the table shows the R^2, the coefficients and the corresponding *t*-stat and *p*-values. The alphas are annualised. The *t*-stats are estimated using the Newey-West method controlling heteroscedasticity and the autocorrelation of residuals. The observation period ran from January 2008 to December 2011.
*significance threshold at 10%, **significance threshold at 5%, ***significance threshold at 1%.

Table A3. Relative Performance of Islamic SRI Portfolios.

Empirical Results of Regressions on Profitability Gaps											
	α	*t*-Stat.	RM – RF	*t*-Stat.	SMB	*t*-Stat.	HML	*t*-Stat.	MOM	*t*-Stat.	Adj. R^2
Strategy A: Responsible portfolios – non-responsible portfolios											
Community	0.96	0.3	−0.28***	−2.62	−0.11	−0.6	−0.05	−0.43	0.01	0.12	0.3
Governance	7.06*	1.86	−0.39***	−4.16	−0.39***	−2.77	0.22*	1.34	0.11	2.23	0.53
Diversity	−4.24	−1.32	0.02	0.19	−0.02	−0.16	−0.16	−1.5	−0.03	−0.69	−0.04
Labour relations	−0.48	−0.12	0.12**	2.03	−0.19	−1.63	0.14	1.2	0.09**	1.49	0.1
Environment	−2.73	−0.57	0	0.01	−0.43***	−2.79	0.04	0.27	0.11**	3.06	0.24
Human rights	−12.11	−0.62	0.08	0.75	0.22	0.77	−0.58	−0.86	−0.06	−0.7	−0.07
Products	4.66	1.01	−0.28***	−2.51	0.23	1.23	0.13	0.81	−0.12	−1.66	0.15
Strategy B: Non-irresponsible portfolios – irresponsible portfolios											
Community	−6.74*	−1.76	−0.1	−1.72	0.74***	5.04	−0.09	−1.09	−0.07	−1.04	0.39
Governance	−1.43	−0.36	0.28***	3.5	0.08	0.54	−0.23*	−1.85	−0.07	−1.08	0.29
Diversity	3.17	0.6	0.05	0.34	0.07	0.38	0.01	0.06	−0.11	−2.17	0.07
Labour relations	−2.02	−0.76	−0.14**	−1.93	0.15	1.03	−0.19*	−1.98	−0.07	−1.33	0.13
Environment	−3.66	−1.17	−0.07	−1.46	0.31**	3.15	−0.06	−0.49	−0.07	−2.33	0.1
Human rights	−6.40*	−1.75	−0.13*	−2.57	0.51***	4.71	0.06	0.57	−0.07	−1.5	0.29
Products	−1.55	−0.39	0.33***	3.99	0.11	0.9	0	0.03	−0.04	−0.65	0.37

Note: This table shows the statistical estimates for linear regression for the performance gaps between portfolios (responsible or irresponsible) and their neural equivalent compared to a benchmark index put together using the MSCI USA Islamic Index. The regressions are described in the following equation: $R(t,p) - R(t,n) = \alpha + \beta[\text{RM}(t) - \text{RF}(t)] + \text{sSMB}(t) + \text{hHML}(t) + \text{mMOM}(t) + \varepsilon(t)$. For each regression, the table shows the R^2, the coefficients and the corresponding *t*-stat and *p*-values. The alphas are annualised. The *t*-stats are estimated using the Newey-West method controlling heteroscedasticity and the autocorrelation of residuals. The observation period ran from January 2008 to December 2011.

*significance threshold at 10%, **significance threshold at 5%, ***significance threshold at 1%.

PART V
CONCLUSION

A PROVISIONAL CONCLUSION: A SHIFT TOWARDS FINANCE AS A COMMONS?

Bernard Paranque

We live in a world where money is the medium underpinning the circulation of goods and services. Without money it is impossible, if not to survive, then at least to have access to basic products, including cultural or educational ones.

However, we need to remember that the means of circulating goods and services that we are familiar with, mainly – if not exclusively – capitalist market-oriented exchanges – are just one of the possible forms of circulation, concealing the specific dynamics of capitalism where the use value is only a medium for exchange value.

That being the case, the vector for capitalist market-oriented exchanges is money. If one wants to institute another register for circulation, it has to be constructed. If one wants to loosen the grip of the exclusive capitalist market-oriented exchange, and the race towards productivity that accompanies it, it is necessary to encourage exchanges for which price and cost criteria alone are not enough to justify entering into the relationship. This is the case for fair trade for example. What then comes into play is the nature of the social link that has been built, to be rebuilt or maintained (Graeber, 2013; Meiksins-Wood, 2009, 2013, 2014; Servet, 2012, 2013).

Finance Reconsidered: New Perspectives for a Responsible and Sustainable Finance
Critical Studies on Corporate Responsibility, Governance and Sustainability, Volume 10, 387–394

ISSN: 2043-9059/doi:10.1108/S2043-905920160000010036

This involves our capacity to put forward not only an analysis of the existing state of affairs but also a utopia – that is another way of exercising our power, to go along with Ricœur – which means looking beyond a growth model that depletes our humanity, that is our relations with each other and with nature – in other words, with ourselves. This means (re-)thinking our relationship with nature. What social relationship to production do we want to build for our lives? We believe that setting man in opposition to his environment will lead to a dead-end because it denies any place for man. This challenge forces us to understand the social relationship within which we embed our activity and which is characterised by the alienation of the majority of people from the conditions under which they exercise 'their own power to act'.

We would like to suggest that the ecological transition, not included in the themes covered in this book, is indeed that political utopia (which is undoubtedly a pleonasm), on the condition that it is not seen as a predefined state or an ideal to which reality has to adjust. The ecological transition has to be seen and promoted as a real movement, the day-to-day political practice that, through its transformation, abolishes the current state of social relationships with regard to production and ownership. This transition should be an opportunity for humankind to reclaim the conditions of their existence, starting with production conditions. It is not therefore an end in itself but a process of emancipation.

We need to break away from the concept of a world handed down to us since Enlightenment where man would be a separate element from nature, dominating it and exploiting it, and the concept rooted in the instrumentalist Marxist vulgate on humankind and nature. The ecological transition we need is, on the contrary, more of a process to create new social relationships that call on our capacity as human beings with a stake in the natural world.[1]

This emancipation refers to the need to reclaim the conditions for our capacity for action, and should draw on collective resource management institutions – financial institutions first of all – and on governance that takes all voices into account.

The construction of the break with the dominant, not to say hegemonic, method of circulation for products (goods and services for the rest of the chapter) is based on our 'constituent capability', in other words our legitimacy to organise the procedures of our collective action. This means we need to clarify the conditions for the existence of the mobilised collective, the definition of the coordination rules, the conditions for their revision, the system of penalties as well as the system for sharing profits and losses, and the distribution of ownership rights underpinning the collective's practices and operation. In brief, it means formalising the whys and the wherefores of the collective and of the cooperation.

Consequently a 'Finance reconsidered' should be based on a 'paradigm of reciprocity' (Giraud, 2012, p. 165; Sahakian & Servet, 2015; Testart, 2007) which one might wish or consider to be necessary is, like any norm or rule, a social construct. If we want to switch from a system of capitalist market-oriented exchange to a market-oriented or non-market-oriented exchange, or even a system of reciprocity, we must construct the underlying norm. This norm refers to the organisation of relationships between people on the basis of uses that they can develop and benefit from (Paranque, 2015). This 'commons' then calls for the definition of the legal ownership framework that allows for the cooperative coordination of the collective action of those involved.

A 'commons' is comprised of an identified resource for which the collection unit is defined (fish for fishing, tree for forest, etc.). It is organised based on a distribution of ownership rights and governance rules characterising a capacity of those involved to institute change.

From this point of view, Giraud insists on two finance functions – ensuring liquidity and allowing credit (2012, p. 143). Finance as a 'Commons'[2] could be organised on the basis of these two qualities of money, one of which makes it possible to free oneself from debt or to make a purchase when one so wishes, while the other lets one plan for the future or face up to uncertainties when liquidity is lacking.

Before specifying this, it is necessary to be sure of understanding the 'Commons' in question, not as a material resource or not but as 'a system of rules governing collective actions, modes of existence and community activities/*un système de règles régissant des actions collectives, des modes d'existence et d'activités de communautés*' (Giraud, 2012, p. 142). This involves a specific ownership regime with distribution of rights of use; for each system of resources there is a corresponding system of ownership rights (bundle of rights) with their system of governance (Chanteau, Coriat, Labrousse, & Orsi, 2013; Coriat, 2015). This therefore means thinking of 'Commons' in the way suggested by Dardot and Laval (2014) as 'the practical activity of men' (p. 49).

Like any other 'Commons', 'Finance as a Commons' is a resource to which access is relatively easy (low exclusion of 'consumers/users') but where rivalry is high (the consumption of one unit reduces the amount available for others). At the same time, this implies reflecting on one's access and thinking about its renewal. The latter can only be guaranteed by the capacity to save that those involved can ensure following mobilisation of the financial resource; in other words, loans produce deposits.

This means that money is not a commons as such; it can only be so through a political decision setting out the conditions and methods for its access and its use. A 'Commons' therefore depends on our constituent capability. What is central is the organisation of our collective action and of its purposes, backed by governance that is appropriate (in both senses of the word – suitable and rightful). This could be established in accordance with the principles setting up the systems for a common pool resources management institution as well as the distribution of associated ownership rights on the resource and its management, distinguishing between management of the resource (liquidity and credit – their formation either by collecting savings, or by creating money as in the case of local currencies) and management of resource units used by stakeholders (the amounts and their type, consumption versus investment).

This therefore means characterising the institution of 'Finance as a Commons' in a twofold dimension that supports the uses and brings in new practices:

– the constitutive principles of such an institution which poses the question of relationships with the banking system and the evolution of its role;
– the ownership rights associated with this management and providing the foundations for the existence of this institution including in its relationships with other stakeholders in financing.

To do this, it is necessary to return to the conditions for access to credit which, as we will see, are varied and, in some cases, present strong convergences in the way they function with the collective coordination set up.

The two qualities of money highlighted by Giraud correspond to two functions but are not at the same level. Freeing oneself from a debit or buying when one wants to is not the same as credit which is an anticipation or the ability to seize an opportunity or a way of facing up to the unforeseen. This is demonstrated well in the work by Hicks (1988) on credit systems or the work on systems of commitment in the economics of agreements (Rivaud-Danset & Salais, 1992).

According to Hicks, the company has two possible methods of financing (Paranque & Rivaud-Danset, 1998). The first is based on the financial autonomy acquired by the allocation of income to reserves which makes cash and cash equivalents available to face up to the problems or opportunities of investment.[3] The second is access to bank loans, in particular to the short-term loans. An implicit or explicit guarantee of access to such loans can provide companies with a financial flexibility equivalent to that provided by the possession of liquid financial assets (Hicks, 1988). However, the mobilisation of one or the other depends not only the company's capacity to generate a surplus, but also on the possibility of access to relatively secure external financing within a committed relationship (Rivaud-Danset & Salais, 1992). But one might say that the generation of a surplus that could be allocated to reserves also depends on the conditions and procedures in place for access to the financing, either via the accumulated reserves, or by means of access to the loan used to finance the investments.

Two types of relationship can then be envisaged depending on whether one manages the financing relationship as pure risk, that is as a calculation of the probability of default and therefore based on the price, or as a social construct in the long term based on a set of joint commitments, and therefore via the collective management of the information, that is of the uncertainty:

- 'The 'commitment-based' banking model sacrifices opportunism and reversibility in favour of a relationship of trust (...)' (Rivaud-Danset & Salais, 1992, p. 89).
- 'The 'procedure-based' banking model excludes any personalised understanding in favour of standardised information on the client in terms of calculation of probability (...)' (idem, p. 91).

In other words, if the exchange relationship is purely market-oriented with the bank, or the lenders in the broadest sense of the term, meaning that only the criteria of price and cost preside over the decision on exchange, then that can only reinforce a relationship that is short term and, what is more, opportunistic. On the other hand, if one wants to ensure this access to credit in the long term, and therefore also to future liquidity, the exchange has to be backed by criteria other than price.[4] For the parties, this means being capable of building up a relationship of commitment (Rivaud-Danset, 1995, 1996; Rivaud-Danset & Salais, 1992). This depends not only on the financial environment, especially the behaviour of banks and shareholders (loans, advances etc.), as well as corporate specificities, but also on the institutional organisation of the financing relationships. One can then consider that firms 'arbitrate' between the internal availability of liquidity and the need for liquidity covered by the current bank credit to obtain funding depending on the existence or otherwise of contractual agreements able to support an exchange in the long term. If the lender needs to be able to estimate the quality of the company's commitment, the company needs to be able to appraise the conditions and procedures of the bank's commitment in line with criteria that are usually only partly common to the 'culture' of each of those involved.

'However this "choice" by companies is not independent of the "social conditions" under which it can be exercised. Literature on the lending relationship (...) clearly demonstrates the difficulty in understanding the demand and supply of credit solely by means of trade relations (...). In a situation of information asymmetry, the decisions and forecasts of agents will be dependent on their cognitive abilities and the degree of uncertainty with which they are confronted (...)/*Mais ce « choix » des entreprises n'est pas indépendant des conditions « sociales » dans lesquelles il peut s'exercer. La littérature sur la relation de prêts (...) montre bien la difficulté de comprendre la demande et l'offre de crédit uniquement au travers des rapports marchands (...). En situation d'asymétrie d'informations, les décisions et les prévisions des agents vont dépendre de leurs capacités cognitives et du degré d'incertitude auquel ils sont confrontés (...)*' (Belletante, Levratto, & Paranque, 2001, p. 408; Rivaud-Danset, 1992, 1995, 1996).

Consequently, the company's proximity to the market supporting the continual renewal of a relationship of trust and of commitment implies the social, if not spatial, proximity of those involved. This proximity can be constructed in the shape of a 'Finance as a Commons' with the rules shown above. This context can enable local funding mechanisms to be assembled (such as La Nef in France, crowdfunding, microfinance, local currency) and also provide stakeholders with the negotiating framework of a shared local financing institution. It could be that of the uses coordinated through mediation of the collective project drawn up with the help of rules adoptable by all, in particular on/for/via finance organised and managed as 'commons'. This no doubt implies the emergence of a possibility of contesting the dominant circulation and production system, provided a governance is ensured giving priority to the human side in relation to capital.

By resuming the criteria advanced by Ostrom and by placing finance structured as a 'commons' at the heart of our development, it might be possible to promote another type of economic growth embedded in social aspects (Polanyi).

A finance as commons could be noted:

- in a circulation of goods and services based on non-capitalist market-oriented exchange, or even non-market-oriented exchange,
- on the basis of a banking relationship of commitment, of proximity, for which the criteria of prices or values are not determinants of the

exchange and therefore hinged on or subject to criteria either of use (needs to satisfy) or of development of links on a territory or between populations sharing the same aspirations and principles of coordination,
- in a coordinated commitment that allows access to liquidity and credit in association with shared and coordinated objectives.

It would rely on a common institution for management of this resource defining the conditions for the collection of savings but also for the mobilisation of credit from other 'external' financial institutions, and would organise the modalities for the unitary extraction of the resource in order to finance the projects validated by the collective that has been instituted. This institution could, subject to specific conditions, manage both functions by promoting a local currency in order to encourage exchanges within the community (which is not necessarily, or even solely, geographical) and mechanisms for micro-credit or credit dedicated to the territory in question, the regulation of which would be carried out via a Forum (Arena in Ostrom's words) along the same lines as those of Banco Palma.

NOTES

1. This issue of man as a stakeholder in nature rather than being exterior to it is found in Descola (2005), in the typology of ontological systems: naturalism, animism, totemism and analogism.
2. It is interesting to note that Ostrom's work never evokes the question of financing for the activities being studied. In fact the issue of financing is absent. We don't know how collective management institutions were financed, any more than the activity of the players themselves, and even less what their relationship is to the market. For example in the case of fisheries (Ostrom, 2010, p. 209), we know nothing of the real or potential interactions between the constraints linked to selling fish on the traditional market and those resulting from collective coordination and compliance with its rules.
3. See Belletante, Levratto, and Paranque (2001, p. 404).
4. See Bachet and Naszályi (2011) for a discussion on the other forms of financing possible and the different role that the banks could play.

REFERENCES

Bachet, D., & Naszályi, P. (2011). *L'autre finance. Existe-t-il des alternatives à la banque capitaliste?* Saint-Malo: Éditions du Croquant.

Belletante, B., Levratto, N., & Paranque, B. (2001). *Diversité économique et modes de financement des PME.* Paris: L'Harmattant.

Chanteau, J.-P., Coriat, B., Labrousse, A., & Orsi, F. (2013). Autour d'Ostrom: communs, droits de propriété et institutionnalisme méthodologique. Revue de la régulation [online], 14 | 2e semestre / Autumn, online since 23 December 2013. Retrieved from http://regulation.revues.org/10365. Accessed on February 17, 2014.

Coriat, B. (2015). Qu'est-ce qu'un commun? Quelles perspectives le mouvement des communs ouvre-t-il à l'alternative sociale? *Les Possibles, 5*.

Dardot, P., & Laval, C. (2014). *Commun*. Paris: La Découverte.

Descola, P. (2005). *Par-delà nature et culture*. Paris: NRF, Gallimard.

Giraud, G. (2012). *Illusion financière*. Paris: Seuil, Collection Poche.

Graeber, D. (2013). *Dette. 5000 ans d'histoire*. Les Liens qui Libèrent.

Hicks, J. (1988). *La crise de l'économie keynésienne*. Paris: Fayard.

Meiksins-Wood, E. (2009). *L'origine du capitalisme*. Québec: Lux/Humanités.

Meiksins-Wood, E. (2013). *Des citoyens aux seigneurs. Une histoire sociale de la pensée politique de l'antiquité au Moyen Age*. Lux/Humanités, Québec.

Meiksins-Wood, E. (2014). *Liberté et propriété. Une histoire sociale de la pensée politique occidentale de la Renaissance aux Lumières*. Lux/Humanités, Québec.

Ostrom, E. (2010). *Gouvernance des biens communs*. Bruxelles: De Boeck.

Paranque, B. (2015). *An alternative to shareholder value creation: Subverting the domination of capitalist exchanges through the production of uses and common pool resources management*. Retrieved from http://ssrn.com/abstract=2466542 or http://dx.doi.org/10.2139/ssrn.2466542

Paranque, B., & Rivaud-Danset, D. (1998). Structures financières des entreprises industrielles françaises: une approche en termes de conventions de financement. *Bulletin de la Banque de France, 57*, 79–100.

Rivaud-Danset, D. (1995). « Le rationnement du crédit et l'incertitude ». *Revue d'Économie Politique, 105* (mars-avril), 223–247.

Rivaud-Danset, D. (1996). « Les contrats de crédit dans une relation de long terme ». *Revue Économique, 4* (juillet), 937–962.

Rivaud-Danset, D., & Salais, R. (1992). Les conventions de financement. Premières approches théorique et empirique. *Revue Française d'Économie, 7*(4), 81–120.

Sahakian, M., & Servet, J.-M. (2015). Separating the wheat from the chaff: Sharing versus self-interest in crowdfunding. In D. Assadi (Ed.), *Strategic managerial approaches to crowdfunding online*. NY: IGI Global Publishers.

Servet, J.-M. (2012). *Les monnaies du lien*. Lyon: Presses Universitaires de Lyon.

Servet, J.-M. (2013). Monnaie: quand la dette occulte le partage. *La Découverte, revue Française de Socio-Economie, 2*(12), 125–147.

Testart, A. (2007). *Critique du don, études sur la circulation non marchande*. Paris: Syllepse.

POSTFACE: LET A THOUSAND FLOWERS BLOOM

Contrary to what some might think, this title is not inspired by or derived from Mao Tse Dong's 1956 slogan, 'Let a hundred flowers bloom'.[1] Given the Chinese communist party's history, it would be pretty cynical for the different authors included here. Instead, I have deliberately taken the title from a paper by Jean Séguy, a sociologist specialising in religions, which came out in 1990 and pleaded for 'variety and freedom in research'.[2] What was true in his field 25 years ago still applies today to the economy.

Today, the economy and finance have abandoned the experimental approach and now apply a dogma. As a result, realities that do not comply with the doxa of the reductive or incorrect models will be 'excommunicated' by modern forms of the court of the sacred Rota, such as the IMF, the central banks and other troikas. As for the people, who are supposed to be at the base of all democratic political action, they are urged to comply with paradoxical injunctions issued by guru economists, even though the latter change direction faster than a weathercock in a wind storm.

However, the 2008 financial crisis demonstrated the failure of one-track economic thinking, the approach that justified subprimes and the theory of shareholder value as the ultimate way of optimising collective action. As a result, dissident voices are now increasingly taken into account and included in higher education institutes like management schools, where there is now an understanding that a single casuistry[3] cannot form the basis of an educational programme.

Let us truly appreciate this book, which gives us food for thought and then for action.

Here, in my capacity as a practitioner in banking and the social and solidarity economy, I would like to emphasise the input and coordination by Bernard Paranque and Roland Pérez.

After the devastation left behind by the overwhelming crisis, the citizen within 'homo economicus' has felt the need to 'take back control' of their destiny through action where everyone is able to contribute to a collective initiative.[4] In this respect, for anyone looking to combine thought and action, this book is much akin to a map, or our more modern-day GPS system, for an orienteering session. Through far-reaching theoretical analysis and the examples quoted, the long-distance hiker is given a few markers for his route. What a pleasure it was to read and meditate on, among other things, the chapters devoted to Socially Responsible Investment (SRI) or the limits of the supposed microcredit cure-all.

Here, I am unable to go over all the different paths that have been drawn, but I would like to highlight one avenue for the future that definitely seems worth exploring: the convergence between the upwelling of thought and actions focused on the notions of common pool resources and the social and solidarity economy.

We are currently witnessing the emergence of numerous academic and practical initiatives through partnerships between researchers and practitioners from both sectors. I'm sure great things will blossom them come to fruition.

In fact, I talked about this during a presentation before the late Nobel economist Elinor Ostrom, where I called on researchers working on the notion of pooled resources and common goods, to extend their analyses to savings.[5] One part of that appeal was heard by the backers of the 'Finance Reconsidered' chair. This thought was turned into action in the form of a new corporate project from Crédit Coopératif, taking 'all co-operators, all bankers' as its theme! It is something that is reflected in the title of the provisional conclusion from Bernard Paranque: 'a move towards "communal" finance?'

Finally, this book recalls Marco Polo's work: 'The Million or the Description of the World'. The famous merchant and traveller is symbolic of the Mediterranean communities that heralded the new economic era – pre-capitalism. As in Fernard Braudel's work, the examples set out show us how the Mare Nostrum remains a place of innovation in the economic and social spheres.

There is evidence that globalisation can also be favourable in economic and social terms, so we need to bear in mind that, when it comes to being strong and retaining control over our destiny, we have to act as global citizens with local roots.

Jean-Louis Bancel
Chairman of Crédit Coopératif and the International Cooperative Banking Association (I.C.A.)

NOTES

1. Mao Tse Dong's slogan 'Let a hundred flowers bloom, let a hundred schools of thought contend'.
2. This was the sub-heading of his paper in *Archives sciences sociales des religions* no. 70 in 1990 (May–June), pp. 185–208.
3. I have voluntarily hijacked this term usually associated with the teaching of morals and human sciences in the classical period, and applied it to management teaching based on case studies which, while they may not offset theoretical teaching complying with the traditional principles of controversy, do affirm the Rabelaisian motto: 'Science without conscience is but the ruin of the soul'.
4. On this point, see my opinion piece on leMonde.fr in the 'voices of the economy' supplement: http://abonnes.lemonde.fr/economie-francaise/article/2015/02/10/pour-une-economie-plus-democratique-par-jean-louis-bancel_4573802_1656968.html?xtmc=jean_louis_bancel&xtcr=1
5. See the report on this conference, held on 23 June 2011, by Jordane Legleye, 'SSE and common pool resources, the same corner between "State and market"?' *in* RECMA http://recma.org/actualite/ess-et-biens-communs-un-meme-coin-entre-letat-et-le-marche. Follow this link to see a video of the presentation: https://www.youtube.com/watch?v=qzNzJo6Swts

APPENDIX A: PRESENTATION OF THE FINANCE AND SUSTAINABILITY PROGRAMME (FAS)

Roland Pérez

PRESENTATION AND CONTRIBUTIONS

At first glance, it is not easy to bring together Finance and Sustainability (F & S), even though a number of works are specifically devoted to this. The worldwide recession that began in 2007–2008 led many research institutions and collectives to start reflecting and debating on themes concerning the links between F & S.

In France, the institutions the most concerned by the crisis were the first to react: the AMF (the French stock market regulator), via its scientific council, or the IFA (French institute of directors), via its research club. Most of the French/French-speaking scientific associations, such as AFFI, AFC, AIMS, RIODD, SFM and the like, turned their attention to themes related to the financial crisis and the ways and means of coming through it thanks to greater sustainability.

The economic and financial downturn was felt across the world so it was natural that the debate it engendered should also be an international one. This was true in the United States where the massive crunch started, but also in Europe which felt its effects. Numerous contributions have already been made; we can quote a few examples from among the researchers who drew attention to the risks incurred well before the current crisis began – the work by the Observatoire de la Finance (H. Dembinski, Geneva), that of economists N. Roubini and R. Shiller, and of S. Keen, anthropologist P. Jorion, sociologist D. A. MacKensie, and mathematician B. Mandelbrot, not to mention the forewarnings – or indeed alarm bells – sounded by practitioners such as G. Soros or N. N. Thaleb.

The international research programme entitled 'Finance and Sustainability' (FAS) was founded in 2009 with a view to contributing to the 10th IFSAM World Conference in Paris in July 2010. It was coordinated by a group of researchers – R. Pérez (U. Montpellier, F), C. Louche (Vlerick Gent-Leuven, B), W. Sun (Leeds Met U., UK) – brought together through a partnership between two networks, the RIODD (International Network for Research on Organisations and Sustainable Development) and CGSIG *(Corporate Governance and Sustainability International Group)*, in relation with a number of other institutions, including the CRIFA (IFA research club), the AAIG (International Academic Association on Governance), the universities of Montpellier 1, Paris Dauphine, Leeds Met, Gent-Leuven, and CNAM Paris.

This joint project resulted in several publications, including a new 'Entreprise et finance' series (KF) by the review *Économies et Sociétés* (ISMEA) and a collective work in a dedicated series from Emerald Publishing.

The conclusive results of this first programme and, above all, the fact that the global crisis was far from over and was in fact being felt even more sharply, shaking the foundations of the world economic system and the models used to analyse it, pushed the participants in FAS 2010 to consider a new programme – known as FAS 2 – with a new timeframe (2015) and content adapted in line with the challenges brought about by the ongoing global recession.

– Just like FAS 2010 – or FAS 1 – FAS 2 is an 'international partnership initiative' as defined by the RIODD, that is involving at least two institutional members (research teams or networks) from different countries. See www.riodd.net. The RIODD's main partner network is CGSIG (Corporate Governance and Sustainability International Group), www.cgsig.net (Pt: W. Sun), already co-coordinator of FAS 1. The IFA www.ifa-asso.com research club, which was pivotal for FAS 1, is also at the origin of FAS 2.
– The ISMEA – Institute for applied mathematical and economic sciences – www.ismea.org. (Pt: R. Borrelly) has also joined the programme. This institute was founded in 1944 by F. Perroux and has retained, alongside its publications activity (applied economy, economy and society, etc.), a coordination mission in the scientific field, contributing to the multifaceted aspect required in economic research. As such, the objectives of the FAS programme seemed to be a good match for its

own goals, which led to the initiative to launch the new 'Entreprise et Finance' (KF) series within *Économies & Sociétés*.

– The French forum for responsible investment (FIR): www.frenchsif.org (Pt: B. Fournier) is another founding member of FAS 2. This forum brings together French stakeholders in SRI and represents the French component in the international SIF (*Sustainable Investment Forum*) network. The French SIF is itself a co-founder of the European network, *Eurosif* www.eurosif.org
– The CNAM, through LIRSA – its research centre, has also joined this founding group with several of its members helping to coordinate the new programme (including Ch. Hoarau, I. Chambost and H. Zimnovitch, editor-in-chief of the KF series).
– Kedge Business School, through the AG2R LA MONDIALE 'Finance Reconsidered' Chair, headed by B. Paranque, has made an active contribution to the new programme, especially for the 'Finance and corporate governance of the social and solidarity economy' theme.
– Other partner institutions of FAS I – in particular the International Academic Association on Governance www.aaig-asso.com, the universities of Leeds, Montpellier, Paris Dauphine, Paris Sud and Audencia Nantes were invited to remain partners of FAS 2. Other research teams and collectives were invited to share ideas, including the seminar entitled 'Finance, Ethics and performativity' – Paris EHESS/ICP (M. Leclerc-Olive, R. Walter), the *Observatoire de la Finance* (OF) in Geneva (P. Dembinsky) www.obsfin.ch;[1] and the *International Observatory on Sustainable Finance* (OIFD), Finance Watch: www.callforfinancewatch, the *European Academy of Management* (EURAM) www.euram-online.org,[2] the *Society for the Advancement of Socio-Economics* (SASE) www.sase.org, and Collège des Bernardins – 'Economy, Man, Society' department, www.collegedesbernardins.fr;[3] the heterodox economists' collectives: AFEP (French political economy association) www.asso-economiepolitique.org, Économistes atterrés www.atterres.org, and Confrontations Europe, www.confrontations.org
– In addition to research groups and teams, the FAS cooperative programme remains open to professionals in the sector, reflected in the sessions organised in 2009 and 2010 by the IFA research club, to develop different perspectives from researchers and practitioners in a field – finance – where each stakeholder's knowledge and experience is questioned and occasionally challenged.

Over these last few years, members of the FAS collective have taken part in a number of scientific meetings or events organised either as part of the programme or on the initiative of partner institutions. There was:

- FAS bimonthly seminar – Paris 2012–2013 and 2013–2014.
- Study days on 'Economic information for employees', CNAM – U. Lille 3: 2012 (Paris), 2013 (Lille), 2014 (Paris).
- RIODD international congress – 2012 (Nantes), 2013 (Lille), 2014 (Bordeaux).
- FNEGE 2004 management week (Marseille).
- INFINITI Conference on international finance 2013 (Aix), 2014 (Prato – Italy), 2015 (Ljubljana – Sweden), on the initiative of Thomas Lagoarde-Segot, professor at Kedge Business School.
- EuroMed Conferences EMBRI 2012 (Montreux – CH), 2013 (Estoril – P).
- EURAM European Congress: 2012 (Rotterdam – NL), 2013 (Istanbul – Turkey), 2014 (Valencia – Spain), 2015 (Warsaw – Poland).
- IFSAM international conferences: 2010 (Paris), 2014 (Tokyo – Japan).

ACTIONS CURRENTLY UNDERWAY ('FAS FINALE')

As we prepare the progress report for FAS 2 and as we look beyond the complete FAS programme, we now consider 2015 as a transitional year between the end of the present programme (which explains the title, 'FAS finale') and a potential new programme, the design and implementation of which would require a new institutional framework and a new coordination team.

In this respect, we believe it would be best to spend 2015 focused on some clearly identified actions which can and should be implemented.

1. Economies & Sociétés
   The launch of a new 'Economies & Sociétés' series as a spin-off from the K series 'Économie de l'entreprise' and devoted to 'Entreprise et finance' has undoubtedly been a remarkable achievement, linked to the FAS programme which provided considerable input but open to other contributions. The four issues already published – K1 (November 2010), K2 (March 2012), K3 (August 2013), K4 (July 2014) are tangible evidence of this achievement. For 2015, a special issue was prepared, with themed

report concerned by FAS program and other contributions (coordinator: R. Pérez). This special issue is planed to be published in 2016 in a new review: "*Entreprise et Soci*été" (Paris, Editions Garnier).

2. EURAM
   The European Academy of Management (EURAM), within its SIG (Special Interest Group), hosted a workshop entitled 'Business for Society', inspired by the FAS 'Finance, Economy and Society' programme; this was headed by C. Karyotis (Neoma, B. S.).

   After the 2014 congress held in Valencia (Spain), the 2015 congress in Warsaw (Poland), the 2016 congress has taken place from 1° to 4 june at Paris (Université Paris Est Créteil UPEC), with a standint track "*Finance Economy and Society: For a Sustainable re-embedding*". Coordinator: C. Karyotis. catherine.karyotis@neoma-bs.fr
3. Finance and the Commons
   This project is one of the most motivating but one of the most difficult to complete. It attempts to reformulate the place and functions of finance, using concepts and analytical frameworks developed by Elinor Ostrom to study common goods resources. The difficulty comes from the fact that finance is, more than any other factor, dependent on both market dynamics and sovereign constraints.

   A discussion forum has been launched via the 'discussion on common pool resources' network at: finance@bienscommuns.org (moderators: N. Alix, R. Pérez, F. Sultan), a forum bringing together researchers, finance professionals and people with an interest in common pool resources.

   This forum took part in the AFEP 2015 congress at Lyon in early July.

   Coordinators: Alix, N., Dupré, D., Paranque, B., Pérez, R., Servet, J.-M.
4. Publications by the 'Finance Reconsidered' Chair
   The 'Finance Reconsidered' Chair, founded by Kedge Business School with support from AG2R LA MONDIALE and headed by B. Paranque, played an active role in FAS 2, especially with regard to the 'Finance and corporate governance of the social and solidarity economy' research theme (bimonthly seminars in Paris over 2012–2013 and 2013–2014, INFINITI 2013 congress round table, FNEGE day in May 2014, themed report in KF4, book by T. Lagoarde-Segot).

   Two publications were planned for 2015: (Coordinator: Paranque, B.):

– First, a special issue of Research in International Business and Finance (RIBAF), published by ELSEVIER.

– Secondly, a collective book, published by Presses Universitaires de Septentrion, setting out the work carried out the last few years within the framework of the 'Finance Reconsidered' Chair.

This reminder of the short history of the FAS programme and the actions planned or supported over 2015, known as the 'FAS Finale', clearly shows the position of this book, and more widely the 'Finance Reconsidered' Chair, within the international partnership programme devoted to a clear analysis of contemporary finance and the ways and means of putting it to the service of society.

THE MAIN PUBLICATIONS AND BOOKS BY FAS MEMBERS AND PARTNERS

(A) Books

(a) Special series on CGSIG from Emerald Publishing www.emeraldinsight.com

The CGSIG support a Book Series, published by Emerald Group, Bingley (UK) Critical Studies on Corporate Responsibility, Governance and Sustainability (Editor: William Sun X.Sun@leedsmet.ac.uk). Among many books:

Volume 1: Sun, W., Stewart, J., & Pollard, D. (2010). *Reframing Corporate Social Responsibility: Lessons from the Global Financial Crisis.*

Volume 2: Sun, W., Louche, C., & Pérez, R. (2011). *Finance and Sustainability: Towards A New Paradigm? A Post-Crisis Agenda.*

Volume 7: Louche, C., & Hebb, T. (2014). *Socially Responsible Investment in the 21st Century: Does it Make a Difference for Society?*

The present book will be the Volume 10: Paranque B., Pérez R. (Eds) (2016), *Finance reconsidered – New Perspectives for a Responsibles and Sustainable Finance.*

A Volume 11 is planed: Alijani S., Karyotis C. (Eds), 2016. *Finance and economy for society: integrating sustainability.*

(b) Among other books:

Lagoarde-Segot, Th. (2014). *La finance solidaire – Un humanisme économique*, De Boeck, Bruxelles.

Servet, J.-M. (2012). *Les monnaies du lien*, Presses Universitaires de Lyon.

Servet, J.-M. (2015). *La vraie révolution du micro-crédit*, Éd. Odile Jacob, Paris.

Sun, W., Steward, J., & Pollard, D. (2011). *Corporate Governance and the Global Financial Crisis: International Perspectives*, Cambridge University Press.

(B) Reviews

FAS members have published numerous papers in various academic reviews over the past few years, in both French and English (a list will be drawn up for the final report at the end of 2015).

a) Special series on "Entreprise et Finance" of the review – *Économies et sociétés*

One publication worth mentioning is the 'Entreprise et Finance' series – *Économies et sociétés (Cahiers de l'ISMEA)*. Reminder of issues published:

N° KF1 – November 2010 (Coordinators: Pérez, R., Louche, C., Sun W) – issue focusing on 'Responsible Finance'.

N° KF2 – March 2012 (Coordinators: Ninet, J., Pérez, R., Zimmnovitch, H.). This issue includes a themed report on 'Banks and the financial crisis'.

N° KF3 – August 2013 (Coordinators: Zimmnovitch, H., Ninet, J., Pérez, R. – guest editor: Hoarau C. – CNAM). This issue contain a themed report on 'Economic and financial information for employees and their representatives', coordinated by I. Chambost. (CNAM) and B. Touchelay (U. Lille 3).

N° KF4 – November 2014 (Coordinators: Zimmnovitch, H., Ninet, J., Pérez, R. – guest editor: Paranque, B. – Kedge, B. S.). This issue contains a themed report on 'Corporate financing, management and governance of the social and solidarity economy'.

b) Other papers: A few exemples:

– Cova B., Paranque B. (2012) "Value Creation Versus Destruction: The Relationship between Consumers, Marketers and Financiers", *Journal of Brand Management*, v. 20, n° 2, pp. 147–158.
– Dupré D, Raufflet E. (2014) « L'enseignement de l'éthique en finance six ans après la crise: constats et perspectives françaises », *Ethique publique*, v. 16, n° 2, p. 11–30.
– Goodman J., Louche C. & al. (2014), "Social Shareholder Engagement: The Dynamics of Voice and Exit", *Journal of Business Ethics*, v. 10, n° 2, p. 193–210.

– Paranque B. (2014) "Private property and collective action: co-operation instead of competition", *EuroMed Journal of Business*, Vol. 9 Iss: 1, pp. 37–59.
– Servet J.M. (2013), « Monnaie: quand la dette occulte le partage », *Revue Française de Socio Economie*, 2 semestre 2013, 12, p. 125–147.

NOTES

1. The OF in Geneva initiated the appeal on 'Renewing research and teaching in finance, economics and management to better serve the common good' http://www.responsiblefinance.ch/

2. In particular, the special interest group (SIG) 'Business for Society', within which a workshop on 'Finance, Economy and Society' (C. Karyotis *et al.*) was set up.

3. And the seminar on 'Entreprise and Society' (B. Roger), in liaison with Université Paris Ouest (O. Favereau) and Mines ParisTech school (A. Hatchuel, B. Segrestin).

APPENDIX B: POST CRISIS FINANCE ASSOCIATION – FROM CRISIS TO VIABILITY: FINANCE RECONSIDERED – FOR A MANIFESTO

The ongoing economic, social and environmental crisis has revealed the need to redefine the finance function. Academic finance's focus on the micro level and its emphasis on econometric modelling at the expense of taking a longer-run view including incorporating the lessons from economic history. Academic finance bears significant responsibility in this process addressing the interaction between finance and society. As a response, many private actors have enlarged their definition of 'value' to include environmental and social elements into their management and asset allocation practices. Such practices, however, appear incompatible with the current theoretical and methodological foundations of academic mainstream in finance, which is heavily influenced by logical positivism and the methodological individualism hypothesis based on the maximization of shareholder's utility function. This paradox challenges us to reconsider the epistemological and theoretical foundations of modern finance, and, in particular, the dominant role played by shareholders. It is our responsibility to question social welfare and ethics simply considered as the result of shareholders value maximization and to enrich finance research, particularly with perspectives and contributions from other social sciences. In particular, we argue there is a need to turn the order upside down: economy and finance have to be embedded in environmental and social welfare to answer challenges we face, rather than the opposite. Should we promote another character, as a substitute to the shareholder? How should we (re)define the concept of value? The network will serve as an interdisciplinary forum for the rethinking of academic finance, with a view to carve out sustainable paths for financial research and practices in the 21st century.

Themes of interest include:

- (Re)defining value(s) and wealth
- Alternatives to shareholder value maximization and promote a long term and sustainable perspective.
- Critical perspectives in accounting
- Economic history and finance
- Finance and comparative capitalism
- Finance and the Global South
- Financialization, networks and interconnectivity
- New metaphors for the study of post crisis finance
- Rethinking education in finance
- Social banking and finance

Keywords: Ethics; financialization; critical perspectives; crisis; sustainability; social impact finance; networks

This initiative has the generous support of:

KEDGE
BUSINESS SCHOOL
CREATED BY BEM & EUROMED MANAGEMENT

ETHOMED
FINANCE RECONSIDERED

ABOUT THE AUTHORS

Belaïd Abrika is Lecturer at Mouloud Mammeri University in Tizi-Ouzou (Algeria). He is known for his militant engagement during the Black Spring of 2001, and is the author of a doctoral thesis entitled "Study into the impact of clientist and/or clannish corruption in developing countries: the Case of Algeria" (*Étude de l'impact du système de la corruption à gestion clientéliste et/ou clanique dans les pays en développement: Cas de l'Algérie*). He now heads a master's course in economics at Mouloud Mammeri University.

Abdel-Maoula Chaar is Professor and researcher at the ESA business school in Beirut. He is head of Research and Development. His research focuses on sustainable development and responsible investment. Abdel-Maoula takes a special interest in Islamic finance, which he sees as a special case providing a practical approach to questions on the reintegration of finance into a socio-economic development ethic.

Bernard Cova is Professor in Marketing at KEDGE Business School, Marseille, where he plays an active role in developing innovative marketing approaches. He also teaches at Bocconi University in Milan. Founded on an ethno-sociological viewpoint that is close to CCT (Consumer Culture Theory), his work on community-focused approaches to consumption go back to the early 1990s, when they laid the foundations for current developments on the role of the market in the development of personal identity (experiential marketing) and the reconstruction of social links between individuals (tribal marketing). His paper, "Working consumers: the next step in marketing theory?" was published in Marketing Theory in 2009 and received a Citations of Excellence Award from Emerald in 2013 for its impact on the scientific community.

Elias Erragragui joined KEDGE Business School in 2011 as a research assistant for the AG2R LA MONDIALE Chair, "Finance Reconsidered: Investment, Solidarities and Responsibility." He has just been awarded a doctorate in economic sciences after his work in the Laboratory for

Economics Applied to Development (LEAD) at Toulon University, supervised by Pr. Reiffers and Pr. Paranque (KEDGE Business School). He has a master's in management science from the IAE school in Montpellier and a master's in Islamic finance from the INCEIF University in Malaysia. He currently teaches on two elective courses on development finance and Islamic finance. His research focuses on ethics applied to financial markets with a special interest in Socially Responsible Investment (SRI) and Islamic finance. His work also covers issues associated with corporate financing. He recently took part in a collective work entitled "Social Impact Finance," directed by Faisal M. Al-Atabani and Cristina Trullols, published in 2014. Prior to his research activities, he was CSR analyst for a CSR rating agency in Malaysia.

Christophe Faugère obtained a PhD in Economic Science from the University of Rochester (USA) in 1993 and a DEA (post-graduate degree) in Economics and Mathematics from Toulouse University in 1987, after a master's in Economic Science at Bordeaux IV University in 1985. He is currently Professor of Finance and head of the Finance and Economics department at KEDGE Business School. He was previously Associate Professor and head of the Finance department at Albany School of Business, New York (USA). Christophe taught on a variety of courses including Investments, Corporate Finance, Derivatives, Bonds, Macroeconomics, Managerial Economics and Monetary Economics on graduate and post-graduate courses in the United States. In 2006, he received the Albany School of Business Harold L. Cannon memorial award for the best teacher on a graduate course and voted best professor on the Albany School of Business MBA programme in 2002.

His research programme focuses on business ethics, financial markets and the monetary economy. More specifically, his research covers the moral and spiritual foundations of financial activity and the creation of valuation models for financial assets (e.g. gold, government bonds, stock market indexes), based on investors' rational and irrational behaviour patterns. He is the co-inventor of the Required Yield Theory, one of the most accurate financial theories used to value the S&P 500 and gold. He has published in the top third publications in the ranking of academic journals, including the *Journal of Portfolio Management and Financial Markets, Institutions & Instruments*. One of his papers on the "Sell Discipline" was covered in two articles published in the New York Times and International Herald Tribune in 2004.

Thomas Lagoarde-Segot holds a PhD in International Finance from Trinity College Dublin and an *Habilitation* in Economics from Aix Marseille Université. He is professor in economics and international finance at KEDGE Business School and a researcher at Aix-Marseille School of Economics (AMSE), CNRS & EHESS. The author of two books and around 20 scholarly papers, his research focuses on emerging economies, financial crises, the social economy, and economic history and philosophy. He is also Editor-in-Chief or Research in International Business and Finance. His full profile, including research activities, consulting and media contributions, can be seen at https://sites.google.com/a/tcd.ie/tls/

Jacques Ninet is Consultant and research advisor for the La Française group and advisor to Convictions AM.

A graduate from ESCP and a former student at the Institut Technique de Banque, his career has been split between the financial markets and the academic world. He has held finance management positions at CEPME and has headed teams of asset management specialists in companies such as Fimagest, Barclays and, more recently, Sarasin France. Throughout his career, he has continued to work as a professor and researcher on master's courses specialised in finance, while contributing to various research groups focused on responsible finance and sustainable development.

He has most notably published: *Les déterminants récurrents de la formation des bulles financières. Économie Appliquée* II-2004; *Analyse des performances de portefeuilles ISR Économies et Sociétés* 2010; *Soutenabilité et crise globale. Économies et sociétés* 2012; *Le XXIe siècle sera coopératif ou ne sera pas. Économies et sociétés* 2014; "Crise économique, complexité financière et responsabilité sociale" *in Risques et complexité.* Institut Fr. Bull. l'Harmattan., March 2003.

Bernard Paranque is Professor of Finance at KEDGE Business School and General Delegate for EuroMediterranean Affairs. He is now Director of "Economy and finance reconsidered – emerging countries" research department. He holds the AG2R LA MONDIALE Chair in "Finance Reconsidered: Investment, Solidarities and Responsibility". He is associate member Institute of Labour Economics and Industrial Sociology LEST-CNRS-UMR 7317.

His research programme covers the issues of and conditions for coordinated economic action, especially in the area of small organisations and their financing. He is interested in all forms of collective ownership, especially companies owned by employees, such as cooperatives, in coordinated collective action taking an approach based on use value or "Commons," and in the dynamics in brand user communities seen through value capture issues. He also works on the social and solidarity economy.

He worked with Bernard Belletante and Nadine Levratto to write *Diversité économique et mode de financement des PME* published by L'Harmattan in 2001. He co-directed the publication of *L'Euro-Méditerrannée: de l'espace géographique aux modes de coordination socio-économiques* with Nadine Levratto and Corinne Grenier, published by L'Harmattan in 2007. He published *Construire l'Euroméditerranée* with L'Harmattan in 2008. Some of his work is online at http://papers.ssrn.com/sol3/cf_dev/AbsByAuth.cfm?per_id=1633

Roland Pérez has been Chairman of the Scientific Council for the AG2R LA MONDIALE Chair "Finance Reconsidered" from 2011 to 2015. He has a PhD in economic science (Paris I University, 1970) and was laureate of national concourse ("aggregation") in economic science and management. He has held successive positions in Lille, Tunis, CNRS Paris, Amiens – where he was university Chairman – then Montpellier I (since 1981) where he was director of the "Economics and Management" graduate school. He has been professor emeritus since 2003.

He has worked successively on corporate finance, the industrial economy and strategic analysis of companies and corporations. He has supervised numerous research programmes in these fields and worked as a facilitator in the scientific realm. He is the author of a hundred or so publications and supervised as many theses for doctorates, MScs and HDR (accreditation to direct research). His recent work covers the industrial and financial strategies of agri-food multinationals and general issues of management, finance and governance with a view to sustainable development. He is currently coordinator of the FAS – Finance and Sustainability international partnership programme and moderator of the "finance and common pool resources" forum.

Pr Pérez has honorary degrees and membership of several academic institutions in France and abroad. He was founder of the French Finance Association (AFFI) and was Chairman of SFM (French Academy of Management) and of RIODD (International Network for Research on Organisations and Sustainable Development).

Cécile Perret is Economist and Lecturer at Université de Savoie, seconded to IREGE and associate researcher at CRDT (Université du Québec). For more than a decade, she has taken an active interest in Kabylia, a territory characterised by the strength of social ties and the survival of a socio-political system of village governance with its roots in tradition. Her work, which makes references to Bourdieu's economics and sociology, led to her proposing an integrated framework for viable development that underpins the importance of respect for traditions and the characteristic values of local populations when governing territories.

She has coordinated or contributed to various university publications (*Les bijoutiers d'Ath-Yenni. La construction d'une attractivité territoriale sur les savoir-faire artisanaux ancestraux*, Éditions Achab, 2010; *Vers un développement citoyen: perspectives d'émancipation pour la Nouvelle-Calédonie*, PUG, 2006; *Perspectives de développement pour la Nouvelle-Calédonie, PUG, 2002*).

Christophe Revelli is Associate Professor at KEDGE Business School. He is a member of the FAS (Finance and Sustainability) collective, of the "Finance Reconsidered" Chair and the "Economics and Finance Reconsidered, Emerging Countries and Shared Resources" research theme.

His work focuses on ethical and sustainable finance and in particular the effect of social ratings and socially responsible investment on financial performance, the relationship between CSR and financial crisis, the impact investing, the critical approach to socially responsible investment and the relationships between Islamic finance and socially responsible investment.

In 2012, at the RIODD (International Network for Research on Organisations and Sustainable Development) conference, Christophe Revelli received the "RIODD-VIGEO" research prize for his thesis entitled "The financial performance of socially responsible investment (SRI): a meta-analytical approach" (*Performance financière de l'Investissement Socialement Responsable (ISR): approche méta-analytique*).

He is the author of several papers published in reviews such as *Business Ethics: A European Review, Finance Research Letters, Research in International Business and Finance, Management International, Revue Française de Gestion*, *La Revue des Sciences de Gestion*, *Recherche en Sciences de Gestion*, and *Finance Contrôle Stratégie*.

Jean-Michel Servet is Professor in development studies, working at the Institute of International and Development Studies since 2003. He teaches in Geneva and Lima. He is an honorary professor of economic science at Université Lumière Lyon 2. He was research director at the Centre national de la recherche scientifique (CNRS/France) and the Institut de recherche pour le développement (IRD/France) seconded to the French Institute of Pondicherry (India).

His main areas of research are the crisis and its solidarity alternatives, financial inclusion and the history of economic and financial thinking and practices from a Polanyian perspective.

He has published more than 200 papers and around 20 books since the mid-1970s. These include *Les Monnaies du lien* (2012), *Le Grand renversement* (2010), *Banquiers aux pieds nus* (2006), *Une économie sans argent* (1999) and *L'euro au quotidien* (1998). He also directed the series of *Exclusion et liens financier*s reports (eight volumes published). He was co-editor of a new translation of Adam Smith's *The Wealth of Nations* (three volumes), and of the complete economic works by Auguste and Léon Walras and the complete works of Jean-Baptiste Say. In 2015, he published *La Vraie révolution du Microcrédit* and co-directed the publication of *Le Marché autrement. Marchés réels et marché fantasmé.*

Hugh Willmott (PhD Manchester University; Honorary PhD, Lund University) is Professor of Management at Cass Business School Research, City University and Research Professor in Organization Studies, Cardiff Business School. He received his PhD from Manchester University and previously held professorial appointments at UMIST (now Manchester Business School) and the Judge Business School, Cambridge and visiting appointments at the Universities of Lund, Uppsala, Sydney, Innsbruck and University of Technology Sydney. Hugh is a Fellow of the British Academy. He has research diverse aspects of organizations including managerial work, culture, control, corporate governance, management education, ethics, regulation and alternative organizations. He is currently Associate Editor of Academy of Management Review and was previous Associate Editor of Organization. He has also served on the editorial boards of Accounting, Organizations and Society, Critical Perspectives on Accounting, Accounting, Auditing and Accountability and a range of management and organization journals including Journal of Management Studies and Organization Studies. Full details can be found on his homepage: https://sites.google.com/site/hughwillmottshomepage